LANGUAGE AND INTERACTION

Routledge Applied Linguistics is a series of comprehensive textbooks, providing students and researchers with the support they need for advanced study in the core areas of English Language and Applied Linguistics.

Each book in the series guides readers through three main sections, enabling them to explore and develop major themes within the discipline.

- Section A, **Introduction**, establishes the key terms and concepts and extends readers' techniques of analysis through practical application.
- Section B, **Extension**, brings together influential articles, sets them in context, and discusses their contribution to the field.
- Section C, **Exploration**, builds on knowledge gained in the first two sections, setting thoughtful tasks around further illustrative material. This enables readers to engage more actively with the subject matter and encourages them to develop their own research responses.

Throughout the book, topics are revisited, extended, interwoven and deconstructed, with the reader's understanding strengthened by tasks and follow-up questions.

Language and Interaction:

- introduces key concepts in language and social interaction
- describes how individuals develop skills in social interaction and shows how people create identities through their use of language
- brings together essential readings in anthropology, discourse studies and sociology.

Written by an experienced teacher and researcher in the field, *Language and Interaction* is an essential resource for students and researchers of applied linguistics and communication studies.

Richard F. Young is Professor of English at the University of Wisconsin-Madison, USA.

D0869355

ROUTLEDGE APPLIED LINGUISTICS

SERIES EDITORS

Christopher N. Candlin is Senior Research Professor in the Department of Linguistics at Macquarie University, Australia and Professor of Applied Linguistics at the Open University, UK. At Macquarie, he has been Chair of the Department of Linguistics; he established and was Executive Director of the National Centre for English Language Teaching & Research (NCELTR) and first Director of the Centre for Language in Social Life (CLSL). He has written or edited over 150 publications and co-edits the new *Journal of Applied Linguistics*. From 1996 to 2002 he was President of the International Association of Applied Linguistics (AILA). He has acted as a consultant in more than 35 countries and as external faculty assessor in 36 universities worldwide.

Ronald Carter is Professor of Modern English Language in the School of English Studies at the University of Nottingham. He has published extensively in the fields of applied linguistics, literary studies and language in education. He has given consultancies in the field of English language education, mainly in conjunction with The British Council, in over thirty countries worldwide. He was recently elected a fellow of the British Academy of Social Sciences and was chair of the British Association of Applied Linguistics (BAAL) from 2003 to 2006.

TITLES IN THE SERIES

Intercultural Communication: An advanced resource book
Adrian Holliday, Martin Hyde and John Kullman

Translation: An advanced resource book
Basil Hatim and Jeremy Munday

Grammar and Context: An advanced resource book
Ann Hewings, Martin Hewings

Second Language Acquisition: An advanced resource book
Kees de Bot, Wander Lowie and Marjolijn Verspoor

Corpus-Based Language Studies: An advanced resource book
Anthony McEnery, Richard Xiao and Yukio Tono

Language and Gender: An advanced resource book
Jane Sunderland

English for Academic Purposes: An advanced resource book
Ken Hyland

Language Testing and Assessment: An advanced resource book
Glenn Fulcher and Fred Davidson

Bilingualism: An advanced resource book
Ng Bee Chin and Gillian Wigglesworth

Literacy: An advanced resource book
Brian V. Street and Adam Lefstein

Language and Interaction

An advanced resource book

Richard F. Young

Routledge
Taylor & Francis Group

LONDON AND NEW YORK

First published 2008
by Routledge
2 Park Square, Milton Park, Abingdon, Oxon OX14 4RN

Simultaneously published in the USA and Canada
by Routledge
270 Madison Ave, New York, NY 10016

Routledge is an imprint of the Taylor & Francis Group, an informa business

© 2008 Richard F. Young

Typeset in Akzidenz Grotesk, Minion and Novarese by
Keystroke, 28 High Street, Tettenhall, Wolverhampton
Printed and bound in Great Britain by
The Cromwell Press, Trowbridge, Wiltshire

British Library Cataloguing in Publication Data
A catalogue record for this book is available from the British Library

Library of Congress Cataloging in Publication Data
Young, Richard, 1948–
    Language and interaction: an advanced resource book/Richard F. Young.
        p. cm.
    1. Sociolinguistics.   2. Social interaction.   I. Title.
    P40.Y68 2008
    306.44–dc22   2007047902

ISBN10: 0–415–38552–0 (hbk)
ISBN10: 0–415–38553–4 (pbk)

ISBN13: 978–0–415–38552–7 (hbk)
ISBN13: 978–0–415–38553–4 (pbk)

Contents

Contents cross-referenced

Figures

Series editors' preface

The Routledge Applied Linguistics series provides a comprehensive guide to a number of key areas in the field of applied linguistics. Applied linguistics is a rich, vibrant, diverse and essentially interdisciplinary field. It is now more important than ever that books in the field provide up-to-date maps of what is an ever-changing territory.

The books in this series are designed to give key insights into core areas of applied linguistics. The design of the books ensures, through key readings, that the history and development of a subject is recognized while, through key questions and tasks, integrating understandings of the topics, concepts and practices that make up its essentially interdisciplinary fabric. The pedagogic structure of each book ensures that readers are given opportunities to think, discuss, engage in tasks, draw on their own experience, reflect, research and to read and critically re-read key documents.

Each book has three main sections, each made up of approximately ten units:

A: An **Introduction** section: in which the key terms and concepts which map the field of the subject are introduced, including introductory activities and reflective tasks, designed to establish key understandings, terminology, techniques of analysis and the skills appropriate to the theme and the discipline.

B: An **Extension** section: in which selected core readings are introduced (usually edited from the original) from existing key books and articles, together with annotations and commentary, where appropriate. Each reading is introduced, annotated and commented on in the context of the whole book, and research/follow-up questions and tasks are added to enable fuller understanding of both theory and practice. In some cases, readings are short and synoptic and incorporated within a more general exposition.

C: An **Exploration** section: in which further samples and illustrative materials are provided with an emphasis, where appropriate, on more open-ended, student-centred activities and tasks, designed to support readers and users in undertaking their own locally relevant research projects. Tasks are designed for work in groups or for individuals working on their own. They can be readily included in award courses in applied linguistics, or as topics for personal study and research.

The target audience for the series is upper undergraduates and postgraduates on language, applied linguistics and communication studies programmes as well as teachers and researchers in professional development and distance learning programmes. High-quality applied research resources are also much needed for teachers of EFL/ESL and foreign language students at higher education colleges and universities worldwide. The books in the Routledge Applied Linguistics series are aimed at the individual reader, the student in a group and at teachers building courses and seminar programmes.

We hope that the books in this series meet these needs and continue to provide support over many years.

THE EDITORS

Professor Christopher N. Candlin and Professor Ronald Carter are the series editors. Both have extensive experience of publishing titles in the fields relevant to this series. Between them they have written and edited over one hundred books and two hundred academic papers in the broad field of applied linguistics. Chris Candlin was president of AILA (International Association for Applied Linguistics) from 1996 to 2002 and Ron Carter was Chair of BAAL (British Association for Applied Linguistics) from 2003 to 2006.

Professor Christopher N. Candlin
Senior Research Professor
Department of Linguistics
Division of Linguistics and Psychology
Macquarie University
Sydney NSW 2109
Australia

and

Professor of Applied Linguistics
Faculty of Education & Language Studies
The Open University
Walton Hall
Milton Keynes MK7 6AA
UK

Professor Ronald Carter
School of English Studies
University of Nottingham
Nottingham NG7 2RD
UK

Acknowledgements

Cicourel, A. V. (1995). Medical speech events as resources for inferring differences in expert-novice diagnostic reasoning. In U. M. Quasthoff (ed.), *Aspects of oral communication* (pp. 364–387). Berlin and New York: W. de Gruyter. Reproduced by permission of the author.

Day, D. (1998). Being ascribed and resisting membership of an ethnic group. In C. Antaki and S. Widdicombe (eds), *Identities in talk* (pp. 151–170). Copyright © 1998 Dennis Day. Reproduced by permission of SAGE Publications, London, Los Angeles, New Delhi and Singapore.

Goodwin, C., and Duranti, A. (1992) Rethinking context: An introduction. In A. Duranti and C. Goodwin (eds), *Rethinking context: Language as an interactive phenomenon* (pp. 1–42). Copyright © 1992 Cambridge University Press, reproduced with permission of the author and publisher.

Hall, J. K. (1995). (Re)creating our worlds with words: A sociohistorical perspective of face-to-face interaction. *Applied Linguistics*, 16, 206–232. Reproduced by permission of Oxford University Press.

Halliday, M. A. K., and Matthiessen, C. M. I. M. (2004). *An introduction to functional grammar* (3rd ed.) (pp. 3–9). London: Arnold. Copyright © 2004 M. A. K. Halliday and Christian Matthiessen. Reproduced by permission of Edward Arnold (Publishers) Ltd.

Hanks, W. F. (1996). Chapter 1: Introduction: Meaning and matters of context. In *Language and communicative practices*. Boulder, CO: Westview. Copyright © 1996 by Westview Press, Inc., a division of HarperCollins Publishers, Inc. Reprinted by permission of Westview Press, a member of Perseus Books Group.

Heath, S. (1983). Excerpts from pp. 201–211. *Ways with words*. Copyright © 1983 Cambridge University Press. Reproduced by permission of the author and publisher.

Hymes, D. (1962). The ethnography of speaking. In T. Gladwin and W. Sturtevant (eds), *Anthropology and human behavior* (pp. 15–53). Washington, DC: Anthropological Society of Washington. Reproduced by permission of the author.

Hymes, D. (1972). Models of the interaction of language and social life. In J. J. Gumperz and D. Hymes (eds), *Directions in sociolinguistics: The ethnography of communication*. Reproduced by permission of Blackwell Publishing.

Ochs, E. (1996). Linguistic resources for socializing humanity. In J. J. Gumperz and S. C. Levinson (eds), *Rethinking linguistic relativity* (pp. 407–437). Copyright ©

1996 Cambridge University Press. Reproduced by permission of the author and publisher.

Ochs, E. (2002). Becoming a speaker of culture. In C. Kramsch (ed.), *Language acquisition and language socialization* (pp. 99–120). London: Continuum. Reproduced by permission of the author and publisher.

How to use this book

The title of this book suggests a combination of two activities that people do but rarely combine in the same thought: language and interaction. Language has been studied for centuries, but what we know about language is strongly influenced by writing and written language and, because writing and reading are most often done in isolation, many theories have ignored the social life of language. Obviously, interaction – social interaction – does not happen in isolation; it involves people doing things and influencing each other by what they do. To combine these two in a single thought means asking: How does social interaction happen through language? And how does our knowledge of language change when we consider it to be primarily a means of social interaction? These are the two questions that this book addresses. It is written for readers who are interested in language and for readers who are interested in society, social institutions, and social relationships. These are often two separate groups of people, and this book has something to say to both.

The presentation of ideas in this book is organized into three parts, titled *Foundations, Analysis*, and *Consequences*. In Part 1 *Foundations*, the main ideas about the relationship between language and social interaction are presented and reviewed. Many ideas have come from philosophers, anthropologists, sociologists, and linguists, and these people have been concerned with spoken language because social interaction is so easy to see when people are speaking to each other. Some of the most exciting and innovative ways of understanding how language works in social interaction, however, have emerged not from studies of conversation but from studies of the novel and other forms of literature by the Russian scholar Mikhail Bakhtin.

In Part 2 of the book, *Analysis*, the fundamental concepts of language and social interaction introduced in Part 1 are applied to analyze actual instances of social interaction through language. The approach that is taken here is not to look first at language but to focus attention instead on the activities that people are doing and only then consider how language helps them to organize those activities. The activities that we consider throughout the book have a recognizable shape that is often repeated and is related to the social and power relations between participants and in the broader society. This approach to language in interaction derives from linguistic anthropology and is called Practice Theory, the focus of which is discursive practice. In the second part of the book, two methods of analyzing discursive practice are presented: one that originated in the linguistic theory known as systemic functional grammar and the other, the procedures of conversation analysis, which had their origin in sociology.

Because language is used in social interaction it has important consequences in people's lives. The third and final part of the book, *Consequences*, examines how people construct their social identities through the language they use, how individuals form communities of people who share similar values and ways of using language, and how people learn to become members of those communities. The analytical frameworks that are presented in Part 2 are used to show the consequences of using language in a certain way.

Depending on your background, you may find that topics raised in the later parts of the book are more interesting than topics discussed earlier and you are, of course, free to pick and choose those pieces of the book that appear to be most relevant to you. But the book is not designed as a buffet, and there is a benefit from consuming the three parts in the order in which they are presented. Part 1 *Foundations* supports the analyses of language and interaction in Part 2, and those analyses inform the understanding of the social consequences of language use in Part 3.

There is somewhat less of an intended sequence in the materials presented in Sections A, B, and C. The three sections of each unit are held together by a common topic as you can see, for example, from the titles of the sections of Unit 2 – A2 *Talk in Context*, B2 *Talk in Context*, and C2 *Exploring the Nature of Context* – or Unit 8 – A8 *Community and Communities*, B8 *Discourse Communities*, and C8 *Discovering Communities*. Each section with the same number is designed to engage the reader with the same ideas in different ways.

In Section A, the main terms and concepts are introduced and exemplified in discursive practices as diverse as a civil rights leader's speech, a music lesson at school, and interaction in an online social networking community. These units are designed for active readers, with tasks interspersed throughout the presentation to help readers relate some of the concepts to their own experience. The material in Section A is presented in ways that are accessible to readers without an academic background in linguistics, anthropology, or sociology. The ideas presented there, however, did originate in the writings of eminent scholars in those fields, and extracts from their writings are presented in Section B. Each unit in Section B contains an overview of the topic and an introduction to the reading. The activity of reading itself is presented in Section B as an interactive process with a set of preview questions that help to familiarize the reader with the theme of the reading, several reflective activities located at key points throughout the text, and a brief discussion of the main points following the reading. A summary of ideas and concerns raised in the readings concludes each unit in Section B.

Section C is where you, the reader, provide most of the input through directed research activities. Each unit is designed to be action-oriented and practical. Units in Section C present a set of data and a variety of activities designed to help readers hone their research skills both in the field (by going out and collecting data) and in the library (by extensive reading and interpretation of key texts). All units in this section contain an introduction, which gives background to the data and includes an overview of some of the methods for collecting and analyzing the data. They include two or three tasks requiring readers to engage with the data, a discussion section with comments on possible interpretations of the data, and a set of questions and tasks to help readers begin similar explorations in their own contexts. The final sections of the C units are titled *Questions and Activities for Future Exploration* and provide suggestions for large-scale research projects.

Some readers may prefer to proceed through these three sections alphabetically, but different routes are possible. Starting with a key reading in Section B provides a basis for evaluating the presentation in Section A, but it would be best done by readers with some background in the academic field from which the Section B author hails. Readers who start with the research projects in Section C and who, only after completing some of the projects, proceed to the other sections will be well grounded in their analyses of social interaction through language and may use that grounding to evaluate the theories presented in the other two sections. This route would be suitable for readers with some previous experience of research in the field or in the library.

Finally, because this book is about language use in social interaction, one of the most effective ways into the field is for readers to interact with other readers in the same study group or with other readers over the internet. Use the book as a springboard for interacting and for reflecting on interaction and how it is achieved through language. By the end of the process, you should be able to take a position on one of the great controversies of modern linguistics: Is language a structured set of forms that are used to represent things and ideas in the world? Or is language a set of meaningful actions and cultural practices through which people intervene in the world (Linnell, 2005)?

SECTION A
Introduction

Unit A1
Language and social interaction

This book provides an introduction to two key concepts in applied linguistics: language and social interaction. In this initial chapter, we will discuss both concepts and argue that language in the context of interaction with others has not been studied as extensively as language as an independent system. Language is, however, the primary means that people use to communicate, to construct identity, and to establish membership in communities, but, without a basic understanding of how language functions in interaction, we cannot make much progress in understanding communication, identity, or community. The study of language in social interaction is therefore a door into understanding how people function in society. This is an important enterprise that has been undertaken by philosophers, historians of literature, sociologists, and anthropologists, some of whose work we will introduce in this chapter.

If you open a book about a language, you are likely to find a lot of information about how to pronounce the language, the vocabulary of the language, meanings of words, how words are made up from smaller parts, and how words are put together into sentences. You might also find out something about the way the language is written, how people use the language to do different things like ask for directions or praise somebody, and how people in different parts of the country speak different varieties of the language.

Here are a few examples of information that you can find about a language. There exist sounds in some languages that you never hear in English; for example, the way that many speakers of Spanish pronounce the 'v' in Venezuela sounds to English ears almost like a 'b.' Even in the same language, there are different pronunciations; for example, Americans and British people pronounce the word 'butter' in different ways. Most people who know a language well can identify words and sentences as belonging to that language. Speakers of English, for example, can recognize words like 'tove' that they have never met before as possible words in English and can distinguish them from impossible ones like 'vtoe.' They can also distinguish combinations of words that form possible English sentences like 'I love going into like clothing stores and stuff' from different but impossible combinations like 'Going love and stuff I like clothing stores into.' And many people have strong feelings about language, about for example the correct spelling of words like 'priviledge,' 'broccolli,' 'accomodate,' and 'embarasment,' and about whether they would say sentences like 'I love going into like clothing stores and stuff.'

It seems like a language has a system of rules that create order out of a mass of sounds and words. If we have spoken the language since childhood and we have been educated in the language, in some sense we know the rules of the language, but unless we have made a linguistic study of the language, we can't say exactly what those rules are. The study of linguistics helps us to articulate those rules because linguistics is a systematic study of what people know about language. It has been around for a long time, at least since the ancient grammarians, who lived in India many centuries before the Common Era. In our own era, the systematic study of language used to be known as 'Philology,' and in the twentieth century some universities had departments of 'Linguistic Science.' All this labor over so many centuries has resulted in a deep understanding of how languages work and, in recent years, linguists have concentrated much attention on language as an innate characteristic of all human beings – what unites us and what distinguishes us from other species. You can recognize how developed the field of linguistics is by examining the technical vocabulary – the jargon if you like. Terms like *morphology*, *phonetics*, *syntax*, *pragmatics*, and *UG* are common in books on linguistics and they are evidence of a mature field with its own way of looking at the world and its own language (!) to talk about it.

And yet, our understanding of one important aspect of how people use language has not kept pace with developments in linguistics. What has not been studied so extensively is how an individual speaker uses language at a definite time in a particular place with other unique individuals for some specific purpose. The *who*, *where*, *when*, *how*, and *why* questions about language use have not received as much attention as the question of *what*. The reason for this difference in understandings is that the *what* of language – the actual words – can easily be removed from the context in which they were produced and then studied at leisure. For centuries, there have existed written records – texts – which are ways in which language was removed from the speaker or writer, from the place, time, and means of its production, and from the original purpose for which the text was produced. Such written records could be – and were – studied and commented on, interpreted and reinterpreted. Then, from the end of the nineteenth century, ways of recording speech were developed which gave a more accurate written representation of how people spoke, and today the permanent record of language includes not only writing but also audio and video tapes. Because of the possibility that writing and tape-recording speech allow people to study language out of context, the linguistic study of language was just that: the study of a self-contained system independent of the context in which it functioned.

Understanding the way that language functions in live interaction is a very different kind of endeavor from the study of the language system because as soon as spoken language is taken out of the online context in which it is used, the who, where, when, how, and why change. Talk becomes text, a process that Greg Urban (1996) called 'the entextualization of talk.' Does this indissoluble relation between language and context mean, then, that we can never understand how talk functions in interaction because we cannot study it apart from interaction? Many scholars in the twentieth century replied in the negative to that question. Scholars of literature such as Mikhail Bakhtin and philosophers of natural language such as Ludwig Wittgenstein have advanced theories that have greatly extended our understanding of language use in interaction. Other scholars have enhanced our understanding by examining the relationship between talk and interaction in cultures very different from our own. In addition, the study methods of ethnography and ethnographic microanalysis that have been developed by linguistic anthropologists provide descriptions of the connections between talk and context, and ethnographers have developed ways of analyzing context that are of a sophistication equivalent to the ways that linguists have developed for analyzing texts.

In the following sections, we will examine the theoretical and practical contributions that have been made by philosophers and anthropologists to understanding language and interaction.

A1.1 SENTENCES AND UTTERANCES

In contrasting a view of language as an abstract system with language as talk-in-interaction, we have said that the *who, where, when, how,* and *why* questions about language use have not received as much attention as the question of *what*. One of the first people to draw attention to these issues was not a linguist but a historian of literature. The Russian philosopher and literary critic Mikhail Bakhtin developed profound insights into the use of language in context through his studies of European literature, especially the development of the novel from classical times to the eighteenth century. We will briefly introduce Bakhtin's contributions under the headings of the who, where, when, how, why, and what of language. A much fuller treatment of Bakhtin's extensive and complex work can be found in Gary Saul Morson and Caryl Emerson's 1990 book *Mikhail Bakhtin: Creation of a prosaics*.

Bakhtin's approach to language in context is founded on his distinction between a sentence and an utterance. These two terms recall the distinction that we made earlier between language as an abstract system and the use that people make of language in context. For Bakhtin, utterances are a different kind of thing from sentences – although sentences are the stuff that makes up language rather like paper and ink are the stuff that make up this book. An utterance can be as short as a sentence or as long as this book, it can also be a turn at talk in a conversation. As Morson and Emerson (1990) put it, the distinction between utterances and sentences is essentially that 'Sentences are repeatable. Sentences are repeatable. . . . But each utterance is by its very nature unrepeatable. Its context and reason for being differ from those of every other utterance' (p. 126). It is now a short step to answering the *who* question: Each utterance is spoken or written by someone and is addressed to someone else. This has the important consequence that the meaning of a word in an utterance is neither the meaning that a speaker originally intended nor the meaning that a listener interprets, it is somewhere in between. Neither is the meaning of a word in an utterance its dictionary meaning. As Bakhtin's colleague

Valentin Voloshinov (1973) wrote, the '*word is a two-sided act. It is determined equally by whose word it is and for whom it is meant. As word, it is precisely the product of the reciprocal relationship between speaker and listener, addresser and addressee* . . . I give myself verbal shape from another's point of view' (p. 86). This relationship is what later scholars have called co-construction.

The *how* and *why* questions are discussed by Bakhtin in his theory of genres. A genre is a pattern of communication that is created in a recurring communicative situation. Genres aid communication by creating shared expectations about the form and content of the interaction, thus easing the burden of production and interpretation. In other words, life is not full of surprises and people use language in routine ways. We see the importance of genres when we move out of our daily communicative routine and try to learn a foreign language. Although we may know the grammar, vocabulary, and pronunciation of a foreign language well, we may nonetheless 'feel quite helpless in certain spheres of communication precisely because we do not have a practical command of the generic forms in the given spheres' (Bakhtin, 1986, p. 80). Genres are crystallizations of earlier interactions, and whenever we communicate we do so in one or another genre. Genres are not simply fixed grammatical structures or combinations of words (although certain words and ways of speaking may be associated with a particular genre), but each implies a set of values, a way of thinking about the world and the appropriateness of a given genre in a particular social context. Genres are also not simply ways of producing talk, they are just as important in interpreting what is said because they help listeners and readers understand social relations between the speaker/writer and others, the speaker/writer's values, their tone, and the purposes of the communication. Later in this book, we will introduce the notion of discursive practices, which recent scholars have developed from Bakhtin's theory of genres.

 Task A1.1.1

➤ As an example of genre, consider the three bumper stickers reproduced here. What messages are the people who drive cars with these bumper stickers trying to communicate? Genres are accumulations of experience that predispose us to forms of thinking, what Bakhtin called 'form-shaping ideology.' Discuss the experiences and ideologies that are accumulated by the generic relations between these three bumper stickers.

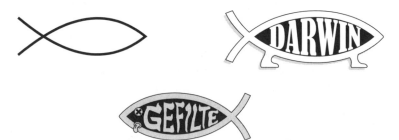

The time and place of an utterance are in one sense the physical circumstances of utterance, but what counts in the interpretation of an utterance is not a physical description of time and place but their meanings for the participants. Bakhtin goes much further in his discussion of *where* and *when* and makes a connection between the actions and interpretations of communication and the time-space context of the interaction.[1] The time-space context, in a similar way to genre, provides possibilities for action and a calculus of likely interpretations of any action. Bakhtin's discussion of time-space context is carried out entirely by reference to the history of the novel in European literature from ancient Greece to the eighteenth century, but can easily be extended to spoken interaction. Take, as an example of the temporal dimension of context, the utterance 'Though the sex to which I belong is considered weak ... you will nevertheless find me a rock that bends to no wind.' In this utterance, the speaker expresses a view of female gender that was prevalent in certain historical periods but is much less common today. A woman in the twenty-first century would be unlikely to claim that women are considered weak. The speaker then goes on to claim for herself an unshakeable determination and strength, in effect claiming a powerful identity in contrast to what her addressee might believe about her gender. Knowing that the temporal context of the utterance is sixteenth-century England helps us understand the reasons why the speaker formulated it in this way. In fact, the remark is attributed to Queen Elizabeth I of England when speaking to the French ambassador.

Another example, provided by John Gumperz (2000) and reproduced in Task A1.1.2, shows the influence of the spatial dimension of context on the inter-pretability of language.

Task A1.1.2

➤ Where do you think the following conversation took place? What is there in the speakers' words that leads you to believe that their conversation occurred in a particular physical location?

```
A:  But she´s a FLAKE.
B:  ((fast tempo)) Ya know we should probably watch it.
    They´re [probably sitt´n there.
A:          [I know
B:  It´s just nice going to cafes now and I feel like
    I don't have [to avoid anybody
A:               [THIS is the LIFE.
```

Besides Bakhtin's insights into the context of utterance, he also provided some observations about the *what* of language use that go beyond a description of a single linguistic system. Bakhtin recognized that a single language like English, Russian, or Japanese has an official form (the standard language), but it has in addition many unofficial forms that are used by different speakers to create identities and establish membership in communities. The term that Bakhtin used for the co-existence of many different varieties within a single language is *heteroglossia*. Dialects of a language are examples of the different varieties of language that make up heteroglossia. Dialects are expressions of a regional identity, of New York or of Manchester, of Paris or of Marseilles, but language also indexes social class within particular communities, so that a working-class New Yorker speaks a different variety of English from an upper-middle-class New Yorker. Other identities that are indexed by different language varieties are gender (women's talk, men's talk, and the talk of other gendered identities), age (teenagers speak very differently from senior citizens), ethnicity (African-American varieties of English differ from Hispanic varieties, and both differ from White varieties). Then of course there are many varieties of language that index the profession of the speaker as a lawyer, as a broadcaster, as a doctor, and so on. Speakers of one language command a number of different varieties of that language and, as we will discuss later in this book, creation of an identity involves use of certain varieties that index that identity. As Bakhtin (1981) put it,

> Consciousness finds itself inevitably facing the necessity of *having to choose a language*. With each literary-verbal performance, consciousness must actively orient itself amidst heteroglossia. It must move in and occupy a position for itself within it. It chooses, in other words, a 'language.'
>
> (p. 295, italics in original)

A1.2 LANGUAGE GAMES

Although Bakhtin provided many insights into the relationship between language and the context of utterance, his work did not become available in English translation until the 1980s and, initially, his influence was felt most strongly in literary studies. Only recently has his work come to the attention of scholars of talk-in-interaction. The same cannot be said of Ludwig Wittgenstein, whose early investigations of the *who*, *where*, *when*, *how*, and *why* of ordinary language influenced a number of linguists.[2] Originally from Austria with a chair in Philosophy at the University of Cambridge, Wittgenstein rejected the prevailing theory that the meaning of a speaker's words in talk-in-interaction involves knowing the objects to which the speaker's words refer and establishing whether the relationship among those objects asserted by the speaker is true. Instead, Wittgenstein argued, meaning involves understanding the function of the utterance in context. Wittgenstein used the term *language game* to emphasize that every moment of speaking is part of a social activity and the meaning of an utterance cannot be established unless one knows which language game is being played and the function of the utterance in the game. Knowing the meaning of an utterance thus involves knowing which move the speaker is making in a language game. Wittgenstein gives an example of the necessity of understanding the language game in which a specific utterance is spoken in order to understand the utterance when he says, 'If I hear someone say "it's raining" but do not know whether I have heard the beginning and end of the period, so far this sentence does not serve to tell me anything' (Wittgenstein, 2001, vol. 1, p. 22).

What are language games? Wittgenstein gives examples, including giving orders and obeying them, making up a story and reading it, requesting, thanking, cursing, greeting, praying, constructing an object from a drawing, telling a joke, guessing a riddle, and many more. In most of these games (requesting, thanking, and so on), language plays a central role but, in others (constructing an object from a drawing, for example), nonverbal communication is involved. The meaning of a word in a language game depends on the nature of the game and, therefore, a word cannot have a fixed meaning outside of the context of the game. To this, you might object that some elements of meaning adhere to words no matter how they are used in language games and this may be the case, but it is not hard to imagine the language game exemplified in Task A1.2.1, in which the meaning of a word is exactly the opposite from its meaning in most games.

Task A1.2.1

➤ Here is an example that Wittgenstein (2001, vol. 1, p. 510) gives of how meanings of words change according to the language game being played. '*Say* "It's cold in here" and *mean* "It's warm in here". Can you do it? – And what are you doing as you do it? And is there only one way of doing it?'

Wittgenstein's philosophy of ordinary language was developed further by philosophers J. L. Austin and John Searle such that by now the theory of *speech acts* which these philosophers originated is well known. Nonetheless the application of their theories was limited by the methods that they used to derive them. Ordinary language philosophers examined their own intuitions about their own languages, and did not look beyond the cultural milieu in which they lived. Understanding the relationship between language and context in all human interaction, however, involves going beyond the everyday context and examining the relationship in a variety of cultures. This work was undertaken by linguistic anthropologists.

A1.3 ANALYZING LANGUAGE IN INTERACTION

A1.3.1 Ethnography

The understanding of talk-in-interaction that linguistic anthropologists provided was based on an analysis of direct, first-hand observation of daily behavior in a tradition known as ethnography. The ethnographer does not attempt to be an impartial outside observer; instead of trying to be a fly on the wall, the ethnographer takes a role in the interaction that is acknowledged by other participants. Because of the participation of the observer in the interaction, this method of studying talk-in-interaction is known as *participant observation*. Observation is also not limited to single bounded interactions but is conducted over a long period of time by a researcher, who often lives with a group of people and tries to understand their ways of speaking and ways of life, not from the perspective of an outsider but from the perspective of the people in focus. Participant observation is a method founded on the idea that no social relationship, including talk-in-interaction, can be understood independently of society as a whole and its parts, and talk-in-interaction happens in a context that is both broader in scope than a single interaction and in a dimension of time that extends into the past before the time of interaction.

Participant observation is therefore a holistic attempt to understand language in the context in which it was produced by unique individuals in specific places at particular times, who use means such as talk or writing for particular purposes. This approach to studying language in interaction was developed by linguistic anthropologists, in particular John Gumperz and Dell Hymes, and came to be known as the *ethnography of communication* or the *ethnography of speaking*.[3] The contrast between the ethnographic approach to talk-in-interaction and the linguistic study of language as a self-contained system independent of the context in which it functions should, I hope, be obvious.

There are, however, two drawbacks to a purely ethnographic approach to language and interaction. The first is that, although ethnographers portray the richness of context in which people use language, the ways of describing context that were originally available to anthropologists were far less developed than the ways of describing language. Hymes (1962/1974) first developed a taxonomy of features of context that included: '1. a Sender (Addresser); 2. a Receiver (Addressee); 3. a Message Form; 4. a Channel; 5. a Code; 6. a Topic; and 7. Setting (Scene, Situation)' (p. 199). Hymes's terms, however, refer to theories or categories that an outside analyst uses, which are not necessarily accepted or understood as relevant by the people participating in the talk being analyzed; they are, however, a way to begin an analysis. They serve as a checklist for an investigator, who can look to see, first, how each of the features is interpreted by participants and, then, whether the participants orient to the features in some way. Later scholars have analyzed some of Hymes's features in greater detail. Erving Goffman (1979/1981), for instance, considered the notions of Sender and Receiver of talk too crude because the question of who sends a message is complex, and there is also differentiation among those who receive it. Goffman also noted that the presentation of self by individuals in interaction is not fixed but may change from moment to moment.

Another feature of context, Setting, was defined by Hymes as 'the time and place of a speech act and, in general, to the physical circumstances' (p. 55). Although this definition seems to be a straightforward description of time and place, what counts in the interpretation of setting is not a physical description of the time and place of interaction, but, as Bakhtin suggested, in order to investigate setting it is necessary to take a perspective that extends beyond adjacent space and contemporary time. In particular, we need to consider features of context that do not belong in the same time period as the focal event but provide a history that influences present talk. In an argument that parallels Bakhtin's discussion of genre, Pierre Bourdieu (1977) argued that participants are not completely free to act or to talk in any way in a particular social situation. Although participants are certainly not automata that respond in pre-programmed ways in social situations, they are nonetheless constrained in their actions and in their talk by their own history, laid down in their formative years by the cultural environment of the home.

The analysis of context thus extends in many directions from the act of speaking itself, and a nuanced analysis of context will involve considerable knowledge of the culture and ways of life of the participants in interaction, an analysis that will be enhanced by the ethnographer's association with the speakers over a long period of time and by comparison of their ways of speaking with other groups.

A1.3.2 Microethnography

The second drawback to a purely ethnographic analysis of talk-in-interaction is that talk is fleeting, and even skilled ethnographers find it hard to analyze what is happening in spoken interaction without the benefit of a record of the event to which they can return many times in order to relate the moment-by-moment development of talk to the effect that it has on the participants and the context. Fortunately, video and audio recordings and subsequent transcription of talk provide that record, and there are two analytic approaches that ensure that the recorded talk does not become entextualized, and is related closely to its original context: microethnography and conversation analysis.

Microethnography – ethnographic microanalysis of social interaction – is an approach developed by Frederick Erickson which involves close study of interaction through ethnographically oriented analysis of audiovisual records. Erickson (2004) recognized that the aim of his approach is to reconcile the immediacy of talk-in-interaction with a social and political context that influences the lives of participants. He summarized the twin aims of his approach as an investigation of (1) the conduct of talk in local social situations as it occurs in real time, crafted by local social actors for the unique situation of its use in the moment of its uttering, and (2) the influence on talk of processes that occur beyond the temporal and spatial horizon of the immediate occasion of interaction.

A1.3.3 Conversation analysis

A different approach to the analysis of talk-in-interaction was developed by sociologists Harold Garfinkel, Harvey Sacks, Emanuel Schegloff, and their colleagues and students at UCLA. Because the primary interest of these scholars was in social life rather than language, the new approach was characterized by an investigation of social actions performed by participants in interaction and did not start from an analysis of language or linguistic form. Their approach, which came to be known as conversation analysis or CA, has found a wide following among researchers who are interested in practical reasoning, in the development of common-sense interpretations of everyday life, and in the construction through talk of social concepts such as identity, stance, and perspective. The methods of CA have also been applied to investigations of how institutions are created and maintained through talk in settings such as hospitals, courtrooms, and classrooms.

This approach shares with ethnography a desire to understand the organization of talk and individuals' experience of it from their own perspective, rather than from the 'objective' perspective of an outsider, but the CA approach eschews the primary concern of ethnography with social and cultural contexts outside the talk in focus. The difference is a methodological one. CA work does not deny Erickson's program to understand the influence on talk-in-interaction of processes that occur beyond the temporal and spatial horizon of the immediate occasion of interaction. The method of CA, however, limits analysis to the talk itself and includes consideration of other contextual processes *only insofar* as participants orient to them through their talk. This does not mean that a CA analysis is identical to a linguistic analysis because, as we have seen, a linguistic analysis considers the *what* of talk as words and structures that exist and have their meaning independently of any context in which language is used. In contrast, the question that CA poses is: *Why this, now?* In other words, each action of talk-in-interaction is examined for what the speaker does in relation to the actions that preceded it and the actions that the speaker expects to follow. In other words, for CA the context of an utterance is its place in the stream of talk – its sequential context rather than a context that extends beyond talk.

The focus of CA on action rather than language also allows us to expand our topic of interest from talk-in-interaction to other means of communication besides language, to what Per Linell (1998) called 'interaction between co-present individuals through symbolic means' (p. 12). Language is the human symbolic system *par excellence* and, because of its centrality in social life and the permanence of written language, it has received a great amount of attention to the detriment of other 'nonverbal' semiotic systems including bodily gesture, facial expression, clothing, spatial positioning, ritual practices, and expressive systems such as the visual arts. However, a communicative social event is much more than the production and reception of language: The relative positioning of participants with respect to each other and to the built environment, their gaze, and their facial expression must all be considered in an understanding of the social organization of participants.

In this chapter, we have presented some of the answers that philosophers, historians of literature, sociologists, and anthropologists have given to the question of the relations between the moment-by-moment development of talk-in-interaction and its social context. Their work has responded to the *who, where, when, how,* and *why* questions about language use and has introduced concepts such as speech genres, meaning as co-constructed, and the extension of context beyond the time and place of utterance. These concepts will be developed further throughout this book.

SUMMARY AND LOOKING AHEAD

The approach to language and interaction that we use in this book draws heavily on microethnography and on conversation analysis. In addition, our analysis of interaction will be inspired by genre theory to examine the discursive architecture of recurrent communicative practices. The approach to language we take is to treat the systemic and interactional features of language as a set of resources that are employed by participants in interaction. Participants' employment of linguistic and interactional resources helps to configure a discursive practice, and discursive practices will be compared in terms of differences between how resources are used, how they are influenced by social processes that occur beyond the temporal and spatial horizon of the interaction, and how practices modify those processes.

The approach to the analysis of language and interaction is developed throughout the remaining units. In Unit A2, we discuss in detail what is meant by context and how we can understand the relation between language and context. In Unit A3, we present the linguistic and interactional resources that speakers employ in creating meaning and participating in conversations. From these resources, participants create discursive practices, and in Unit A4 we define discursive practice and show how participants in discursive practices employ linguistic and interactional resources in order to create them. In Unit A5, we put all the resources together to show how they construct an interaction between two people: a music teacher and his student. We present a systematic way of describing the practice. We do so by analyzing participants' employment of linguistic and interactional resources, and how those resources combine to construct identity for the participants and how they establish a meaning for the practice. In Unit A6, we consider the relation between social constructions achieved through interaction in discursive practice and the cognition of individual participants. This relationship is considered as interactional competence, which is based on the psychology of intersubjectivity and the sociology of interaction.

The final three units of Section A apply the framework of discursive practice and interactional competence that we have laid out in Units A1 through 6 to develop an understanding of identity, community, and learning. In Unit A7, we focus on identity as constructed by the self and others. We consider the role of individual agency in identity construction and the imposition of identity by powerful others that is coercively applied through political, economic, and educational systems. Talk helps us to construct identity, and one aspect of identity is membership in a community of people with whom we feel we have something in common. In Unit A8, we discuss various ways in which individuals identify themselves as members of communities through shared linguistic resources and, more often, through shared ways of doing things.

Introduction

Throughout the book we discuss how people use language in social interaction with others in order to perform actions and to create contexts, meanings, stances, identities, and membership in a cultural community. How did they learn to do so? To complete the picture, the development of skills in social interaction is the topic of the final unit, which we discuss under three headings: language socialization, situated learning, and classroom interaction in schools.

Unit A2
Talk in context

PROLOGUE AND ROADMAP

An important feature of the way people use language in interaction is that the language we use is never taken in isolation but is always associated with a context. The place and time the interaction happened and the backgrounds of the people involved in the interaction all have an important influence on who says what to whom. It may be more surprising to learn that, by using language, people don't simply take context as a given, but also create their own context in which what we say is understood. The relationship between talk and context is a very complex one and we know much less about the relationship than we do about the talk itself. The aim of this unit is to examine systematically what we know about that relationship, and consider context first as a spatiotemporal construct, then as a sociocultural phenomenon, and third to consider that what we say in this moment is related to what we and others have said before and to the history of the social group to which we belong. The historical context of language does not only relate to words, events, and activities that happened long ago, but also to what was just said in interaction, and an important insight into conversation is that any utterance is influenced by utterances immediately preceding it. After this survey of the influences of context on talk, we will turn in the second half of the unit to consider the ontological status of context; that is, is context really 'out there'? Or do we construct psychological contexts that encourage us to fit our interpretations of language into the context that we create? The answer to both questions is yes.

A2.1 UNDERSTANDING CONTEXT

The word 'context' is one that we use quite often in everyday language. Here are some examples of contemporary uses of the word taken from the World Wide Web:

1. At the age of seven I joined the village church choir and from that time on the parish church was the main *context* of my life.
2. Students should apply mathematical knowledge and skills in a problem solving *context.*
3. The products themselves succeed or fail in the *context* of a global information industry.

In each of these examples, 'context' seems to mean some sort of background or container for an activity. In (1) the parish church is the background to the author's life activity; in (2) applying mathematical knowledge and skills is the activity that students are told to use when they solve problems; and in (3) the global information industry is the place where the activity happens – where the products succeed or fail. These examples show the common meaning of the noun 'context' in this dictionary definition.[1]

> the part or parts of a written or spoken passage preceding or following a particular word or group of words and so intimately associated with them as to throw light upon their meaning

An example of this would be the way readers interpret a word in the context of a sentence. Take the context of the word 'lie' in the sentences 'Lie down' and 'Don't tell a lie.' The words preceding or following the word 'lie' tell readers to interpret it as a verb meaning 'move your body to a horizontal position' or as a noun meaning 'falsehood.' The words before and after the group of words that we choose to focus on have been called the *sequential context*. A second dictionary definition of the word 'context' is:

> the interrelated conditions in which something exists or occurs

Examples of this meaning are sentences (1)–(3) in which the context is a different kind of thing from the activity: the author's life is a different kind of thing from the parish church, mathematical knowledge and skills are a different kinds of thing from problem-solving activity, and the success or failure of products is one thing and the global information industry is another.

In the common use of the word, then, the context refers to a place, a time, or conditions in which other things happen. The thing that happens is the focal event and the context is the background within which that event happens.

A2.1.1 Setting as spatiotemporal context

Linguists, too, have differentiated between activity and the context in which the activity occurs. One way in which linguists have understood context originates in the writings of Roman Jakobson (1960) and Dell Hymes (1974). Hymes recognized that any communicative activity in any modality – speech, writing, computer-mediated communication, signing, etc. – has features of context that share the same modality, i.e., some other speech can be a context for the speech we wish to focus on and some other email a context for a specific email message. At the same time, however, we can recognize features of context in a modality different from the focal event. For example, a particular speech event happens at a particular place and at a particular time between people who have particular relationships and a specific email message is written or read by certain people on different computers in different places at different times.

Hymes used the term *setting* to identify some features of context in a different modality from that of the focal event. Specifically, he defined setting as 'the time and place of a speech act and, in general, to the physical circumstances' (1974, p. 55).

Task A2.1.1.1

➤ Take your reading of a page of this book as the focal event and try to first identify features of the context of that event that share the same modality and then identify features that are from different modalities. For example, what did you read before you read this page? And what are the physical and temporal circumstances of the act of reading?

Hymes's distinction between those features of contexts that share a modality with a communicative event and those features that do not is similar to the distinction made in the two dictionary definitions cited above. The first definition identifies 'the part or parts of a written or spoken passage preceding or following a particular word or group of words,' and thus refers to features of context that share the same modality as the focal event. The second definition refers only to 'the interrelated conditions' when the communicative event occurs, conditions such as temporal and spatial location which do not share the same modality as a communicative act. In fact, a third dictionary definition of 'context' makes this meaning even clearer.

> things or conditions that serve to date or characterize an article (as a primitive artifact)

A2.1.2 Social and cultural context

While there is a clear distinction between features of sequential context that surround a focal event on the one hand and its spatial and temporal location on the other, there are further features of context that entice us to a deeper understanding of language in context. In order to illustrate some social and cultural features of context, Ray Birdwhistell (1960, 1970) reported a conversation between a mother and child that he heard one day on a bus. He reproduced the words of the conversation as follows.

```
1   Child:   Mama ((pause)) I gotta go to the bathroom
2  Mother:   ((pause))
3   Child:   Mama ((pause)) Donnie´s gotta go
4  Mother:   Sh-sh
5   Child:   But ((pause)) mama
6  Mother:   ((softly)) Later
7   Child:   ((whining)) Ma ma
8  Mother:   ((rasping voice)) Wait
```

```
 9   Child:   Oh mama mama mama
10   Mother:  ((loudly)) Shut up ((softly)) will yuh
```

In this conversation, we can quite easily identify the two features of context that we have discussed so far: sequential context and setting. The child begins the conversation with a request and repeats the request four times. Part of the sequential context of each repetition is the preceding request, and in this way we can understand why the child says 'Donnie's gotta go' in line 3 and he does not specify where he's got to go because he's already specified that in line 1.

The sequential context of his mother's 'Sh-sh' in line 4 also helps us to understand what she is doing. In other sequential contexts, a mother hushing a child could be interpreted as a request to be quiet or the mother's attempt to comfort the child. But in this conversation the mother produces 'Sh-sh' after two requests from her child, and we know that if someone makes a request of another person the first person expects the reply to mean that the request has been either granted or refused. So, in this sequential context, Donnie understands his mother's 'Sh-sh' as a refusal, which sets up a new sequential context for his contestation of his mother's refusal in line 5: 'But mama.'

The setting of the conversation is also easy to specify. Birdwhistell observed the conversation at about 2:30 p.m., April 14, 1952 on a bus in Arlington, Virginia. But beyond the spatiotemporal data, Birdwhistell (1970, p. 283) goes on to give further information about the context.

> Mother and child spoke with a tidewater Virginia accent. The bus route on which the event was recorded leads to a middle-class neighborhood. The way in which the mother and child were dressed was not consistent with the dress of other riders.

Birdwhistell's description gives information about some other contextual features of the conversation – the participants' accents and dress – that distinguish them from the middle-class neighborhood through which they are passing; the implication being that mother and child are from a different socioeconomic class than the other riders on the bus. This description of the social context tells us that this conversation between mother and child did not take place in private, and the context – on a bus in front of other participants from a different (perhaps higher) social class – also allows us to interpret the mother's refusal of her son's request. It is not possible to go to the bathroom on a bus and talking loudly about such things can cause embarrassment, especially if the talk is overheard by other people.

 Task A2.1.2.1

➤ In line 2 of the conversation between the mother and child, Birdwhistell reports a pause, and he attributed the pause to the mother. In other words, there was silence. Why not simply ignore the silence and continue with the child's talk in line 3? Why attribute the silence to the mother?

In describing the social context of this conversation, we have informally specified the participants as the mother, the child, and the other people on the bus. In doing so, we have extended the meaning of context to include participants, and by doing so we do not mean simply Donnie and his mother, the people whose talk we have chosen as the focal event. Erving Goffman (1979, 1981) criticized the simple idea that we can identify speaker and hearer simply by looking at the names that are indicated on the left-hand side of a transcript, and he distinguished among several different social roles that hearers and speakers can play. Goffman distinguished among hearers as follows. The person or persons being addressed by a speaker are ratified by the speaker as official participants in the encounter, although some or all of them may not be paying conscious attention to the speaker. In addition, many other people may hear the conversation even though the speaker does not ratify them. These unofficial participants may be engaged in the encounter in one of two socially different ways, as Goffman (1981, pp. 131–132) described:

> Either [the hearers] have purposely engineered this, resulting in 'eaves-dropping,' or the opportunity has unintentionally and inadvertently come about, as in 'overhearing.' In brief, a ratified participant may not be listening, and someone listening may not be a ratified participant.

If we now examine the participants in the conversation on the bus, Birdwhistell told us that there were other people on the bus, who were dressed differently from Donnie and his mother, and some of these riders may have overheard Donnie and his mother's talk. Why should we be interested in these non-ratified participants? Although they do not contribute their own voices to the conversation between Donnie and his mother, they do in fact exert an influence. We see, for example, that a lot of the work that the mother tries to do in the conversation is to get Donnie to be quiet. In line 2 she tries to ignore him, in line 4 she shushes him, in line 6 she speaks softly, in line 8 she produces just the single word 'wait' in a rasping voice, and in line 10 the mother loudly tells her boy to shut up and immediately reverts to a low volume 'will yuh.' One way of interpreting the generally low volume of the mother's talk and her desire to shut Donnie up is that she recognizes the fact that the other riders on the bus are overhearing a conversation that she does not wish them to hear, perhaps because she feels embarrassed about talking about bathroom functions and perhaps because she perceives a social class difference between herself and the other riders. The unofficial participants in a conversation therefore influence the talk of the official participants and we must include them as participants in order to understand the social context of the conversation.

Besides distinguishing several roles for hearers, Goffman also distinguished among three different production roles that participants play as *animator*, *author*, and *principal*. The participant out of whose mouth words flow is the 'animator,' an individual engaged in the activity of speech production. But the words spoken may not originate in the mind of the animator, who may simply give voice to the expressed thoughts and actual words of another. An 'author' is someone who has selected the sentiments being expressed and the words in which they are encoded. And then, in any interaction, there may be a participant whose 'position is established by the words being spoken, someone whose beliefs have been told, someone who is committed to what the words say' (p. 144), a participant Goffman called the 'principal.' These participant roles take the context far beyond the people who produce the talk. An example of a principal can be clearly identified in the following conversation between a pharmacist and a client in a community pharmacy (Nguyen, 2003). In this conversation, a client has given a prescription to a pharmacist, the pharmacist has filled the prescription, and is now conducting a patient consultation, in which he is advising the client on how to use the medication.

```
 1 Pharmacist:   have you had doxycycline before:;
 2     Client:   u:::h. nn (.) <I think that I might have
 3               I´ve had, (.) something for this,>
 4               this similar type of allergy. so.
 5 Pharmacist:   okay. they want you to have one tablet
 6               (.) twice daily (.) ten day supply. this is
 7               one of those has some warnings that come
 8               with it, probably the most important one
 9               that I can think of is to take it with (.)
10               at least one full glass of water coz when
11               it´s stuck and doesn´t get all the way down
12               it can cause (.) a lo:t of burning.
13     Client:   right.
```

Throughout this patient consultation, the pharmacist takes the role of animator because it is through his words that the patient consultation is achieved, but he also invokes another participant in turn 3 with 'they want you to have one tablet twice daily.' It is not clear here whether the pharmacist is invoking the doctor or the person who wrote the information relating to the drug; it is clear, however, that the pharmacist is invoking 'their' authority in advising the client. By invoking this authority, the pharmacist has established a role for a different participant in this conversation: the principal. The principal is not physically present in the pharmacy during the patient consultation, but nonetheless forms part of the context in which the consultation takes place.

 Task A2.1.2.2

➤ At the time of this patient consultation, the pharmacist was in fact an advanced student at a School of Pharmacy doing his internship in the community. What evidence does the consultation provide for his status as a student? What differences would you expect to find between this consultation and one conducted by an experienced, qualified pharmacist?

The role of 'author' is much easier to identify than principal because the animator invokes an author by using the author's words to express the author's position. The role of author is clear in the email below from the chair of a department at an American university to the members of his advisory committee.

1   In response to Anna's question in AC yesterday, I called Peter Chandler this
2   morning and asked him whether it was necessary for the chair to seek
3   permission from the department's executive committee to negotiate
4   counteroffers for faculty who receive offers from other institutions.
5   He cited FPP 3.77.a, which says:

6   The executive committee may, by annual vote, delegate to a subcommittee
7   or to the chair the authority to make recommendations with respect to any
8   or all of the following matters, except as noted in 3.77.C.:

9   1. salaries;
10 2. faculty recruitment;
11 3. nonfaculty personnel actions;
12 4. equipment and supplies.

In this email communication, the department chair reports that he had requested some guidance on a matter of personnel policy. He invokes another participant, Peter Chandler, in the role of author, and he reports that Peter Chandler in turn invokes (and the invocation is made explicit by the word 'cited' in line 5) a university governance document called 'Faculty Policy and Procedures' (FPP) as an authoritative source of information on personnel matters, i.e., as the principal. Neither Peter Chandler nor the FPP document were physically present in the spatiotemporal context of the department chair composing the email to his colleagues, but they nevertheless have an effect on the focal event – the email – and must be considered as participants.

In this discussion of social context, we have expanded the notion of participant roles from those individuals who are physically present during an interaction to those whose roles are invoked as unofficial or non-ratified hearers, as well as authors and principals of the production of talk. This broader view of participant roles allows us to understand certain kinds of discourse where participants are clearly not physically present. When Christians say the Lord's Prayer, for example, they invoke God as an official hearer by referring to God with the second person singular pronoun possessive 'thy' in:

Our Father who art in heaven, Hallowed be thy Name.

When Muslims read a surah from the Qu'ran or begin a formal lecture or public discourse, they do so by invoking Allah as principal with the Arabic phrase 'In the name of Allah, most gracious, most merciful':

Bismillah AlRahman AlRaheem

And when Buddhists recite of The Heart of Prajna Paramita sutra, they animate the words of the Buddha, who is both author of the words and the principal, who addresses his disciple, Shariputra thus:

> Shariputra, form does not differ from emptiness; emptiness does not differ from form. Form itself is emptiness; emptiness itself is form. So, too, are feeling, cognition, formation, and consciousness.

Physical presence is therefore not a requirement for a participant in communicative activity, and we need to look outside the here-and-now to understand the influence that non-present or unofficial participants have on the language and the meaning of the event.

A2.1.3 Historical context

In the previous section, we presented evidence that some important features of the context of communicative events are not physically present at the event. We follow this observation with a further expansion of the idea of context: We need to consider features of context that do not belong in the same time period as the focal event, in particular those that happened before the focal event. This idea of the importance of historical context in understanding communicative events is brought out in Birdwhistell's description of the context of the conversation between mother and child on the bus. Birdwhistell gives contextual information about the accents and dress of the participants. Why is this relevant in understanding their conversation?

The French sociologist Pierre Bourdieu argued that participants are not completely free to act or to talk in any way in a particular social situation. Although participants are certainly not automata that respond in pre-programmed ways in social situations, they are nonetheless limited in their actions and in their talk by their own history, laid down in their formative years by the cultural environment of the home. Participants' predispositions to act and to talk in certain ways in particular situations, Bourdieu (1977) called *habitus*. Habitus refers to participants' socially acquired predispositions, tendencies, propensities, or inclinations, which are shown in mental phenomena such as opinions and outlooks, linguistic phenomena such as ways of talking, and physical phenomena such as deportment, posture, as well as ways of walking, sitting, and dressing.

Accent is a good example of what Bourdieu meant by habitus. The term accent refers to how people pronounce certain words, so if one speaker pronounces the final 'r' after vowels like in 'car' and one doesn't, making the word sound like 'cah,' then we recognize two different accents. Everyone has an accent, not just people who speak a foreign language; although we notice accents more when they are different from our own. Although it is possible for people to change accents throughout a lifetime, most features of pronunciation that we recognize as an accent are formed in childhood and adolescence, and they reflect the geographical and social background of a speaker. When we talk about 'a Texas accent' or 'a British accent' or we say that 'The customers will love your Italian accent' we are referring to what we perceive to be the geographical origin of the speaker. Linguists have observed that a person's accent also correlates with their social class. In a famous study carried out in department stores in New York City, William Labov (1972b) found that store clerks' pronunciation of 'r' after vowels varied according to their social class. In the pricier stores in the upmarket neighborhoods, clerks pronounced postvocalic 'r' much more often than clerks in the cheaper stores in less affluent neighborhoods.

A third major influence on a person's accent is ethnicity. White Americans tend to speak differently from African Americans, and both groups tend to speak differently from Latinos. For example, many white Americans pronounce two consonants in final consonant clusters such as 'lift' but many African Americans will produce a single consonant, 'lif'. And bilingual Latinos often alternate rapidly between their two languages and play on the differences between the Spanish and English pronunciation of words, as in this performance by Guillermo Gómez-Peña (1996).[2]

1   kiss me, kiss me my chola
2   como si fuera esta noche the last migra raid
3   kiss me, kiss moi mi chuca
4   que tengo miedo perderte somewhere in L.A.

5   watcha' que maybe mañana yo estaré en la pinta
6   longing for your ass (digo eyes)
7   y que quizá me deporten de nuevo a Tijuana
8   por ser ilegal

Rapid switching between two languages as exemplified in this performance also involves changing from an Anglo accent to a Spanish one, a difference that Gómez-Peña makes explicit in line 6 when 'eyes' in a Spanish accent sounds like 'ass' in an Anglo accent.

These examples show that where you grew up and the people from the social class and race that you have hung out with all influence how you speak in a particular conversation. These are all features of your personal history that allow other people to categorize you as belonging to a larger group of people who share your geographical, class, and ethnic background; in Bourdieu's terms accent is habitus, and habitus is something which does not generally reach conscious awareness and, unless it does, it limits the ways in which we can act and talk. We only become aware of our own accent when someone else points it out to us, usually with praise ('I love your British accent') or blame ('Children can't speak properly any more').

Although Bourdieu (1990) recognized the predispositions to act and think in certain ways that are consequences of habitus, he did not think of habitus as a fixed essence operating to determine thoughts or behavior. Instead, he recognized 'the social agent in his true role as the practical operator of the construction of objects' (p. 90). That is to say: Human actors are agents in the construction and interpretation of their own actions.

Through the concept of habitus we can see that the context of a focal event extends way back into the past histories of all participants in the event. In order to understand how the passengers on the bus interpret the actions and dress of the mother and child in Birdwhistell's example, we have to know something about their personal histories as well as about Donnie's and his mother's home culture.

A2.1.4 Language as its own context

In discussing context so far, we have shown that the concept extends beyond the speaking participants in a conversation to other participants who may or may not be physically present, and to the personal histories of all participants. We also noted that language itself provides a context for interpreting words such as 'lie' in 'lie down' and 'don't tell a lie,' which we have termed sequential context. But there is another way in which we interpret talk-in-interaction by means of the talk that precedes or follows it, and that is through the processes of conversational implicature identified by H. P. Grice (1989) and conversational inference identified by John Gumperz (1982).

Grice recognized that, if we look only at the words of some conversations, participants seem to be behaving irrationally. Imagine, for example, that one evening two people, Harry and Sally, are hosting a party at their house. It is about nine o'clock when Harry asks Sally 'What time is it?' and Sally replies 'Some of the guests are leaving already.' Although Harry requests information about the time, Sally does not appear to provide it; instead she replies that some of the guests are leaving. Why is Sally being apparently uncooperative? Grice tells us that Harry can interpret Sally's utterance perfectly well because both of them observe the Cooperative Principle, which can be simply stated as follows: 'Make your conversational contribution such as is required, at the stage at which it occurs, by the accepted purpose or direction of the talk exchange in which you are engaged' (Grice, 1989, p. 26). If Harry assumes that Sally is observing the Cooperative Principle, then he knows that her statement about the guests leaving implies that (1) it is quite early in the evening, and (2) their party is not the social success that they had hoped it would be.

Grice further specifies that four maxims (or rules) operate within the Cooperative Principle. Participants in conversations expect their conversation partners and themselves to say just the right amount and to say what they believe to be true, and they expect the contributions to be relevant and to be unambiguous. Sally's response to Harry's inquiry about the time clearly violates the maxim of relevance because it does not appear to provide an answer to Harry's question. But precisely because it apparently violates a conversational maxim and Sally appears to be acting uncooperatively, Harry has to search for a different interpretation that does not violate the maxim and, through the process of conversational implicature, arrives at the conclusion that Sally *really means* that it is quite early in the evening and their party is not the social success that they had hoped it would be.

Task A2.1.4.1

➤ In this exchange between a high-school teacher and student, what does the teacher imply by his reply? How can the student use the Cooperative Principle to arrive at an understanding of what the teacher 'really means'?

Student: Tehran's in Turkey, isn't it, teacher?
Teacher: And London's in Armenia, I suppose.

Conversational implicature is the process by which conversational participants resolve apparently illogical meanings by recourse to the assumption that all parties to the conversation are following the Cooperative Principle. That is, if the meaning of conversational participants' utterances cannot be arrived at by considering the everyday meaning of their words, then we must seek outside everyday meanings in order to interpret them. There are also occasions when speakers imply meanings without explicitly stating them, such as in political discourse. If, for example, a challenger to an incumbent politician promises to produce better-paying jobs, to improve education and to cut health care costs, the meaning that we can derive from his use of the words 'better-paying,' 'improve,' and 'cut . . . costs' is that he wants us to believe that (under the rule of the incumbent) jobs don't pay enough, educational standards are low, and health care costs too much. The challenger's implied criticisms of the incumbent don't follow from any apparent violations of the Cooperative Principle, but they are inherent in the everyday meanings of the words.

We have tried to show with these examples that the meaning of an utterance is not fixed, and can be interpreted in myriad ways. John Gumperz showed that people make decisions about how to interpret an utterance based on their understanding of what is happening at the time of the interaction. In other words, each utterance is understood in an interpretive frame (Goffman, 1974), and people's belief in or knowledge of the frame determines their understanding of the utterance. Participants in conversations offer a frame in which interlocutors can interpret their utterances. Sometimes they indicate a frame explicitly by naming it when they say something like 'I was only joking!' or 'This is off the record,' but more often frames are signaled by intonation, facial expressions or gestures, and constellations of surface features of the form of a message, signals that are sometimes very subtle and can be easily misinterpreted. These subtle signals of the frame in which a participant wishes an interlocutor to interpret an utterance, Gumperz called *contextualization cues.* When participants share a common background, the contextualization cues are easy to understand, as in this conversation between two students sitting in a coffee shop gossiping about their landlords (Gumperz, 2000, p. 127).

```
1   A:   But she´s a FLAKE.
2   B:   ((fast tempo)) Ya know we should probably watch
         it. They're probably sitt´n there.
3   A:   (overlapping B´s last three words) I know.
```

```
4   B:   It´s just nice going to cafes now and I feel
         like I don't have to avoid
         anybody.
5   A:   (overlapping B´s last three words) THIS is the
         LIFE.
```

In this conversation, A's overlapping of the end of B's turns and her statements of agreement in turns 4 and 6 indicate that she shares with A the frame of the conversation as an opportunity to complain about powerful adults like landlords and to take youthful pleasure in the freedom of the coffee shop. As Gumperz comments, 'To those familiar with American student culture, the exchange seems perfectly understandable.'

But contextualization cues can also be misunderstood and lead to bad feelings. As an example of this, Gumperz (1982, pp. 134–135) provides the following scenario.

> A husband sitting in his living room is addressing his wife. The husband is of middle class American background. The wife is British. They have been married and living in the United States for a number of years:

```
Husband:   Do you know where today´s paper is?
Wife:      I´ll get it for you.
Husband:   That's O.K. Just tell me where it is. I´ll get it.
Wife:      No, I´LL get it.
```

The husband begins this conversation in line 1 with a question that interpreted literally is an inquiry about the location of today's newspaper. His wife does not accept this frame and offers instead to get the paper and indicates the change of frame by means of an accented '*I'll*' in line 2. The change of frame from an inquiry to an offer is then contested by the husband in line 3 with a counter-suggestion and another stressed '*I'll*.' The wife then repeats her offer within this frame of contestation with strong stress on 'I'LL' in line 4 to indicate her annoyance with the change of frame.

Contextualization clues are subtle and frames can change rapidly in the course of a conversation. Getting on the same wavelength as a conversational partner requires a lot of work that hardly appears to be work at all when the participants share a cultural background, but when they don't a lot of work may result in very little understanding. In his work among Asian immigrants to Britain in the 1970s (Twitchin, Gumperz, Jupp, and Roberts, 1979), Gumperz has shown that the work of inferring frames from contextualization clues is a particular challenge for participants who come from different cultural backgrounds, and the failure of immigrants to understand the frames of their employers and vice versa have serious economic consequences.

Task A2.1.4.2

➤ Here is another example of misinterpretation of contextualization cues from Gumperz (1982, p. 133).

> The graduate student has been sent to interview a black housewife in a low income, inner city neighborhood. The contact has been made over the phone by someone in the office. The student arrives, rings the bell, and is met by the husband, who opens the door, smiles, and steps towards him:

> *Husband*:   So y're gonna check out ma ol lady, hah?
> *Interviewer*:   Ah, no. I only came to get some information. They called from the office.

> (Husband, dropping his smile, disappears without a word and calls his wife.) The student reports that the interview that followed was stiff and quite unsatisfactory. Being black himself, he knew that he had 'blown it.'

> What were the contextualization cues that the student missed and what did they mean? How could the student have replied to the husband to show that he was on the husband's wavelength?

In this section we have further expanded the concept of context to include the inferences that participants draw from the talk of others and the interpretative frames that they attempt to create and within which meaning of talk is understood. Goffman's notion of *frame* as a way of understanding talk-in-interaction is similar to the idea of context with which we began this unit. In distinguishing a focal event from its context, we are in effect placing a frame around the event, to isolate it and to interpret it. But it would be a mistake to think of the frame and the focal event as independent entities, because in fact, as we have seen, the frame influences our interpretation of the event, and the event itself can help to construct a frame for its interpretation. The interrelationships between context and focal event will be the subject of the concluding sections of this unit.

A2.2 THE ONTOLOGICAL STATUS OF CONTEXT

In discussing context, we have adopted a visual trope by talking about it as a 'frame,' rather like the frame surrounding a classical portrait in which we distinguish between the central figure and a peripheral ground. Pursuing this trope, the focal event is seen like the figure in a classical portrait painting, in which we view it as a central figure in a background of peripheral interest. In the portrait in Figure A2.1, for instance, the central figure of Elvis is clearly distinguishable from the background, and our attention is focused on the figure of Elvis although we scan the background scenery in order to put Elvis 'in context.' The visual separation of figure from ground and the centrality of the figure in a peripheral background in a portrait is a remembrance of the basic concepts of focal event and context that we have described throughout this unit so far.

Figure A2.1 Portrait of Elvis Presley by Ralph Wolfe Cowan. Source: National Portrait Gallery, Smithsonian Institution; gift of R. W. Cowan

The clear separation between figure and ground reinforces the separation and independence of a focal event and context, and there is a tradition in the study of context in which we assume that context is given and can be described, and the distinguishable focal event is correlated with the context in some way. As the context changes, so the focal event changes in some way, and our task is to understand the correlation between the two. There is, however, another way of understanding the relationship between context and the focal event that stress the interconnectedness of the two. In a different tradition, the focal event shapes the context of the event itself; rather like if we replaced Elvis in the portrait with a different figure, then that change would also change the background. We will discuss these two ways of understanding context in the next sections.

A2.2.1 Context as a given

One notion of context is that it is just out there: It is a given that we may know and describe. In the examples of language-in-interaction that we have discussed so far, we can see this view of context as the physical setting in which talk takes place. The conversation between Donnie and his mother took place on a bus, the patient consultation took place in a pharmacy, and the conversation between the students took place in a coffee shop. Each of the settings can be described and each of them has a different effect on the talk. It's likely that many patient consultations take place in a pharmacy, for example, and it's unlikely that many take place in different settings. The correlation between the other two conversations and their settings is less clear. Students complain about their landlords and children ask their mothers to go to the bathroom in many different settings, although certain aspects of the conversations (the mother's desire to quiet Donnie and the student's remark that 'It's just nice going to cafes') may be more closely correlated with the context than others.

Labov's work in the department stores that we mentioned above also took context as given, but in this case the given context was the socioeconomic class of the store clerks and it was their pronunciation of postvocalic 'r' that was the focal event. Many other studies of language variation have correlated features of context with pronunciation, but most have taken the contextual features as a given, existing independently of the language that was studied. Peter Trudgill, for example, studied how gender correlated with the pronunciation of '-ing' in Norwich, England. In this community people pronounce words like 'sitting' or 'talking' in two different ways. One pronunciation of the final consonant is the non-standard [n], which we can write as *sittin'* or *standin'*, and the other standard pronunciation is with the same velar nasal that we hear in the pronunciation of 'ng' in 'English,' which we write in phonetic script as [ŋ]. Trudgill (1974) found that three features of context correlated with the pronunciation of '-ing': the task that the speakers were doing, the socioeconomic class of the speakers, and their gender. Figure A2.2 shows the correlations that Trudgill found.

The gender of these middle-class speakers had an influence on their pronunciation of -ing. Men tended to produce more non-standard pronunciations as their speech style became more informal, but women were unaffected by the formality of the speech style and pronounced all their -ing's in the standard way. The contextual features of gender, speech style, and socioeconomic class that Trudgill reported in this study are assumed to exist independently of the pronunciation of -ing; that is to say, before they opened their mouths, speakers were men or women, came from a certain class, and during the recording sessions used the same speech style. These features of context were, in a way, like the physical settings of the other examples we discussed: They did not change as a result of how the speakers talked and they remained the same before and after the focal event. In this view of context, it is a given and the task of the linguist is to correlate the language of the focal event with the various fixed features of context.

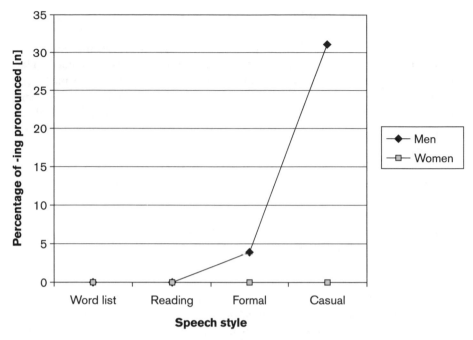

Figure A2.2 Pronunciation of '-ing' by middle-class speakers in Norwich as a function of task and gender. Source: Trudgill (1974)

A2.2.2   Context as constructed by language in interaction

Studies of how language correlates with the features of social context in specific speech communities have produced much valuable information about how working-class people speak differently from middle-class people, how older people speak differently from younger people, and how men speak differently from women, among many other findings. But in all of this work, the actual speaker is assumed to simply respond to the context. What is lacking is a sense of individual agency: How I can speak in a more or less gendered way if I want to, how I can say things that are at least odd and even sometimes inappropriate for a person of my age, and how I as a middle-class professor can express my solidarity with working-class people by taking on pronunciations characteristic of the working class if I choose to? In other words, through my use of language I can create context, not simply respond to it.

The use of language to help people create and play with new identities has been discussed at length by Ben Rampton, in his work on *language crossing*, which we discuss at length in Section A7.6. Crossing is the use of a conspicuous out-group language and involves a speaker attempting to move across quite sharply felt social or ethnic boundaries. The phenomenon of language crossing is found often among white middle-class American teenagers who have been influenced by hip hop language. Black youth language creates an aura of toughness and street smarts; essentially, it has become a prestige language for young people in the early twenty-first century, just as hip hop fashions and music have come to dominate adolescent buying habits. Crossing into African American Vernacular English (AAVE) allows young people to experiment with alternative identities and has the potential for breaking down ethnic barriers by creating new forms of youth culture. Cecilia Cutler (1999) described an example of this kind of language crossing in her study of 'Mike.'

Mike lived in a wealthy New York City neighborhood and attended an exclusive private school. Mike and most of Mike's friends were white. At around age 13, he began to identify quite strongly with the hip hop culture. He wore baggy jeans, a reverse baseball cap, designer sneakers, and developed a taste for rap music. At around the same time he began to change the way he spoke, crossing into AAVE. His family members said he 'sounded like a street kid or hoodlum.' At age 16, Cutler recorded Mike speaking to some of his white friends:

```
You ever hear of Frank Frazetta? Dis is some phat shit, yo.
Yo, when the dude dies, this book will probably be worth
like a thousand dollars. Yo tell me that shit is not phat!
```

By Mike's use of pronunciations like 'dis' for this, intensifiers like 'yo,' and words like 'phat,' Mike created for himself and his friends an imaginary identity of a black hip hop emcee. Looking at the interaction from a distance, of course, we see a bunch of middle-class white kids but, for the participants themselves, the context that Mike creates is very different.

An individual human agent cannot create contexts alone; at least some of the co-participants in an interaction co-construct the context that is being created. You may remember a scene from the movie *Rush hour* starring black actor Chris Tucker and Hong Kong born Jackie Chan. Tucker's character has entered a bar and is passing out some friendly greetings to his brothers, slapping palms and using the phrase 'Whaassup, mah nigger?' Later in the scene, Jackie's character – who is fresh off the plane from Hong Kong and new to this American jive – attempts to imitate his partner's culture to fit in better. He flashes a silly grin at the black bartender, says 'What's up, my nigger?', and almost gets a bar stool broken across his teeth.

SUMMARY AND LOOKING AHEAD

In this unit we have taken a very broad perspective on the relationship between language and context, between utterance and beliefs, and between talk in the present moment and talk in the past. Unit B2 contains passages from the writings of Charles Goodwin and Alessandro Duranti, in which the relationship between language and context is explained systematically. In Unit C2 you have the opportunity to explore the relationship of two narratives to the contexts in which they were told. Although we know far more about language than we understand about context and its relationship to talk, there are two analytical approaches that have been successful in increasing our understanding. These are systemic functional grammar and conversation analysis, which we introduce in Unit A3.

Unit A3
Interactional resources

PROLOGUE AND ROADMAP

In this unit we will consider a number of different communicative events – a famous speech and snippets from a number of conversations – with a view to explicating the relationship between these events and the contexts in which they occur. We will introduce two methodologies which provide a way to understand that complex and shifting relationship: systemic functional grammar and conversation analysis. Known by their acronyms of SFG and CA, these two methodologies focus on two sides of the problem: how linguistic resources are employed by speakers to create meaning in text, and how interactional resources allow participants in the ongoing flow of conversation to do social actions and to respond to the social actions of others. In introducing SFG, we will highlight the importance of constituency in the analysis of texts, and consider how texts create interpersonal, ideational, and textual meanings. Turning to conversational interaction, we will introduce how CA explains how speakers sequence their conversational actions, how they take turns, and how they repair trouble in interaction. The unit concludes with a discussion of how participation in interaction creates identities and how those identities form, dissolve, and reform through the course of an interaction.

A3.1 LANGUAGE AS A RESOURCE FOR MAKING MEANING

Consider a communicative event. We'll take for example Dr Martin Luther King Jr's famous speech 'I have a dream,' which he delivered in front of the Lincoln Memorial on August 28, 1963, at the March for Civil Rights in Washington, DC. Figure A3.1 shows Dr King speaking.

There are many aspects to Dr King's speech that combine together to make it a communicative event, some of which you can see in the photograph: Dr King, the speaker, and a number of people who are listening to him speak. Things that you can't see in the photograph include the time and place of the speech, the reasons for the event, and its effect on the struggle for civil rights in the United States. What most people focus on, of course, is the speech itself and for linguists the language of the speech is the prime aspect of the communicative event.[1] Here is an excerpt.

Figure A3.1 Dr Martin Luther King Jr speaking at the March for Civil Rights in 1963.
Source: http://www.drmartinlutherkingjr.com/ihaveadream.htm

I have a dream that one day this nation will rise up and live out the true meaning of its creed: 'We hold these truths to be self-evident: that all men are created equal.' I have a dream that one day on the red hills of Georgia the sons of former slaves and the sons of former slave owners will be able to sit down together at the table of brotherhood.

Although we have mentioned several different aspects of the communicative event, the language of the speech being only one, and although language is only one method of communication its importance must not be underestimated. Here is a dictionary definition of the word *language*:

The words, their pronunciation, and the methods of combining them used and understood by a considerable community and established by long usage <French *language*> <Bantu group of *languages*> <classical Latin is a dead *language*> <*language* barrier between two countries>[2]

Human languages, both spoken and written, can also be described as a system of symbols and the rules by which the symbols are manipulated. Many people accept a view of language as a set of clearly delineated and internally coherent structures that are best understood as a self-contained system. And in some modern linguistic theories, the coherent nature of language, the similarities that can be seen between all human languages, and the differences between human languages and forms of animal communication are taken as evidence that linguistic phenomena arise from uniquely human mental states. From this point of view, linguistics is in fact a subfield of psychology. Although this is no doubt true of all human languages, this view does not emphasize the primary use of language in communicative events, where it is used as a resource for making meaning.

One linguistic theory that does not start from the forms of language but considers it first and foremost as a resource for making meaning is Systemic Functional Grammar or SFG (Halliday and Matthiessen, 2004). In the sections that follow, we will introduce some basic principles of systemic functional grammar and show how they can be applied to the understanding of the role of language in communicative events.

A3.1.1 Levels of language

The basic unit of language in SFG is the text. A text is any instance of language produced in speech or in writing. It can be as short as a single word or longer than the 'I have a dream' speech, but in most texts we can recognize that they make meaning at different levels of organization and that these levels are in a hierarchical relationship, which means one level is composed from units at another level, which in turn are composed from units at a lower level, and so on. This property of texts is called *constituency*, and it is a fundamental organizing principle of language. In the 'I have a dream' speech, Dr King pauses and his listeners respond and applaud at certain places in the speech, as in this representation.[3]

I have a dream *((Pause))* that one day *((Shout of 'Yeah!' from crowd and pause))* this nation will rise up *((Pause))* and live out the true meaning of its creed: *((Pause))* 'We hold these truths to be self-evident: *((Pause))* that all men are created equal.' *((Applause, shouts of 'Hear! Hear!' and pause))* I have a dream *((Pause))* that one day on the red hills of Georgia *((Shout of 'Yeah!' and pause))* the sons of former slaves and the sons of former slave owners *((Pause))* will be able to sit down together at the table of brotherhood.

Those pauses and audience responses coincide with divisions of the spoken text into units called *melodic lines* or *tone units*. Each tone unit is composed of rhythmic units or *feet*. For instance, in the tone unit *I have a dream*, the louder volume and the stretched vowel of *I* are of similar length to *have a dream*, and thus allow us to identify two feet in the tone unit. Within each foot there are a number of smaller units called syllables, and the division of a foot into syllables is represented as in this example: *the+true+mea+ning+of+its+creed*. Within the syllable itself, we recognize two constituents, one of which allows the syllable to rhyme with other syllables. We refer to this simply as the *rhyme* and the proceeding sound to which it is attached (if any) as the *onset*. This we can see in *creed* in which -*eed* which rhymes with *need*, *seed*, *freed*, and *lead*; and these syllables are distinguished from each other by their onsets: *cr-* in *creed*, *n-* in *need*, *s-* in *seed*, and so on. These elements have their own constituents, called *phonemes*, for example the long 'e' sound in -*eed* and the final 'd' sound. The phonological system is thus a hierarchy of constituents: from phoneme to onset and rhyme, from onset and rhyme to syllable, from syllable to foot, and from foot to tone unit.

Task A3.1.1.1

➤ Take another tone unit from the 'I have a dream' speech, for example 'the sons of former slaves and the sons of former slave owners,' and identify its constituent structure in terms of feet, syllables, onsets, and rhymes.

Just as we recognize constituent structure in spoken language, we can recognize the same kind of structure in writing and in lexicogrammar. The graphological constituents of writing are letter, word, subsentence, sentence, and paragraph; and the constituent structure is indicated by punctuation and spacing. In the 'I have a dream speech' as it is written in the first excerpt, we can see that the constituents of the paragraph are sentences, and the sentences are bounded by periods. The first sentence has two subsentences bounded by the colon, and words are the constituents of each sentence and subsentence. Words are bounded by white space and their constituents are letters, which are also bounded by space. Because the boundaries of each constituent in the written text are conventional in modern English, we have no difficulty in distinguishing one constituent from another. In early forms of writing, however, these indications were absent. For example, Figure A3.2 shows the initial page of St Mark's Gospel in the Lindisfarne Gospels of the seventh century CE.[4] In this Latin text, there is no punctuation, there are no spaces between the words and, although boundaries between letters are mostly as we would recognize them today, in some cases letters are written within and across other letters. In modern writing, the Gospel opens with letters taken from the Roman and Greek alphabets:

LIBER GENERATIONIS IHU XPI FILII DAVID ΦLII ABRAHAM

We can easily recognize the graphological constituents of this modern text, which helps us to translate the text into Modern English as: 'The book of the genealogy of

Jesus Christ, the son of David, the son of Abraham.' You may also notice that, in the margins, a scribe has added translations of the Latin text in Old English.

Besides speech and writing, one other important dimension of language in which we see the principle of constituency is lexicogrammar. Grammar refers to how words are organized into phrases, and how phrases are organized into clauses. The lexicon is the properties of words, both how words are built up from smaller units and also the relationships between words. In order to capture both levels of organization into

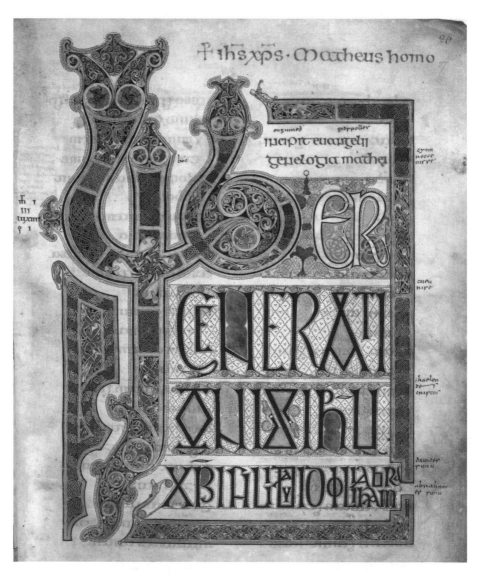

Figure A3.2 The initial page of St Mark's Gospel in the Lindisfarne Gospels of the seventh century CE. Source: © The British Library Board. All Rights Reserved Cotton Nero D. IV, f. 27.

one system, SFG calls that system *lexicogrammar.* The system of lexicogrammar is different from the graphological system and from the phonological system, and we use different terms to identify the constituents of the three systems. 'Sentence' and 'letter' are constituents of the graphological system; 'syllable' and 'phoneme' are constituents of the phonological system; and 'clause' and 'phrase' are constituents of lexicogrammar. The only term that is shared is 'word,' but we must be careful to distinguish between a written word and a word in lexicogrammar; for example the *'ll* in *I'll* and the *n't* in *can't* function as words in the lexicogrammar, but most people would not call them words in the writing system.

In the first lines of the 'I have a dream' speech, these two clauses are constituents of a clause complex: *I have a dream* and *that one day this nation will rise up and live out the true meaning of its creed.* The constituents of the first clause are two phrases *I* and *have a dream,* and the constituents of the phrase *have a dream* are *have* and another phrase *a dream.* The words that are constituents of the phrases in some cases have their own constituents, called morphemes. In the first lines of 'I have a dream,' each word is a single morpheme, but in the second clause complex, *the sons of former slaves and the sons of former slave owners will be able to sit down together at the table of brotherhood,* four words have two constituent morphemes each: *son-s, slave-s, owner-s,* and *brother-hood.*

When we look at the language of a communicative event as text, we analyze it in terms of three systems: the phonological system if it is a spoken text, the graphological system if it is a written text, and the lexicogrammar for both written and spoken texts. Although each of these systems is described by different terms and in different ways, the basic organizing principle of all linguistic systems is the same: a hierarchical organization of constituents.

A3.1.2 Meaning as constructed

We have discussed linguistic systems in Section A3.1.1 in terms of the properties of each system and the hierarchical relationship between constituents of a system, but we have not indicated their role in realizing meaning. The study of linguistic meaning is a part of a more general theory of signs, or semiotics, and it is to a discussion of semiotics that we now turn.

Two major theories of semiotics were developed in the twentieth century: one associated with the Swiss scholar Ferdinand de Saussure and one with the American philosopher Charles Sanders Peirce. In Saussure's theory, a sign has two components, the signifier and the signified. A signifier is the element of the sign that we use in communication. For example, a red traffic light, the direction of a weather vane, and a word like *house* are all signifiers. The complements of these signifiers are their signifieds, or what we commonly term their meanings. So, if you are in a car, a red traffic light 'means' stop; the direction that weather vane is pointing 'means' the direction that a wind is blowing, and the word *house* 'means' a building for human habitation. Saussure believed that the relationship between the signifier and the signified is purely arbitrary, and he illustrated this point with examples of the relationship between signifier and signified in different languages. The signifier of 'a building for human habitation' in English is *house*, but in French it is *maison*, in Italian it is *casa*, and in Chinese it is 房子 (fángzi), so there is no way to predict the form of the signifier by looking at what it signifies. And in just the same way, if you look at a particular signifier, there is no way to predict what it signifies. For example when the sound 'lee' is spelled *Lee* in English it is a family name, when it is spelled *lea* it means grassland or pasture, but the sound is written *lit* in French and means 'bed', and in Chinese it is written 里 (lì) which means 'in' or 'inside.'

Given that the relationship between signifier and signified (between word and meaning) is arbitrary, Saussure wondered how it was that people who speak the same language can communicate because, in principle, when you say a word, how am I to know its meaning? The answer that Saussure proposed was that people in the same speech community shared a kind of social contract, which he called 'la langue' and one clause, if you like, in that social contract was that the members of the community all accept a particular relationship between signifier and signified, between word and meaning. Of course, when we meet people who have not 'signed the contract' (very young children or foreigners), we do have trouble communicating with them because their word–meaning relationships differ from our own.

Saussure's semiotic theory with its abstract 'langue' implied that all members of the same community shared the same way of making meaning from language, but this is one place where Peirce's theory differed from Saussure. Unlike the two components of the sign that Saussure envisioned, Peirce recognized three: object, representamen, and interpretant. The object is the referent of the sign or what the sign 'stands for.' The representamen is the form that the sign takes, and in many ways it is similar to Saussure's signifier. But where Peircean semiotics diverges from Saussure is in the interpretant. This is not the person who interprets the sign but it is the sense that someone makes of the sign. So, in principle, the relationship between representamen and object differs from the relationship between interpretant and object. In other words, the meaning of a sign produced by a speaker may differ from the meaning interpreted by the receiver. One way in which this becomes apparent is if we consider the diversity of properties that constitute meaning. As Nation (2001) points out, knowing a word involves knowing not only its referential meaning but also its associations with other words.

 Task A3.1.2.1

➤ Work individually to discover which words you associate with the following words. Then compare your associations with those made by other people. Are they the same or different? What do the similarities or differences in people's word associations say about Saussure's and Peirce's semiotic theories? Here are the words: *deep, hair, moon, mother, music, Paris, purple, scissors, soft, table.*

If, as Peirce suggests, the meaning of a word used by a speaker may differ from its meaning for a hearer, then the people involved may (or may not) do interactional work in order to arrive at what they think is a common meaning. This interactional work has been called *co-construction* by Jacoby and Ochs (1995) and refers not only to work on the meaning of words but, more generally, to the joint creation of a form, interpretation, stance, action, activity, identity, institution, skill, ideology, emotion, or other culturally meaningful reality. Making meaning in a communicative event is therefore not simply a question of using a linguistic system that members of a speech community share. The shared system may help with communication at some level, but communication is not simply a matter of an idea arising in one brain and being transferred by means of language to another brain as Saussure envisioned it in Figure A3.3.

Making meaning in a communicative event is a process of co-construction which involves all those who participate in the event. Take, for example, the 'I have a dream' speech. The meaning of the speech was certainly different for those people who participated in the civil rights march on Washington, DC, than from the meaning constructed by people who clung to racist views of the role of Blacks in the United States of the early 1960s.

A3.1.3 Modes of meaning

In a communicative event, people use spoken or written language – texts – for some purpose. Often that purpose is communicative: to inform, to persuade, or to cajole other people, in some way to influence others people's thoughts, beliefs, or actions. The purpose of text is not necessarily communicative, though; for as Noam Chomsky (1976) once wrote,

> As a graduate student, I spent two years writing a lengthy manuscript, assuming throughout that it would never be published or read by anyone. I meant everything I wrote, intending nothing as to what anyone would believe about my beliefs, in fact taking it for granted that there would be no audience. (p. 61)

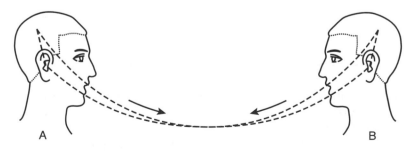

Figure A3.3 The speaking circuit. Source: Saussure, Bally, Sechehaye, and Riedlinger (1966, p. 11)

Chomsky refers to the purpose of writing as the expression of his own ideas, not a communicative purpose, and in many other instances of speech the intended recipient is our self and not an audience. In some other forms of speech we are talking to ourselves with no intention of communicating with others, such as when we are trying to solve a problem by ourselves. This kind of speech is called private speech but it, too, has a purpose. As Vocate (1994) asserts, its purpose is cognitive adaptation: 'The "I" makes choices, and the interpretive, critical process that follows from the "Me" allows us to adapt ourselves . . . before we think or act further' (p. 12).

The various purposes of texts are considered in SFG to fall within three basic areas: interpersonal, ideational, and textual. Each of these areas is called a metafunction, and each metafunction corresponds to the social, individual, and cultural contexts of language. We consider these three purposes in turn in the following sections.

A3.1.3.1 The interpersonal metafunction

When we focus on language in its social context – that is, in its communicative function of influencing others people's thoughts, beliefs, or actions – we identify the interpersonal metafunction. This has to do with the relationships between speakers and hearers, between writers and readers, and with those linguistic resources that allow people to create social roles for themselves and others through interaction. The grammatical system which realizes interpersonal meaning is the system of mood. A statement is typically realized by declarative mood, a question is realized by interrogative mood, a command realized by imperative mood, and a nomination by vocative mood. The interpersonal metafunction is about the social world, especially the relationship between speaker and hearer, and is concerned with clauses as *exchanges*. And there are two main constituents of a clause that realize the mood element: a noun-like element that we call the *subject*, and a verb-like element that we call the *finite*. In the 'I have a dream' speech, the clause *the sons of former slaves and the sons of former slave owners will be able to sit down together* has a subject *the sons of former slaves and the sons of former slave owners* and a finite *will*. The interpersonal function of this clause is to influence the behavior of others, to express Dr King's desire that two groups of people – the sons of former slaves and the sons of former slave owners – do something that they are not used to doing: sit down together.

A3.1.3.2 The ideational metafunction

In addition to influencing the thoughts, beliefs, and actions of other people, it is clear that one primary function of language is to construe our experiences of the world, including our experiences of our own thoughts and feelings. Construing experience means describing experience, representing it, analyzing it, and explaining it, and this way of using language is analyzed in SFG as the ideational metafunction.[5] In the ideational metafunction, a clause is analyzed into *process*, *participants*, and *circumstances*, with different participant types for different process types. Processes are often realized by a verbal group, and the processes themselves may be material, mental, verbal, or relational. As an example of a material process, Chomsky wrote *As a graduate student, I spent two years writing a lengthy manuscript*. In this clause, the process of writing is material, the participant is 'I', and the circumstances are *as a graduate student I spent two years*, and the circumstances of the manuscript that he wrote is *lengthy*. The verbal group has a grammatical tense associated with it, which is also a representation of the material process of writing: Chomsky *spent two years writing* indicates that the writing happened in the past.

However, processes do not always occur in the external world. They may also report internal experiences, and in this case a representation of a mental process would be by means of a psych verb like *believe, think, remember*, or an expression like *I have a dream*. Verbal processes are realized by verbs of telling such as *ask, tell, say*, etc. A famous expression of verbal process is in the phrase used in the United States military to describe the official policy regarding homosexual or bisexual acts by members of the American armed forces. Such acts are forbidden, but as long as gay or bisexual men and women in the military hide anything that could disclose their sexual orientation, commanders will not try to investigate their sexuality. The policy is well described by a phrase that realizes verbal processes but does not mention material processes: *Don't ask, don't tell*.

Another type of process that differs from those realized by material, mental, and verbal clauses is relational process. Relational process clauses allow us to express identity and classification. The verbal groups in these three clauses are relational.

You are the same size as your sister.

The three major languages in the United States are English, Spanish, and French.

What does 'relational' mean?

In the first clause, the verb *are* expresses an identical relationship between your size and your sister's size. In the second clause, *are* allows us to classify the three major languages in the US as English, Spanish, and French. And in the third, the verb *mean* asks for the identity of the word *relational*.

A3.1.3.3 The textual metafunction

The interpersonal metafunction of language helps us to enact social relationships, the ideational metafunction allows us to construe a model of experience, and now the textual metafunction allows us to connect utterances to their linguistic context, so that separate clauses hang together to make a coherent text. In other words, the textual metafunction allows us to create textuality within a message. The grammatical system that realizes the textual metafunction is theme and rheme. Theme is 'the starting point for the message: it is what the clause is going to be about' (Halliday and Matthiessen, 2004, p. 64). And since a message generally begins with what is assumed to be familiar to the listener or reader, theme generally contains information that has already been mentioned or is available in the nonlinguistic context. As we saw in Unit A2, in talk-in-interaction people can respond to contexts, and they can also create contexts by their own talk.

By examining theme, it is possible to discover the kind of context that is being invoked. Consider, for example, the patient consultation in a pharmacy that we described in the Section A2.1.2.

```
Pharmacist:  Have you had doxycycline before?
Client:      I think that I might have.
```

In this conversation, the pharmacist asks the patient, 'Have you had doxycycline before?' The theme is what is familiar to both patient and pharmacist: the patient, who the pharmacist invokes with 'you.' The rest of the clause is a request from the pharmacist for new information: 'Have . . . had doxcycline before?' and is the rheme. As Susan Eggins puts it, 'The definition of the Rheme is that it is the part of the clause in which the Theme is developed. . . . the Rheme typically contains unfamiliar or 'new' information' (Eggins, 2004, p. 300).

Texts hang together in three different ways. The simplest form of textuality is when a theme is reiterated, and this is seen in oratory such as Dr Martin Luther King's speech with which we opened this unit. The theme of a 'dream' – a major aim, goal, or purpose the attainment of which the Civil Rights movement ardently desired is reiterated throughout the speech. In other types of talk-in-interaction, however, textuality is created by means of a zigzag pattern of Thematic development, in which the rheme of a preceding clause becomes the theme of the next clause and so on, as illustrated below.

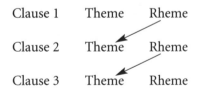

The patient's reply to the pharmacist's inquiry about his experience with doxycycline takes that as a new theme and provides new information about it: 'I think that I might have.' Notice that the theme in this case is so completely known to both participants that the patient does not even mention it; he has no need to say 'I think that I might have had doxycycline before.'

While zigzag thematic development is common in informal conversation, a third type of development is sometimes found in expository writing or more formal speech: the multiple-rheme pattern, in which the theme of one clause introduces a series of different pieces of information, which are then developed sequentially in subsequent clauses. At the beginning of this section, I introduced the topic by writing: *The various purposes of texts are considered in SFG to fall within <u>three basic areas</u>: interpersonal, ideational, and textual. <u>Each of these areas</u> is called a meta-function, and each metafunction corresponds to the social, individual, and cultural contexts of language.* The phrase *three basic areas* is the Rheme of the first clause, which then becomes the Theme of the second clause: *Each of these areas.* The text then continues by describing using each of the three rhemes sequentially as Themes of new clauses which in turn define and exemplify interpersonal, ideational, and textual metafunctions.

A3.2 INTERACTIONAL RESOURCES

The account of communicative resources that we have presented so far has considered text as the central feature of a communicative event, and we have presented a linguistic view of text in terms of hierarchy, constituency, and the modes of meaning that text embodies. Yet, there are other important features of a communicative event that go beyond the features that we have isolated as text. A communicative event is done in real time and in constantly varying social contexts. While our linguistic analysis of communication as text has treated a text as an object, and we have assumed that the meaning of texts is not in dispute, in this section we will consider that, in constructing spoken texts, speakers are doing conversation in real time and that throughout the constantly evolving interaction, meanings are not fixed but are negotiated by speakers. The framework for understanding com-municative events as talk-in-interaction that we will take is that of conversation analysis, or CA; and it is quite different from the linguistic analysis that we have presented so far. The contrast between CA and the linguistic approach is indicated by Hutchby and Woofitt (1998, p. 14).

> CA is only marginally interested in language as such; its actual object of study is the *interactional organization of social activities*. CA is a radical departure from other forms of linguistically oriented analysis in that the production of utterances, and more particularly the sense they obtain, is seen not in terms of the structure of language, but first and foremost as a practical social accomplishment.

Conversation analysis originated in the work of Harvey Sacks, an American sociologist who was trained in ethnomethodology, a discipline that focuses on the way people make sense of the world and display their understandings of it. This approach is very different to the linguistic approach of SFG that we discussed in the first part of this unit because, while SFG assumes that a linguist's understanding of the meaning of a text is the same meaning that is intended by the producer of the text, ethnomethodology takes it for granted that the individuals who participate in a conversation are constantly attempting to make sense of what they are doing. From the point of view of ethnomethodology, the analyst's interpretation is just another participant trying to make sense of the interaction, and it has no priority over the interpretations made and displayed by the participants in the conversation.

How, then, does an analyst interpret the actions of conversational participants? In order to do so, a foundation of CA is that conversation is systematically organized and ordered. Participants in conversations orient to the underlying organization of talk, so that when an action appears to a participant not to be organized, the participant will display a reaction in some way. To take an example, we noted in the conversation between the mother and child in Unit A2 that the child oriented to his mother's lack of response to the child's call as unexpected and undesired, and so the child repeated his call.

```
Child:   Mama ((pause)) I gotta go to the bathroom
Mother:  ((pause))
Child:   Mama ((pause)) Donnie's gotta go
Mother:  Sh-sh
```

The underlying organization that we can see in this short conversation is that the participants expect two actions to occur adjacent to one another. In this case, the actions are Call and Response. When the child receives no response to his call 'Mama', he tries again, . . . and again until he receives a response.

By carrying out detailed analyses of talk-in-interaction, conversation analysts have identified three different aspects of the organization of the talk. We have just shown an example of the first aspect of organization, and that is that social actions in a conversation are sequenced, and participants orient to certain kinds of action sequences, especially when one type of action is expected to follow another. A second aspect of organization is that when communicative events involve more than one participant, the participants do not all speak at once but take turns to speak. It happens, of course, that two participants do on occasion speak at the same time, but such overlapping talk is soon resolved into the talk of a single speaker. And a third aspect of conversational organization is that the smooth production of talk and turn-taking is sometimes disturbed by some kind of communication trouble. The source of trouble is often a word or phrase that one participant does not under-stand or cannot hear or that one participant feels is inappropriate. Participants' reactions to the trouble are called *repair* in CA. These three aspects of conversational organization – action sequences, turn-taking, and repair – will be discussed in detail in the following sections.

A3.2.1 Action sequences

In ordinary talk-in-interaction somebody says something and then another person says something else. In other words, one action follows another, and one of the basic insights of conversation analysis is that actions do not happen randomly; in many cases they follow a fixed sequence. Consider the following four turns at talk taken from the same conversation: the speakers are labeled as 'A' and 'B', and the turns are listed in alphabetical order of the first word in each turn:

```
B:  are you over twenty-one?
A:  can I have a bottle of Mich?[6]
A:  no
B:  no.
```

If these turns are listed alphabetically, the conversation doesn't seem to make sense. Why does A ask for a bottle of beer as a reply to B's question about his age? And why do A and B both say 'no'? These four lines don't seem to make sense because when we look at conversation, we have certain expectations about which actions happen first and which actions follow. If we look now at the conversation as it was originally reported in Levinson (1983, p. 304), it seems to make a lot more sense.

```
A:  can I have a bottle of Mich?
B:  are you over twenty-one?
A:  no.
B:  no
```

In the original conversation, A makes a request, and the expectation of both A and B is that a request requires a reply either granting or refusing the request. B does not immediately reply to A's request; instead B asks A a question about A's age, and again the expectation of both A and B is that a question requires an answer. After A answers B's question, B is able to reply to A's request in the first line by refusing it. These pairs of actions fit together in a sequence called an adjacency pair: A request is the first part of one pair and the refusal is the second part; a question is the first part of the other pair and the answer is the second part. There are other sequences of conversational actions that occur in pairs in this way, for example a call and a response such as 'Cecilia!' / 'Yes?' or a pair of greetings such as 'How are you?' / 'Fine. How are you?'

Task A3.2.1.1

➤ Here are some more turns from a conversation between a mother and daughter.[7] The mother, Lyn, is sitting at the kitchen table at home and Zoe, her daughter, has just come in. The turns are listed in alphabetical order by the first word of each turn. Rearrange the turns so that they make sense as a conversation. What knowledge of adjacency pairs do you use to help you rearrange the turns into a conversation?

```
Zoe:  hello
Lyn:  hello I'm here
Lyn:  hi
Lyn:  in the kitchen
```

```
Zoe:  mum
Zoe:  okay
Zoe:  where's the cigarettes
```

We have discussed here actions that occur in pairs, and the dependence of the second pair part on the first pair part seems clear to conversationalists; in fact, if the second pair part is not forthcoming, speakers often react to its absence by a verbal action that sanctions the other speaker. But there are sequences of actions that are longer than the pairs that we have been discussing, and in these longer sequences the sequential dependence of one action on others is not so strict but nonetheless can cause misunderstanding. A good example of a longer sequence of actions was reported by Susan Ranney (1992), who described the sequence of expected actions that together compose a visit to a doctor at a clinic in the United States. The sequence of actions by the doctor and the patient follows a script that many American adults recognize. A clinic visit involves well defined roles for participants and consists of a series of speech acts in a well defined sequence. For example at the end of the clinic visit, the doctor presents treatment options to the patient, the patient informs the doctor of conditions that indicate one option rather than others, and the doctor directs the patient to return to the clinic for a follow-up visit. Such a normative series of actions and expected roles can be misinterpreted if the cultural background of the patient is different from the doctor. Ranney described the sequence expected by Hmong patients. The closing script of the clinic visit expected by the Hmong patients included prescription of medication and it did not include a choice of treatment options, so the expectations of different scripts by the two participants may lead to dissatisfaction by the Hmong patients and to lack of comprehension by their American doctors.

In the examples of act sequences that we have presented in this section, the linguistic form of the action has not been our primary concern; instead we have focused on the normative expectations that conversational participants have about the sequences themselves. And for the sake of simplicity, we have also associated each act with one turn-at-talk in a conversation. Of course, a speaker can perform more than one action within a single turn, but the system of turns and turn-taking nonetheless underlies the sequential organization of conversation. It is to a description of this system that we now turn.

A3.2.2 Turns and turn-taking

One of the most amazing things about conversational interaction is that most of the time a single participant talks and other participants do not. It is certainly true that there are occasions when more than one speaker talks at the same time but when that happens, one speaker soon ceases to talk and a single speaker holds the floor. Holding the floor is achieved by a single speaker when that speaker talks and the other participants in the conversation choose not to. There are also occasions in most conversations when speaker change occurs; that is, one speaker stops talking, and another one begins. This system of turn-taking in conversation was first described in detail by Sacks, Schegloff, and Jefferson (1974), who answered two basic questions about turn-taking: (1) How is the next speaker selected? And (2) how do participants know when to end one turn and when to begin another?

The question of how to select the next speaker was answered by Sacks *et al.* by means of the following algorithm.

1.   If the current speaker selects the next speaker, then that party has the right and obligation to speak.
2.   If no next speaker is selected, then self-selection may (but need not) occur. The first starter acquires rights to the turn.
3.   If no next speaker is selected, then current speaker may (but need not) continue.

(cf.) Sacks, Schegloff, and Jefferson (1974, p. 704)

The current speaker may select the next speaker by means of the mechanisms of adjacency pairs that we discussed in the previous section, so if the current speaker produces a first pair part (a question or a greeting, for instance), then another speaker is obliged to produce the second pair part (an answer or a response). In a multi-party conversation, the selection of the individual to be next speaker may be done by linguistic means such as naming or by gestural means such as gaze and orientation of the upper body. The difference between current speaker selects next and next speaker self-selects is an important way in which communicative events differ. In informal conversation, for instance, the next speaker often self-selects, as in this example from Sacks *et al.* (1974, p. 707).

```
Lil:     Bertha´s lost, on our scale, about fourteen
         pounds.
Damora: Oh [::no::.
Jean:       [Twelve pounds I think wasn´t it.=
Daisy:  =[Can you believe it?
Lil:    =[Twelve pounds on the Weight Watcher´s
        scale
```

In many institutional settings, however, the preferred technique is current speaker selects next, as in this example from the pharmacy consultation.

```
Pharmacist:  Have you had doxycycline before?
Client:      I think that I might have.
```

The selection of next speaker is one way in which participants create a power differential among speakers because, in order for a single speaker to hold the floor, the other speakers must desist from taking turns and, if there is one individual in a group that can select the next participant, the individual who does the selection has that power.

Task A3.2.2.1

➤ How does the selection of the next speaker vary across these different communicative events? A courtroom trial, the 'I have a dream' speech, a wedding
ceremony, a first date, a university class. Is there one participant in these events
who has more power than others?

The second question that Sacks *et al.* asked about turn-taking was: How do
participants know when to end one turn-at-talk and when to begin another? They
answered the question by invoking the notion of the turn-constructional unit or
TCU. Such a unit may be a unit of the lexicogrammar, of intonation, or a pragmatic
unit (a complete idea), and as Ford and Thompson (1996) pointed out, these units
often coincide to make a complex TCU. The place at which a transition between
speakers occurs is not necessarily at the boundary of a TCU, but speakers are able
to predict when a boundary is forthcoming and are therefore able to project the
completion of the TCU. Transitions between speakers occur at such places when
participants project the completion of the TCU, projecting not only the form of the
next word but also the completion of larger lexicogrammatical, intonational, and
pragmatic units. Prediction is thus an important part of what recipients do when
listening to talk in progress, and the place in an ongoing turn when participants are
able to project the completion of the TCU is called a transition-relevance place or
TRP. That is to say, participants do not necessarily take a turn *at* a TRP but, if they
do, then they are more likely to do so at a TRP than elsewhere. In the following
conversation between a tourist and two Londoners, the Parky waits until the old
man has finished to take a full turn, but he attempts to do so at two TRPs that he
perceives in the old man's turn, projecting the completion of two clauses (Sacks *et
al.*, 1994, p. 721).

```
Tourist:   Has the park cha:nged much,
Parky:     Oh:: yes,
           (1.0)
Old man:   The Funfair changed it ´n [ahful lot [didn´
           it.
Parky:                                [Th-      [That-
           That changed it,
```

 Task A3.2.2.2

➤ Here is a long turn from a conversation.[8] No other participant took a turn while
this turn was under way, but is that because there are no transition-relevance
places in this long turn?

Ken: I still say though that – if you take if you take uh a big fancy car out on the
road and you're hotroddin' around, you're – you're bound to get – caught you're
bound to get caught, and you're bound to get shafted.

The organization of turn-taking in talk-in-interaction is therefore systematic. The selection of who will take the next turn depends on the sequence of conversational actions, the nature of the communicative event, and the relative power of the participants. When the next speaker self-selects, the next turn begins at a place in the current turn when participants project the completion of a turn constructional unit, and such a place may be at the completion of a TCU or prior to it. When the current speaker selects the next speaker, however, the new turn may often begin at or after the completion of the current speaker's TCU. Conversational participants orient to the turn-taking system in a normative way, just as participants orient to the sequence of actions in an adjacency pair by commenting when there is a change or a violation of the rules. The actions that participants perform in such a case comes under the general heading of conversational repair.

A3.2.3 Repair

Repair is the treatment of trouble in talk-in-interaction. Trouble can be anything in the talk to which participants in the interaction orient as problematic. One participant may use a word that is misunderstood or misheard by another participant, one participant may realize that a phrase that they have just used is less preferable than another phrase. Although the source of trouble is often a word or phrase, it may in principle be anything that participants orient to as repairable. Thus, the absence of the second pair part of an adjacency pair may elicit 'an apology,' or when a listener projects a TCU and takes a turn while the current speaker wishes to continue, this may be oriented to by one or more participants as 'an interruption.' In many cases, however, the source of trouble in a repair is a choice of words or phrasing and, in understanding repair, conversation analysts have focused on two questions about the participants in the repair: In whose turn did the trouble occur? And who initiated the repair sequence? Beyond the participants, the analysis focuses on the sequence of actions in the repair. Here is an example of a repair recorded by Maria Egbert (2004).

```
Thom:   the newspapers are wet
        (0.5)
Rob:    sorry?
Thom:   the newspapers are wet
Rob:    yeah, there was a:: hole in thee mail bag
        mine was soaked as well
```

In this conversation, the trouble source is in Thom's first turn. The repair is initiated by Rob with 'sorry?', and the repair operation is completed when Thom repeats his original comment. Rob signals that the repair is complete by continuing the conversation and adding new information. Such a repair is called an *other-initiated self-repair* because the repair was initiated by a different participant from the one in whose turn the trouble source occurred, and the repair is completed by the same participant in whose turn the trouble source occurred. Three other kinds of repair are labeled in the same way according to the participant who initiates the repair and the participant who completes the repair; they are *other-initiated other repair*, *self-initiated self-repair*, and *self-initiated other repair*.

 Task A3.2.3.1

➤ Identify the kinds of repair that occurs in the following four conversations.

(1) *Al:*   I need a new disk for my computer.
    Brett: *disk?*
    Al: I mean a new memory.

(2) *Alan:*   I need a new TV for my computer.
    Bob: You mean a *monitor?*
    Alan: Yeah.

(3) *Cecilia:*   I want to get one of those pen –, uh flash memory drives.

(4) *Art:*   I need one of them whatchamacallits.
    Bill: Network cards?
    Art: Yeah.

Although it is reasonably straightforward to identify the types of repair based on who initiates the repair and who completes it, the four types have quite different implications for the social relationship between participants. By making an other-initiated repair, a participant is requiring the other participant to do what they would not otherwise do: carry out a repair. In ordinary informal conversation such a request is dispreferred and, in consequence, other-initiated repair is less frequent in this context than self-initiated repair. In communicative events where there is greater social distance between participants and one participant has more power than another, the threat to negative face is mitigated and other-initiated repair is more common. Such social contexts include foreign language classrooms, where teachers often perform other-initiated repairs of students' talk. An example of this is given by Patsy Lightbown and Nina Spada (1993, p. 76).

```
Learner:  it bug me to have =
Teacher:  =it bugs me. it (bugzz) me
Learner:  it bugs me when my brother takes my bicycle.
```

In this exchange, the trouble source is the learner's omission of the *–s* inflection on the third person singular present tense of the verb *bug* in the learner's first turn, and the repair is initiated and completed by the teacher in the next line. Although this is an other-initiated other repair, the learner goes on to repeat the repair in the third turn.

The three aspects of conversational organization that we have discussed – action sequences, turn-taking, and repair – are the fundamental building blocks of intersubjectivity in conversational interaction. We have, however, also mentioned relationships between participants as one way in which the patterns of sequence, turn-taking, and repair differ from one communicative event to another. We will look in greater detail at the ways in which participation in communicative events differs on the social dimension in the next section.

A3.2.4 Participation framework

In discussing conversation analysis, we remarked that adjacency pairs are common features of conversational interaction, but that longer action sequences such as those described by Ranney (1992) are specific to a particular kind of communicative event: the doctor–patient interview. When we discussed turn-taking, we recognized that the procedure for selection of next speaker in informal conversation between peers differs from the procedure used by participants in a courtroom trial, in the 'I have a dream' speech, in a wedding ceremony, in a first date, and in most school classrooms. And we also recognized that the face-threatening nature of other-initiated repair is a factor encouraging its use in contexts of unequal power distribution between speakers and discouraging its use in informal conversations. One way of describing and explaining these differences among communicative events is through the concept of participation framework developed by Erving Goffman (1979, 1981).

Goffman recognized that a simple model of a communicative event involving a speaker and a hearer was inadequate. In Goffman's (1981) words, 'Our common-sense notions of hearer and speaker are crude, the first potentially concealing a complex differentiation of participation statuses, and the second, complex questions of production format' (p. 146). He distinguished between several roles involved in the production of talk and several more roles of hearers. Three production roles are: *animator*, the talking machine, an individual engaged in the role of utterance production; *author*, someone who has selected the sentiments being expressed and the words in which they are encoded; and *principal*, someone whose position is established by the words being spoken, whose beliefs have been told, and who is committed to what the words say. As an example of the three roles, take the pharmacy consultation we have examined in Unit A2. Figure A3.4 shows an image from the interaction.

The animator in this conversation is the pharmacist because it is out of his mouth that the words come, and the patient is clearly an official and ratified participant because he is addressed by the pharmacist, but notice that both the pharmacist and the patient are gazing not at each other but at the medication. One way in which we can identify a participant who is not physically present in talk-in-interaction is by the gaze and gesture of the physical participants and the way they address those who are not present.

Although author and animator may not be physically present at a communicative event, the roles of hearers generally involve co-participation of some sort, as an

Figure A3.4 A patient consultation in a pharmacy. Source: Nguyen (2003)

official hearer, an unofficial hearer, a ratified participant, or an unratified participant. An official hearer is a participant who is overtly addressed by a speaker and a ratified participant is one whose presence is acknowledged by a speaker but who may not be overtly addressed.

Goffman not only identified these roles for participants but recognized that their roles may change quite quickly in interaction. Individuals in a communicative event play many roles, and the roles that they play during a single event (what Goffman called 'footing') frequently change, and as their footing changes so participants' attitudes toward the interaction (their 'stance') also change.

The participation framework of an interaction is thus the identities of all participants, present or not, official or unofficial, ratified or unratified, and their footing or roles in the interaction, recognizing that the footing of co-present participants may change from moment to moment.[9]

 Task A3.2.4.1

➤ Teenagers, when talking to each other on the phone, often use language and expressions that their parents don't understand. And when you are in a foreign country, it is often an advantage to be able to speak to your friends in a language that the people around you don't understand. How do the participation frameworks of these two communicative events affect the language that teenagers and foreigners use?

When we consider the participation frameworks of some of the communicative events that we described earlier in this unit, the importance of this perspective becomes clear. The doctor–patient interactions described by Ranney involve individuals with certain expectations about the footing that they should take in the event. We expect doctors to take a role that is consistent with the specialist knowledge that they possess and we expect patients to take the role of clients in a service encounter. If a doctor were to use very familiar and colloquial language when addressing a patient or if a patient were to display some specialist knowledge about their condition, this would involve the participants in a change of footing in the interaction. In a conversation between a service provider and a client, such as between a doctor and patient or between a teacher and a student, we expect that in turn-taking the selection of next speaker would be made most frequently by the service provider rather than by the client although, once again, a change to self-selection of next speaker or to selection by the client may indicate a change of footing. And finally as we have seen, the initiation of repair involves a threat to the negative face of one of the participants in an interaction: Consider the change of footing that would result from a patient initiating a repair to a doctor or a student to a teacher.

A3.3 HOW INTERACTIONAL RESOURCES DIFFER FROM LINGUISTIC RESOURCES

In the first part of this unit we described the role that language plays in communicative events by providing the framework of systemic functional grammar to explain how meanings are constructed by a speaker's selection of elements from different levels of linguistic structure, and how the selection of different kinds of text organization foregrounded the interpersonal, ideational, or textual ends to which a text is put. Our analysis began with the language of the text, which was treated as an object, and we assumed that the meaning of texts is not in dispute. In the second part of the unit, we put forward the idea that when talk-in-interaction occurs in real time, the meaning of a speaker's actions is always potentially in dispute and participants display their understanding of those actions by their ongoing contributions to the conversation, specifically through the sequence of actions, the organization of turn-taking, and conversational repair. In concluding the second part of the unit, we began an analysis of the social relationships among participants in a communicative event using the notion of participation framework.

To what extent are the linguistic resources available to speakers compatible with the interactional resources that we have described here? Or, to put the question more appropriately, is an analysis of the linguistic resources for making meaning compatible with an explanation of the interactional resources? At first glance, it would seem as though the interactional resources are appropriate for describing talk-in-interaction, while the linguistic resources are appropriate for describing written texts or monologues, and it is true that in the following chapters we will make more use of SFG in analyzing written texts and more use of CA to analyze conversations. But this is not to say that the two approaches are incompatible. In fact, SFG can make significant contributions to our understanding of talk-in-interaction: first, by allowing analysis of the register of a communicative event – the words and grammatical structures that characterize it; and second, by allowing us to analyze the ways in which participants in a communicative event make meaning. And the methods of CA will clearly be of greatest help when we analyze conversation, but even those spoken events, such as the 'I have a dream' speech which appear monologic are in fact co-constructed by all participants, even those who remain silent (and thus allow Dr King to have the floor) and especially by those members of the audience who punctuate the speech with cries of 'Yeah' and 'Hear! Hear!' A more fundamental (and controversial) application of CA is to written texts because of the view put originally forward by Mikhail Bakhtin (1981) that all language production is dialogic, in the sense that the mutual participation of speakers and hearers, readers and writers is necessary in the construction of utterances and the connectedness of all utterances to past and future expressions. Clearly, the analysis of texts is far from the original intentions of the founders of conversation analysis, but recent research into private speech has shown that the methods of CA can be used to further our understanding of texts that had been considered monologic (Lee, 2006). We hope to show in the following units how SFG and CA are complementary in furthering our understanding of communicative events.

SUMMARY AND LOOKING AHEAD

The method of SFG that we have introduced in this unit is explained in greater detail in Unit B3 in an excerpt from the writings of the founder of this approach, Michael Halliday. In the second reading in Unit B3, Joan Kelly Hall considers an approach to understanding talk-in-interaction which, like CA, recognizes that all utterance must be understood in context. Kelly Hall's work is inspired by the Russian literary critic and philosopher Mikhail Bakhtin's theory that there is no fixed meaning to utterances, and that the same words, the same grammar can be used by different individuals to create new meanings, identities, and stances. In Unit C3, you will have the opportunity to develop your skills in SFG and CA. An understanding of SFG is necessary for a systemic analysis of part of the 'I have a dream' speech; very attentive listening to talk-in-interaction and transforming talk into text by means of transcription are the basis of every conversation analysis. Skills in the tools of analysis provided by SFG and CA are essential to the topic that we turn to next in Unit A4: discursive practice.

Unit A4
Discursive practices

PROLOGUE AND ROADMAP

Since the 1960s, one of the dominant developments in social anthropology has been Practice Theory, and it is this theory which inspires the notion of 'discursive practice,' which is developed in this unit. Practice Theory is an important reconceptualization of ideas such as identity, membership in social groups, action, learning, competence, and power. In this unit, we will define discursive practice and show how participants in discursive practices employ linguistic and interactional resources in order to create the practices. In many practices, some participants control and constrain the contributions of others and, when this occurs, we perceive a difference between powerful and less powerful participants. The important issue of discursive power is addressed at the end of this unit.

A4.1 DEFINING DISCURSIVE PRACTICE

Life is not full of surprises. The way most things happen is routine. The work week has five days in most places, you get up at around the same time each day, you might shower, get dressed, eat breakfast, leave the house, do your work or your study, break for lunch at around noon, return to work or study for a few more hours, pack up, go home, eat an evening meal, maybe go out with friends, maybe watch TV, go to bed at around the same time most nights, get undressed, sleep, and then it begins again. Your routine at weekends is probably made up of different activities, but the weekend will see you mostly doing things that you've done before. The same goes for interaction. Some interactions are so routine that they have become rituals. For example, after you have checked out and paid for your groceries at a supermarket in the United States, the clerk usually says 'Have a nice day.' When somebody proffers their hand in greeting, you normally respond by grasping it with yours in a handshake. In some countries, when somebody greets you with a kiss on one cheek, they follow it with a second kiss on the other cheek.

We are not born with the knowledge of such actions because one of the things that parents have to teach their children is how to behave in such routines: how to dress, what to wear, how to behave at mealtimes, when to say 'please,' when to say 'thank you,' and so on. When we move to a new community, either a foreign country or to a different group of people within our own country, one of the first things we notice is how different the interactional routines in the new community are and, if you want to pass as a member of the new community, you have to make an effort to learn not only a new way of speaking but also the new interactional routines. How are new routines learned? There are two ways in which children or newcomers learn new routines. They do so either by having somebody teach them the new routine explicitly, or they learn the new routine implicitly by watching what other people do. In Task A4.1.1, there is an example of two ways of learning something new: by following instructions or by looking at a picture. Some people prefer learning by watching others, and some people prefer learning by doing. Which do you prefer?

★ Task A4.1.1

➤ Try to learn the following yoga pose. Choose either to follow the instructions or to imitate the pose in Figure A4.1. What is the difference between the explicit and implicit methods of instruction?

Downward Facing Dog (*adho mukha svanasana* in Sankrit) is one of the most widely recognized yoga poses. It is an all-over, rejuvenating stretch. Here are two ways to learn it published on the Yoga Journal website.

1. Come onto the floor on your hands and knees. Set your knees directly below your hips and your hands slightly forward of your shoulders. Spread your palms, index fingers parallel or slightly turned out, and turn your toes under.
2. Exhale and lift your knees away from the floor. At first keep the knees slightly bent and the heels lifted away from the floor. Lengthen your tailbone away from the back of your pelvis and press it lightly toward the pubis. Against this resistance, lift the sitting bones toward the ceiling, and from your inner ankles draw the inner legs up into the groin.
3. Then with an exhalation, push your top thighs back and stretch your heels onto or down toward the floor. Straighten your knees but be sure not to lock them. Firm the outer thighs and roll the upper thighs inward slightly. Narrow the front of the pelvis.
4. Firm the outer arms and press the bases of the index fingers actively into the floor. From these two points lift along your inner arms from the wrists to the tops of the shoulders. Firm your shoulder blades against your back, then widen them and draw them toward the tailbone. Keep the head between the upper arms; don't let it hang.

The activities that we do on a regular basis we learn by observing and participating in activities performed by members of the community in which we grow up. The way we perform these activities is something that we learned very early on, and individuals differ in their actual performance of an activity because each individual grew up in slightly different circumstances. Nonetheless, we recognize the origins of an individual's performance of an activity as indexing that individual's member-

Figure A4.1 The yoga pose 'Downward Facing Dog'. Source: iStockphoto. File Number 3491632

ship in a particular social class, professional group, ethnic group, dialect community, gender, age or any other socially significant grouping. People in different social classes tend to speak differently; professional people such as teachers, carpenters, construction workers, and pizza makers perform different activities in their professional lives; teenagers interact very differently when they are interacting with other teenagers than when they are interacting with their parents; and there are many other ways in which membership in a social group is indexed by the kinds of activities that people perform and how they perform them.

The activities that we perform regularly make up an important aspect of our lives. Activities are important in establishing who we are, how what we do creates culture, how relations of power are created and maintained among individuals, and therefore how we understand the world. In the 1970s, the French sociologist and anthropologist Pierre Bourdieu and the British sociologist Anthony Giddens developed a theory of these activities, which they called *Practice Theory*. By 'practice' they meant activities that have their own rules, their own constraints, and their own structures; and these theorists sketched the relations among practice, performance, and culture (see Ortner 1984 for a full discussion of Practice Theory). In this book, we will focus on those practices in which language is a central feature. We will examine the linguistic and social structure of recurring episodes of social interaction in context, episodes that are of social and cultural significance to a community of speakers. Such episodes have been called interactive practices (Hall, 1995) and communicative practices (Hanks, 1996), and I will refer to them here as *discursive practices.*

Practice is anything that people do, and one of the most accessible definitions of discursive practice is given by Karen Tracy (2002, p. 21), who describes discursive practices as 'talk activities that people do.' She continues,

> A discursive practice may refer to a small piece of talk (person-referencing practices) or it may focus on a large one (narratives); it may focus on single features that may be named and pointed to (speech acts) or it may reference sets of features (dialect, stance). Discursive practices may focus on something done by an individual (directness style) or they may refer to actions that require more than one party (interaction structures).

The structure of a practice includes what actions you perform, the forms of language that you use, and also gesture, eye gaze, and ways of positioning the body – how close you stand to the person you are talking to, for example. Figure A4.2 is a picture of a practice that is familiar to many people, and we can tell a lot about the practice and the people in it just by carefully examining the picture.

The two individuals in Figure A4.2 have short hair and are wearing clothes that are typical of males. We can tell from their physical size and the skin coloration that

Figure A4.2 Father and son playing a video game. Source: Downloaded from iStockphoto. File Number: 401030

their ages are different, but their white skin and similar facial features indicate a similar ethnicity; the one on the right looks older than the one on the left. They are sitting side by side and are not gazing at each other; their smiles indicate pleasure and both of their gazes are focused on a single object. Both individuals are holding in their hands identical black objects with a cord attached to each one; the two cords seem to lead toward the object of their joint attention.

All this information is summarized in the caption of the photograph as 'Father and son playing a video game.' The caption is a description of the social roles of the individuals and the caption names the practice – the culturally significant activity in which they are engaged – but in order to understand the practice and the social roles invoked by the caption we must first have knowledge of family and gender roles in a particular society and cultural artifacts such as video games. When we observe a practice, one of the first things that we do is to interpret its social values in this way. To see how important our social interpretation of a practice is, try to interpret a practice that is described with very little social information in Task A4.1.2.

Task A4.1.2

➤ Here is a description of a picture of a practice that is of cultural significance among members of a particular community. Use the description to draw a picture and write a caption that identifies the social roles of the participants and names the practice.[1]

The two individuals in the picture have long black hair; they are wearing earrings and brightly colored clothes that are typical of females. Their physical size suggests that they are of a similar age and their skin texture shows that they are not yet adult; their light brown skin, dark brown eyes, and similar facial features indicate a similar ethnicity. Their heads are very close together; the one on the left is in profile, facing the one on the right. The one on the left is smiling and holding her right hand open between her mouth and the right ear of the one on the right. The one on the right has wide open eyes and a half-open mouth. Besides the earrings and clothes, there are no other physical artifacts in the picture.

So far, we have described activities and behaviors of people from the outside, what we can physically perceive of an interaction – the audio and video of an interaction – but we have begun to argue that these physical perceptions have their roots in social history. History is something that we cannot immediately perceive in an interaction but which we infer on the basis of our own life experience. Such inferences are values, and each aspect of physical behavior has a value associated with it. When we say that someone 'speaks well,' 'looks like a movie star,' is 'verbally deprived,' or has 'an accent' we are expressing values about the way that person speaks, looks, or behaves. So an important dimension of a discursive practice is not only *what* you do but *how* you do it and the judgments that people make about it. Bourdieu (1977) recognized that a person's ways of speaking and acting in a practice have their origins in the person's upbringing, education, group membership, and value system. Those ways are not usually subject to conscious inspection; they are in Bourdieu's term *habitus*. To illustrate the connection between an individual's present practice and that individual's history, Bourdieu quotes Émile Durkheim (1969, p. 16) as follows.

> in each of us, in varying proportions, there is part of yesterday's man; it is yesterday's man who inevitably predominates in us, since the present amounts to little compared with the long past in the course of which we were formed and from which we result. Yet we do not sense this man of the past, because he is inveterate in us; he makes up the unconscious part of ourselves.
>
> (Quoted in Bourdieu 1977, p. 79)

Durkheim does not mean that we are automata, nor does he imply that in present practice we are simply reproducing the behaviors and attitudes that have been inculcated in us as children; he does in fact recognize the role of individual agency in creating and resisting habitus, but nonetheless the effect of history – of 'yesterday's man' (and, of course, yesterday's woman) – is very strong, both in influencing behavior in discursive practice and conditioning attitudes toward that behavior. An example of the way that history conditions attitudes towards people and their practices is this remark by a woman from Mississippi in the American South about people from the North (Kolker and Alvarez, 1987).

> I don't think they [people from the North] perhaps have the same values of hospitality that we do in the South. And so I associate all of that with the sound of their voice. And it's um, grating on your ears. Maybe our sound is also, but it's usually their nasal, um, and a lot of times the things they say are not kind.

Interaction in discursive practices is therefore not just about communication of information; every interaction involves a complex network of power relations among participants. When a person speaks or writes, that person makes a bid for social authority, and the person who hears or reads decides to what degree to recognize that claim to authority. Bourdieu introduced the concept of *linguistic capital* to describe the respect or authority that is claimed or enjoyed by a speaker. The notion of linguistic capital is similar to the idea of 'capital' in economics because, the more you have, the more power you have over your own life and the lives and opinions of others. Those with high linguistic capital speak with 'command' – they have the power to influence a listener toward the desired interpretation.

 Task A4.1.3

➤ Read the following story told by a Boston woman of how her fiancé lost linguistic capital during a drive to his home in the South of the United States.

Describe how much linguistic capital her fiancé had at the start of the journey and how he lost it by the time they arrived (Kolker and Alvarez, 1987). What is the relationship between *habitus* and *linguistic capital*?

I was engaged for a while to a Yalie, who sounded like a Yalie to me, although he had a trace of a Southern accent.[2] I thought sort of Bill Faulkner, Truman Capote accent, you know. When you're twenty you don't, you know, make these distinctions, and I went home to meet his family, ah, at Christmas. And as we drove further south from New Haven, his accent got heavier and heavier. It became filled with all these hillbilly kind of regionalisms, you know, this real kind of 'you-all' stuff and as well a lot of the hand gestures. This was, this man was becoming a different person as we went – mostly the language. By the time we got to Sparta,[3] um, I had had it. I just knew that someone with those little accents was not gonna crawl around inside of me. I was not gonna have little Southern babies who talked like that and I got on a plane home. No question.

In this section, we have discussed the importance of practice in people's lives and we have described practices as recurrent activities that have their own structures. Structure in discursive practices includes the ways that participants use linguistic resources, but structure also includes the configuration of gestural resources, gaze, and ways of positioning the body in a practice. Because a community's practices have social and cultural significance, the attitudes of participants and observers toward the use of linguistic and non-linguistic resources in a practice are always present. Those resources and the attitudes toward them are rooted in *habitus* – past experience, upbringing, and membership in social groups. All relations between individuals involve power – either approval or disapproval of a course of action, either influence by or resistance to the power of another. Power that is created, adapted, and asserted through language can be seen as linguistic capital, and it is therefore important to understand the ways in which language provides resources for individuals to exercise power in discursive practices. The following section will describe the linguistic resources that are available to participants in discursive practices.

A4.2 HOW LINGUISTIC RESOURCES ARE USED TO CONSTRUCT PRACTICES

One dimension that participants use in order to create a discursive practice is a characteristic and high-frequency use of particular linguistic forms. Linguistic features such as pronunciation, vocabulary, and grammar may combine to characterize a specific register for the practice. A register is a recognizable repertoire of such linguistic features that is associated with a specific discursive practice and with the people who engage in the practice.[4] Many registers are associated with practices that are of such importance in a culture that the practice has a name, and that name is also used to refer to the register that indexes it. So the register that lawyers use in a courtroom is called *courtroom language* and the language of legal documents is called *legal language*, just as the repertoire of certain other people who might sometimes be found in courtrooms is called *thieves' argot*.

High-frequency use of certain vocabulary is a feature of register that marks some practices. Thus, a broadcast commentary of a sporting event such as tennis or golf in which the participants are easily identifiable includes a high-frequency occurrence of the players' names as well as vocabulary descriptive of the event such as *net, ball, serve, volley,* and *baseline* in tennis and *tee, drive, putt, birdie,* and *par* in golf. In fact, one definition of register is 'the means whereby contextual predictability . . . is reflected in the lexico-grammar' (Trappes-Lomax, 2004). This definition implies both that the context predicts lexical frequency, and that frequent use of certain vocabulary helps in the identification of a discursive practice. Not all members of a society have access to the same registers, and socialization to a social role often involves acquisition of the appropriate register. Those people who have not been socialized to the relevant roles may reject the registers that index them by referring to such registers as *jargon, gobbledygook,* or by saying *It's Greek to me*.

 Task A4.2.1

➤ Here is list of words associated with *two* different registers. The words are listed alphabetically. Divide them into two groups and name the practices and identities that they index.

boi, butch, cache, cgi, cookie, femme, ISP, MTF, surf, tranny

In addition to the high-frequency use of particular linguistic forms, discursive practices are also characterized by specific ways in which participants make meaning in those practices. In unit A3, we identified three modes of meaning – ways in which people use language to create certain kinds of meaning: The interpersonal metafunction includes linguistic resources that allow people to create identities for themselves and others; the ideational metafunction includes ways in which people use language to represent and analyze their experiences; and the textual metafunction makes connections between one part of a text and another. These interpersonal, ideational, and textual metafunctions are also features of register, and one register may show a predominance of one metafunction over or to the exclusion of others. Take, for example, the passage in Task A4.2.2 from the online *Physics classroom* (Henderson, 2004).

 Task A4.2.2

➤ The text below is intended for instruction in physics. Which mode of meaning predominates in the text? The interpersonal metafunction (the communicative function of language to influence others people's thoughts, beliefs, or actions)? The ideational metafunction (the function of language is to describe, represent, analyze, and explain our experiences of the world)? Or the textual meta-function, which allows us to connect utterances to their linguistic context?

The Law of Reflection
Light is known to behave in a very predictable manner. If a ray of light could be observed approaching and reflecting off of a flat mirror, then the behavior of the light as it reflects would follow a predictable law known as the law of reflection. The diagram below illustrates the law of reflection.

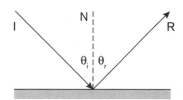

In the diagram, the ray of light approaching the mirror is known as the incident ray (labeled I in the diagram). The ray of light which leaves the mirror is known as the reflected ray (labeled R in the diagram). At the point of incidence where the ray strikes the mirror, a line can be drawn perpendicular to the surface of the mirror; this line is known as a normal line (labeled N in the diagram). The normal line divides the angle between the incident ray and the reflected ray into two equal angles. The angle between the incident ray and the normal is known as the angle of incidence. The angle between the reflected ray and the normal is known as the angle of reflection. (These two angles are labeled with the Greek letter 'theta' accompanied by a subscript; read as 'theta-I' for angle of incidence and 'theta-r' for angle of reflection.) The law of reflection states that when a ray of light reflects off a surface, the angle of incidence is equal to the angle of reflection.

Although the high-frequency occurrence of linguistic features and predominant modes of meaning may distinguish spoken or written discursive practices from each other, discursive practices are not distinguished in these ways alone. In fact, most of the attention that researchers have directed at spoken discursive practices has focused on their interactional nature and, in particular, dimensions such as how participants manage to organize who speaks when and who speaks next.

A4.3 HOW INTERACTIONAL RESOURCES ARE USED TO CONSTRUCT PRACTICES

When two or more people are talking together, a remarkable thing happens: Most of the time one person talks and the other person remains silent. There are of course overlaps when two or more people speak at the same time, but the overlapping talk doesn't generally last too long. This remarkable and remarkably consistent fact about people taking turns at talk in conversation was first described by Harvey Sacks,

Emanuel Schegloff, and Gail Jefferson in a classic article published in 1974. They identified two ways in which participants in talk-in-interaction orient to turn-taking. These were: (1) how participants decide who will speak next and (2) at what point in the current speaker's turn a transition to a new speaker may occur. In Sacks, Schegloff, and Jefferson (1974) and in several subsequent studies, the organization of turn-taking in talk-in-interaction was shown to be systematic. The possibilities of allocating who will take the next turn-at-talk were listed by Sacks, Schegloff, and Jefferson as:

- A current speaker may select the next speaker.
- Another person or persons may self-select by starting to talk.

And if another speaker does not take a turn, then the current speaker has the right (but not the obligation) to continue talking. The allocation of the next turn to a particular speaker depends on the sequence of conversational actions, the nature of the communicative event, and the relative power of the participants. An example of a sequence of conversational actions is the question-and-answer sequence. If two people are in conversation and one of them asks a question of the other person (i.e., that person is selected by the current speaker to take the next turn), then both people in the conversation expect the next turn to be taken by the person to whom the question was addressed. In a communicative event such as requesting a pharmacist to fill a prescription, the patient may begin the event by giving the pharmacist the prescription written by a doctor. Although the patient has not said anything, both patient and pharmacist expect the next turn to be taken by the pharmacist. And finally, the system for selecting the next speaker has been shown to be very different in institutional contexts (such as a courtroom, a classroom, a radio call-in program, or a political debate) from the pattern in informal non-institutional contexts, and the practice of selecting the next speaker is a way in which institutional power is realized in interaction. In questioning of a witness in a courtroom, for example, the attorney is the participant who selects the witness to answer questions; the witness is not permitted to ask questions of the attorney.

In addition to explaining how a next speaker is selected in conversation, Sacks, Schegloff, and Jefferson also discussed the place in a current turn that participants perceive a transition from one speaker to the next as possible. A transition-relevance place in the current speaker's turn is a place of possible turn-completion where transition to the next speaker may occur. This place is often thought of as marking a boundary between grammatical, intonational, or pragmatic units (or a place which marks a boundary of all three types of units). Sometimes, there is a hearable silence between the conclusion of one speaker's turn and the beginning of the next speaker's turn as in this example (Sacks *et al.*, 1974, p. 702).

```
Jeanette:   Oh you know, Mittie— Gordon, Gordon, eh-
            Mittie's husband died.
            (0.3)
Estelle:    Oh whe::n.
```

In this conversation, Jeanette's turn completes a grammatical unit, 'Mittie's husband died,' with a falling intonation indicated by the period (.), and is a pragmatically complete piece of information. The transition-relevance place is recognized by Estelle who waits three-tenths of a second before she begins the next turn. In many cases, there is no hearable silence between the end of one turn and the beginning of the next and the subsequent turn is latched on to the previous one.

But when the next speaker self-selects, very often the subsequent turn begins before a unit boundary in the previous turn because an upcoming boundary can be projected. Here is an example of a second turn taken before the completion of the first (Wells and Macfarlane, 1998).

```
M:  they´ve got ↑n:uts in[side.
J:                       [yes. but you can buy them,
```

M and J are mother and daughter from the West Midlands in England. They are engaged in unwrapping Christmas presents. In the conversation, M's turn reaches a grammatical, phonological, and pragmatic completion point after she utters 'inside.' 'They've got nuts inside' is a grammatically complete clause, it ends with a falling intonation indicated by the period (.), and it is a pragmatically complete piece of information. Yet the aligned square brackets indicate that J does not wait until her mother's turn is complete before beginning the next turn: She begins to speak before her mother is finished and her 'yes' overlaps with the final syllable of her mother's turn. In other words, J projects the completion of her mother's turn shortly before it is actually complete.

Discursive practices differ in the ways that participants allocate turns and decide at which point in the current speaker's turn a transition to a new speaker may occur. We have seen that institutional power in interaction is exercised by the participant who regularly selects the next speaker, but the participant who refuses to cede the next turn to others also exercises power in conversation. As Bales (1970, p. 76) commented,

> To take up time speaking in a small group is to exercise power over the
> other members for at least the duration of the time taken, regardless of the
> content. . . . Within the small group, the time taken by a given member in
> a given session is practically a direct index of the amount of power he has
> attempted to exercise in that period.

In discursive practice, then, certain linguistic forms such as vocabulary, grammar, and pronunciation characterize a practice; and in addition, practices are characterized by the ways in which participants make meaning. In oral interaction in particular, the ways that participants organize turn-taking create not only the practice itself but also the relations of power among the participants. Task A4.3.1 is an activity in which you can discover for yourself some of the ways that discursive practices are created.

Task A4.3.1

> Imagine the following discursive practices. How do participants in these practices allocate the next turn? When do participants recognize that a transition from one speaker to the next is possible? What does your analysis of turn-taking in these practices indicate about the power of the participants in these practices?
>   ■ a courtroom trial
>   ■ a wedding ceremony
>   ■ a first date
>   ■ Dr Martin Luther King's 'I have a dream' speech

A4.4 POWER IN PRACTICE

'Power' is a powerful word. The word has the sense of control or dominion of one group over another, an essential inequality between dominant and subordinate, an inequality that has been resisted by many people working in critical discourse analysis. From this perspective, some people have power over others and they exercise that power through certain face-to-face interactions and through discursive practices. Doctors, teachers, and lawyers are able to exert power over patients, students, and witnesses by the ways that they use language. They do so by frequent use of technical terms that are little known to others, by using language to create identities for themselves and others, by representing and analyzing their own experiences as more real than others, and by controlling turn allocation in examination rooms, classrooms, and courtrooms. The practical result of the power that they exercise is to get patients to follow a prescribed course of treatment, to get students to follow a course of study prescribed by the teacher, and to get witnesses to pursue topics and inferences suggested by the lawyer. As Norman Fairclough (2001) has pointed out, power in discourse involves 'controlling and constraining the contributions of non-powerful participants' (pp. 38–39). But it is not discourse alone that creates these results, power is also created by 'the system' – organized social situations and political institutions that create enduring master identities for individuals as doctors and patients, as teachers and students, and as lawyers and witnesses, and expectations for their roles in society. Language – more specifically, discursive practice – is the construction and reflection of these social expectations through actions which invoke identity, ideology, belief, and power.

How do powerful participants exercise power in discursive practices? How do they control and constrain the contributions of the non-powerful? One answer to those questions is that power in discourse is co-constructed by all participants – both the powerful and the non-powerful. When a student reads the text on the law of reflection from *The physics classroom* (Henderson, 2004) reproduced earlier in this unit, the student may not understand some of the technical terms such as 'angle of incidence' or 'normal line' because words like 'incidence' may be unfamiliar or words like 'normal' are being used in an unusual way. When a classroom teacher controls talk by means of allocating next turn to the students, the students' rights to speak are limited. In both cases, however, the non-powerful may co-construct power by accepting the constraints imposed upon them: The student who doesn't understand a word may decide to search for the meaning in a dictionary or to ask somebody to explain it; and the students in a classroom may simply accept the fact that their discursive contributions will be limited. In these cases, the structures of discursive practices appear to be universally followed and thus necessarily accepted by all participants.

There are, of course, instances where non-powerful participants resist the constraints imposed on them in a discursive practice and struggle against the power exerted over them. One example of that is when students ask questions of a teacher. Normally in a classroom, the teacher allocates turns-at-talk by selecting the next speaker, but the students may sometimes select the next speaker by asking a question of the teacher. The teacher may then try to re-impose the normal turn-allocation system by repeating the question, and by so doing selecting another student as the next speaker. An example of such a struggle for the right to allocate turns is the transcript in Task A4.4.1 adapted from Markee (2000, p. 172).

Task A4.4.1

➤ In the following classroom conversation, what rules of turn allocation is the teacher (T) trying to impose on classroom discourse? How do the students (L1, L2, and L3) resist the power of the teacher?

```
 1 L1:  ok (0.2) excuse me (0.2) uh: what what does it mean
        hab— (0.5) habi-
 2      (0.4)
 3  T:  habitats
 4 L1:  habitats
 5  T:  yeah (.) you had that word as well (0.2) what do you
        think it means
 6      (0.8)
 7 L2:  hhh [hh      ]
 8  T:      [yours   ] talked about habitats didn't it
 9      (0.4)
10 L2:  uh:m
11  T:  the [m]ost important (1.2) habitat
12 L2:      [I]
13      (1.0)
14 L2:  I think (.) the habitats is the: /em/ (1.0)
        e[nvironment uh] and uh
15 L3:   [environment  ]
16 L2:  (0.8) environment and uh (2.0) uhm 'h
17      (1.2)
```

```
18  L3:  is it [is it  ] the: nearest [environment]
19  L2:        [for for]              [for the fish] you (mea
                                be:) hh
20   T:  ˙h yeah what would be another word for a habitat then
         (0.7)
21       it´s like
22       (1.3)
23   T:  [it´s hli—  ]
24  L1:  [I ha       ]ve ↓no idea↑
```

SUMMARY AND LOOKING AHEAD

The concept of discursive practice that we have introduced in this unit is not only a way of categorizing different human activities but it is also a way of explicating how participants in discursive practices create identities, display group membership and competence, learn, and exert power. We are able to understand how these social realities are created by observing how participants employ linguistic and discursive resources. The reading in Unit B4 is written by an anthropologist who contributed to the development of Practice Theory. But unless this discussion of theory becomes too rarefied, Unit C4 contains transcripts of two discursive practices that will be familiar to many: story telling among friends and a radio call-in program. Both of these practices are recorded and can be accessed over the internet. Now we have the main tools in place for understanding language in interaction: an understanding of the relationship between language and context, the tools of systemic functional grammar and conversation analysis, and an appreciation of how discursive practices are co-constructed by participants. In the next unit, A5, we will put all these charms together to analyze a complete discursive practice and to begin thinking about what learning means in Practice Theory.

Unit A5
Describing discursive practices

PROLOGUE AND ROADMAP

In the previous units we have introduced a procedure for analyzing talk in interaction, paying careful attention to the context in which talk occurs, the linguistic and interactional resources that participants employ, and the discursive practice that they co-construct. In this unit, we put all this together in a detailed analysis of an interaction between two people: a music teacher and his student. We lay out a systematic way of analyzing the practice by analyzing participants' employment of linguistic and interactional resources, and how those resources combine to construct identity for the participants and a meaning for the practice. The practices that we have chosen to analyze in this unit and in Unit C5 all involve some kind of teaching–learning interaction and we have done so in order to present an interactional view of learning. Learning in discursive practice is analyzed very differently from the way that learning is conceived in other disciplines; learning is not the changing cognition of an individual learner, but it is considered, rather, as changing participation by the learner and the teacher in a discursive practice: What is learned is not 'the topic' of the lesson but the practice.

A5.1 A FRAMEWORK FOR DESCRIBING DISCURSIVE PRACTICES

Discursive practices are talk activities that people do. People do them all the time and for this reason it is quite difficult to step back from activities that are so common in order to analyze what they are and to understand how people manage to do them. Because in our everyday lives these activities are so common, in order to understand them we need to get outside our everyday experience. That is why anthropologists study exotic societies in far flung parts of the world; they do so in the belief that all human societies share common practices, and by understanding practices in societies which are very different from our own we will come to greater insight into the practices that we do every day and which constitute the society in which we live. We may not have the opportunity or the resources to conduct anthropological research on distant societies, but we can perhaps get an outsider's perspective on our everyday activities by imagining that we are aliens or we come from a different species. In other words, can we take the role of the monkey in Figure A5.1?

Figure A5.1 Learning a new discursive practice. Source: Monkey thinking 'Conversation – What a Concept!' by Jack Ziegler. Published in *The New Yorker*, November 25, 1991. Available from www.cartoonbank.com ID: 31811

The discursive practice shown in the cartoon is an informal social conversation among middle-class white adults in the United States. The humans in the picture obviously know what they are doing, but the monkey is perplexed, probably because he has not learned the patterns of this particular discursive practice. But the monkey's problem is not just because he is not a human; the problems of understanding how unfamiliar discursive practices work and how to participate in them face most of us throughout our lives as we move from one community to another and discover unfamiliar practices. Our problem is really two problems: how to understand what is going on in the practice and how to participate in the practice ourselves.

The three units that preceded this one have prepared us to understand what is going on, and in the units that follow we will discuss how people learn to participate in unfamiliar practices. A framework for understanding practices includes understanding both the linguistic and the interactional resources that participants use. The linguistic resources include the register of the practice, which we defined as a recognizable repertoire of pronunciation, vocabulary, and grammar that often occurs with high frequency in certain practices, the combination of which is associated with a specific activity, place, participants, or purpose.[1] Another linguistic resource that participants adopt is certain kinds of meaning that participants create through the practice: meanings through which we influence others; meanings with which we describe, represent, and analyze experience; and meanings that help participants connect one part of a discourse to another.[2]

The interactional resources that participants use to construct a discursive practice also include some of the features of talk-in-interaction that we have presented in earlier units, including the selection and sequential organization of acts, the turn-taking system that participants use to manage transitions from one speaker to another, the ways in which participants repair interactional trouble, and how participants construct identities for themselves and others and in so doing construct a participation framework.[3] In addition to these four interactional resources, one resource that we have not discussed so far is the ways in which participants construct boundaries of a practice. In order to identify a practice, it is necessary to distinguish it from other talk. This is done by means of locating the boundaries of the practice – the opening and closing moves in the sequence of acts in a practice. Not all practices begin and end abruptly within a few moves and, in fact, boundaries of a practice may be vague, may be negotiated, or may be resisted by one or more participants; nonetheless, boundaries are essential in identifying discursive practices. In summary, then, we can describe a discursive practice by specifying the ways in which participants avail themselves of the following seven resources.

- Identity resources
  - *Participation framework*: the identities of all participants in an interaction, present or not, official or unofficial, ratified or unratified, and their footing or identities in the interaction

- Linguistic resources
  - *Register*: the features of pronunciation, vocabulary, and grammar that typify a practice
  - *Modes of meaning*: the ways in which participants construct interpersonal, experiential, and textual meanings in a practice

- Interactional resources
  - *Speech acts*: the selection of acts in a practice and their sequential organization
  - *Turn-taking*: how participants select the next speaker and how participants know when to end one turn and when to begin the next
  - *Repair*: the ways in which participants respond to interactional trouble in a given practice
  - *Boundaries*: the opening and closing acts of a practice that serve to distinguish a given practice from adjacent talk

The configuration of these seven resources may be conceived as an interactional architecture unique to a specific discursive practice. The word 'architecture' gives a very solid feel to the notion of a discursive practice although, as we have seen, practices are constructed, modified, and changed by participants on the fly, so it is more accurate to consider participants as the architects and this list as seven resources they use in order to construct a practice.

Later in this unit we will use this framework in order to analyze in detail one authentic discursive practice, but in order to get a feel for the framework, let's take a look at the problems that the monkey has with the imaginary practice of 'conversation over drinks with friends in a bar' that is illustrated in the cartoon. We don't know what the people are talking about but it looks to be a fairly informal conversation; the people are adults – two females and two males (including the monkey) – and all of them are dressed formally so it looks like the conversation is taking place in a public place, probably a bar or a restaurant because they are gathered around a table with drinks in front of them. From our experience of the culture, we also know that gathering around a table for drinks in American society constructs an egalitarian status among participants. Even though status differences may exist among these four people at their workplaces, the practice in which they are engaged here is one in which such status differences are downplayed.

Although the group looks to be focused (that is, the four people are not unknown to each other), there appear to be two conversations going on at the same time. By observing the direction of their gaze, we can infer that the females appear to be talking to each other and the man appears to be addressing the monkey (who is quite nonplussed). By this close observation, we have already begun to specify the participation framework of the practice: Gender identities seem to be relevant for participants and this appears to influence their turn-taking organization. Females are talking to females and males to males, so gender identities appear to influence the selection of the next speaker. In addition, we can surmise that power relations among participants are not crucial in determining the kind of discourse in this practice.

We cannot specify the linguistic resources used by participants in this practice and, depending on what they are talking about, they may construct meanings in different ways. If one of the participants invites others for dinner, for example, the mode of meaning is likely to be interpersonal; if another participant tells a story about what happened at work today, the mode of meaning may be experiential; and, as participants respond to topics that they or others have previously introduced, the mode may be textual. Although we may not know how participants are constructing meaning or what the participants are saying, the observation that they are dressed formally and they are sitting in a public place influences the register of the practice.

 Task A5.1.1

➤ What are the kinds of topics and vocabulary that are likely to be used in an informal conversation among formally dressed adults in a public setting? How does that differ from the register of informal conversation among informally dressed adults in a private setting?

Interactional trouble may occur during the conversation; in fact, it probably does because interactional trouble such as misunderstanding or mishearing by one participant of what another participant said is very common in conversation. When participants perceive interactional trouble, they may orient to it by means of repair. In Section A3.2.3 we discussed three aspects of repair in conversation: the source of the interactional trouble, the participant who initiates the repair, and the participant who completes the repair. The four types of repairs are known by reference to the participants involved as *other-initiated self-repair*, *other-initiated other repair*, *self-initiated self-repair*, and *self-initiated other repair*. As we have discussed, however, the two types of other-initiated repairs present threats to the negative face of a participant and thus, when there are no clear power or status distinctions between participants, such threats are often mitigated in some way. The best way to mitigate such a threat is, of course, not to do it; that is, not to repair trouble in another participant's talk: and so other-initiated other repair is found very infrequently in informal conversation.

We see in the cartoon only one snapshot of the conversation, but this practice had a beginning and will have an end. Although we cannot know what opening and closing acts the participants use to create a boundary between this practice and adjacent talk, we can infer a side-sequence in their talk in which they ordered the drinks which we now see on the table in front of them. The practice of 'ordering drinks in a bar' is quite circumscribed and routine, which means that the practice includes the same acts in a very similar sequence, beginning with an opening act and ending with a closing act.

Task A5.1.2

> Write a dialogue for the practice of 'ordering drinks in a bar,' and identify the acts that characterize the practice. Now compare your dialogue with one written by someone else. How do the acts that you selected for your dialogue compare with the acts that another person selected? Does the sequence of acts differ?

We have speculated about the resources that participants employ in the practice of 'conversation over drinks with friends in a bar' that is illustrated in the cartoon. Let us summarize how our imaginary participants utilize the seven resources that we identified. First, participants employ resources of register and semiotics (modes of meaning) to construct the linguistic dimension of the practice. Second, a certain turn-taking organization and pattern of repair is likely to characterize the inter-actional dimension of the practice, while the gender and status identities that participants play are discussed as the participation framework. Finally, although in a long and complex practice like this it is difficult to speculate about the selection and sequence of acts by participants, in shorter and more routine practices such as 'ordering drinks' the selection and sequence of acts is perhaps easier, as is the identification of acts which bound the practice itself and distinguish it from adjacent talk.

Has this listing of the resources that participants employ in the practice of 'conversation over drinks with friends in a bar' made it easier for the monkey to participate in the practice? That will probably depend on whether he prefers to learn implicitly by observing the practice as a legitimate peripheral participant (as seems to be illustrated in the cartoon), or whether he prefers to learn the new practice by paying explicit attention to the resources that we have listed, or by a combination of implicit and explicit learning. Which do you prefer?

A5.2 WHAT DO DISCURSIVE PRACTICES LOOK LIKE?

When the configuration of resources that participants use in one practice differs from those used in another practice, we have good reason to say that the two discursive practices differ. So far in Units A2 through A4, we have studied a number of different activities (we haven't called them discursive practices yet) and if we revisit two of those activities now from the perspective of the discursive practice framework, we can see how they shape up as practices.

In Unit A2.1.2, we presented a conversation between a mother and her child on a bus and, in discussing this conversation, we introduced Erving Goffman's idea that participants in an interaction are not only those who speak but also non-speaking participants because non-speaking participants such as overhearers may influence what is said. In that conversation, we also recognized that the identities of the speaking participants were invoked by the participants themselves as a mother and her son, Donnie. There was also clearly a power difference invoked by the speaking participants: Donnie wanted to do something (go to the bathroom) and his mother didn't permit him to do so. What we have done in identifying participants and in describing the roles that they play in creating the discourse is in effect to specify the *participation framework* of the interaction. We can go on to identify and describe the other resources that participants invoke. The *register* used by Donnie and his mother includes their accent, which Birdwhistell identified as 'tidewater Virginia'; that is, an accent that identifies them as from a different social class from the other people on the bus. It also includes the whining and rasping tone used by Donnie that helps to construct for him the less powerful identity of the two speakers. In their *modes of meaning*, both speakers are primarily trying to influence the behavior of each other and are thus constructing interpersonal meanings. The *acts* that they carry out involve a sequence of requests by Donnie, each one of which is followed a refusal of some kind by his mother. The way that they take *turns at talk* is also quite clear. Donnie assigns the next turn to his mother, who initially declines to take a turn until Donnie repeats his request. There is no overt interactional trouble in the dialogue because it seems that both participants share intersubjectivity: They both know what Donnie wants and they both understand his mother's refusal to grant it. And since there is no interactional trouble, there is no occasion for *repair*. The *boundaries* of the conversation are also quite clear – an initial request by the child opens the reported conversation and a loud 'Shut up' from the mother concludes it – although Birdwhistell does not give any information about what happened before and after the short conversation that he reports. In Karen Tracy's definition of discursive practices as 'talk activities that people do,' the conversation between Donnie and his mother is clearly an instance of a small piece of talk, or a person-referencing practice. But we have also noted that a discursive practice is a culturally significant activity, an activity that has a name in the community where it is practiced, or an easy caption that we can attach to an image of the activity. We are able to label some public activities quite easily, like Dr Martin Luther King's 'I have a dream' speech in Section A3.1, and we can also easily label some more homely activities such as 'Father and son playing a video game' in Figure A4.2.

Task A5.2.1

➤ Is the conversation between Donnie and his mother a culturally significant activity? Would you give a name to such an activity? If so, what would you call it?

A more institutional discursive practice that we observed in Sections A2.1.2 and A3.2.4 has a name: the patient consultation in a pharmacy. It is a culturally significant activity because as Nguyen (2003) reported, in Schools of Pharmacy in the United States, the patient consultation is a part of the curriculum for all pharmacy students. We noticed in this practice, too, that the participation frame-work included a non-present participant. Both the pharmacist and the patient in Figure A3.4 gaze at the medication in the pharmacist's hand because they recognize a non-present participant in the interaction, a principal who gives authority to the pharmacist's instructions to the patient. The identities of pharmacist and patient are also co-constructed in the discourse by the pharmacist's long turn (lines 5–12 in Section A2.1.2) and the patient's shorter turns; by the pharmacist's use of the technical term 'doxycycline' and by the patient's avoidance of technical terms; and by the interpersonal meanings that the pharmacist creates in order to instruct the patient on how to administer the medication and the patient's use of experiential meaning to describe his experience with doxycycline or a similar medication. The pharmacist selects and sequences the acts in this practice, beginning with a question about the patient's prior experience with doxycycline, which he follows with instructions about how much medication to take (one tablet), how often to take it (twice daily), and how to take the medication (with water). The organization of turn-taking in the patient consultation is similar to many professional–client interactions in which the professional takes turns whenever he wants, and selects the client as next speaker. There is apparently no interactional trouble and thus no repair in this conversation, and, because the excerpt in Section A2.1.2 is taken from a longer patient consultation, the opening and closing moves of the practice were not reported.

Both Donnie's conversation with his mother and the patient consultation in the pharmacy are instances of discursive practice in which participants create and manage their identities and adopt certain linguistic and interactional resources in order to do so. The structure of the patient consultation seems to be more routine than the conversation between Donnie and his mother because, as we have remarked, the patient consultation is an interaction which pharmacists are explicitly taught to do and it follows a routine sequence of acts and the resources called upon by the pharmacist are well known to him. The conversation between Donnie and his mother is not routine, and certainly neither participant has been explicitly taught how to act in this practice, but there are nonetheless aspects of this practice which may well be re-used from other practices. The desire of a young child to use the bathroom is something that both participants are familiar with and also the communication of that desire by the child to his mother is also likely to have happened before. Life is not full of surprises.

These two examples of discursive practices are presented for illustration purposes, and they are necessarily brief. In the next sections, we will discuss a longer practice in a school setting and show how the framework of discursive practice provides us with insights into how these three practices help participants create identities.

A5.3 AN INSTRUCTIONAL PRACTICE

The practice that we will analyze in this section is perhaps familiar to you. It is a practice that occurs in many schools around the world and involves a student learning to play a musical instrument with a teacher. Music is a part of school life in many elementary, middle, and high schools in the United States. Music instruction is offered in kindergarten through twelfth grade and students in grades 6 and 7 are able to choose whether to participate in band, chorus, general music, or orchestra. Besides whole-class instruction, students who play in an orchestra or band receive short periods of individual instruction from a music teacher. The practice we examine here is an individual music lesson between a teacher and his middle school-student. The teacher is male in his 30s and the student is female age about 11; her instrument is the clarinet, and teacher and student meet once a week for about five minutes. Between lessons, the student (S) is supposed to practice playing music assigned to her each week by the teacher (T), who has written the assignments on a 'blue sheet.' The lesson we examine here was videotaped in November when the student was preparing for an orchestra performance at a Christmas concert. The whole of their five-minute lesson is transcribed below, and in Figure A5.2 you can see an image from the middle of the lesson.

A5.3.1 A clarinet lesson

```
1       ((S is sitting holding her clarinet. A music stand with
        the score of ´I´ll be home for Christmas´ is in front of
        her. T walks around her, then claps his hands.))
2  T:   ALRIGHT. let´s do a lesson here. (1.0) what are you
        gonna do for me. let´s see your blue sheet? (3.0)
```

Figure A5.2 Participants in the clarinet lesson. Source: Kelley, W. (2000). *Instrumental music lessons* [VHS video]. Madison, WI: University of Wisconsin-Madison

```
 3      ((T places the blue sheet on the music stand in front of
        him and sits down next to S.))
 4  T:  alright let´s play I´ll be home for Christmas.
 5  S:  I hate this one.
 6      (2.0)
 7  T:  go ahead and begin it.
 8      ((S reads from the score on the music stand in front of
        her and plays a few measures from ´I´ll be home for
        Christmas´ for 17 seconds. T also looks at the score.))
 9  T:  good. how m´ny beats does this have. ((T points to a
        note on the score.))
10  S:  three.
11  T:  three. d´you give it three beats?
12  S:  ↓No:↑
13  T:  why not.
14  S:  (1.0) ↓I don´t know:↑
15      ((T reads from the score on the music stand in front of
        S and plays the same measures on his trumpet for 7
        seconds.))
16  T:  let´s play it again at the begin— (2.0) one, two, three,
        go.
17      ((S and T play the measures together for 22 seconds, S
        on her clarinet, T on his trumpet.))
18  T:  you gotta hold that for all four beats.
19  S:  I ↓did.
20  T:  you didn´t. for all eight beats I´m sorry. ((sniffs))
        now.
21      ((T leans over and marks a note on S´s score.))
```

22 T: listen you gotta do something with this note. (1.0) so
        let's say: like this. you put an eff here. so I want you
        to crescendo and de— decrescendo. so you get big and
        then you get little. so you go ((sings)) daaa°aaaa°. can
        you do that?
23   ((S nods.))
24 T: do that over eight beats for me.
25   ((S puts clarinet to her lips but does not play.))
26 S: so you get louder then you get softer?
27 T: yeah. get loud for four beats and then get soft for four
        beats.
28   ((S plays for 6 seconds.))
29 T: okay that's good. play this ((T points to S's score.))
        all by yourself. °from the beginning.°
30   ((S plays for 20 seconds.))
31 T: good. now this measure is the only one you're still
        having trouble with. one, and two, three. and I've put a
        little breath here, ((T marks S's score.)) and then go
        ((T sings.)) baa dee-dee-dee ((T ends singing.)) this is
        like all one phrase play:: play a meas— two measures
        before seventeen. a bee flat.
32 S: (3.0) oh right— here? ((S points to her score.))
33 T: yeah.
34   ((S plays for 4 seconds.))
35 S: what? (0.5) okay,
36 T: ((sarcastic voice)) we went over this la:st wee:k.
37 S: so(hh)?
38   ((S plays for 7 seconds.))
39 T: okay play bee flat ((picks up his trumpet)) want me to
        play it for you? finger along.
40   ((T plays on his trumpet for 5 seconds, S fingers the
        notes on her clarinet.))
41 T: you do that. let's play it together. (1.0) one, two.
42   ((T and S play together for 7 seconds.))
43 T: now this is what note.
44 S: bee, flat.
45 T: what note is this.
46 S: bee sharp.
47 T: it's not bee ↑sharp↓.
48   ((S looks at T.))
49   (3.0)
50 S: bee?
51 T: regular bee. so y'go y'go bee flat ei bee flat bee
        natural, and then you— you play see plus your gee sharp
        key, (1.0) with this.
52 S: yeah right here.

```
53  T:  yeah. do that for me.
54      ((S plays for 7 seconds. T watches S´s fingering.))
55  T:  now you got to (    ) one more time.
56      ((S plays for 3 seconds.))
57  S:  I´m goin´ too fast here ain´t it?
58      ((T marks time with hand beats while he sings.))
59  T:  ba: ba: ba: ba: [ba:
60                      [((S plays for 7 seconds.))]
61  T:                              there you go.] now here
        you have the melody, (1.5) so you have that part.
        (1.0) alright. ALRIGHT EH:M let´s see so we got that
        far. (    ) next week I wanna hear the rest of this.
        then I wanna hear little drummer boy (0.5) and with any
        lu:ck, (0.5) we´ll have uh the grinch right next to it.
        otherwise it´s gonna be a GRINCH ((T hands S the blue
        sheet.)) for Mr Anderson´s Christmas. is this your
        pencil?
62  S:  ye:s:
63  T:  good I brought one in so I don´t have to rip that off.
        (1.0) alright thank you. have a nice day.
64  S:  thank you for the lesson.
```

The first thing to notice before we begin to analyze this discursive practice is that we need to include in the transcription as much information as possible about the different ways in which participants do the practice. The words they use are important, of course, but just as important is how they speak and the analysis must take into account pauses, intonation, and the gaps and overlaps between participants' turns. The reason for paying so much attention to the details of the interaction is that, as we have seen in Units A2 and A3, the participation framework of the practice, the roles that participants play, and their interactional footing are all created by <u>how</u> participants speak as much as by <u>what</u> they say. In addition, although analysis may focus on both the how and what of the language used, many of the resources that participants bring to interaction are nonverbal, including how they gesture with their hands and bodies, their facial expressions, their clothing, and their positioning in space. As Erving Goffman (1979) originally explained, a communicative social event is much more than the production and reception of speech: The relative positioning of participants with respect to each other and to their environment, their gaze, and their facial expression must all be considered in an understanding of the social organization of participants. For this reason, data for an analysis of discursive practice will include a description of the nonverbal resources and, where possible, a visual representation of the interaction. The level of detail required in this analysis can be achieved only by repeated listening and viewing of the recording and, although this may at first seem tedious, it is only through such a process that certain phenomena of the practice appear to the ears, eyes, and mind of the transcriber. Thanks to several decades of work in conversation analysis, analysts have developed conventional ways for transcribing talk-in-interaction, and in Sections C3.2.1 and C3.2.2 you can find the conventions used here to transcribe and present talk-in-interaction. If you want to learn how to do CA transcription, a full and detailed description of the process of transcription can be found in Chapters 4 and 5 of Paul ten Have's 1999 book *Doing conversation analysis*.

A5.3.2 Boundaries

Let's start our analysis by distinguishing this practice from the surrounding talk. The clarinet lesson lasts about four-and-a-half minutes and is distinguished from surrounding action by opening and closing moves. Before the talk begins, the student is seated with her clarinet at the ready and a music score in front of her. The teacher begins the practice at turn 2 with a very loud 'alright' and then wonders aloud about the content of the lesson: 'what are you gonna do for me. let's see your blue sheet?' The blue sheet is a list of practice activities that the student is supposed to prepare for the lesson, and at the conclusion of the practice in turn 61, the teacher hands back to the student the blue sheet on which he has written the material that he wants her to prepare for the following week's lesson. He marks the conclusion of the practice in the same way that he marked the beginning: with very loud volume on 'alright' in turn 61. The exchange of the blue sheet and the teacher's very loud 'alright' separate this practice from other instances of the same practice with different students.

Immediately after the clarinet lesson, the teacher begins another lesson with a young boy, whose instrument is the trumpet. Because the discursive resources that participants employ in the clarinet lesson and in the trumpet lesson are very similar, we can say that both are instances of a middle-school music lesson practice. That is, the practice consists in the configuration of the resources that participants employ and not their use on any specific occasion. The reason why it is important to identify the boundaries of a practice is because in this way we can separate one instance of the practice from another adjacent instance of the same practice, or distinguish an instance of one practice from an instance of a different practice. People repeat instances from a range of practices in their daily lives, and in this way they create a sense of community with other people who participate in the practices with them.

A5.3.3 Participation framework

The first step in analyzing a discursive practice is to consider the evidence in the transcript of a participation framework. First we need to identify participants, recalling that participants may be physically present or not, they may be official or unofficial, and they may be ratified or unratified. Then we need to consider the identities that participants construct in the practice and their footing in the interaction, recognizing that within a practice participants may change footing, and a change of footing is a change in the alignment they take to themselves and to the others present. But in analyzing the participation framework, we must be aware of our own biases. Because we have ourselves participated in very similar practices to the ones we analyze, we approach the data with a lot of preconceived ideas: How would *we* act in the same situation? How would *the people we know* act? What is the meaning of the practice in *the community with which we* are familiar? But if we analyze the data as if we were familiar with the practice, then we will not find anything new in it, and for this reason we should try to take the perspective of an alien, or of the monkey that introduced this unit. The monkey's way is to pay very careful attention to the details of the practice and to try to understand what the actions of participants mean to them, not to us.

Let's begin, then, with the participants. In Figure A5.2 we can see those that are physically present: the student and the teacher. But both student and teacher spend much of their time gazing not at each other but at the music score in front of the student. Not only do they gaze at it and orient their upper bodies to it, but both teacher and student point to the score and use words to refer to it like 'this' in turn 9: 'how m'ny beats does this have' and 'that' in turn 18: 'you gotta hold that for all four beats.' Words that point to something are called indexicals and include 'here,' and 'there' as well as 'this' and 'that.' When physical participants orient to something which remains in the same place and which they index with language and gesture, that something is also considered to be a participant. In Goffman's categorization of production formats as animator, author, and principal, it also appears that the music score (or the composer) that the student and teacher invoke is an author; that is, both student and teacher are attempting to animate the score or, more simply put, they are attempting to play the music. There are thus three participants in this practice: the student, the teacher, and the score.

Task A5.3.3.1

➤ Participants are not only invoked by their physical presence but are indexed by gaze, gesture, and addressee status. Identify all the indexicals in the clarinet lesson. Who uses them? Do the indexicals invoke non-present participants? When different people use the same indexical at different times the indexical meaning changes and this can lead to misunderstanding. Are there any indexicals in the clarinet lesson that give rise to misunderstanding between teacher and student? If so, explain the sources of the misunderstanding. If not, why is there no misunderstanding?

A5.3.4 Speech acts

The identities of teacher and student are constructed by the interactional resources that they bring to the practice. These identities are complementary in the sense that in a discursive practice a teacher needs a student in order to play the role of a teacher, and a student needs a teacher in order to play the role of a student. These complementary identities are constructed in several ways, and one way is by the distribution of speech acts between participants. There are certain acts that only one participant performs and some of these are listed below.

```
let's do a lesson here (turn 2)      so you get louder then you
                                     get softer? (turn 26)
let's see your blue sheet            oh right— here? (turn 32)
(turn 2)
let's play I'll be home for          I'm goin' too fast here ain't
Christmas (turn 4)                   it? (turn 57)
go ahead and begin it (turn 7)
you gotta hold that for all
four beats (turn 18)
```

The acts on the left are all requests for action and are done by the teacher while the student follows each request with the action that the teacher required. The acts on the right are requests for confirmation of an interpretation – attempts by one participant to repair interactional trouble – and all those acts are performed by the student, and each repair initiation is completed by the teacher with 'yeah' (turns 27 and 33) or by the teacher marking time with his hand (turn 58). The student does not perform any requests for action and the teacher does not request any confirmation from the student, and the division of these actions helps to create complementary identities for the two participants.

Another sequence of acts which helps to create complementary identities for the two participants is illustrated in the exchange in turns 45–47.

```
45  T:  what note is this.
46  S:  bee sharp.
47  T:  it's not bee ↑sharp↓.
```

This sequence of three acts is known as an initiation-response-evaluation. In the first act, one participant elicits a response from another participant, often by means of a question as in this example. The second act is a response to the initiation and the third act is the means by which the first participant evaluates the response. The third act is also known as 'feedback' or 'follow-up,' but I prefer the term 'evaluation' here and I will use a shorthand name for the sequence: 'IRE.' Although this act sequence was first identified by John Sinclair and Malcolm Coulthard in 1975, anybody who has been in a classroom will recognize it as a common way that teachers and students construct classroom practice. The evaluation act in the third position in the sequence is possible only if the teacher knows the answer to the question posed in the first act and the IRE sequence is thus a way in which one participant (the teacher) constructs himself or herself as having greater knowledge than the other participant (the student). Because of the differential identities that the IRE sequence constructs, it is not found very often in discursive practices outside the classroom in which participants prefer to construct roles that are more equal.[4]

Task A5.3.4.1

➤ In what practices outside the classroom have you witnessed (or participated in) an IRE sequence? Who were the participants in the practice? What was the participation framework?

A5.3.5 Turn-taking

When we examine how participants employ turn-taking resources, we need to identify how participants select the next speaker and how participants know when to end one turn and when to begin the next. Recall that Sacks, Schegloff, and Jefferson (1974) identified three ways of allocating a turn to the next speaker selection:

1. If the current speaker selects next, then that party has the right and obligation to speak.
2. If no next speaker is selected, then self-selection may (but need not) occur. The first starter acquires rights to the turn.
3. If no next speaker is selected, then the current speaker may (but need not) continue.

In the clarinet lesson, the two participants allocate turns to the next speaker in two different ways. In most cases, the teacher allocates the next turn to the student, whose turn may consist of talk or, more often, by playing her clarinet. The teacher does that, as we have seen, by requests for action that are taken by the student as an opportunity to take a turn at talk or at the clarinet. He also allocates the next turn to the student by means of questions, as we saw when discussing the IRE sequence, but also by his final farewell in turn 63.

```
63  T:  . . . alright thank you. have a nice day.
64  S:  thank you for the lesson.
```

In contrast, the student allocates the next turn to the teacher much less frequently. And when she does so, she does not use requests for action but for information, as in turn 26.

```
26  S:  so you get louder then you get softer?
27  T:  yeah. get loud for four beats and then get soft for four
        beats.
```

Most of the time, though, the student does not select the next speaker at the completion of a turn. The teacher simply self-selects as in turns 4 and 7.

```
4  T:  alright let's play I'll be home for Christmas.
5  S:  I hate this one.
```

```
6    (2.0)
7 T: go ahead and begin it.
```

When the student has finished playing, the teacher also self-selects, often with an evaluation as in turn 9 'good' and turn 29 'okay that's good.'

The three ways of allocating a turn to the next speaker are interactional resources that both participants in the clarinet lesson can employ, yet in this practice the teacher predominantly employs current-speaker-selects-next-speaker, while the student employs next-speaker-self-selects. The different allocation of interactional resources by the participants also contributes to the participation framework; that is, the turn allocation helps to construct the identities that we have come to associate with teacher and student, roles in which participants' selection of acts and their allocation of turns are complementary.

A second aspect of turn-taking is how participants know when to end one turn and when to begin the next. As we saw in Section A3.2.2, places where transitions between speakers are possible are signaled by a combination of lexicogrammar, intonation, and pragmatics. The next speaker does not have to wait for the current speaker to finish their turn before beginning a new turn because transition-relevant places can be projected, and such projection may result in overlap between the current and subsequent turns. Overlaps are very common in casual conversation among friends, but in the clarinet lesson the only overlaps that occur are in turns 59–61, when the student begins to play on the last beat of the teacher's turn, and the teacher begins his turn before she has completed playing. (The beginning and end of overlap are transcribed by square brackets in the adjacent turns.)

```
59 T: ba: ba: ba: ba: [ba:
60                    [((S plays for 7 seconds.))]
61 T:                               there you go.] now here
      you have the melody,
```

No other transitions between speakers in this practice involve overlap; in fact almost all transitions occur immediately after the conclusion of a turn-constructional unit, or after a short silent pause. The pauses in turns 14, 32, and 49 represent time taken by the student before responding to questions or instructions from the teacher; in contrast, the teacher does not pause before taking a turn.

A5.3.6 Repair

When considering repair, we analyze the ways in which participants manage interactional trouble in a practice. We first identify the source of the trouble, then the participant who initiated the repair, and finally the participant who completes the repair. In the clarinet lesson, the source of trouble is often the student's playing and sometimes it is the words used by one of the participants. An example of a source of trouble in the student's playing is in turns 17–20. In turn 17, the student does not hold a note long enough and the repair is initiated by the teacher in line 18. After much discussion, the student eventually completes the repair in turn 28 by holding the note for fully eight beats. A second source of trouble, this time language trouble, is in the teacher's response in turn 18 'four beats,' which he repairs in turn 20 with 'eight beats.'

```
17      ((S and T play the measures together for 22 seconds, S
        on her clarinet, T on his trumpet.))
18  T:  you gotta hold that for all four beats.
19  S:  I ↓did.
20  T:  you didn´t. for all eight beats I´m sorry.
```

When identifying who participates in the repair, there are four possibilities: other-initiated self-repair, other-initiated other repair, self-initiated self-repair, and self-initiated other repair. In the first repair, the trouble source is in the student's playing in turn 17, an OTHER person (the teacher) initiates the repair in turn 18 and the student eventually completes the repair herSELF in turn 28. This repair is thus an *other-initiated self-repair*. In the second repair of language, the trouble source is the word 'four' in the teacher's turn. He identifies the trouble himSELF in line 18 and repairs it himSELF with the word 'eight,' making this a *self-initiated self-repair*.

The following repair sequence in turns 22–27 follows a different path.

```
22  T:  listen you gotta do something with this note. (1.0) so
        let´s say: like this. you put an eff here. so I want you
        to crescendo and de– decrescendo. so you get big and
        then you get little. so you go ((sings)) daaa°aaaa°. can
        you do that?
23      ((S nods.))
24  T:  do that over eight beats for me.
25      ((S puts clarinet to her lips but does not play.))
26  S:  so you get louder then you get softer?
27  T:  yeah. get loud for four beats and then get soft for four
        beats.
28      ((S plays for 6 seconds.))
29  T:  okay that´s good.
```

In the repair sequence in turns 22–27, the source of the trouble is the teacher's use of the technical terms 'crescendo' and 'decrescendo,' for which the student attempts a candidate repair with 'so you get louder then you get softer?' and the teacher concludes in the following turn: 'yeah. get loud for four beats and then get soft for four beats.' The trouble source was in the teacher's turn, the repair was initiated by the student, and it was concluded by the teacher: an example of an *other-initiated self-repair*.

Task A5.3.6.1

➤ In the clarinet lesson, find other instances of trouble sources and analyze how they are repaired. How are the trouble sources and repairs distributed between the teacher and the student?

In the preceding pages we have identified the boundaries of this instructional practice, and we have analyzed the selection and sequencing of acts, the turn-taking organization (including allocation of next turn and placement of turn transitions), the sources of interactional trouble, and the ways that participants repair the trouble. By means of a close analysis of the interactional resources that the participants employ and a consideration of which resources are employed by which participant, we may also understand the participation framework of this instructional practice. Although from the very beginning of our analysis, we have identified the participants as 'teacher,' 'student,' and 'music score,' if we take the monkey's perspective, we would have no idea what these words mean and we would not know what roles these participants play. On the other hand, by examining the interactional resources that they employ we are able to see how these participants construct identities for themselves in the practice. In other words, just because we label a participant as 'a teacher,' that does not mean that the participant plays the role of teacher in an automatic, deterministic sort of way. Instead, in every interaction, by employing interactional and linguistic resources participants attempt to create identities, and in many cases the other participants help them in the creation of these identities by attempting to create complementary roles for themselves: The identity of 'teacher' cannot be created without the willing construction by another participant of the complementary identity of 'student.' The complementary distribution of acts between speakers, the complementary ways in which participants allocate turns, and even participants' complementary strategies for repair combine to co-construct this practice and to co-construct the identities of the participants.

We have made our analysis of the participation framework of the clarinet lesson on the basis of the interactional resources that participants employ, but when we turn to analyze their linguistic resources (the features of pronunciation, vocabulary, and grammar that they employ, and the ways in which participants construct interpersonal, experiential, and textual meanings) we will see that these, too, are employed in a mutually dependent way by the two participants.

A5.3.7 Register

Register is a recognizable repertoire of linguistic features that participants in a discursive practice employ, one that becomes associated with that practice. Linguistic features of register include vocabulary, grammatical structures, and pronunciations, and one way to identify these features is to do a corpus analysis: to see if there are linguistic items that occur frequently and other items that never occur and to compare the corpus with other corpora to find out what distinguishes one practice from others. In the clarinet lesson we have less than five minutes of data, which are not enough to identify what linguistic features distinguish it from other practices, so we will have to proceed more intuitively in order to describe the register.

The first thing that appears from the transcript of the clarinet lesson is that the teacher talks more than the student: A word count reveals that he uses about eight times as many words as the student does. One reason for this difference in quantity of talk of course is that the student spends a total of one minute forty seconds out of the four-and-a-half-minute practice playing her clarinet. When we examine the vocabulary that they use, although this is a music lesson in which the student is learning to play the clarinet, neither participant uses the word 'music' nor the name of any musical instrument. Probably because this is a practice that both participants have done before, these items are taken for granted. On the other hand, some words do occur frequently and they serve to characterize the practice. The most frequent word is 'you,' occurring a total of 25 times in the conversation (used 22 times by the teacher and 4 times by the student); in contrast, 'I' occurs 12 times (used 8 times by the teacher and 4 times by the student). The second most frequent word is 'this' (used 12 times by the teacher and only once by the student) followed by 'that' (used 9 times by the teacher). Most of the time, 'this' and 'that' index parts of the music score as in turn 9.

```
9  T: good. how m´ny beats does this have. ((T points to a
       note on the score.))
```

From this simple snapshot, it is already possible to deduce that the interaction involves the teacher talking a lot about the student and what she is doing, and that the teacher often indexes parts of the music score. Participants also employ the technical vocabulary of music: 'beats,' 'measure,' 'sharp,' 'flat,' and 'natural,' for example, as well as the names of notes, B, C, F, G, and the numerals one through eight, which participants use to measure time.

Turning from vocabulary to grammatical structures, we noticed already that the teacher made a lot of requests for action and most of these are encoded by imperatives, sometimes second person imperative as in turn 39 and sometimes first person plural as in turn 41.

```
39  T: okay play bee flat ((picks up his trumpet)) want me to
        play it for you? finger along.
41  T: you do that. let´s play it together. (1.0) one, two.
```

Imperative structures are, however, absent from the talk of the student, who, instead, utilizes affirmative and negative statements and occasional interrogatives.

Task A5.3.7.1

➤ Count the imperative, affirmative, negative, and interrogative structures used by the teacher and student in the clarinet lesson. What differences do you find between the teacher's and the student's use of these grammatical structures?

Finally, one phonological aspect of register which appears in the transcript is the teacher's differential use of volume. Throughout the lesson, his talk is louder than the student's and he uses extra loudness (indicated in the transcript by words underscored or capitalized) to emphasize ten words throughout the lesson. The student uses this resource just once in line 5, when she says she *hates* 'I'll be home for Christmas.'

The register of this practice can be summarized as use by two participants of technical musical vocabulary, frequent use of first and second person pronouns, and reference to the third participant, the music score, by means of indexicals. As we noticed with the interactional resources, the teacher and student continue to co-construct their identities in the practice by their complementary use of linguistic resources. The teacher talks more, talks louder, and uses imperatives in contrast with the student, who co-constructs the practice by talking less and softer, and avoiding imperatives.

A5.3.8 Modes of meaning

In order to understand how participants use linguistic resources to create meanings in a practice, we perform a semiotic analysis using the tools of systemic functional grammar. In any practice, meaning is constructed in three different ways: the interpersonal, ideational, and textual metafunctions described in Section A3.1.3. The interpersonal metafunction of language helps participants to enact social relationships, the ideational metafunction allows participants to construe a model of experience, and the textual metafunction allows participants to create textuality by connecting utterances to their linguistic context.

The grammatical system that realizes interpersonal meaning is the system of mood, and, as we found in analyzing the register of the clarinet lesson, the teacher employs imperative mood throughout the practice in order to influence the behavior of the student. The subject employed by the teacher in most of the clauses in the practice is 'you' referring to the student or an indexical like 'this' referring to the music score as in turn 51.

```
51 T: regular bee. so y´go y´go bee flat ei bee flat bee
        natural, and then you– you play see plus your gee sharp
        key, (1.0) with this.
```

The student never uses 'you' to refer to the teacher, but instead uses 'I' to contrast her behavior with that requested by the teacher as in turns 18–20.

```
18  T:  you gotta hold that for all four beats.
19  S:  I ↓did.
20  T:  you didn´t.
```

In addition to influencing others, a primary function of language is to describe experience, represent, analyze, and explain our experiences of the world, including our experiences of our own thoughts and feelings. This way of using language is analyzed in systemic functional grammar as the ideational metafunction and this function is realized by processes in the verbal group. Consider, for example, the processes in turn 22.

```
22  T:  listen you gotta do something with this note. (1.0) so
        let´s say: like this. you put an eff here. so I want you
        to crescendo and de– decrescendo. so you get big and
        then you get little. so you go ((sings)) daaa°aaaa°. can
        you do that?
```

The processes in this turn involve putting in an F, crescendoing and decrescendoing, getting big, getting little, and going 'daaa°aaaa°'. All these are physical processes involved in playing the music, and they are realized by unmarked tense verbs referencing processes in the past, present, or future. Throughout the body of the practice, processes described by participants are unmarked for tense except in turn 36, when the teacher reminds the student of material that they had gone over last week. Utterances at the boundaries of the practice, however, do reference processes in time and allow participants to plan what will happen in this lesson and to connect this lesson with the lesson next week, as in turn 2 'what are you gonna do for me' and in turn 61 'next week I wanna hear the rest of this. then I wanna hear little drummer boy (0.5) and with any lu:ck, (0.5) we'll have uh the grinch right next to it.' In addition to construing external experiences, the ideational metafunction includes describing, representing, analyzing, and explaining internal experiences (feelings and thoughts), but in this practice the student is the only participant who does this with 'I hate this one' in turn 5 and 'I don't know' in turn 14.

Another type of process is relational process. Relational process clauses allow participants to express identity and classification, and the teacher employs relational processes in order to compare the student's playing with the music score. An example of this is in turns 45–51, in which the copula *be* is used by both participants to contest the interpretation by the student of a note in the music score.

```
45  T:  what note is this.
46  S:  bee sharp.
47  T:  it´s not bee ↑sharp↓.
48      ((S looks at T.))
49      (3.0)
50  S:  bee?
51  T:  regular bee.
```

The third and final part of a semiotic analysis of this practice involves understanding how utterances are connected to one another and how participants create textuality. As we saw in Section A3.1.3, this involves analyzing the thematic structure of clauses and the relationship between themes and rhemes, and we identified three modes of textuality: thematic repetition, thematic development, and multiple rhemes. The thematic structure of this practice appears to be a series of themes introduced in turn throughout the practice by the teacher, each of which is then developed as multiple rhemes. The first example of this is in turns 4–9, where the theme introduced by the teacher is the tune 'I'll be home for Christmas,' and this theme is reinvoked as a rheme by the student in turn 5 with 'I hate *this* one' and again by the teacher with 'go ahead and begin *it*' in turn 7 (the rhemes are italicized). A new theme introduced by the teacher in turn 9 is the number of beats to hold a certain note on the music score: '*how m'ny beats* does this have.' The theme is reinvoked as a rheme until turn 20, when the teacher invokes a new theme in turn 22: 'this note' on the music score to be played crescendo and decrescendo. This is then the rheme until turn 31, when the teacher begins a new theme: the student's trouble with a measure on the music score. This is the rheme until turn 41, when the teacher introduced a new theme in turn 43, which lasts until turn 55. The resource that the teacher uses to mark transition to a new theme is a discourse marker: a word or phrase used in a conversation to signal the speaker's intention to mark a boundary (Schiffrin, 1987). Transition to a new theme is marked by the teacher employing the discourse markers 'alright,' 'good,' or 'now.' An example of this is in turns 20–22 in which the teacher follows the discourse marker 'now' by marking a new theme 'this note' on the music score.

```
20 T: you didn´t. for all eight beats I´m sorry. ((sniffs))
      now.
21    ((T leans over and marks a note on S´s score.))
22 T: listen you gotta do something with this note. (1.0) so
      let´s say: like this. you put an eff here. so I want you
      to crescendo and de— decrescendo. so you get big and
      then you get little. so you go ((sings)) daaa°aaaa°. can
      you do that?
```

The complementary ways in which the participants create their identities in this interaction is thus also through textuality, with all new themes introduced by the teacher, and none by the student.

Our analysis of the clarinet lesson has used the framework for describing discursive practices presented in Section A5.1. We began by identifying the boundaries of the practice and using them to distinguish this practice from adjacent talk and discussing how the clarinet lesson is one instance of a more general practice that we might call 'middle-school music lesson.' We then identified three participants in the practice and, by careful analysis of the interactional, linguistic, and semiotic resources that they employed, we demonstrated how two participants co-constructed identities, which we are familiar with as 'teacher' and 'student' by the mutually dependent way in which they employed those resources.

SUMMARY AND LOOKING AHEAD

The methods that we have shown here in the analysis of the clarinet lesson can be used also in the analysis of four teaching–learning interactions that we have included in Unit C5. The theoretical foundations for a discursive practice approach to talk-in-interaction were laid down by Dell Hymes in his article on the ethnography of speaking that we have excerpted in Unit B5, and the view of learning as changing participation is discussed by Elinor Ochs in her presentation of language socialization, which we have also excerpted in Unit B5. If we accept this view of learning, though, the question remains of whether what we observe in discursive practice is all that there is in learning. If we are radical empiricists, then what goes on inside learners' heads is something that we cannot talk about, but to do so would ignore much research that has been done in psychology, applied linguistics, and performance assessment to understand learners' knowledge. The idea of 'competence' is one that has its roots in cognitive psychology and is related to the belief that individuals carry knowledge and skill with them from one practice to another. The question of how to resolve the practice approach to learning in interaction and the cognitive approach to competence is the issue that we will address in the next unit.

Unit A6
Interactional competence

PROLOGUE AND ROADMAP

What does it mean when we say that someone is 'competent' or that they have 'competence'? Discussion of these two terms has occupied linguists and applied linguists for many years and has led to fine distinctions between 'competence' and 'performance,' between 'linguistic competence' and 'communicative competence,' between 'communicative competence' and 'communicative language ability,' and between 'competence' and 'expertise.' In this unit, we will try to steer a course through these distinctions because of the important connection that must be made between the social and cultural constructions achieved through interaction in discursive practice and the cognition of individual actors. We conclude with a presentation of interactional competence, which will help to make that connection because it is based on the psychology of intersubjectivity and the sociology of interaction.

A6.1   THE MEANING OF 'COMPETENCE'

In Units A2 through A5 we analyzed a number of discursive practices and described the resources that participants in these practices have employed in order to construct actions, meanings, and identities. In the patient consultation in the pharmacy, the patient was successful in getting the pharmacist to fill his prescription and the pharmacist successfully gave the patient advice on how to take the medication. In his 'I have a dream' speech, Dr Martin Luther King Jr eloquently presented to his audience his vision of a future in the United States where racial discrimination would be a thing of the past. And in the clarinet lesson, the teacher was skilled in getting the student to hold certain notes for a full eight beats and to execute crescendo–decrescendo on another note. In these three examples, individual participants were successful in achieving their aims, and it is common to relate their success to some ability that these individuals possess. So we say that the pharmacist is a good communicator, Dr Martin Luther King is an eloquent speaker, and the clarinet teacher is a good teacher; in other words, we relate something that these people do in interaction with some ability that they possess that makes them different from other pharmacists, orators, or teachers. One word to describe what we believe that these individuals possess is *competence* and we say that they are *competent* to do certain things. The word competence, however, has taken on several different meaning in discussions of language and social interaction over the past hundred years, and before putting forward a definition of interactional competence, we'll review here some previous definitions of the word.

Let's start with ordinary language. Here are three examples of how people have used the word 'competent' to describe what they believed certain individuals possess.[1]

> 'Justice Ginsburg is a very *competent* justice, and it is a joy to have her on the court, but particularly for me it is a pleasure to have a second woman on the court.' – Justice Sandra Day O'Connor

> 'I was amazed at how organized the Palestinian election authority was, how *competent* they were in setting up their polling places and the poll workers they had.' – US Senator Joe Biden

> 'I consider myself to be an inept pianist, a bad singer, and a merely *competent* songwriter. What I do, in my opinion, is by no means extraordinary.' – Billy Joel

In the first quote, Justice Sandra Day O'Connor, who for many years was the only female justice on the United States Supreme Court, welcomes her first female colleague and says that she is 'a very competent justice.' In doing so, she relates something that Justice Ginsburg possesses (her knowledge, her scholarship, and her judgment) to her performance as a justice on the Supreme Court. In the second quote, US Senator Joe Biden, a senior member of the Senator Foreign Relations Committee, evaluates people in the Palestinian election authority as having performed their duties surprisingly well. These two statements of competence are made by people about other people, but in the third quote, singer and songwriter Billy Joel modestly evaluates his own abilities, saying in the practice of writing songs, he is 'merely competent' and implying that he is an incompetent singer and pianist.

In these examples, the meaning expressed by the word 'competent' is a relationship between an individual, the individual's ability, and that individual's performance. And the focus on the individual can be observed in a sense of the related word 'competence,' when it is used by linguists. This sense was introduced by Noam Chomsky in 1965, when he wrote, 'We thus make a fundamental distinction between *competence* (the speaker-hearer's knowledge of his language) and *performance* (the actual use of language in concrete situations)' (p. 4).

In Chomsky's sense, then, a person's linguistic competence must in principle be separated from that person's use of language. But Chomsky's use of the word differs from the meaning of the word in ordinary language, for if at some point Justice Ginzburg's performance on the Supreme Court began to be very incoherent, her colleagues might call her 'incompetent,' or if the Palestinian election authority failed to set up polling places and train poll workers, then perhaps Senator Biden might call them 'incompetent.' Not so with the language of Chomsky's speaker/hearer, however, because there is a conceptual disconnect between competence in

Chomsky's sense and the speaker/hearer's performance. One feature, however, that 'competence' in Chomsky's sense does share with ordinary usage is in the location of competence in a single person, and not in that person's ability in interaction with others. So it is Justice Ginsburg who is competent, independently of how the other members of the Supreme Court vote or react; it is Billy Joel who is a competent songwriter independently of how any singer performs his songs; and it is 'the speaker/hearer' whose competence Chomsky wishes to investigate independently of interlocutors.

Linguists before Chomsky did not always make such a neat conceptual distinction between competence (what someone knows) and performance (what someone does), although the idea of language as an abstraction from the hurly-burly of performance has been accepted by many. As we have seen in Section A3.1.2, in the *Course in general linguistics*, a summary of Ferdinand de Saussure's lectures delivered at the University of Geneva between 1907 and 1911, Saussure recognized that 'language' had two senses. Because he wrote and lectured in French, Saussure called one sense of language 'la langue' and the other he called 'la parole.' Here is Saussure's definition of these two terms (Saussure *et al.*, 1966, p. 14).

> [La langue] is a well-defined object in the heterogeneous mass of speech facts [la parole] . . . It is the social side of speech, outside the individual who can never create nor modify it by himself; it exists only by virtue of a sort of contract signed by the members of a community.

Although Saussure's langue and Chomsky's competence are similar in the sense that they are abstractions from performance or parole, Saussure's langue is distinguishable from Chomsky's competence in one important respect: It is the result of a social contract, formed through social action and not by individual cognition. For Chomsky, however, competence is located in an ideal realm far from the tumult of social interaction, a principle that he made clear. Linguistic theory, according to Chomsky should be concerned with 'an ideal speaker-listener, in a completely homogeneous speech-community, who knows its language perfectly' (Chomsky, 1965, p. 3).

A6.1.1 Communicative competence

Chomsky's idealization of the concept of competence was criticized by Dell Hymes, who made the case that, even in language, there exists great individual variation in competence. Hymes (1971/1972) held up Leonard Bloomfield's portraits of two members of the Menominee tribe of Native Americans in Wisconsin as examples of bilinguals who seemed to have very different competences in their languages. Bloomfield told first of Red-Cloud-Woman (1927, p. 437).

> Red-Cloud-Woman, in the sixties, speaks a beautiful and highly idiomatic Menominee. She knows only a few words of English, but speaks Ojibwa

and Potawatomi fluently, and, I believe, a little Winnebago. Linguistically, she would correspond to a highly educated European woman who spoke, say, French and Italian in addition to the very best type of cultivated, idiomatic English.

He then went on to contrast Red-Cloud-Woman with White-Thunder.

> White-Thunder, a man around forty, speaks less English than Menomini, and that is a strong indictment, for his Menomini is atrocious. His vocabulary is small; his inflections are often barbarous; he constructs sentences of a few threadbare models. He may be said to speak no language tolerably. His case is not uncommon among younger men, even when they speak but little English.

The knowledge that these two individuals possess of Menominee, their native language, seems to be very different, and just as Billy Joel admitted different competences as a singer, pianist, and songwriter, these two native speakers of Menomini can be said to have different competences in their mother tongue. As Hymes (1971/1972) suggested, 'Social life has affected not merely outward performance, but inner competence itself' (p. 274). Arguing further against the idealization of linguistic competence, Hymes put forward the notion that not only does an individual's competence refer to the individual's knowledge of the forms and structures of language, but competence extends to how the individual uses language in actual social situations. That is, Hymes rejected Chomsky's dichotomy between competence and performance and argued that using language in social situations required as much knowledge and skill as knowledge of language as an idealized system. In Hymes's famous words, 'There are rules of use without which the rules of grammar are useless' (p. 278). Hymes then went on to specify the knowledge that speakers must have of at least four ways in which language is used in social situations: what is possible to do with language, what is feasible, what is appropriate, and what is actually done. These are rather like constraints on language use in social situations.

First, in certain discursive practices, only certain actions and certain uses of language are formally *possible*. By 'formally possible,' Hymes meant the kind of social action that would elicit a response to language use like 'Oh you don't say it like that' or a response to a cultural behavior such as 'Oh, we don't do that sort of thing around here.' Language use that is not formally possible is ungrammatical, and social action which is not formally possible within a community is 'uncultural.' In the context of the clarinet lesson that we analyzed in Unit A5, for example, the teacher's use of a different language, Italian say, would not be formally possible, and if the student brought a trombone instead of a clarinet to the lesson, a clarinet lesson could not happen. Second, in the social use of language, only certain actions or uses of language are *feasible*. Hymes related what is feasible with cognitive limitations on speaking such as memory and perception, so, in the patient consultation in the pharmacy, memory limitations may not render it feasible to have the patient repeat word-for-word the instructions given to him by the pharmacist, and it may not be feasible for the pharmacist to diagnose the patient's condition because he may not have the medical expertise to do so. The third aspect of social use of language that Hymes revealed is whether (and to what degree) something is *appropriate* in the social situation in which it is used and evaluated. Appropriateness is a relationship that participants in a discursive practice perceive between a particular linguistic action and the context in which it is performed. So something may be appropriate or inappropriate for an individual participant, for a particular place, or for a particular practice. Language or social action that is believed to be inappropriate may result in overt sanctions by other participants. What would you do for example, if you heard a 3-year-old scream at his mother, 'I HATE you mommy!' when the mother refused to let him eat his Halloween candy before supper?

 Task A6.1.1.1

➤ What language actions by the patient or the pharmacist would you consider to be inappropriate in the patient consultation? How do you think the other participant would react? Why do you consider the actions inappropriate?

Finally, Hymes considered whether (and to what degree) something is actually done in communicative interaction. By this he meant that it is important to consider that, even when linguistic actions are considered by participants to be impossible, unfeasible, or inappropriate, those actions may actually be done, and so the concept of competence must include things which participants may believe are otherwise prohibited. To sum up, then, in Hymes's theory, a theory of competence must show the ways that what is possible, what is feasible, and what is appropriate are related to the production and interpretation of actually occurring linguistic and cultural actions. This ability and knowledge Hymes called *communicative competence*, which many people contrasted with Chomsky's theory, which came to be known as *linguistic competence*.

The ideas behind Hymes's communicative competence were the basis for views of *communicative competence* put forward by Michael Canale and Merrill Swain in 1980 and *communicative language ability* introduced by Lyle Bachman in 1990. These scholars tried to relate linguistic acts in social situations to an individual person's underlying knowledge, and their views became very influential in foreign-language teaching and language testing. In both these applied linguistic theories, competence is recognized as something that an individual person possesses to a greater or lesser extent than another person, and a person's competence is a complex construct composed of several component parts.

The communicative competence framework of Michael Canale and Merrill Swain (1980) includes three different components: grammatical competence, sociolinguistic competence and strategic competence. Sociolinguistic competence is further divided into two parts: appropriateness and discourse competence. A person's grammatical competence is very similar to the linguistic competence theorized by Chomsky and includes a person's knowledge not only of grammatical rules but also rules of phonology and knowledge of lexical items. What that means is that if a speaker uses words and grammar according to the accepted rules of the language and speaks with an accepted pronunciation, then that person's speech actions indicate that they have some degree of grammatical competence. Equally, if another person recognizes the difference between grammatical and ungrammatical sentences, between words used with their dictionary meanings and words used with idiosyncratic meanings, between an acceptable pronunciation and an unacceptable pronunciation, then the opinions of that person indicate their degree of grammatical competence.

The sense of appropriateness that is part of sociolinguistic competence in the Canale and Swain framework is the same sense that Hymes described when he said that participants in a discursive practice perceive a relationship between a particular linguistic action and the context in which it is performed. The example of sociolinguistic competence that Canale and Swain give is of a waiter in a restaurant commanding diners to order a particular dish. People in many cultures would regard the waiter's action as inappropriate and, if their judgments correspond to the norms of the community (and the waiter's actions do not), then we could infer that those people have a degree of sociolinguistic competence. The knowledge of rules of discourse that Canale and Swain include in sociolinguistic competence is very similar to the sequential context that we discussed in Unit A2; that is, the relationship of certain words and structures to words and structures that preceded them in a written text or in a conversation. If, for example, you (the reader) understand that this paragraph and the next are organized in the sequence that is laid out in the first two sentences of the preceding paragraph, then you recognize the author's discourse competence. Thank you!

The final component of Canale and Swain's model of communicative competence is strategic competence, and this component has less to do with knowledge than with performance. In Canale and Swain's words, strategic competence is 'made up of verbal and nonverbal communication strategies that may be called into action to compensate for breakdowns in communication due to performance variables or to insufficient competence' (p. 30). An example of a communication strategy might happen if a reader comes across a word that they do not know in a book they are reading ('solipsism,' say) and they turn to a dictionary to look up the meaning of the word. If they do not turn to the dictionary or use some other strategy such as asking someone else to explain the meaning of the word, then their lack of action would be evidence of a degree of strategic *in*competence. Strategic competence differs from the other components in Canale and Swain's framework because it is called into play only to compensate for difficulties in communication. Although speakers may well have difficulty in implementing grammatical or sociolinguistic competence, those components of knowledge exist independently of any trouble. The existence of strategic competence, in contrast, depends on there being some trouble in communication.

The framework of communicative competence that Canale and Swain built clearly goes beyond the theory of competence put forward by Chomsky. In fact, we could say that they simply added components of communicative competence to Chomsky's original formulation of grammatical competence. In fundamental respects, however, the framework of Canale and Swain is identical with Chomsky's thinking. The concepts at the foundation of both theories are, first of all, abstract. That is, competence, even communicative competence, is not simply a record of performance but rather an inference from performance to an individual's knowledge. Second, the competence of an adult native speaker of a language is considered to be fixed and stable, and it is to this unchanging standard that the communicative competence of learners of a language (either children or foreigner) is compared. And last, competence is considered to be a property of individuals, just as in the ordinary language examples with which this unit began. It is, in effect, an ability that individuals possess in unequal measures; and, in fact, differences in ability between individuals are in principle measurable. It is this sense of competence as an ability of individuals that was theorized in language testing by Lyle Bachman, and it is to Bachman's theory that we now turn.

A6.1.2 Communicative language ability

Language testing involves discriminating among people. In a test at the end of a course of study of a foreign language, for example, a test will tell the teacher and students who has learned what the teacher taught and who has not. It may also rank students on a scale from those who learned most to those who learned least. In a test of foreign language given to people who wish to become citizens of a country, the test will say this person knows or does not know enough of our language to function as a citizen of our country. Language tests have very practical outcomes for test takers, and the people who design tests have very practical concerns about relating what test takers can do on a test with what they know. For this reason, the theory of communicative language ability put forward by Bachman (1990, Bachman and Palmer, 1996) was a serious attempt to bridge the divide set up by Chomsky between competence and performance. As Bachman (1990, p. 84) wrote,

> *Communicative language ability* (CLA) can be described as consisting of both knowledge, or competence, and the capacity for implementing it, or executing that competence in appropriate, contextualized communicative language use.

Bachman accepted all of the components of grammatical and sociolinguistic knowledge that Canale and Swain had provided, but he integrated them all into the first component of his communicative language ability as 'language competence.' In the second component of communicative language ability Bachman included 'strategic competence' and the 'psychophysiological mechanisms' for psychological and physical production and interpretation of language. Although Bachman used the same term as Canale and Swain, his meaning of 'strategic competence' was very different. Bachman did not limit strategic competence to situations of communication difficulty but extended the term to apply to all social interaction. In all communicative contexts, according to Bachman, individual participants must decide what they are going to do, they must take stock of possible constraints on their action, and they must decide how they are going to employ the resources at their disposal. Strategic competence, in other words, involves an individual participant in *setting goals* for interaction, *assessing* what resources they have and what resources other participants have, and *planning* to use those resources. These processes do not necessarily happen in this or in any sequence, and actual implementation of communicative resources is left to an individual's psychophysiological mechanisms. Because the processes included in Bachman's strategic competence all involve higher order thinking – that is, they involve a person's active control over their own processes of language production and comprehension – they can be called metacognitive strategies. That does not mean necessarily that these individuals are conscious of these processes, although they may be.

Task A6.1.2.1

➤ In William Shakespeare's play *The tragedy of Hamlet Prince of Denmark*, the title character talks aloud to himself about some future action. In Hamlet's famous soliloquy, identify evidence of his metacognitive strategies: What goals does he set? What resources does he think he has? What resources does Hamlet believe others to have? How does he plan to use those resources?

> To be, or not to be: that is the question:
> Whether 'tis nobler in the mind to suffer
> The slings and arrows of outrageous fortune,
> Or to take arms against a sea of troubles,
> And by opposing end them? To die: to sleep;   5
> No more; and by a sleep to say we end
> The heart-ache and the thousand natural shocks
> That flesh is heir to, 'tis a consummation
> Devoutly to be wish'd. To die, to sleep;
> To sleep: perchance to dream: ay, there's the rub;   10
> For in that sleep of death what dreams may come
> When we have shuffled off this mortal coil,
> Must give us pause: there's the respect
> That makes calamity of so long life;
> For who would bear the whips and scorns of time,   15
> The oppressor's wrong, the proud man's contumely,
> The pangs of despised love, the law's delay,
> The insolence of office and the spurns
> That patient merit of the unworthy takes,
> When he himself might his quietus make   20
> With a bare bodkin? who would fardels bear,

To grunt and sweat under a weary life,
But that the dread of something after death,
The undiscover'd country from whose bourn
No traveller returns, puzzles the will   25
And makes us rather bear those ills we have
Than fly to others that we know not of?
Thus conscience does make cowards of us all;
And thus the native hue of resolution
Is sicklied o'er with the pale cast of thought,   30
And enterprises of great pith and moment
With this regard their currents turn awry,
And lose the name of action. – Soft you now!
The fair Ophelia! Nymph, in thy orisons
Be all my sins remember'd.   35

Bachman's communicative language ability differs from Canale and Swain's communicative competence because Bachman recognized that individuals utilize metacognitive strategies in implementing their linguistic competence, and one important strategy involves ascertaining the abilities and knowledge of their interlocutors. Bachman is thus one of a group of scholars since Saussure who discuss the possibility that competence involves more than an individual secluded from social interaction. Saussure wrote about a social contract, and Bachman wrote about assessing where one's interlocutors are at, a point that was made forcefully by Claire Kramsch (1986, p. 367).

> Whether it is face-to-face interaction between two or several speakers, or the interaction between a reader and a written text, successful interaction presupposes not only a shared knowledge of the world, the reference to a common external context of communication, but also the construction of a shared internal context or 'sphere of intersubjectivity' that is built through the collaborative efforts of the interactional partners.

Kramsch called the basis of successful interaction 'interactional competence.' It is Kramsch's theory that forms the basis for contemporary understandings of the competence that is created by all participants in social interaction, and this is the topic to which we now turn.

A6.2 INTERACTIONAL COMPETENCE

In the discussion of competence in the Section A6.1, we have identified several fundamental differences between scholars who have theorized the concept. One difference is between those who take 'competence' to refer only to the grammatical, morphological, lexical, and phonological systems of language and those who expand the concept of competence to include pragmatic systems of language use such as speech acts and knowledge of the relation between language forms and the social contexts in which they are used. This is the difference between formal linguists and sociolinguists. A second difference is between those who use 'competence' as a methodological tool to distinguish an abstract concept that pertains to a language (or in general to all languages) and not to a person, and those who maintain that competence has more to do with an individual person's ability, an ability which may differ from one person to the next. That is a difference between people who want to relate competence to language and those who want to relate it to people. The third and final difference is between those who recognize competence as an ability belonging to one individual who employs the ability in all social contexts and those who recognize that social contexts involve at least two participants and, for this reason, an individual's competence varies according to what the other participants do. This last is the difference between individual competence and interactional competence. Because in this book we focus on the use of language in social inter-action, the meaning of competence that we will use here is that of sociolinguists and interactional competence. As we will use it here, interactional competence is a relationship between the participants' employment of linguistic and interactional resources and the contexts in which they are employed; the resources that interactional competence highlights are those of identity, language, and interaction that we have described in Units A4 and A5. Interactional competence, however, is not the ability of an individual to employ those resources in any and every social interaction; rather, interactional competence is how those resources are employed mutually and reciprocally by all participants in a particular discursive practice. This means that interactional competence is not the knowledge or the possession of an individual person, but it is co-constructed by all participants in a discursive practice, and interactional competence varies with the practice and with the participants.

A6.2.1 Interactional competence and intersubjectivity

A few examples will illustrate the concept of interactional competence more clearly. Let's take a simple conversational interaction as a first example.[2] Ms Allen and Mr Bunch are two teachers at an American school. They are acquaintances and the following conversation happens as they are walking toward each other along a school corridor. They see each other for the first time today.

```
Ms Allen:  How are you?
Mr Bunch:  Fine.
Ms Allen:  That's good.
```

In starting to talk, Ms Allen shows an understanding that a previous turn was finished or that no previous turn had occurred, and, when Mr Bunch replies, he recognizes that Ms Allen's turn is complete, something that she must also recognize. If not, there would be overlap between Ms Allen's and Mr Bunch's turns. Mr Bunch's reply also shows that he understands that Ms Allen has asked a question and he expects that she will hear his next turn as an answer. Mr Bunch also shows that he understands Ms Allen's question to be a wh-question, one which requires an answer that gives more information than a simple 'Yes' or 'No.' If Mr Bunch replies with 'Yes,' it's likely that in the next turn Ms Allen might seek some repair. In Ms Allen's rejoinder, 'That's good,' she expresses an understanding that Mr Bunch's turn is complete and that he had indeed provided an answer to the question that she posed, which was interpreted by Mr Bunch as a response to Ms Allen's question. Why didn't Mr Bunch take the opportunity to provide an extended report of his medical, emotional, and economic conditions? Mr Bunch could have provided a longer and more substantial response but, if he had done so to his colleague in the school corridor, he would be attempting to construct a different discursive practice such as a visit to a doctor's office or to a therapist. That would have been an answer to Ms Allen's question, but it would have shown a misunderstanding of her intentions – a pragmatic failure that occurs often in communication across cultures.

The two teachers are well acquainted with each other's intentions, however, and Mr Bunch shows Ms Allen that he has interpreted her question as a formulaic greeting. In fact, Ms Allen's rejoinder is interpreted by both Ms Allen and Mr Bunch to effect closure of the practice of greeting as they walk past each other.

In this simple interaction between two participants, both individuals are demonstrating that they have a common understanding of the process of turn-taking in conversation and that they are interpreting the discursive practice as an exchange of greetings. The timing of each participant's turn shows their mutual understanding of three aspects of turn-taking: selection of next speaker, identification of turn-constructional units (TCUs), and projection of transition relevance places (TRPs). The practice is co-constructed by both participants and in their skillful co-construction they are displaying interactional competence. Interactional competence arises from the interaction and is based on knowledge of procedure and practice that is shared by participants. This shared knowledge has been called by philosophers, sociologists, and psychologists *intersubjectivity*, and it is the basis for interactional competence. This example is one that clearly involves two people taking turns at talk and it is easy to see how intersubjectivity is the basis of their actions, but let us consider a second example, in which apparently only a single participant is involved. Do intersubjectivity and interactional competence still apply?

The ancient Greek historian Plutarch remarked about listening to lectures, 'The mind is not a vessel to be filled, but a fire to be kindled,' but many of us have sat through lectures in which no intellectual fires were kindled. A boring lecture is a practice in which a lecturer talks at great length without relating what they are saying to the interests of the members of the audience. Here are some things that Christopher Thomas (1994) suggested to do during a boring lecture. (He assumes that you are not the lecturer.)

> There are many games one can play in a lecture. Games like 'I Spy,' 'Charades,' 'Basketball,' or 'Boxing' are usually quite noisy, and can distract the toffee-nosed note-scribbling scum-bag party-poopers who do not wish

to play or who are in no need of an increase in brain activity. A less obtrusive and altogether quieter form is required. Observation showed that most students attending lectures will have at least one sheet of paper and a pen. The application of the one on the other is, usually, quite quiet, which then indicated to me that using them was the best course of action.

This led me to compile a list of games which can be played with a pen and paper, between two people (or more in some cases): Noughts and Crosses (a.k.a. Tic-Tac-Toe), Alphabetic Variation of Noughts and Crosses, Connect Four, Squares/Boxes, Tetris, Oxo, Lecture Bingo, Bok.

Although the lecturer is a single speaker in this practice, it is nonetheless possible to identify intersubjectivity and interactional competence. Apparently, the lecturer is giving his lecture as if they were alone in the room, in effect constructing a very long turn at talk. This very long turn is, however, co-constructed by the students, who are choosing to play games quietly, which means that they are not attempting to take a turn-at-talk in interaction with the lecturer. They also stay in the same room as the lecturer; although they could leave, they do not do so, and a lecture hall in a school with a lecturer talking and bunch of students is a discursive practice called a lecture. The practice of a lecture – boring or not – is one in which all participants co-construct a very long turn-at-talk by one participant and, by their co-presence in the room with the lecturer, co-construct a participation framework that demonstrates shared knowledge of procedure and practice by all participants. The students demonstrate interactional competence by not taking turns while the lecturer takes his long turn and they demonstrate intersubjectivity by sharing with the lecturer an understanding of the discursive practice of a lecture.

In the first example of a greeting, both participants talked; in the lecture, the students didn't talk while the lecturer took a long turn. In the third example of intersubjectivity and interactional competence, no participant needs to talk. This is the case of pointing. When one person points to a distant object and another person follows with their gaze in the direction indicated by the gesture of pointing, although neither person speaks there is a very clear evidence of intersubjectivity. Figure A6.1 illustrates this.

Figure A6.1 shows a mother and her son. Something in the distance has caught the mother's attention and she is pointing to it. Her son gazes in the direction that she is pointing. The reciprocal behavior of the mother's pointing and her son's gaze following in the direction pointed is a very good example of intersubjectivity. The physical hand gesture of pointing is a nonverbal sign and is a cardinal example of the indexicality that we introduced in Section A5.3.3. We introduced the idea of indexicality to illustrate the semiotic theory of Charles Peirce. According to Peirce, the actor creates a sign that in the actor's mind is a relationship between a physical or linguistic action and an object, while the observer creates a sign in the observer's mind which is a relationship between the physical or linguistic action and an object. The two signs are not identical: the actor's sign is representamen and the observer's

Figure A6.1 Mother pointing and son looking. Source: iStockphoto. File Number 3822925

sign is interpretant – the sense that an observer makes of a sign made by an actor. In the act of pointing that we see in Figure A6.1, the mother is creating an indexical sign that is the relationship between a distant object and her own position. In order for her son to interpret his mother's sign, he has to take his mother's point of view: that is, he has to imagine that he is in the same physical position as his mother and direct his gaze in the direction of his mother's gesture. This taking of another's point of view is intersubjectivity.

Psychologists who have studied pointing by mothers and infants have found that 9-month-old infants are able to follow their mother's point when the object pointed at is in the infant's visual field. Those who have studied other evidence of inter-subjectivity in infants have found that it develops even earlier: two to three months of age. Intersubjectivity between infants and their mothers goes beyond simple responses to pointing and includes mutual attention to objects, shared rhythm, facial expressions, and emotion. These examples of shared mental control by infants and their mothers were first noticed by University of Edinburgh researcher Colwyn Trevarthen, who described intersubjectivity as follows (1977, p. 241).

> a correct description of this behavior, to capture its full complexity, must be in terms of mutual intentionality and sharing of mental state. Either partner may initiate a 'display' or 'act of expression' and both act to sustain a sharing and exchange of initiatives. Both partners express complex purposive impulses in a form that is infectious for the other.

Although pointers often accompany the gesture of pointing with expressions like 'Lookit,' language is not necessarily involved. Whether language is involved or not, pointing demonstrates intersubjectivity in which the observer interprets the pointing gesture as an intentional creation of a sign and then interprets the sign from the point of view of the pointer. This is what Trevarthen means by sharing of mental state, by one participant's 'infecting' the other. Interactional competence is displayed by both participants by their co-construction of pointing and following the point.

These three examples of competence show a relationship between language forms, gestures, and the social contexts in which they are used. Interactional competence, however, is not the ability of a single individual such as Mr Bunch, the imaginary lecturer, or the mother pointing to employ those resources in any and every social interaction; interactional competence is how those resources are employed mutually and reciprocally by all participants (both Mr Bunch and Ms Allen; the lecturer and the students; the mother and her son) in a particular practice. This means that interactional competence is not the knowledge or the possession of an individual person but it is co-constructed by all participants in a discursive practice, and, in order to describe interactional competence, it is necessary to carefully analyze the participation framework of the practice.

Task A6.2.1.1

➤ In this interaction reported by Deborah Tannen (2004), analyze the participation framework in order to discover how (or whether) participants construct intersubjectivity. What evidence exists of their interactional competence?

A couple who live together are having an argument. The man suddenly turns to their pet dog and says in a high pitched, baby-talk register, 'Mommy's so mean tonight. You better sit over here and protect me.' This makes the woman laugh – especially because she is a petite 5 ft, 2 in.; her boyfriend is 6ft, 4 in. and weighs 285 lb.; and the dog is a 10-lb Chihuahua mix.

SUMMARY AND LOOKING AHEAD

In this unit we have provided a number of views on 'competence,' most of which have been developed by applied linguists in trying to assess how well a learner knows a foreign language. We follow these threads in an activity in Unit C6 when we present two data segments from oral interactions between native and nonnative speakers of English as a way of comparing the competence in the practice of assessment with competence in ordinary conversation.

Interactional competence builds on the theories that preceded it, but it is a very different notion to communicative competence and communicative language ability. Interactional competence involves knowledge of the relation between language forms and the social contexts in which they are used. Interactional competence recognizes an individual's competence varies according to what the other participants do; that is, interactional competence is distributed across participants and varies in different interactional practices. And the most fundamental difference between interactional and communicative competence is that interactional competence is not what a person *knows*, it is what a person *does* together with others. Because of this, interactional competence presupposes intersubjectivity, something that infants at a very early age develop through interaction with the caregivers. In Unit C6, we examine cases where intersubjectivity is not acquired by children and where we cannot see development of interactional competence.

In this unit we have placed much emphasis on the importance of interaction in understanding competence, and in Units A7 and A8 we will present further evidence of the importance of interaction in the construction of identity and in the formation of community.

Unit A7
Talk and identity

PROLOGUE AND ROADMAP

The Orkneys are a group of islands lying off the northern tip of Scotland where the North Sea and the Atlantic Ocean meet. In the sea around the Orkneys, seals are very common – their heads bobbing above the waves, watching inquisitively with uncannily human eyes. Seals, or the selkie-folk as they are known in the Orkneys, have become an important part of Orcadian folklore, and there are many stories about selkies transforming into people. In many such stories an Orcadian girl falls in love with a stranger, whom she later discovers is in fact a selkie. One of Orkney's best-known and most haunting ballads, *The Great Selkie o' Suleskerry*, is in the form of a dialogue between a mother and a selkie, who had fathered her child when he had taken the shape of a man. The shapeshifter explains:

> I am a man upon the land;
> I am a selkie on the sea,
> and when I'm far frae ev'ry strand,
> my dwelling is in Sule Skerry.

It is perhaps remarkable that the man who walks on land and fathered the child is the same as the selkie who swims in the sea. Clearly something has changed but something has remained the same, and this same-but-not-the-same is the paradox at the heart of identity. *Webster's third new international dictionary* alludes to this paradox in defining 'identity' as 'sameness of essential or generic character in different examples or instances.' What we will investigate in this unit is how uses of language in different situations and activities with different interlocutors construct different facets of an identity that we perceive as essentially the same. Our first task will be to define the word 'identity' by presenting four characteristics of persons that are different aspects of person-hood. We will then go on to examine how identity is constructed in social interaction, first by looking at the work that individuals do in order to claim an identity for ourselves, and then by investigating the work that other people do to construct our identity by what they say to us and what they tell people about us. Finally, there is almost always a moment of negotiation between ourselves and others when we work to resolve disagreements about our identity.

We focus on identity as constructed by the self and others, but we should not delude ourselves into believing that free individual agency is all that there is in identity construction. Some identities are imposed by powerful others and are coercively applied through political, economic, and educational systems, and those identities are very hard to disavow. Even so, all identities, even those coercively applied, involve lifestyles, and those people who have greater freedom in defining themselves sometimes choose to 'cross' into the identities of others in order to perform a new and unexpected lifestyle.

A7.1 DEFINING 'IDENTITY'

The sense that we have of our identity and the identity of other people is a sense that seems at times confusing. If we have known a person for a long time and interacted with that person in many different contexts, we feel that although this is always the same person, sometimes they seem to be different, and we remark on this by saying things like 'You were acting weird last night,' 'You're so nice to her, why can't you be nicer to me?' or 'When I first knew him, he had a very strong accent, but now I hardly notice it.' Identity, then, has two contradictory meanings. In one sense it is the stable sense of self-hood attached to a physical body which, although it changes over time, is somehow the same; in a second sense, it refers to what we *do* in a particular context, and of course we do different things in different contexts. The first sense of identity helps us to distinguish one person from another, even two people with the same name. My telephone directory has two listings for 'Jennifer Hamilton,' but I don't expect that this is the same person with two different telephone numbers. Although this sense of identity helps us to distinguish among individuals, individuality may be more important in some cultures than in others. In some cultures, individuals value their unique identity by wearing different clothes, by speaking differently, and by competing in order to distinguish themselves from others. In other cultures, it is more valued *not* to distinguish yourself from others, to wear the same clothes, to talk in similar ways, and to work as part of a team.

Task A7.1.1

➤ When we meet people for the first time, we often try to make sense of our experience by putting them into categories, and these categories help us to distinguish them from other people. Figure A7.1 shows some pictures of people you probably don't know. Write down your description of the people in these pictures. What categories do you use to describe them? Then compare your descriptions with those made by someone else.

When we identify people in this way, we tend to put them in categories. For example, you probably described the people in Figure A7.1 in terms of the categories of gender, race or ethnicity, age, and profession. You may also have mentioned categories like religion, physical ability, nation of origin, sexual orientation, and so on. These are the kind of categories that you find on census forms, and these are aspects of a person that Karen Tracy (2002) called *master identities*, which she

Figure A7.1 Who are these people? Source: Downloaded from iStockphoto, File
Numbers: 2192770, 2857064, 3169937, and 2903632

defined as 'those aspects of personhood that are relatively stable and unchanging'
(p. 18). Because they are stable, many people may think they know what these
categories represent, but often those representations are contested. For example,
Queen Elizabeth I attempted to disabuse the French ambassador of his understanding of her gender when she said, 'Though the sex to which I belong is considered weak . . . you will nevertheless find me a rock that bends to no wind.'

Master identities are indexed by Pierre Bourdieu's notion of *habitus*. Habitus refers
to socially acquired predispositions, tendencies, propensities, or inclinations, which
are revealed in many ways, including ways of talking. In Unit A2, we gave an example
of habitus as a person's accent, and it is accent that contributes much to the master
identity of individuals by allowing us to categorize a person's national origin or
ethnic identity.

Task A7.1.2

➤ Listen to recordings of three people reading the 'Please call Stella' passage below.
The recordings are archived on the web at *The speech accent archive* maintained
by Steven H. Weinberger at George Mason University. What master identities
do you assign to the speakers? Now make an audio-recording in which you read
the same passage, and then compare your recording with one made by another

person. What features of voice allow listeners to identify the speaker and distinguish one speaker from another?

➤ http://accent.gmu.edu/searchsaa.php?function=detail&speakerid=191
➤ http://accent.gmu.edu/searchsaa.php?function=detail&speakerid=260
➤ http://accent.gmu.edu/searchsaa.php?function=detail&speakerid=323

Please call Stella. Ask her to bring these things with her from the store: six spoons of fresh snow peas, five thick slabs of blue cheese, and maybe a snack for her brother Bob. We also need a small plastic snake and a big toy frog for the kids. She can scoop these things into three red bags, and we will go meet her Wednesday at the train station.

The features of master identity such as gender, ethnicity, age, and nationality are stable, but there are other stable aspects of identity that are more often contested. These aspects are exemplified in descriptions of characters in literature taken from SparkNotes Online Study Guides.[1]

> Old, fat, lazy, selfish, dishonest, corrupt, thieving, manipulative, boastful, and lecherous, Falstaff is, despite his many negative qualities, perhaps the most popular of all of Shakespeare's comic characters.

> Hamlet is melancholy, bitter, and cynical, full of hatred for his uncle's scheming and disgust for his mother's sexuality. A reflective and thoughtful young man who has studied at the University of Wittenberg, Hamlet is often indecisive and hesitant, but at other times prone to rash and impulsive acts.

> Kitty is sensitive and perhaps a bit overprotected, shocked by some of the crude realities of life, as we see in her horrified response to Levin's private diaries. But despite her indifference to intellectual matters, Kitty displays great courage and compassion in the face of death when caring for Levin's dying brother Nikolai.

> Hester is passionate but also strong – she endures years of shame and scorn. She equals both her husband and her lover in her intelligence and thoughtfulness. Her alienation puts her in the position to make acute observations about her community, particularly about its treatment of women.

The features of identity that are described in these four quotes, Tracy (2002) called *personal identities,* by which she meant the kinds of identities that are attributed to people on the basis of their attitudes and behavior toward some issue and also those aspects of people that index the way they talk and usually conduct themselves. Hamlet's 'disgust for his mother's sexuality' and Hester's 'acute observations about . . . treatment of women' are examples of personal identities based on the character's behavior toward some issue. Falstaff's personal identity is characterized as 'selfish, dishonest, corrupt, thieving, manipulative, boastful, and lecherous' on the basis of the way that he normally talks and his routine behavior. In contrast to master identities, personal identities involve other people creating an identity for someone on the basis of how they perceive that person to talk and behave. This creation of an identity for someone else has been termed *altercasting* by social psychologists such as McCall and Simmons (1978). Personal identities are, of course, not only altercast by others but claimed by ourselves, and often these two constructions of identity may be in conflict. If, like Falstaff, you are altercast as selfish, dishonest, corrupt, and so on, you would likely contest this identity, just as Kitty may have rejected being altercast as overprotected and shocked by some of the crude realities of life.

We mentioned earlier that the uniqueness of individuals may be important in some cultures, and it is aspects of personal identity that contribute most saliently to distinctions between individuals. Master identities, on the other hand, are social categories that construct an individual as belonging to a group, whose members all share the same master identity. If people talk frequently about aspects of personal identity, their talk may indicate that they attend to and value individual differences.

While master and personal identities are considered to be fairly stable, there are other aspects of identity that are more dynamic and situated in specific inter-actions. Karen Tracy refers to these as *interactional identity* and *relational identity*. Interactional identities are specific roles that people take on in interaction with specific other people. For instance, Joey is my next-door neighbor, he is my friend Dan's oldest child, he works for Gumby's Pizza, he is friends with my daughter Jenni, and he shares an apartment with some buddies from high school. His identities in interaction with other people are: next-door neighbor in interaction with me, son in interaction with his father, employee in interaction with his boss at work, and roommate in interaction with the people he lives with. The way that Joey talks in these different interactional identities is likely to differ: What he talks about (his register), his modes of meaning, his choice and sequencing of speech acts, the way that turn-taking is organized, and the trajectories of repair are all likely to create participation frameworks that differ from one interactional identity to another.

The role that a person plays in interaction with another person, as neighbor, son, roommate, and so on does not *determine* the kind of interaction that occurs. Joey is not an automaton and he can decide the kind of role that he wishes to play in each interaction, although those interactional roles are likely to be related to his interactional identity. The agency that an individual exerts in creating an identity in a particular conversations is an effort to create what Tracy calls a *relational identity*, which she defines as 'the kind of relationship that a person enacts with a particular conversational partner in a specific situation' and she remarks that 'relational identities are negotiated from moment to moment and are highly variable' (p. 19).

In previous units we have studied several examples of people who attempt to create relational identities with specific conversational partners. In Unit C2, we met Philip, the young man from the North End of Boston who told us how he creates a certain relational identity when he's in a club 'talkin' to a babe,' which is a very different relational identity from the one that he creates when he is talking to a guy. Even with the same conversational partner, relational identities can change over the course of a conversation, as we saw in the story in Unit A4 told by a middle-class Boston woman who drove down South with her boyfriend to meet his family. By the time they reached their destination, the woman's relational identity with her boyfriend had changed dramatically, and she decided that she 'was not gonna have little Southern babies who talked like that,' and she got on a plane home. These two examples reveal that people use strategies to create relational identities in conversations, like Philip's Italian accent when chatting up women and his bravado when confronting men, but these strategies are not always successful because identities are co-constructed by conversational partners. An example of failure to construct a relational identity is the conversation between the Black graduate student and the family in the low-income inner-city neighborhood that we studied in Task A2.1.4.2. In that conversation, the husband tried to altercast the student as a 'brother,' but the student rejected the relational identity, a strategy that he later regretted when he reported that his interview with the wife was 'stiff and quite unsatisfactory.'

We have identified at least four ways in which identities can be conceptualized: as master identities, as personal identities, as interactional identities, and as relational identities. Identity is thus a complicated notion. We have seen that some identities are stable, while others are dynamic and change with the context of interaction; and some identities result from individuals belonging to a social group while others are personal, and we like to feel that they are unique to a particular personality. We have observed that individuals do interactional work to create some aspects of their own identity, but that their conversational partners also do interactional work to altercast the identity of the individuals with whom they interact. Identity is co-constructed in this way, just as Jacoby and Ochs (1995) described. In the following sections, we will discuss ways in which individuals construct their own identities, how others altercast identities, and how identities are co-constructed through talk. The relationships among the four different aspects of identity that we have presented are summarized by Tracy in Figure A7.2.

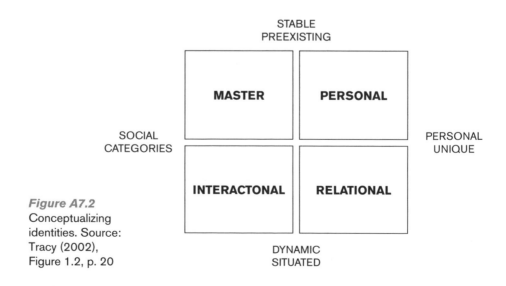

Figure A7.2
Conceptualizing identities. Source: Tracy (2002), Figure 1.2, p. 20

A7.2 HOW DO INDIVIDUALS CONSTRUCT THEIR OWN IDENTITY?

In this section, we will discuss interactional work that individuals do in order to construct their own identity, and the emphasis will be on identities actively produced – whether through deliberate, strategic manipulation, or through out-of-awareness practices. Consider, first, some aspects of master identities such as age, gender, ethnicity, and national origin. In many developed societies, individuals are categorized according to different stages in the life cycle. Shakespeare wrote a soliloquy for a melancholy Jaques in *As you like it* in which Jaques categorized 'The Seven Ages of Man' (he didn't include women) as Infant, Schoolboy, Lover, Soldier, Justice, Pantaloon (a foolish old man), and Second Childhood. In contemporary societies, at least five ages seem to be culturally distinguishable by the ways in which individuals use language: infancy, childhood, the teenage years, adulthood, and old age. Task A7.2.1 shows an example of how two individuals use language to create their age identity.

Task A7.2.1

➤ Here is an imaginary instant-message interaction between two individuals.[2] What age category do they belong in? How do they create that master identity?

Juliet:	romeo u there
Romeo:	yo wassup
Juliet:	nothin, u?
Romeo:	school sucked 2day
Juliet:	heard wylander got mad at u
Romeo:	what a jerk I usedd purple ink on the sci test, he g5ot pissed he looks like jiminy cricket
Juliet:	lol
Romeo:	going to nicks party
Juliet:	cant im grounded

A lot of research in the past fifty years has focused on gender differences in language. One of the best known researchers is Deborah Tannen, who described differences that she observed between men's and women's talk-in-interaction. In her videotaped lecture, *He said, she said*, Tannen showed that females and males orient their bodies to each other differently in same-sex conversations: Females face each other and prefer a direct gaze and keep looking at each other the whole time that they are talking to each other, while males sit either at angles or with their bodies parallel and rarely gaze directly at each other. She also mentioned a number of different conversational styles that help to create a gendered identity, including a male preference for directness and a female preference for indirectness, a male preference for public talk contrasting with a female preference for talk in private, and preference by males for ritual opposition in interaction which contrasts with avoidance of opposition by females. Tannen's descriptions of gender differences in talk-in-interaction should not be taken to reinforce stereotypes about the ways that men and women talk, but ignoring them risks one kind of conversational style being labeled as 'wrong' or 'bad.' Although gender is considered an aspect of master identity, there is no one-to-one correspondence between gender and a particular conversational style. Many other factors influence conversational styles including regional background, social class, ethnicity, age, sexual orientation, profession, and individual personality.

As we have seen in the previous discussion of accent as an index of regional origin and social class, a master identity implies that a person belongs to a certain social group. When membership in a social group is well defined, the linguistic and interactional indices of membership may be highly restricted or even unique. This is the case of language varieties such as *Polari*, a form of argot[3] used in the gay subculture in Britain during periods when homosexual activity was illegal. This language variety was used to disguise forbidden activity while at the same time acting as a badge of membership in the gay community. Polari (sometimes called *Palare*) used English grammar and common English vocabulary, but was identified by use of certain words that were unique, as can be seen in this excerpt from Peter Burton's *Parallel lives*.

> As feely ommes . . . we would zhoosh our riah, powder our eeks, climb into our bona new drag, don our batts and troll off to some bona bijou bar. In the bar we would stand around with our sisters, vada the bona cartes on the butch omme ajax who, if we fluttered our ogle riahs at him sweetly, might just troll over to offer a light for the unlit vogue clenched between our teeth.[4]

The above examples of teenage talk, gendered interaction, and gay men's argot are linguistic and interactional resources that individuals can employ in order to create an identity for themselves. It is important to note, however, that they are *resources* and not constraints on individuals. Teenagers don't always speak like Romeo and Juliet even when they I.M., women and men are not obliged to interact in the gendered ways that Tannen described, and you couldn't always identify gay men in the London of the 1950s by their use of Polari. As Bourdieu observed when theorizing habitus, these ways of speaking index certain identities, but when they reach the level of an individual's conscious awareness, they become resources that the individual can use at will, resources that permit an individual agent to attempt to construct a desired identity in specific interactions. And these attempts do not always succeed because other people with whom we interact co-construct our identity.

A7.3 HOW DO OTHERS ALTERCAST AN INDIVIDUAL'S IDENTITY?

Work on identity construction is never a one-person job. The way that we think about the people we know is not necessarily the same as the way that they would wish us to regard them, but we don't keep our attitudes to ourselves. We help to create the identity of others by altercasting: by employing naming practices, honorifics, by telling stories about them, and finally (when they no longer have an opportunity to contest our construction of their identity), by writing their obituary.

One of the most common ways of using language to altercast identity is by naming a person. We all have the names that we were given by our parents that appear on our birth certificates, but these are often not the names by which other people name us. People with whom we have different relationships address us differently and, as our relationships with them change, they may change the way that they address us.

Task A7.3.1

> Imagine calling these people up on the phone and identifying yourself. How do you name yourself . . . to your parents? To your friends? To your teachers? To your best friend? To your partner? How do these people name you? Has your name changed over time?

In many languages, naming practices reflect the relationship between individuals in a systematic way. Here are two examples. As a young university professor who had just received his Ph.D., I was used to being called by my first name by most people I knew at university, so I was quite taken aback when my students started calling me 'Professor,' which is the standard term of address for anybody who teaches at an American university. I soon realized, however, that my students were altercasting me in a different identity to the one I was used to. Another example of the power of naming began in the early days of the women's liberation movement. In the 1960s and 1970s, people who wanted to change the subordinate status of women in society abandoned addressing women as 'Miss' or 'Mrs' So-and-so and began using 'Ms' instead because Ms (pronounced MIZ) is a form of address for females that does not reflect their marital status. In 1971, the term became the title of the first national feminist monthly, *Ms* magazine, which gained extensive media attention and introduced this form of address to a wider public. Although Ms is intended as a neutral counterpart to Mr, it creates identities for those women who are addressed in this way. As Margot Mifflin (2000) wrote,

> Ms. is larded with sticky, often contradictory associations. For example, a 1998 survey of 10,000 Midwesterners revealed that women who use Ms. were perceived as better educated and more independent, outspoken and self-confident than those who use Mrs. or Miss. But they were also presumed by the respondents to be less attractive and less likely to be effective wives and mothers.

A very common way in many languages of indicating relative status of the speaker and addressee is to use different address pronouns. In French, you must choose whether to address someone as *tu* or as *vous*, in Spanish as *tu* or *usted*, in German as *du* or *Sie*, and your choice of pronoun influences the form of the verb that follows. Linguists refer to the binary distinction in these languages by the initials of the pronouns of address in French as *T/V*. In Japanese, Korean, and many other languages, the resources for indexing status differences are more extensive than the binary T/V distinction; these resources, called 'honorifics,' influence not only how you address someone but also how you refer to them in the third person. The use of T/V forms and honorifics constructs social scales of respect, familiarity, and relative status that are important and specific to a culture which learners of the language often find it difficult to accept. For instance, the way that age creates high status in many cultures and the ways that status is indexed by use of T/V pronouns or honorifics is a linguistic and cultural lesson that many foreigners find it hard to learn.

When another person uses names to insult us, a children's saying gives the victim some encouragement: 'Sticks and stones may break my bones but words will never hurt me.' The cheerful view of naming practices in this saying, however, underestimates the power that others have to altercast us by their use of language. At the opposite end of the spectrum to the children's rhyme is a ballad written by Shel Silverstein and sung by Johnny Cash about 'A Boy Named Sue.' Here is the first verse. You can easily find the remaining verses on the internet.

> My daddy left home when I was three
> And he didn't leave much to Ma and me
> Just this old guitar and an empty bottle of booze.
> Now, I don't blame him cause he run and hid
> But the meanest thing that he ever did
> Was before he left, he went and named me 'Sue.'

Being called Sue caused many problems for the song's male protagonist. As Johnny Cash tells it, 'Some gal would giggle and I'd get red / And some guy'd laugh and I'd bust his head, / I tell ya, life ain't easy for a boy named "Sue."' The altercasting of a gender identity different from the gender that a child is born into is not just the stuff of country-and-western ballads. In his research on disruptive behavior in a large Florida school district in the school years 1996 through 2000, David Figlio (2005) found that boys with names like Taylor, Dominique, or Alexis that are more commonly given to girls were more prone to be suspended from high school for disruptive behavior than boys with conventionally 'masculine' names.

The examples that we have examined so far show that individuals can resist altercast identities and that the creation of personal identity is a process of co-construction. This happens in all cases except one – when the self has no opportunity to negotiate identity because it is dead. An obituary is the final moment of altercasting, and is in fact a way in which others will remember us. Here are two obituaries that create memorable identities retold by Marilyn Johnson in her book *The dead beat: Lost souls, lucky stiffs, and the perverse pleasure of obituaries* (2006). The first identifies a priest's feisty old housekeeper by recalling aspects of the interactional identity that she took on in relation to other people.

Clementine Werfel blessed priests at St. Joseph Catholic Church in Strongville with heavenly desserts, memorable meals and seemingly miraculous coffee. The retired parish housekeeper, who died Aug. 2 at 96, routinely walked around the dining table in the rectory, offering coffee to each priest.

'Would father like regular or decaf?' the 4-foot-something Werfel asked them one by one.

Regardless of the priests' individual preferences, she filled all their cups with coffee from the same pot. The coffee drinkers silently accepted what they got, as though Werfel really could turn regular coffee into decaffeinated, much the way that the biblical Jesus turned water into wine.

(p. 116)

The second obituary constructs an identity for a woman by a series of adjectives describing aspects of her personal identity and characteristic practices.

Described fondly as demanding, disorganized, unpunctual and 'dotty,' [Anat Rosenberg] was at the same time intelligent, loving, witty, supportive and loyal and obsessed with buying bags, jewellery and shoes.

(pp. 180–181)

A7.4 HOW IS IDENTITY CO-CONSTRUCTED?

In the previous two sections, we have discussed how individuals attempt to create an identity for themselves by using language that constructs their membership in social categories such as gender, class or rank, profession, ethnicity, and sexual preference. Because identity construction is never the work of a single individual, we have also shown how others altercast identities by the use of naming practices, address forms, and honorifics; and we have shown how narratives construct relational and interactional identities in obituaries. In this section, we ask: How do the self's construction and the altercasting of others interact? Or, as Jacoby and Ochs (1995) termed it, how is identity co-constructed? To answer that question we will discuss co-construction of identity that results from speech accommodation, resistance to ascribed identity, and identity confusion.

Speech accommodation is selection of linguistic forms and interactional patterns by a speaker in response to the identity or identities that the speaker perceives in the audience. An individual speaker creates identity with the linguistic and interactional forms that are employed, and each speaker commands a range of variation – of pronunciations, of accents, of vocabulary, and of other linguistic and interactional resources. The way that these resources are assembled in a particular context is known as language style or speech style. Allan Bell (1984) showed that the selection by a speaker of one style over another is influenced by the speaker's perception of the identities of hearers, a theory that became known as 'Audience Design.' Bell's theory builds on the framework of participation that we introduced in Unit A3. In theorizing participation framework, Goffman (1979, 1981) described the production roles of participants and he also identified several roles for hearers, all of whom may affect a speaker. The main hearer role is the *addressee*, who is the person known, ratified, and directly addressed by the speaker, but other persons in the audience may also influence the speech style of the speaker. These include those who are known and ratified but not directly addressed or *auditors*, as well as those *overhearers* that the speaker knows to be there but has not ratified, and *eavesdroppers* – persons whose presence is unknown. Bell pictures audience members positioned in concentric circles, as in Figure A7.3, with those participants closer to the speaker in the center having a potentially greater influence on the speaker's style.

Bell based his theory of Audience Design on his observations of how broadcasters in the mass media change their speech styles according to the audience they believed they were addressing. Although audience design explains how identities are co-constructed, the motivation for style shifting is the speaker's *perception* of the audience, and that perception may in fact be mistaken. Such misperception can lead to an identity construction for the speaker which diverges from the audience rather than converging. Hypercorrection is often the result of such misperception. Hypercorrection from below refers to the alteration of a speaker's normal usage based on the speaker's mistaken interpretation of a prestige linguistic form, while hypercorrection from above results from a speaker's mistaken avoidance of stigmatized speech. Hypercorrection from below was found by Labov (1966, 1972b) in his work on the social stratification of English in New York City. In his study of the relationship between social class and the pronunciation of English by speakers in New York City, Labov observed that New Yorkers' pronunciation of 'r' after a vowel in words like 'thirty,' 'fourth,' and 'car' varied systematically with the speaker's social class. The higher the socio-economic class

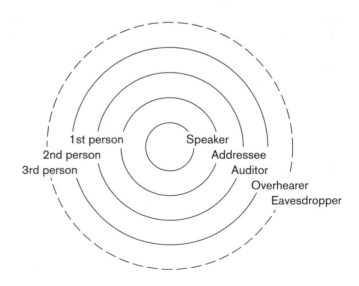

Figure A7.3
Roles and identities
in interaction.
Source: Bell (1984),
Figure 5, p. 159

of the speaker the more frequent r-coloring of the vowel occurred, while speakers from the lower socioeconomic classes produced far less r-coloration. The correlation between socioeconomic class and pronunciation of 'r' was consistent in all cases except for lower-middle-class speakers, who recognized the prestige value of 'r' but hypercorrected by producing r-colored vowels *more often* than upper-middle-class speakers. The parallel process of hypercorrection from below is observed in British English when speakers avoid the stigmatized dropping of an initial 'h' from words like 'have' and 'Harry' but hypercorrect by pronouncing an 'h' in words where it does not exist in the prestige form, for example pronouncing an initial 'h' in [ə´hɑːmfʊl] for 'an armful.'

As Jacoby and Ochs (1995) point out, 'co-construction does not necessarily entail affiliative or supportive interactions' (p. 171). In fact, identity claimed by one participant may be rejected by another, and an identity that is altercast may be resisted. An amusing example of how participants negotiate their way out of this kind of identity confusion is the following scene from the long-running TV comedy series *Seinfeld*. The scene is Monk's Diner, where Elaine is sitting at a table waiting for her boyfriend, Darryl. The Black waitress hands Elaine a menu.[5]

1   *Elaine, to the black waitress*: Long day?
2   *Waitress*: Yeah, I just worked a triple shift.
3   *Elaine*: I hear ya, Sister.
4   *Waitress*: Sister?
5   *Elaine, as Darryl comes into Monk's*: Yeah. It's okay. My boyfriend's black.
6   Here he is. See?
7   *Darryl*: Hi, Elaine.
8   *Elaine*: Hey.
9   *Waitress*: He's black?
10 *Elaine*: Yeah.
11 *Darryl*: I'm black?
12 *Elaine*: Aren't you?
13 *Waitress, leaving*: I'll give you a couple minutes to decide.
14 *Darryl*: What are you talking about?
15 *Elaine*: You're black. You said we were an interracial couple.
16 *Darryl*: We are. Because you're Hispanic.
17 *Elaine*: I am?
18 *Darryl*: Aren't you?
19 *Elaine*: No. Why would you think that?
20 *Darryl*: Your name's Benes, your hair, and you kept taking me to those
21 Spanish restaurants.
22 *Elaine*: That's because I thought you were black.
23 *Darryl*: Why would you take me to a Spanish restaurant because I'm black?
24 *Elaine*: I don't think we should be talking about this.
25 *Darryl*: So, what are you?
26 *Elaine*: I'm white.
27 *Darryl*: So, we're just a couple of white people?

28 *Elaine:* I guess.
29 *Darryl:* Oh.
30 *Elaine:* Yeah. So do you want to go to The Gap?
31 *Darryl, leaving with Elaine:* Sure.

Elaine first attempts ethnic solidarity with the Black waitress by calling her 'sister' in line 3, an attempt that the waitress queries in the following line. Elaine then justifies her attempt by telling the waitress that her boyfriend Darryl is black. As Darryl arrives, in line 11 he challenges Elaine's altercasting him as Black. The waitress retreats, while Darryl and Elaine try to work out their ethnic identities. Darryl says that he altercast Elaine as Hispanic because of her name, her frizzy black hair, and because she kept taking him to Spanish restaurants, but in line 22 Elaine claims that her choice of restaurants was based on her belief that Darryl was Black, a reasoning that Darryl doesn't accept. After much confusion of their ethic identities, Darryl and Elaine finally realize in lines 27–29 that they are not an interracial couple and agree that they do in fact share an ethnic identity – White. The scene ends as they repair to a store that is well know for marketing preppy clothing to Whites.

A7.5 IDENTITY AND AGENCY

In the previous section, we have focused on an individual's freedom to manipulate a flexible system of identities but, as Paul Kroskrity (2000) points out, this fails to adequately take into account that some identities – notably race, caste, and gender – are imposed and coercively applied. There are indeed political and economic constraints on processes of identity-making. The terms 'race' and 'ethnicity' distinguish groups of people based on certain characteristics. The most widely used human racial categories are based on visible traits (especially skin color, facial features, and hair texture), as well as self-identification and beliefs about common ancestry. Perhaps because of the visibility of these traits, the master identity of race or ethnicity has a greater permanence than others. Related to race is caste, which is used to distinguish groups that are identified by traditional, hereditary systems of social restriction and social stratification, systems that are often enforced by law or common practice. Finally, gender is a social (not a biological) identity that has begun to lose its coercive force in contemporary Western societies after the feminist revolution of the 1960s. In many societies, however, gender remains a master category that is applied coercively to women, as this story told of a meeting held in Tehran in preparation for the UN-sponsored World Conference against Racism in 2001 illustrates (Sorabji, 2001, March 4).

In Iran, ladies are required to cover their heads with a scarf in public. Some women delegates inadvertently omitted to observe this injunction during the conference. The result was an angry public demonstration and a demand for the resignation of the Minister who organised the conference!

Organized social situations and political institutions, often referred to pejoratively as 'the system,' are responsible for imposing and coercively applying identities to groups with the aim of maintaining their subordinate status in society. Such power is not necessarily exercised by violent means but often through mystification of the individuals to whom power is applied and even of those individuals tasked with enforcing systemic power. An example of how this applies in education is provided by Nikhat Shameem (2007) in her description of social interaction in multilingual classrooms in Fiji.

In multilingual Fiji, the community language of Fijians of Indian ancestry is Fiji Hindi, a common language that evolved over the years from the dialects of Hindi spoken by indentured laborers brought to the Fiji islands by the British in the nineteenth century. Fijians of Indian ancestry constitute 38 percent of Fiji's population but there has always been a political and economic struggle between Indians and native Fijians to the extent that Fijian citizens of Indian descent are officially referred to simply as 'Indian.' Fiji Hindi today has diverged significantly from the varieties of Hindi and Urdu spoken on the Indian subcontinent, but the colonial government of Fiji established a different variety of Hindi, known as Shudh (or 'pure') Hindi as the standard because this variety enjoyed the status of official language in India. Although it was a variety that was already codified and was incorporated as a language of education in Fiji, it was not the variety used by the majority of Indians. The diglossic situation of Fiji Hindi and Shudh Hindi is complicated by the colonial language, English, which is the official language. Shameem reports that after Fijian independence from Britain in 1990, the official language education policy has been to use Shudh Hindi for teaching Indo-Fijian children in the first three years of primary school before transitioning to English in the later years of schooling, although the community language is Fiji Hindi, which differs from the standard variety. Shameem's research shows that, in their responses to questionnaires, primary-school teachers reported much greater use of Shudh Hindi than was the case when she observed actual language use. She reports that 'while three [first grade] teachers had reported using English and three a combination of English and F[iji] H[indi] as language of instruction in their English lessons, observation showed that in fact six of the eight teachers were using only English while the other two used both' (p. 209). The divergence between reported and actual language use has two important implications when viewed from the perspective of identity coercively imposed by official policy on a subordinate group. First, although 'the system' may constrain language choice by these teachers to some degree, the constraint is much more effective on their consciousness; that is, what they believe about their own language choice. The system provides a ready-made mystification for these teachers of their own practice, a practice which actually diverges from their own beliefs about what they do. Second, the systematic encouragement of teachers' preference for the High variety of Hindi over the variety that the children know best appears to do little to maintain either variety as a community asset and, in fact, encourages maintenance of the colonial language – English. The Fijian situation thus appears parallel to many postcolonial situations, where the use of English is encouraged at the expense of the languages of indigenous peoples.

A7.6 CROSSING

In the preceding section, we have discussed how certain aspects of master identity are coercively applied and shown that individuals have very few options to elude the master identities of race, caste, and gender that are ascribed to them. The groups to which such identities are ascribed are those on the lower rungs of society whose lower social position is enforced by others higher up. Curiously perhaps, the master identities which some individuals cannot elude are precisely those which others choose to adopt, albeit for a relatively short span of time. Members of more prestigious social groups may adopt the identity of the subordinate groups for several reasons: They may do so in order to express their rejection of the systemic hierarchy or, in a time when lifestyles are commodified, because they find some aspects of the subordinate group's identity attractive. Such appropriation of the language, interaction, and other symbolic codes of the subordinate group is known as 'crossing' and has been researched extensively by Ben Rampton (1998, 1999, 2005).

Examples of crossing into a lower socioeconomic class are shown in Part 3 of the PBS video *People like us: Social class in America* (Alvarez *et al.*, 2001). The segment was shot in Baltimore, Maryland, once well known as a working-class city with friendly corner bars and waitresses who called everybody 'Hon' (short for 'Honey'). Now, with most of the big factories gone, middle-class families are moving into the old neighborhoods or dropping in from the suburbs for a visit. The newcomers are crossing into the old working-class identities in a spirit of fun, games, and nostalgia celebrated every year at 'The HonFest.' The HonFest is an annual event in Baltimore when middle-class women don beehive hairdos, cat-eye glasses, pink poodles, and feather boas to compete in a competition to see who has the most authentic working-class accent in public speaking performances of lines like 'Hi hon, how you doin?' 'Hon, you want coffee?' and 'Hey hon, you goin downey ocean?'

The HonFest is an opportunity for middle-class people to 'cross' into a different and lower social class, but there is a much wider phenomenon of crossing across racial and ethnic boundaries that has been documented by Cecilia Cutler (1999). Most people who have listened to Black rappers and hip hop music will recognize that Black youth language creates an aura of toughness and sexuality. In the chorus of the hit song *In da club* by Black rapper 50 Cent, for example, the message comes over loud and clear: 'You can find me in da club, bottle full of bub / Look mami i got the X, if you into takin drugs / Im into havin sex i aint into makin love / So come give me a hug if you into gettin rubbed.' Essentially, hip hop has become a prestige language for today's youth just as hip hop fashions and music have come to dominate adolescent buying habits. Linguistic crossing into the African American Vernacular English (AAVE) used in hip hop allows young people to experiment with alternative identities and has the potential for breaking down ethnic barriers by creating new forms of youth culture. The potential for this sort of development among the droves of White hip hop fans in suburbia exists even in the face of substantial opposition from other Whites and Blacks.

SUMMARY AND LOOKING AHEAD

Talk helps us to construct an identity for ourselves and to cast others in a certain identity. Identity has many facets, primarily those identified by Karen Tracy as master, personal, interactional, and relational identities, and different aspects of a person's identity can change while others aspects remain fixed over a long period of time. A person's talk – their accent, in-group vocabulary, tone of voice, and preferred topics of conversation – is one of the primary means by which other people construct an identity for a person, an identity that sometimes we welcome and sometimes we resist. Telling a story about a person's deeds and misdeeds, likes and dislikes, friends and foes is one of the most powerful ways in which identities are constructed, and if we don't like the identity constructed for us in the narrative, we can always tell a different story – unless, of course, the narrative is an obituary. The way that we project an identity for ourselves is partly strategic and partly, perhaps mostly, out of our control. If we strategically project an identity, then we design it for an audience, but there are some aspects of our identity that it is very difficult to escape such as race, gender, and age – although we may playfully cross into an identity that we prefer by copying some stereotypes of speech and clothing of the target group.

Much of the work we do to construct an identity for ourselves and for others is done to locate an individual within a social group. If those groups are ones with which we identify, we often refer to them as communities and one of the ways in which we identify communities is by the shared speech styles, appearances, beliefs, and discursive practices of their members. In the next unit will we investigate further how those identity characteristics help to create a community.

Unit A8
Community and communities

PROLOGUE AND ROADMAP

As we saw in Unit 7, talk helps us construct identity, and one aspect of identity is membership in a community of people with whom we feel we have something in common. In this unit, we will discuss various ways in which individuals identify themselves as members of communities. Sometimes we do that through a shared language but, more often, membership in a community is achieved and maintained through shared ways of doing things as well as ways of speaking. In the first section we will examine the notion of a *speech community*, which is one way in which linguists have come to grips with the idea of a community. In the second section we will present groups of people who definitely feel a sense of community but who don't necessarily speak the same language and don't always live in the same place. Because it is what they do and how they interact that defines these communities, these groups of people form *communities of practice*.

What make these groups of people into communities are shared ways of interpreting the world and especially shared ways of organizing how they talk. The organization of talk-in-interaction as a way of understanding how communities work and how members differentiate themselves from other communities is the focus of the third section of this unit, where we discuss *discourse communities*. In this section, we look closely at how the discourse of two very different groups of people helps create community: an Italian-American family at the dinner table and the children of the Warm Springs Indian tribe at home and at school.

A8.1 IDENTITY AND COMMUNITY

If you have a passport or an identity card, you will know that it says something about your identity and about the community to which you belong. It probably contains a rather unflattering photo of you together with a list of some of the master identities that we discussed in Unit A7: your name, your nationality, your gender, and your age (which can be calculated from your date of birth). This document provides some evidence of the community to which you belong, and in order to obtain a passport you have to go through quite a troublesome procedure to demonstrate that you are in fact a member of the community from which you need the document. In the United States, for example, you have to provide a document that shows that you were born in the US, or a report of your birth from a US consulate abroad. If you cannot claim citizenship by birth, you need to provide evidence that you have been naturalized (i.e., become a citizen later in life). There are several other requirements but these do not include your level of education, the languages that you speak at home, or the car that you drive. Place of birth is very important in establishing membership in one of the communities that we know best: a country, or to be more precise, a nation-state. The state is a political community and the nation is a cultural and/or ethnic community. The term 'nation-state' implies that they geographically coincide. A nation-state is one of the most familiar communities to which almost everybody belongs and, because the place of birth of citizens is so important, one of the primary defining characteristics of the national community is its geographical location.

Place is one of the easiest ways of defining a community. A nation-state such as Israel and a city such as Manchester are physical locations that lend their names to identify individuals (Israelis and Mancunians) who live or work there. There is a problem with using physical locations to define communities, however, because people who live and work in a place do not necessarily feel a sense of community with other people who live or work in the same place. As Barbara Rogoff (2003) points out, the 'box' approach to community does not describe anything about how people participate in their communities; it only specifies their location. The same criticism applies to other ways of defining community that are not so closely linked to a physical location. Other kinds of boxes that you might check off on a census form or some other document include your religion, the language or languages you speak, your current employment, your membership in clubs, the motorcycle that you ride, and so on. If we take these as criteria for communities, we would have to talk for instance about the community of Baptists, the community of speakers of Japanese, the community of pizza delivery drivers, the community of members of the Hong Kong Club, as well as H.O.G.s (members of the Harley Owners' Group). If people say 'I'm a Baptist,' 'I speak Japanese,' 'I deliver pizza,' 'I'm a member of the Hong Kong Club,' or 'I'm a H.O.G.,' then their statements go some way to defining what they do and the kind of people they interact with, but their statements do not imply that all members of these communities do the same thing or hold the same beliefs. The sense that a group of people form a community is often felt more strongly by outsiders than by members of the group themselves. If you don't speak Japanese, then it surely seems that people who do so are fluent in the language, but among those who do speak Japanese (especially those who learned it as a second language) there are many who would deny fluency in the language. Another example is the group of people who gather together to ride their Harley-Davidson motorbikes to a Hogfest. An outsider would see a bunch of middle-age people dressed in biking outfits riding down the road on bikes that emit a distinctive full-throated deep rumble. They certainly look and sound the same to outsiders, but whether the H.O.G.s feel themselves to be a community is an open question.

A8.2 SPEECH COMMUNITIES

Membership in a community is closely related to doing the same things that other members of the community do, and one of the most frequent indices of membership is languaging – using the same language or language variety in the same way as other people. The idea of a community has been very important in the history of linguistics because it has been invoked in order to explain the apparent fact that groups of people are able to communicate because they speak the same language. The *speech community* is a concept that helps to explain a connection between psychology and sociology: how what seems to be a psychological fact – an individual's knowledge of a linguistic system – connects with a social fact – interactive communication using that system among a large group of people. In this section, we will consider what speech community has meant for different linguists and how the various interpretations of the term shed light on the concept of community.

We presented in Unit A3 the semiotic theory of Ferdinand de Saussure, who invoked the idea of a contract signed by members of a community to accept the arbitrary nature of the relation between word and meaning and to do nothing by individual action to change that relationship. Underlying Saussure's theory is a community that is homogeneous in the sense that every member accepts the same arbitrary semiotic conventions. A very similar interpretation of speech community was accepted by Leonard Bloomfield, who wrote 'A group of people who use the same set of speech signals is a *speech community*' (1933, p. 29). Homogeneity is also fundamental to Noam Chomsky's approach to linguistic theory which, as we saw in Unit A6, is concerned with 'an ideal speaker-listener, in a completely homogeneous speech-community, who knows its language perfectly' (1965, p. 3). Claiming that a speech community is homogeneous has at least two advantages. Politically, it simplifies the connection between community and language and this corresponds to a view of the nation-state as a single entity: We can conveniently assume that all Koreans speak Korean, all Poles speak Polish, and all Saudis speak Arabic. For a linguist, the advantage of considering a speech community as homogeneous is that there is only one object to study and to describe, so when you look in a reference book such as *The world's major languages* (Comrie, 1987), there is only one chapter on Korean, one on Polish, and one on Arabic.

The disadvantage of considering a speech community as homogeneous is, of course, that it's simply not true. People within the frontiers of the same nation-state speak different varieties of a language, whose grammar, vocabulary, and pronunciation vary geographically and socially and, in many countries, different groups of people speak different languages. There is no necessary connection between citizenship and language, and I don't know of a passport application procedure in any country that requires the applicant to state the language that they speak as a condition of citizenship. The geographical boundaries of nation-states rarely coincide with the boundaries of languages. This was recognized some years ago by European linguists who used the German term *Sprachbund* ('language area') to describe parts of the world where a number of different languages are spoken that mutually influence one another, and where languages cross national boundaries. One example of a language area is the Balkans where five language families – Macedonian, Balkan Slavic, Albanian, Greek, Balkan Romance, and Romani – are spoken and where languages do not stop at national frontiers.

Geographical boundaries do not make languages and languages alone do not make communities. There is a sense, however, in which communities are defined not by what common language people speak but by how people use their languages. People who speak different languages may nonetheless share ways of using their languages such as in greetings, judgments about what topics are acceptable in polite conversation, or how to organize turn-taking. On the model of *Sprachbund*, this combination of shared knowledge of ways of speaking and values regarding speech across language boundaries has been called *Sprechbund* or 'speech area'.[1] It can be quite surprising when people who speak very different languages seem nonetheless able to communicate effectively because of their shared ways of speaking. Marycliena Morgan (2004, p. 6) provides the following example of the hip hop Sprechbund that unites the French hip hop artist MC Solaar and the American hip hop artist Guru.

> In the prelude to their music video 'Le Bien, Le Mal – The Good, The Bad,' MC Solaar telephones Guru to arrange a meeting . . . MC Solaar is in Paris and speaks to Guru in French using *verlan* – urban French vernacular that incorporates movement of syllables and deletion of consonants. Guru is in New York and uses hip hop terminology and African American English . . . as he talks to MC Solaar.

Paris

MC Solaar:	C'est longtemps depuis qu'on a vu Guru Gangstarr. *(It's been a long time since we've seen Guru from Gangstarr.)* C'est pas cool, s'il venait a Paris? *(It will be fly [very cool] if he comes to Paris.)*
Friend:	Ouais. *(Yeah)*
MC Solaar:	On essait de l'appler *(Let's give him a call.)*

New York

Guru (on phone):	Hello – who dis? Solaar! What up Man? Yeah! No I'm comin' man. I know I'm late Yo! Hold up for me al(r)ight. Baby! I'm on my way now al(r)ight! Peace!

At the end of the conversation, Guru leaves to meet MC Solaar and descends stairs into a New York subway. When he ascends the subway, he is in Paris!

The Sprechbund is a particularly useful concept for describing hip hop. Hip hop has linguistic characteristics like rapping, rhyme, and human beatboxing, but these features can be used in any language. Nonlinguistic features of hip hop also extend beyond language boundaries and include musical style, clothing, and association with minorities. Although hip hop transcends national boundaries, the idea of a hip hop community has been invoked by H. Samy Alim (2004), who reminds us of the traditional relationship between language and nation by referring to it as 'Hip Hop Nation Language.' There is of course no geographical entity called Hip Hop Nation, and Hip Hop Nation Language has been defined as 'a universoul-sonic force being adopted and adapted by youth around the planet, in countries as distant and diverse as Mexico, Cuba, France, Bulgaria, Ghana, Pakistan, Japan, Australia and many more' (Cran and McNeill, 2005).

Communities like hip hop do not have physical boundaries. Other communities without physical boundaries are the virtual communities provided by user groups, chat rooms, and many other virtual communities on the internet. Communication among members of these communities is not face to face but is mediated by computers. Apart from that, communication among members of online communities is very similar to communication face to face. As one of the most active and experienced critics of virtual communities Howard Rheingold (2000) writes,

> People in virtual communities use words on screens to exchange pleasantries and argue, engage in intellectual discourse, conduct commerce, exchange knowledge, share emotional support, make plans, brainstorm, gossip, feud, fall in love, find friends and lose them, play games, flirt, create a little high art and a lot of idle talk. People in virtual communities do just about everything people do in real life, but we leave our bodies behind. You can't kiss anybody and nobody can punch you in the nose, but a lot can happen within those boundaries. To the millions who have been drawn into it, the richness and vitality of computer-linked cultures is attractive, even addictive.
>
> (pp. xvii–xviii)

A8.3 COMMUNITIES OF PRACTICE

We have so far discussed communities in terms of what people do including, to a large extent, how members of a community use language and other semiotic systems in order to communicate with other members. We have also noted the differences between insiders and outsiders, and how a community seems much more unified when looked at from the outside than from the perspective of insiders. Because of the sense that, in communities, activities (or practices) are shared and interpreted in similar ways, Etienne Wenger (1998) extended the meaning of community beyond the geographical communities that we have discussed earlier to what he called a *community of practice*. As Wenger defined it, a residential neighborhood, though often called 'the community,' is not a community of practice. Instead, a community of practice is formed by three essential dimensions: (1) mutual engagement in activity with other members of the community, (2) an endeavor that is considered to be of relevance to all members of the community, and (3) a repertoire of language varieties, styles, and ways of making meaning that is shared by all members of the community. Wenger illustrated how these three dimensions are related in a community of practice in Figure A8.1.

Wenger was concerned only peripherally with how language helps to construct communities and focused his attention instead on how organizations function by means of these three dimensions. His theory is nonetheless relevant to the ways that language creates and maintains communities, and we will consider here his explanation of those three dimensions before we go on to see how communities of practice are created through talk-in-interaction in the family and in the classroom.

Mutual engagement of participants is a defining feature of communities of practice. Geographical proximity, participants' identities, and networks of communication do not define a community of practice. Instead, whatever it takes for members to mutually engage in an endeavor is a necessary component; this may include talking on the phone, exchanging email in a workplace community or it may involve sharing meals together and taking trips together as a family. Relationships among participants in a community of practice are necessary but these relationships are not necessarily affiliative. As Wenger puts it, 'Peace, happiness, and harmony are . . . not necessary properties of a community of practice . . . mutual relations among participants are complex mixtures of power and dependence, pleasure and pain, . . . fun and boredom, trust and suspicion, friendship and hatred' (p. 77).

The second defining characteristic of communities of practice Wenger calls the negotiation of a joint enterprise. Because the word 'enterprise' may be interpreted

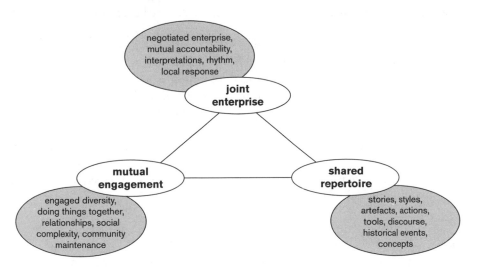

Figure A8.1 Dimensions of practice in a community of practice. Source: Wenger (1998), p. 73, Figure 2.1

as referring to a commercial organization and because communities of practice are found in all human activity, not just in business, I have preferred to use the term 'endeavor' in place of 'enterprise.' A joint endeavor, then, does not mean that everybody in a community of practice shares the same goals, or that they work on the same problems, or create similar solutions. What it does mean is that the goals, the problems, and the solutions are interrelated in some way. The ways in which they are interrelated are often influenced by the history, traditions, and culture of the community, which in turn are related to the history, traditions, and culture of the broader society in which the community exists. The way that participants work to achieve their goals is influenced but not determined by the historical and social context, so that each community in fact evolves local practices and local ways of achieving participants' goals. Wenger's final comment on the endeavor of a community of practice is that it is 'a resource of coordination, of sense-making, of mutual engagement; it is like rhythm to music' (p. 82).

Communities of practice come closest to a linguistic characterization in their third defining feature, which is a repertoire of language and nonlinguistic resources such as tools, gestures, stories, and genres that are shared by participants. Just as in the ways of working to achieve the goals of an endeavor, the resources that participants utilize in constructing a community of practice are influenced by the history, traditions, and culture of the community, which in turn are related to the history, traditions, and culture of the broader society in which the community exists.

Finally, a community of practice need not necessarily be recognized as such by participants; that is, although participants may be mutually engaged in a joint endeavor, they may not focus explicit attention on what they are doing, and insiders and outsiders may not name it and thus mentally convert a community of practice into something concrete or objective. In this sense of community, we have come a long way from the concrete sense of place with which we began this unit.

The two examples of communities that we have presented so far – hip hop and virtual communities – can be described from the perspective of Wenger's model of communities of practice. Let's first consider hip hop as a community of practice. The first dimension of practice is mutual engagement, which recognizes that hip hop artists interact with one another, just as we saw in the interaction between MC Solaar and Guru, and that members of online communities maintain complex networks of communication with one another. The joint endeavor of the Hip Hop Nation is the creation of rap music, which often incorporates the rhythms of other MCs. The third dimension is a shared repertoire, which is clearly seen in the shared rhythms and musical styles of hip hop artists.

An even clearer example is the virtual community developed through Facebook, the social networking website for college students. Anybody who registers and builds a profile on Facebook participates in the community, although the networks of communication with other participants are very varied and can include private messages, public messages, shared pictures, and shared music with other members who share a school, a region, a company, or an interest. The joint endeavor that members of Facebook pursue is – as the site defines itself – social networking: to meet people for a wide variety of purposes. Social networking is so popular that Facebook was named by Associated Press in 2006 as the second most 'in' thing among undergraduates, tied with beer and sex and losing only to the iPod. The repertoire that Facebook members share includes all aspects of computer-mediated communication such as web pages, blogs, emails, chat, and file sharing.

A8.4 DISCOURSE COMMUNITIES

Communities of practice are defined by the activities or practices of members and, for our purposes, the most relevant of those practices is the repertoire of language varieties and speech styles that participants in a community utilize. As we have presented it in Unit A5, a repertoire is a collection of resources that includes linguistic, interactional, and identity resources. Linguistic resources include the features of pronunciation, vocabulary, and grammar that frequently characterize practices and also the ways in which participants in practices construct inter-personal, experiential, and textual meanings. Interactional resources include the selection of speech acts in a practice and their sequential organization, how participants select the next speaker and how participants know when to end one turn and when to begin the next, the ways in which participants respond to interactional trouble in a given practice, and the opening and closing acts of a practice that serve to distinguish a given practice from adjacent talk. Together, linguistic and interactional resources form the participation framework of a practice, in which the footing or identities of participants are constructed in interaction.

For many years, research in sociolinguistics and discourse analysis has considered communities in terms of the linguistic and interactional resources that participants utilize in order to construct and maintain a community and how those resources are used to differentiate members of one community from others. Pioneering work in this area contrasted home and school communities with the aim of under-standing the poor performance of some groups of children in schools. The most extensive early work was Shirley Brice Heath's (1983) study of Black and White working-class children and their families in the Piedmont Carolinas, and Susan Urmston Philips's (1970) study of the participation structures at home and school on the Warm Springs Indian reservation in central Oregon. Many other studies followed of the mismatch between the ways that talk is organized in schools and the discursive practices of the family, the home, and the community beyond the school walls. This work came to be known as the study of *discourse communities*. The emphasis on ways of using language in discourse communities clearly differentiates this work from Wenger's theory of communities of practice in organizations. Because, in studying a discourse community, the analyst focuses on how participants use talk-in-interaction to create, maintain, and characterize a community it is also a different way of approaching the study of community from the work on speech communities that we discussed earlier in this unit. In the sections that follow, we will show examples of how a discourse approach helps us to understand how a family constructs community and how the identification of contrasting discourse organization in different communities explains problems for minority communities at school.

A8.4.1 Family

The first example of a discourse approach to community to consider is Frederick Erickson's (1992, 2004) analysis of a conversation over an evening meal at the Pastores, a lower-middle-class Italian-American family. Thirty-six turns from the very lively conversation are transcribed below and represent contributions from a total of eight participants, who, while talking, were passing food and eating.[2] Erickson points out that all of this activity was rhythmically oriented so that the gestures and passing movements matched the cadence of the conversation. Erickson situates the topic of the conversation within the family's socioeconomic situation in 1974 when he recorded the conversation.

The participants in the Pastore family dinner were the father, the mother, five children, and a guest. Mr Pastore worked as an industrial arts teacher at a neighboring high school. Mrs Pastore had been an elementary school teacher before her children were born but at the time of filming she was a full-time home maker and did not earn a salary. In birth order, their children were Joe Junior, Louie, Al, Anna, and Jimmy. Joe Junior was the oldest child, an eighth grader. His two brothers, Al and Louie, were in the late grades of elementary school. The two youngest children were Anna, in third grade, and Jimmy in first grade.[3] The family sat at dinner around a rectangular table at which they hosted Erickson's graduate assistant, Susan Florio, while Erickson filmed the dinner from a camera positioned behind the mother's chair. The seating arrangement is shown in Figure A8.2.

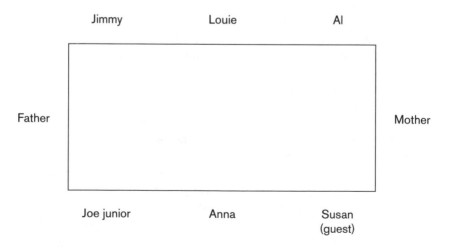

Figure A8.2 Seating positions at the Pastores' family dinner table. Source: Erickson (2004), p. 24

The topic of the slice of conversation transcribed below is the cost of living. All the children displayed their knowledge of the family budget situation and displayed similar ways of talking about it. The topic had been introduced earlier when referring to the cost of repairing Jimmy's bicycle and, just before the opening of the segment transcribed below, Mrs Pastore had mentioned that her husband's planned overnight stay at a workshop for teachers would cost $75. This amount impressed the youngest son, Jimmy, whose turn begins the transcript, and who expressed his feelings in a loud and astonished voice, 'Seventy five dollars!' Responding to his kid brother's surprise, the eldest son, Joe Junior, displayed that he was more realistic about the cost of things with an ironic rejoinder in turn 3. Joe Junior then continued to display his worldliness about money matters to the female guest in turn 6 by commenting that 'Seventy five dollars goes in a day.' The topic continued with a touch of sibling rivalry as Louie recalled to his sister Anna that the money paid for her bike and her wheels was much less – only two dollars. Anna repeated the cost of her bike to the female guest without the irony with which Louie had loaded his words, to which Susan replied in turn 12 with less irony than Joe Junior's initial comment, 'You're a big spender.'

The cost of living was a topic that Joe Junior used to pursue his display of worldliness with a question to his mother about shopping for food in turn 13. Erickson interprets his mother's reply, 'Ah well we won't talk about that . . OK?' as in fact a playful invitation to continue talking on the topic, which Joe Junior accepts. He displays to Susan that, although he is familiar with the family's expenses for food, taxes, and the mortgage, he doesn't have to pay them, and so he could buy a lot with $75. The father is evidently pleased that his son has learned about his family's financial outflows and he remarks 'he's learnin' huh?' to Susan in turn 17. This is evidently a clue for the other children to chime in with their own displays of knowledge of family expenses. Anna names the water bill, Al mentions the cost of the car and insurance, Louie the electric bill, and gas for the car. Then he and Joe Junior seem to vetriloquate their father when, in turns 24 and 27, they agree that Joe Junior doesn't have to support five kids. After their contribution, even little Jimmy displays in turn 28 that he knows that his brother doesn't have to pay for gas. Within the current topic of expenses, Louie now takes the opportunity in turn 30 to introduce a related matter dear to his heart: shoes and clothes. In fact, he claims that he needs some new moccasins (a type of traditional North American footwear fashionable in the early 1970s). His brother's request is ignored by Joe Junior, who simply summarizes the previous topic by saying in turn 33, 'So *I* could do a lot with *seventy . . seventy five dollars.*' Louie's new topic is, however, picked up by his kid brother who, in turn 36, echoes to his mother Louie's request, 'Mom *I* need some new moccasins.' Perhaps doubtful whether there is enough money to go around for two pairs, Louie effectively quashes Jimmy's request, saying 'You don't even know what moccasins *a::re.*'

A8.4.2 'They know all the lines'

```
 1          Jimmy:    (very loud) SEVENTY FIVE DOLLARS!!
 2          Louie:    He has to work . . .
 3          Joe Jr:   [WO::::w . . a-mazing . . . ] it is?
 4   Louie to Jimmy:  [he has to work three days
                               to get you a bike]
 5          Anna:     It cost even more than that to get his
                      bike, didn´e?
 6   Joe Jr to Guest: Seventy [five dollars goes in a day
 7    Louie to Anna:          [Your bike and wheels we got
                      for two dollars
 8  Guest to Joe Jr:  m hmhmhm hm (laughs)
 9          Anna:     I know
10          Joe Jr:   today it will
11   Anna to Guest:            my bike cost only two
                      dollars
12    Guest to Anna:  You´re a big spen[der
13  Joe Jr to Mother:                 [How ´bout last time
                      . . how ´bout last time you went /eh
                      foo:d shoppin´?
14          Mother:   Ah well we won´t talk about tha:t . .
                      OK?
15          Guest:    But you still could buy a lot with
                      seventy five dollars . .
                      you could buy a lot
16          Joe Jr:                      I could yeah . .
                      ´cause
                      I don´t have to pay taxes on a house
                      I don´t have to pay a mortgage
                      I don´t have to [pay all kinds/
17  Father to Guest:                 [he´s learnin´ huh?
18          Mother:                  [hehehe he
19          Anna:     a water bill
20          Joe Jr:   I don´t have to pay all kinds of stuff
                      like that
21          Al:       You don´t have to pay for a car
                      [´n´ the insurance
22          Louie:    e[lectric bill I don´t
                      I don´t have to keep two cars on the
                      road
23          Mother:   electric bill gas insur[ance
24          Louie:                          [you don´t
                      support [five kids
25          Guest:            [you´re right . . small change
                      that´s all it is
```

```
26          Mother:    food for [(
                                 )
27          Joe Jr:            [I don't support five kids
                       either
28          Jimmy:     You don't have to pay for gas
29             Al:     Not yet anyway
30          Louie:     Shoes 'n' clothes
31          Guest:     Mhmhmhm . .
32          Louie:                 Speakin' of shoes I need
                       some new moccasins
33          Joe Jr:    So I could do a lot with seventy . .
                       seventy five [dollars
34  Father to Guest:              [shows they hear me
                       complainin' a lot . . eh?
35          Guest:     mhmhmh . . . .
36          Jimmy:     Mom I need some new moccasins
37  Guest to Father:   They know all the lines
38  Louie to Jimmy:    You don't even know what they
                       a::re
```

What evidence can we see in the organization of this conversation that the Pastores constitute a community? From the perspective of community of practice, the conversation displays its three defining features by mutual engagement in a joint endeavor by individuals who share a repertoire of stories, styles of speaking, artifacts, and concepts. Mutual engagement is evident in the practice of sharing food at the same table and everyone participating in a fast-paced conversation on a common topic. The joint endeavor appears to be the concern that everyone around the table expresses about the cost of living for members of that family and how far $75 would go in a day. Erickson (2004) argues that the joint concern that family members express about the cost of living was shared with many other lower middle-class families in their neighborhood and in the surrounding towns – families that had traditionally voted for Democratic Party candidates in local and national elections. It was his sensitivity to this concern that, according to Erickson, Republican Party candidate Ronald Regan was able to use in the 1980 presidential election campaign to draw traditionally Democratic voters like the Pastores to vote Republican.

The linguistic and nonverbal repertoire that the participants in this dinner table conversation share is the point at which the community of practice approach and the discourse approach to community intersect. Erickson (1992) points out that the people at the dinner table utilize three different resources in order to produce the conversation, and each individual's use of each resource is carefully coordinated with its use by the others. The resource that appears most readily in the printed transcript is their use of common syntactic structures in order to collaboratively construct listing routines. The first example is in turns 4 and 5 when Louie and Anna use the same grammatical structure in successive turns.

```
4       Louie to Jimmy:    [he has to work three days to get you a
                            bike]
5                  Anna:   It cost even more than that to get his
                            bike, didn´e?
```

The second example is the extended sequence in turns 16 through 28 when the children and their mother list all the things that could be bought with $75, if . . .

```
16              Joe Jr:   I don´t have to pay taxes on a house
                          I don´t have to pay a mortgage
                          I don´t have to [pay all kinds/
                          . . .
28              Jimmy:    You don´t have to pay for gas
```

The other two shared resources that Erickson identifies are more difficult to see in a conventional transcript because they are the coordination of prosody and information focus and the timing of passing of dishes and the movement of food from the plate to the mouth. The coordination of the prosodic feature of sentence stress with the introduction of new information is most obvious in the listing routine from turn 16 through turn 28. Underscoring of syllables in the transcript such as 'I don't have to pay *taxes* on a *house*' in turn 16 indicates that the syllables are spoken at either greater volume than the surrounding talk or with prominent pitch height or extended pitch movement. In all cases, prosodic prominence coincides with a new piece of information produced within the same syntactic frame that other speakers had used in precious turns.

Erickson demonstrates the rhythmic production of stressed syllables by transcribing the conversation in musical notation, where each speaker's contribution is on a separate line, just as in an orchestral score each instrument's part is written on a separate line. The musical transcription is also valuable in displaying the carefully coordinated timing relations between talk and the nonverbal business of passing food and eating it. As Erickson (2004, p. 48) summarizes it, there is

> a functional connection between the verbal and nonverbal behavior that
> occurred at the dinner table. Forks waited in mid-air for the completion
> of utterances with list item nouns. The salad bowl moved across the table
> in concert with the speech rhythms of those engaged in the conversation
> accompanying the ingestion of food.

This coordination of verbal and nonverbal behavior is an index of community that is particularly noticeable during focused group activities such as family mealtimes. Timing of nonverbal activity in relation to the timing of talk is a general phenomenon found in all human interaction, but it is an index of a discourse community when participants treat timing as a shared resource. That means that when we observe focused face-to-face interactions in which participants' movements are out of sync with each other, we may begin to doubt the existence of a community.

In the discussion of the family dinner table conversation, we have most recently focused on how verbal and nonverbal resources in one participant's production are coordinated with the resources of other participants. The family discourse community that we have considered shows how those resources are coordinated among community members. There are, however, interactions in which such interactional resources are not shared. The lack of match between one participant's interactional style and that of others can have serious consequences, particularly in the classroom, because the style to match is the style imposed by the school through the teachers. Mismatch between ways of speaking at school and ways of speaking in the home and community environment outside the school has been studied extensively because of the belief by many scholars that in it may be discovered the cause of underperformance by minority children at schools. It is to a discussion of this work that we now turn.

A8.4.3 Contrasting communities: Classroom and home

The conversation of the Pastore family over dinner provides a view of community that is defined by participants' shared use of linguistic and interactional resources. Some of the resources used by people around the table were also nonverbal. Participants coordinated the passing of plates and the consumption of food with their own talk and with the talk of others. In this section, we will now consider a very different kind of discourse community and contrast the differences between the way talk and nonverbal behavior are organized in that community with discourse organization in a community perhaps more familiar to readers of this book. The community that we will examine is the Warm Springs Sahaptin Indians who live on a reservation in central Oregon. The ways that talk-in-interaction by Warm Springs Indians differ from its organization in middle-class White American society was described in a book (1982) and a number of articles by Susan Urmston Philips (1970, 1972, 1976, 1985). The purpose of Philips's research was not, however, simply to contrast the discourse organization of talk of two communities. She was primarily concerned to explain the consequences in those differences for the education of Warm Springs Indian children and for the perpetuation of inequality between Whites and Indians.

The basis that Philips uses to contrast discourse organization in the two communities is *participation structure*. Participation structures are not the same as the participation framework of talk-in-interaction that we have presented in Unit A5; instead, a participation structure is a way of organizing verbal interaction. Since Philips's research focused on classroom interaction in schools, she provided examples of four different participation structures that are commonly found in interaction among students and teachers in elementary school classrooms. The first structure is when the teacher interacts with all the students in the class, either by addressing them all or by addressing a single student in the presence of the rest; student responses are expected to be directed to the teacher. A second structure is when the teacher interacts with a small group of students while the remaining students are working in other groups or independently; again, student verbal responses are expected to be directed to the teacher. A third structure consists of all the students working independently at their desks while the teacher is available for individual consultations which must be initiated by students raising their hands or approaching the teacher's desk. A fourth structure occurs very infrequently in primary grades and hardly ever in the lower grades: It consists of the students being divided into small groups, in which they organize their own activity among themselves with more distant supervision by the teacher.

These participation structures are ways of organizing talk in classrooms with which many people who have participated as students or teachers in formal British or American education are familiar. The participation of Indian children in the four structures is however markedly different from the way that non-Indian children from outside the reservation participate. As Philips (1970) reports, 'In the first two participant structures where students must speak out individually in front of the other students, Indian children show considerable reluctance to participate, particularly when compared to non-Indian children' (p. 84). When the teacher is working with a small group of students, the Indian children frequently refuse to respond when called upon and, unlike the non-Indians students, hardly ever urge the teachers to call on them. If the Indian children do speak, they do so very softly, 'often in tones inaudible to a person more than a few feet away, and in utterances that are typically shorter' than those of the non-Indian students (ibid.). In the third structure, when the teacher is available for student-initiated consultations during a lesson when the whole class is working independently on reading or writing assignments, the Indian children often take the opportunity to initiate contact with the teacher, and their participation increases such that by sixth grade, 'Indian students initiate such relatively private encounters with teachers much more frequently than non-Indian students do' (ibid.).

The participation structure in which the Indian students become most fully involved in classroom activity is when they themselves are able to control and direct the interaction in small group projects. In this context, they appear to concentrate fully on their work until the task is completed, 'talking a great deal to one another within the group, and competing, with explicit remarks to that effect, with the other groups' (pp. 84–85). To summarize Indian children's participation in the classroom, several features stand out. First of all, they appear much less willing than other students to speak or to participate when they are asked to do so in front of other students. Second, they appear much less willing to speak when the aim of the speaking activity is determined by the teacher, as it most often is in small group work. Last, Indian children appear considerably less willing than non-Indians to assume a leadership role which requires them to dictate actions to their peers in a similar way to the teacher's direction of activity in the whole class.

It is clear that the participation of Warm Springs Indian children in their classrooms on the reservation is different from participation of non-Indian children outside the reservation. After six grades of schooling on the reservation where all classmates are Indian and their teachers are White, for the remaining grades, the Indian children are bussed to the town of Madras, where they encounter White students for the first time, and where Indian children are outnumbered by Whites five to one. The differential participation of Indian children in class is a very important aspect of their lack of success at school. They fare much worse academically than non-Indians and by the time they reach high school in ninth grade, their problems at school become really serious and it is at this time that hostility between Indians and non-Indians is expressed openly. The Indian children's participation at school is interpreted by their White teachers, whose interpretative framework is dominant and sanctioned by the school authorities. As Philips (1985, p. 316) remarks,

> Teacher and student do not meet on an equal basis and work out between them what is meaningful, or what is right and wrong. It is the teacher who defines what is meaningful, what is appropriate, what is true and what is false.

It is therefore the Indian children's participation in the structures of classroom interaction that is interpreted by their teachers as uncooperative and unlikely to lead to academic success.

The educational and social consequences of Indian children's participation in classsrooms result from the different way that talk-in-interaction is organized in the children's home community on the Warm Springs reservation and the normative expectations of their White teachers and classmates. To understand the reasons why the Warm Springs children speak readily under some conditions and fail to do so under others, it is necessary to understand how talk is organized in the Indian community. Philips conducted participant observation among the Warm Springs Indians and found that the participation structures in which the children spoke in school were those contexts which were prevalent ways of organizing talk-in-interaction in their home community. On the other hand, the participation structures at school where Indian students were required to verbally display before their classmates or to take leadership roles were not found by Philips in their interactions at home, and this was the reason why the Indian children were disinclined to participate in this way in class. Philips also reported that the leadership role taken by the teacher in the elementary school classroom was very different from the way that leadership was exercised in the Warm Springs community.

Warm Springs children learn skills around the home and outdoors at a much earlier age than non-Indian children. Children are present at many adult interactions as silent but attentive observers and it is through such silent observation that they learn skills. 'Girls, for example, learn to cook some foods before they are eight, and by this age may be fully competent in cleaning a house without any aid or supervision from adults' (Philips, 1972, p. 385). An image of a Warm Springs child observing adult activity is reproduced in Figure A8.3. A second way in which learning in the Warm Springs community differs from learning at school is the absence of any form of assessment of the child's skill by an adult before the child exercises the skill

Figure A8.3 A Warm Springs Indian girl is a silent and attentive observer as an adult
weaves a basket. Source: Photo by Peg Herring, News and
Communications, Oregon State University

unsupervised. The child demonstrates the skill in public only when it is fully
developed. Some of the most dramatic examples of this apparent 'instant learning'
are the ritual songs that individuals perform for the first time in full and complete
form in the presence of others, which they report as having been received and
learned through dreams and visions.

Learning takes place in the Warm Springs community in a very different way from
its organization in the school. In the community, it can be seen as a process of three
steps: (1) silent listening and patient observation of the activities of adult family
members, (2) supervised participation, and (3) private, self-initiated assessment.

In all three stages, children's use of speech is minimal. The contrast between learning in the community and learning in the classroom is highlighted by Philips (1972, p. 388):

> In the classroom, the processes of *acquisition* of knowledge and *demonstration* of knowledge are collapsed into the single act of answering questions or reciting when called upon to do so by the teacher . . . The Indian children . . . have no opportunity to 'practice,' and to decide for themselves when they know enough to demonstrate their knowledge; rather their performances are determined by the teacher. And finally, their only channel for communicating competency is verbal, rather than non-verbal.

A discourse approach to community is a way in which we can understand how members of a family like the Pastores construct themselves as a community and it is also a way in which we can contrast the discourse organization of one community with another. As Philips has argued, however, the comparison between two discourse organizations is not a comparison among equals, especially when there is a tradition of inequality and discrimination against members of one of the communities. Lack of understanding by teachers and other powerful individuals of how talk is organized in interaction in different communities contributes to perpetuating discrimination.

SUMMARY AND LOOKING AHEAD

People identify with communities by means of ways of speaking, modes of dress, practices, and values that they share with other people. And a person's identity is closely connected with the community or communities in which they have or seek membership. Communities are united by a common language in a language area (although members may not be citizens of the same country) and by common ways of speaking and pragmatic values in a speech area (although members of a speech area may not speak the same language). A shared repertoire of language and speech styles is also one characteristic of a community of practice, although members of a community of practice are also mutually engaged in the accomplishment of a joint endeavor.

Communities are created actively and in real time by collaborative construction of discourse by coordinating individual members' interactional, linguistic, and non-verbal resources – coordination which is timed to the split second and which creates a symphonic image to the outsider in which individual voices play different instruments. This is music to some but discord to others. Discord is created when individuals from different communities come together; when, for instance, respectful silence by one group is interpreted as lack of interest by another or when one group's dislike of displaying skill in public is interpreted by another group as evidence that they lack the skill to be displayed. Such differences among discourse communities are the root of some social ills, but they need not be. Learning to understand the discourse of a different community from your own involves developing new skills in social interaction, which is the topic of the next and final unit.

Unit A9
Developing skills in social interaction

PROLOGUE AND ROADMAP

Throughout this book we have studied how people use language in social interaction with others in order to perform actions and to create contexts, meanings, stances, identities, and membership in a cultural community. In the early units, we overheard an embarrassing conversation between Donnie and his mother on a bus, and later we admired Dr Martin Luther King Junior's eloquent speech at the March for Civil Rights. In Unit A4, we observed a struggle for discursive power between an ESL teacher and her students over the meaning of the word 'habitat', and in Unit A5 we analyzed the interaction between a clarinet teacher and his student. In Unit A6, we marveled at how very young infants demonstrate intersubjectivity while, at the opposite end of a life span, we recognized in Unit A7 that an obituary is a very powerful means of altercasting a person's identity. In Unit A8, we watched the skill with which members of an Italian-American family coordinated their talk and their bodily movements to create a sense of community and we witnessed the discursive processes that perpetuate discrimination against American Indian children in schools.

In all these interactions, we observed people who have developed interactional skills. In many cases their interactional skills helped these individuals to achieve a desired outcome and, in some other cases, we observed people employing their interactional skills to demonstrate their cultural differences. What we have touched on only lightly so far is how people develop the skills that they use so effortlessly and effectively in interaction. To complete the picture, the development of skills in social interaction will be the topic of this final unit. We will first consider what is learned: Is it language, interactional skill, actions, stances, identities, or some combination? Do individuals develop strategies for participating in specific discursive practices or do they acquire knowledge that is independent of the context of interaction? We will discuss these questions under three headings: language socialization, situated learning, and classroom interaction in schools.

Before we start, we should be aware of a question of focus. 'Learning' is the most general term for what we will examine in this unit but 'learning' is often associated primarily with particular practices in which young people participate at school. We want, however, to look beyond schooling to consider a process that happens throughout a lifetime and both inside and outside of school.

A9.1 METAPHORS FOR LEARNING

Let's begin with an example of how skills in social interaction develop. You have probably had an interaction with a doctor at a doctor's office, at a clinic, or at the hospital. Doctors are highly trained professionals and their knowledge of human health care is vastly greater than most of their patients. This difference can cause problems of communication when doctors interact with patients. Have you ever left a doctor's office wondering just what you were told about your health, or what exactly you were supposed to do to relieve or prevent a health problem? If you are a typical patient, you remember less than half of what your doctor tried to explain. How can you learn to be a better patient? One way is to learn the technical vocabulary of medicine. Task A9.1 is an activity designed to test the current state of your medical knowledge.

Task A9.1.1

➤ The Rapid Estimate of Adult Literacy in Medicine (REALM) is a screening instrument designed to assess an adult patient's ability to read common medical terms. Here are 66 words. How many can you pronounce correctly, each within five seconds?

fat	fatigue	allergic	flu
pelvic	menstrual	pill	jaundice
testicle	dose	infection	colitis
eye	exercise	emergency	stress
behavior	medication	smear	prescription
occupation	nerves	notify	sexually
germs	gallbladder	alcoholism	meals
calories	irritation	disease	depression
constipation	cancer	miscarriage	gonorrhea
caffeine	pregnancy	inflammatory	attack
arthritis	diabetes	kidney	nutrition
hepatitis	hormones	menopause	antibiotics
herpes	appendix	diagnosis	seizure
abnormal	potassium	bowel	syphilis
anemia	asthma	hemorrhoids	obesity
rectal	nausea	osteoporosis	incest
directed	impetigo		

Check your answers with a health professional

A9.1.1   Learning as knowledge acquisition

The activity of pronouncing the 66 words in the REAM test is an assessment of one kind of knowledge and one kind of learning, which has three characteristics: (1) What you learn you do so independently of social context, (2) Learning happens in the mind-brain of a single individual, and (3) Increases of knowledge happen incrementally. Let's consider these three characteristics in turn. First, knowledge of medical vocabulary is not specific to a particular interaction. If you were able to pronounce the medical terms in a classroom context, you could probably also pronounce them in a different context such as a doctor's office. Second, your knowledge does not depend on who you say the words to; it only depends on your own individual ability. And third, if you don't pronounce all 66 words correctly, you can learn the words that you don't know and your knowledge of medical vocabulary will increase incrementally. This metaphor of learning as independent of context, as located in a single individual, and incrementally increasing is an image familiar to many people. It is, however, just that – a metaphor for a process that we need to represent in a familiar way in order to understand it. Anna Sfard (1998) called it the 'acquisition metaphor,' and suggested that it makes us think of learning in a particular way: 'The language of "knowledge acquisition" and "concept develop-ment" makes us think about the human mind as a container to be filled with certain materials and about the learner as becoming an owner of these materials' (p. 5).

A9.1.2   Learning as changing participation

Acquiring knowledge of medical terms is one way in which we can learn to be a good patient. There is, however, another way in which learning to communicate does not remain the patient's responsibility alone. Doctors can learn to be better communicators by using plain language in place of medical jargon, by saying for example 'chest pain' instead of 'angina' or 'You don't have H.I.V.' instead of 'Your H.I.V. test was negative.' In a visit to a doctor's office, however, we find ourselves face to face with the doctor and we don't have time to wait for the doctor to learn better communication skills. As a patient, we can take the initiative in interaction by doing other-initiated self-repair. If the doctor says something we don't understand, we can ask that it be repeated in simpler language. If we are given a new set of instructions, we can repeat them back to the doctor in order to confirm our understanding. We can also try to enhance our confidence in interaction and minimize the power and status differential between ourselves and the doctor by ensuring that conversations about serious medical matters take place when we are fully clothed.

This kind of learning involves not simply change in an individual patient's knowledge. It involves both the patient and the doctor. In order for the patient to ask questions about treatment, the doctor must allow time and encourage questions, not simply by saying 'Do you have any questions?' but rather 'What questions do you have?' Doctors can also encourage patients to confirm their instructions by saying things like, 'I always ask my patients to repeat things back to make sure that I have explained them clearly.' Learning to be a good patient then involves learning to participate in doctor–patient interaction, a process that Sfard referred to as the 'participation metaphor' for learning.

Considering learning in this light means recognizing a process very different from knowledge acquisition. Learning activities are never considered independently of the social context in which they take place – a context that is, as we have recognized in many places in this book, rich and co-constructed by learners. Some aspects of learning to participate as a patient in doctor–patient interactions are specific to that context, and it is a question that merits further investigation which aspects of learning to participate in one context are portable to a different context. Learning also does not occur in a single individual. It is not development of an individual's cognition that we observe but interaction between an individual and a complex sociocultural environment that affects an individual's learning and is in turn influenced by it. This environment includes both the other participants in the interaction and the tools and implements that are available to an individual. In the doctor–patient interaction, we have seen that the doctor can provide affordances for the patient's learning by encouraging questions and allowing time for discussion. Contributions of the environment to patient learning may also include a written summary of treatment provided in the doctor's office as well as internet websites that provide further information. In the participation metaphor for learning, cognition is distributed because 'people think in conjunction and partnership with others and with the help of culturally provided tools and implements' (Salomon, 1993, p. xiii).

The path of learning as changes in participation is quite different from the incremental learning which characterizes the acquisition metaphor. The participation metaphor characterizes learning as becoming a participant in a community, developing from peripheral participation to full use of the interactional and linguistic resources that are available as a veteran member of the community. As we have seen in Unit 5, interactional and linguistic resources are configured in ways that are specific to a discursive practice, and this makes it inappropriate to view the participation metaphor for learning as the accretion of skill in one specific resource. There are certainly differences in the interactional competence of novice and veteran members of a discourse community but those differences cannot be represented on a trajectory of accretion.

The differences between the ways that the learning process, learners, and teachers are mapped in the acquisition metaphor and in the participation metaphor are summarized in Table A9.1.

Neither of the two metaphors for learning that Sfard presents should be considered exclusive. The goals and processes of learning, the role identities of student and teacher, and conceptions of what is to be learned and what knowing it means differ from one learning context to another and, equally, both metaphors can reveal useful

Table A9.1 A comparison of the acquisition and participation metaphors for learning
(Sfard, 1998, p. 7)

Acquisition metaphor		Participation metaphor
Individual enrichment	Goal of learning	Community building
Acquisition of something	Learning	Becoming a participant
Recipient (consumer), (re-)constructor	Student	Peripheral participant, apprentice
Provider, facilitator, mediator	Teacher	Expert participant, preserver of practice/discourse
Property, possession, commodity (individual, public)	Knowledge	Aspect of practice/ discourse/activity
Having, possessing	Knowing	Belonging, participating, communicating

insights into a single learning context. Laying out the two metaphors for learning side by side, however, allows us to see what can go wrong with one kind of learning from the perspective of the other. One example of how the two metaphors complement each other can be seen in interpretations of the role of the teacher. In the acquisition metaphor, where knowledge is viewed as the possession of an individual, that individual's task as a teacher is to transmit knowledge to students and to evaluate the students' acquisition of that knowledge according to criteria of which the teacher is guardian. The situation viewed from the participation metaphor is rather different, however, because, as Douglas Barnes (1976) wrote, 'It would be a mistake to think that what a teacher teaches is quite separate from how he teaches' (p. 139); that is, students are learning to participate in a learning practice at the same time as they are acquiring knowledge. In this context, the social context of transmission of knowledge is one in which an identity as knower is created for the teacher, and very different identities are created for the students. If, moreover, the students' knowledge is evaluated by criteria established by the teacher, then knowledge is quite literally power, and what the students are learning in addition to official knowledge specified in a curriculum are values and attitudes toward people who have knowledge. In other words, what is being learned and implicitly taught is a social hierarchy in which a knower is in a better position than a consumer of knowledge – a difference that parallels the hierarchy of producer and consumer of commodities in the society outside the classroom.

Another example of the value of comparing learning in the two metaphors and the dangers of choosing just one is a weakness of the participation metaphor that is made clear by the acquisition metaphor. The emphasis on knowledge as an aspect of practice and of learning as becoming a participant in a practice in the participation metaphor strongly emphasizes the context-bound nature of learning as participation. What learners learn is to participate in one practice. But is that learning – that participation – portable to other practices? From the point of view of the acquisition metaphor, porting knowledge from one situation to another and using it in the new context does not present a problem because knowledge is abstracted from the situation in which it was acquired. But if what you learn is how to participate in a given practice, what do you do when you encounter a different practice? In one view of participation, the dependence of learning on context is far too great to allow for transfer of participation from one context to another. To a certain extent, this must be true, of course. When we find ourselves participating in a completely novel practice, we often try to participate in ways that we have learned in other practices. But are practices so different one from another that daily practices are completely new and we find ourselves at a loss in a new and different context? This is surely not the case. Life is not full of surprises and, in fact, the essence of learning is being prepared to deal with new contexts that we encounter tomorrow. If learning occurs in a participation framework, then that framework has a structure and elements of structure can be found, albeit in different configurations, in different contexts. Comparing the participation frameworks of different practices is an activity that we have done throughout this book and the bases for making comparisons are the resources that we described in Unit A5: identities co-constructed within a participation framework, the register of the talk participants use, how participants construct meaning, what actions they do through talk, how they organize turns at talk, how they repair interactional troubles, and how they construct boundaries between one practice and another.

The two metaphors for learning that we have discussed here are two different and complementary ways of understanding the same phenomenon. Although the acquisition metaphor may be more familiar, that does not imply that the newer participation metaphor is better. We do need, however, to investigate the participation metaphor in more detail because it is perhaps less familiar, and this investigation is the topic of Section A9.3, where we describe Jean Lave and Etienne Wenger's theory of Situated Learning (also known as Legitimate Peripheral Participation or LPP).

Before we discuss Situated Learning, we need to consider what is learned in a universal process that is a prime site of learning but which has until recently been very rarely studied: how children learn the ways of speaking of the community into which they are born, how those ways of speaking index the values and beliefs of a group, and how those values are reproduced in a new generation of speakers. Young children learn language and ways of speaking that characterize interaction in the community into which they are born, and it is through these interactions that they learn not only language but the also the culture of the adult community. This process in which learning language cannot be separated from learning culture has been investigated by linguistic anthropologists since the 1980s. The approach to learning has come to be known as 'language socialization' – a new field established by Elinor Ochs, Bambi Schieffelin, and Karen Watson-Gegeo. It is to their work that we now turn.

A9.2 LANGUAGE SOCIALIZATION

In Unit B5 there is a discussion of language socialization in the reading extracted from Ochs's (1996) essay 'Linguistic Resources for Socializing Humanity' in Unit B5. In that essay, Ochs proposed two basic goals of language socialization research: (1) to explain how language practices encode and socialize information about society and culture and (2) to go beyond a description of the relationship of a language to a local culture to establish associations between languages and cultures that are common to all human social groups.

The first principle is a question of pragmatics and envisages a function for language that goes far beyond the representation of factual information. Language socialization researchers acknowledge that through language children learn the beliefs and attitudes of their community toward ways of acting, feeling, and knowing. They learn how to act in certain social contexts not only by explicit instruction but by interacting with others and observing their language and actions. The connection between language and action is brought into relief when two or three communities are compared, which Ochs and Schieffelin (1984) do in their comparison of adult–child interaction in White middle-class Anglo-American communities and among the Kaluli people in the southern highlands of Papua New Guinea. Most of the research on child development in White middle-class Anglo-American communities has focused on the interaction between a single infant and a single caregiver, a dyadic interaction which is considered to be primary within this social group. In addition, the caregiver's language has been described as a simplified Baby Talk register (Ferguson, 1977), and many believe that the purpose of Baby Talk is to simplify speech in order to aid the infant's comprehension. In contrast, Schieffelin's (1979) research showed that Kaluli mothers organize interaction among three or more participants in which the infant is oriented away from the mother and the Kaluli adults do not simplify their speech when addressing the infant because they believe it will inhibit the child's speech development.

Because interactions between infants and caregivers in these two communities are so different, what the White MC infant and the Kaluli infant learn also differs. For example, learning the tactics of turn-taking in a dyadic interaction – including selection of next speaker and recognition of transition relevance places in an ongoing turn – is a very different task from learning the tactics of turn-taking in a multi-party interaction. The construction of social identities by means of the interaction for the infant and caregivers also differs. In White MC dyadic interaction the individual child and adult co-construct clear and reciprocal identities, while in the multi-party Kaluli interaction the individual roles are more complex.

When we consider the focus of language socialization research from the perspective of Sfard's two metaphors for learning, it appears at first that infants are learning to become participants in a social group rather than acquiring knowledge of the ways of speaking in the group. This is, however, an impression that Watson-Gegeo and Nielsen (2003) reject when they point out that 'Cognition *originates* in social interaction. Constructing new knowledge is therefore *both* a cognitive *and* a social process' (p. 156). This view of learning that bridges Sfard's two metaphors and recognizes cognitive acquisition and increased participation as aspects of the same learning process originates in the work of the psychologist L. S. Vygotsky. Vygotsky's work in the Soviet Union of the 1920s and 1930s showed how young children's knowledge of spatial, temporal, and mathematical concepts originated in spoken interaction with adults or with older children. The importance of language for children is that utterances are a concrete phenomenon that a child can manipulate in action and in memory and serve as a tool for thinking. The function of language as a meditational tool for thought can be seen when children (or adults) are required to solve a difficult problem in isolation. Even without an interlocutor, the child will produce utterances that have no intended hearer besides the child itself. Vygotsky (1978) interpreted such private or egocentric speech as a tool to help the child's thinking; that is, even in social isolation human infants create a participation framework in which the child takes two social roles. As we argued in Unit A3, the function of the 'I – Me' dialogue in private speech is to create a participation framework in which 'I' makes choices with regard to what to talk about and 'Me' interprets and critiques these choices.

As we have discussed in Unit A7, one way in which cultural knowledge is created in interaction and mediated by language use is the acquisition of forms of address. In many cultures, people mark social distinctions between speaker and addressee by means of second-person pronouns and verb forms. The distinction in French between the pronouns *tu* and *vous*, for example, encodes a speaker's social knowledge about the relative social rank or familiarity of participants. The use of *vous* typically shows the speaker's reverence or respect for the person being addressed, but it also shows the social distance between speaker and addressee and the formality of the situation. From the initials of the French pronouns, such resources, which are available in many European languages, are known as T and V forms. In many other languages, including Japanese and Korean, the linguistic marking of social categories applies not only on pronouns and verbs but also on nouns and is used not only to persons being addressed but also *about* persons to whom the speaker refers in the third person. These linguistic resources, which are prevalent throughout the grammar, are known as *honorifics*. Such linguistic and cultural distinctions must be learned by children growing up in the society and may cause great difficulty for foreigners learning the language because the cultural values that are indexed by honorifics often have different meanings for foreigners. Task A9.2.1 provides an opportunity for you to examine your own knowledge about such forms and to reflect on how you have used them in your own participation in interaction.

Task A9.2.1

➤ How have you learned to use T and V forms in languages such as French, Spanish, German, Italian, or Russian? Do you know languages such as Korean and Japanese which use honorifics? If so, consider what form you would use in addressing (or talking about) the following participants. Have you ever experienced an interaction in which you realized that you had used the incorrect form? In English today, we have lost the distinction between the T-form *thou* and the V-form *you*. Are there other linguistic resources that we use in contemporary English to show respect or familiarity and social distance or solidarity?

Your teacher	Your elder brother
Your best friend	Your younger sister
Your parents	Your doctor
The waiter	The baker
Your auntie	Your partner
A stranger you ask for directions	The king, queen, or president of your country

Language socialization research has been carried out primarily to investigate how infants and young children achieve membership in an adult social group, and it has focused on the intimate connection between language and culture. Language socialization researchers, however, have claimed that language socialization continues throughout a lifespan and that learning is both a social and a cognitive process. We turn next to an approach to learning that in some respects differs from language socialization in its emphasis on the apprenticeship of adults to a new community of practice and on learning as a change from peripheral to fuller participation in the community.

A9.3 SITUATED LEARNING

A theory of learning that is very far from conventional views of learning in schools was put forward by Jean Lave and Etienne Wenger (1991) in their book *Situated learning: Legitimate peripheral participation*. Situated learning is fundamentally a social process far from the process of acquisition that happens solely in a learner's head. Lave and Wenger maintain that learning viewed as situated activity has as its central defining characteristic a process they call legitimate peripheral participation. This term describes the incorporation of learners into activities of communities of practice, beginning as a newcomer – a legitimated (recognized) participant on the edges (periphery) of the community of practice – and moving through a series of increasingly expert roles as a learner's skills develop. A community of practice is formed, as we saw in Unit A8, by mutual engagement of individuals in an endeavor that is considered relevant by all members of the community, an endeavor that requires a repertoire of language and skills that are shared by all members. The notion of community of practice was put forward by Etienne Wenger, while the social anthropologist Jean Lave collected and wrote ethnographies of how people in many different parts of the world become members of different communities of practice. Five communities are described in the Lave and Wenger's book: Mayan-speaking midwives in Mexico, tailors in Liberia, quartermasters in the US Navy, meat cutters in American supermarkets, and nondrinking alcoholics in Alcoholics Anonymous. Lave and Wenger describe the processes by which newcomers become members of these communities, processes that may include some formal schooling but mostly involve personal and physical involvement of both newcomers and old timers in a formal or informal apprenticeship.

As an illustration of situated learning, Carol Cain (1991) described in detail how newcomers to Alcoholics Anonymous learn to become nondrinking alcoholics. It is her description of the process that we summarize here because it shows clearly the following features of situated learning.

- the characteristics of the community of practice
- the transition from newcomer to old timer
- the help that both newcomers and old timers provide each other
- the repertoire of skills that the learner develops, and
- the acquisition of a new identity.

The change that men and women undergo in becoming members of the new community is much more than a change in behavior. It is a transformation of their identities, from drinking non-alcoholics to nondrinking alcoholics, and it affects how they view and act in the world. In the extended excerpt from her article below, Cain describes this process of situated learning and focuses our attention on the means that help mediate this: telling personal stories.

> There are two important dimensions to the identity of AA alcoholic. The first distinction that AA makes is between alcoholic and non-alcoholic, where alcoholic refers to a state that, once attained, is not reversible. The second is drinking and non-drinking, and refers to a potentially controllable activity . . . There are therefore two aspects of the AA alcoholic identity important for continuing membership in AA: qualification as an alcoholic, which is based on one's past, and continued effort at not drinking. The AA identity requires a behavior – not drinking – that is a negation of the behavior that originally qualified one for membership. One of the functions of the AA personal story is to establish both aspects of membership in an individual.
>
> In personal stories, AA members tell their own drinking histories, how they came to understand that they are alcoholics, how they got into AA, and what their life has been like since they joined AA . . . In AA, personal stories are told for the explicit, stated purpose of providing a model of alcoholism, so that other drinkers may find so much of themselves in the lives of

professed alcoholics that they cannot help but ask whether they, too, are alcoholics. Since the definition of an alcoholic is not really agreed upon in the wider culture, arriving at this interpretation of events is a process negotiated between the drinker and those around her. AA stories provide a set of criteria by which the alcoholic can be identified . . . 'Personal stories' play a large part in helping people identify themselves as alcoholics. AA recognizes their importance and dedicates a significant amount of meeting time and publishing space to the telling of these stories. In personal stories, AA members tell their own drinking histories, how they came to understand that they are alcoholics, how they got into AA, and what their life has been like since they joined AA. From the founding of the AA program, the telling of personal stories has been both the major vehicle for 'carrying the message to alcoholics who still suffer' (the 'Twelfth Step'), and an important tool for maintaining sobriety.

AA members tell personal stories formally in 'speakers' meetings.' Less formally, members tell shortened versions of their stories, or parts of them, at discussion meetings. The final important context for telling personal stories is in 'Twelfth Step calls.' When AA members talk to out-siders who may be alcoholics in a one-to-one interaction, they are following the last of the Twelve Steps . . . Ideally, at these individual meetings, the member tells his story, tells about the AA program, tries to help the drinker see herself as an alcoholic if she is 'ready.' [Members] have claimed that telling their own stories to other alcoholics, and thus helping other alcoholics to achieve sobriety, is an important part of maintaining their own sobriety.

Telling an AA personal story also plays an important role in helping members acquire the identity of AA alcoholic, through signaling real membership, and through a process of transforming the member's self-understanding . . . Telling an AA story is not something one learns through explicit teaching. Newcomers are not *told* how to tell their stories, yet most people who remain in AA learn to do this. There are several ways in which an AA member learns to tell an appropriate story. First, he must be exposed to AA models . . . The newcomer to AA hears and reads personal stories from the time of early contact with the program – through meetings, literature, and talk with individual old timers . . . In addition to learning from the models, learning takes place through interaction. All members are encouraged to speak at discussion meetings and to maintain friendships with other AA members. In the course of this social interaction, the new member is called on to talk about her own life . . . This may be in bits and pieces, rather than the entire life. For example, in discussion meetings, the topic of discussion may be 'admitting you are powerless,' 'making amends,' 'how to avoid the first drink,' or shared experiences in dealing with common problems . . . One speaker follows another by picking out certain pieces of what has previously been said, saying why it was relevant to him, and elaborating on it with some episode of his own . . . Usually, unless the interpretation really runs counter to AA beliefs, the speaker is not corrected. Rather, other speakers will take the appropriate parts of the newcomer's comments and build on this in their own comments, giving parallel accounts with different interpretations, for example, or expanding on parts of their own stories that are similar to parts of the newcomer's story, while ignoring the inappropriate parts of the newcomer's story.

In addition to the structure of the AA story, the newcomer must also learn the cultural model of alcoholism encoded in them, including AA propositions, appropriate episodes to serve as evidence, and appropriate interpretations of events . . . Simply learning the propositions about alcohol and its nature is not enough. They must be applied by the drinker to his own life, and this application must be demonstrated . . . In AA, success, or recovery, requires learning to perceive oneself and one's problems from an AA perspective. AA members must learn to experience their problems as drinking problems, and themselves as alcoholics . . . Stories do not just describe a life in a learned genre, but are tools for reinterpreting the past and understanding the self in terms of the AA identity . . . Internalization of the identity takes place as the initiate begins to identify with AA members . . . She comes to understand herself as a non-drinking alcoholic, and to reinterpret her past life as evidence.

Learning to be a nondrinking alcoholic member of AA seems to be far removed from the kind of learning at school that we are used to thinking about – learning a foreign language, learning calculus, or learning to drive a car, for instance. And yet, in many ways the processes that the learner and the community go through are similar both in situated learning and in schooling, and by considering the process of legitimate peripheral participation as an AA member we can gain some insights into the kind of learning that happens in more conventional contexts. The first thing to consider is the community of practice which the learner wishes to join. As Wenger described it, the community of practice is not simply a group of people who know something but a group focused on a mutual endeavor, which for AA members is to maintain both the behavior and the identity of a nondrinking alcoholic. Members of AA consider this endeavor to be relevant for all, both newcomers and old timers. This endeavor requires that members define themselves as alcoholics and maintain an effort at sobriety. Membership in this community also involves participation in a central practice: the personal story. AA members tell their stories at informal discussion meetings, at formal speakers' meetings, and at Twelfth Step calls on outsiders. Personal stories are drinking histories and, according to Cain, individual members' stories follow a similar format that demonstrates the cultural model of alcoholism and they provide appropriate episodes to serve as evidence of AA propositions, including: alcoholism is a progressive disease, the alcoholic is powerless over alcohol, the alcoholic drinker is out of control, AA is for those who want it not for those who need it, and AA is a program for living not just for not drinking.

Newcomers to AA transition to old timers by regular attendance at AA meetings, by listening to the personal stories of others, and by telling their own. There is no explicit instruction in how to tell a personal story, but most people who remain in AA learn to do so. For their part, the old timers acknowledge the newcomer as a legitimate peripheral participant by encouraging her to tell her own story and by picking out certain pieces of what the newcomer said, saying why it was relevant to them, and elaborating on it with some episodes of their own. In this way, newcomers and old timers provide each other with help in maintaining the community of practice.

The repertoire of skills that the learner develops includes not only attending meetings and telling the personal story, but also recognizing 'the cultural model of alcoholism encoded in them, including AA propositions, appropriate episodes to serve as evidence, and appropriate interpretations of events.' These behaviors and beliefs form part of the acquisition of a new identity by the learner because learning the genre of the AA personal story also requires that the newcomer acknowledge that her experience and situation are similar to the drinking experiences of old timers. She does not simply have a drinking problem, but she is an alcoholic as construed by AA, and telling her personal story in the AA genre also involves reinterpreting the past through the story.

Learning in Lave and Wenger's theory, like learning in other theories, involves changes over time. The scope of change in situated learning is, however, broader than we are used to seeing because it involves not only changes in the learner's behavior but also changes in the learner's identity as she becomes a member of the new community of practice. At the same time, it is not only the newcomer that changes but also the old timers, who change in order to accommodate the newcomer by recognizing her as a legitimate peripheral participant and by incorporating the newcomer's personal stories into their own. As we have seen, in situated learning explicit instruction is not a necessary part of the process of transformation and some people have criticized this approach because of its lack of attention to pedagogy and formal instruction. As Lave and Wenger admit, 'we do not talk . . . about schools in any substantial way, nor explore what our work has to say about schooling' (p. 39). In any discussion of how individuals develop skills in social interaction, however, schooling cannot be ignored, and it is to this important topic that we now turn.

A9.4 CLASSROOM INTERACTION IN SCHOOLS

The focus of most research on learning in schools has been on the classroom. The classroom is one of the primary sites for social interaction in schools and, because it is public and because the classroom is considered to be the place where teachers teach and learners learn, classrooms have been the focus of most attention. Classrooms are also places where talk happens, and so the interest of researchers had been on the relationship between talk in classrooms and learning – as a matter of fact, one of the earliest studies of classroom learning in British secondary schools was entitled *Talking to learn* (Britton, 1971). Some of the early studies of classroom interaction focused on the amount of talk by teachers and students and suggested that teachers talk too much and learners talk too little. Other studies distinguished between teachers' views of what constitutes knowledge on a dimension called transmission-interpretation (Barnes and Schemilt, 1974). The transmission teacher '(1) believes knowledge to exist in the form of public disciplines which include content and criteria for performance; (2) values the learners' performances insofar as they conform to the criteria of the discipline,' while the interpretation teacher '(1) believes knowledge to exist in the knower's ability to organize thought and action; (2) values the learners' commitment to interpreting reality, so that criteria arise as much from the learner as from the teacher' (p. 223). Such different views by teachers of what constitutes knowledge of their subject may influence the kind of talk that happens in their classrooms and, in fact, Margaret Falvey (1983) found just that. Falvey reported that a teacher who held interpretation views spent three times as much classroom time on student–student interaction as a transmission teacher. She also found that students asked questions more often in the interpretation teacher's class, and another difference was that the interpretation teacher asked her students far more questions that elicited new information than display questions to which she already knew the answer.

A characteristic of spoken interaction in all classrooms was first described by John Sinclair and Malcolm Coulthard (1975). They identified a very common sequence of three actions in which a teacher interacts with an individual student or with the whole class. The sequence is initiated by the teacher, often in the form of a question. The second action is performed by one or more students in response, and the sequence is concluded by the teacher in the form of an evaluation of the student's response. Here is one example from Tsui (1995) of what has come to be known as the initiation-response-evaluation (IRE) or initiation-response-feedback (IRF) sequence.

```
Teacher: After they have put up their tent, what did the boys
         do?
Student: They cooking food.
Teacher: No, not they cooking food, pay attention.
Student: They cook their meal.
Teacher: Right, they cook their meal over an open fire.
```

The teacher initiates this exchange by asking a question to which a student responds. The teacher expresses a negative evaluation of the student's response, at which point the student hazards a second response. The teacher expresses a positive evaluation of the second response and expands it.

We have discussed in Unit A4 the social implications of the teacher's control of turn-taking. It is a way in which power is created in discourse by controlling and constraining the contributions of non-powerful participants, and a way in which non-powerful participants co-construct power by accepting the organization of talk. In the IRE/IRF sequence, we can see that the co-construction of power in a classroom is not only by turn allocation (as happens in the first two acts of the sequence in which the teacher selects a student as the next speaker) but also by means of the teacher's third act: evaluation of the student's response. What is being learned in this sequence is thus much more than the subject matter of the lesson. As we have affirmed earlier in this unit, the students are being socialized to a social hierarchy in which a knower (the teacher) is in a more powerful position than a consumer of knowledge (the student) – a difference that parallels the hierarchy of producer and consumer of commodities in the society outside the classroom.

Many recent investigations of the relationship between classroom talk and learning have adopted the methodology of conversation analysis to provide insight into what is happening in classrooms – in particular, classrooms in which a foreign or second language is the subject matter. Led by Paul Seedhouse (2004) and Numa Markee (2000), this line of research has shown yet another relationship between teachers' beliefs and the organization of talk in their classrooms. Seedhouse showed that a teacher's pedagogical goals influence the organization of talk. Different pedagogical goals correspond to four different contexts that teachers create in foreign-language classrooms: (1) form-and-accuracy contexts, (2) meaning-and-fluency contexts, (3) task-oriented contexts, and (4) procedural contexts. In a form-and-accuracy context, the teacher expects learners to produce linguistic forms and patterns of interaction that correspond to the pedagogical focus of the lesson. In a meaning-and-fluency context, the teacher's aim is to maximize the opportunities for spoken interaction in the target language. In a task-oriented context, the teacher introduces a pedagogical focus by allocating tasks to the learners and then generally withdraws, allowing the learners to manage the tasks themselves. Tasks are activities where the target language is used by learners for a communicative purpose and include activities in which learners work together to find missing items in a picture, directions to a place, make an airline reservation, or arrive at a medical diagnosis, and so on. These three contexts may or may not occur in a lesson and, in a single lesson, more than one context may be created. The fourth context, however, is one that occurs at least once in every lesson. In the procedural context, the teacher's aim is to transmit procedural information to the students regarding the activities that are to be accomplished during the lesson. Seedhouse argues that the organization of classroom interaction differs according to the pedagogical focus of the lesson. Thus interactional patterns of turn-taking, sequential organization, and repair are inextricably intertwined with the pedagogical context created by the teacher in what Seedhouse calls a mutually reflexive relationship.

The methodology of conversation analysis provides an insightful way of looking at conversations in classrooms, and has revealed many interesting ways in which talk is organized in classrooms. The question remains, however: what does this close analysis of classroom talks tell us about learning? Given that a methodological foundation of CA is to ask 'Why this now?' and to search for the answer to that question within the participants' talk, it is not surprising that most CA analyses of learning in language classrooms have focused on specific interactional events, often with a focus on repair initiated by the learner or the teacher and completed by the learner. Most often the focus of such events is linguistic form and learning has been construed within Sfard's 'acquisition metaphor.'

The study of language learning must surely go beyond such individual moments of acquisition of linguistic forms to consider what Catherine Brouwer and Johannes Wagner (2004) called a 'systematic and structural change of knowledge and skills' (p. 32). How can an analysis talk in classrooms provide evidence of learning over the long term rather than in a single 'light bulb moment'? And how can it provide evidence of how learners integrate knowledge of one particular aspect of the new language with related aspects – say how they integrate learning of new vocabulary with pronunciation or learning of new grammatical items with how to use them in interaction? The answer to how this may be accomplished is, first, to integrate a close CA analysis of talk in classrooms in a longitudinal study of the same learners over time and, second, to observe the learners in the same discursive practice over time. This means identifying how the participation of the same learners changes over time in different manifestations of the same discursive practice. It involves observing how the participation framework of a discursive practice changes, and how an individual learner's identity develops. It is, in effect, an application of CA to understand changes of participation and it involves recognizing the development of learners from legitimate peripheral participants to fuller participation in a community of practice. Such investigations of changing participation and developing identities have been investigated by Hanh Nguyen (2003) in her study of how students of pharmacy learned skills in advising patients and by Richard Young and Elizabeth Miller (2004) in their study of how a single learner and his ESL teacher developed skills in talking about the student's writing over four weekly writing conferences.

SUMMARY

We use language in many different ways in social interaction in order to create meanings, identities, and membership in communities for ourselves and for others. Until we experience a new and unfamiliar culture and language, we take such skills for granted. It is only by looking beyond our everyday interactions that we become aware of how complex such skills are and we marvel at how people learn them. In this unit we have presented learning skills in social interaction with the help of two metaphors: learning as acquisition of cognitive skills and learning as changing participation. The two metaphors are different ways of looking at the same phenomenon because cognition originates in social interaction and learning is both a social as well as a cognitive process. We have, nonetheless, focused here on three different frameworks for understanding learning, all of which describe changes of participation. Language socialization, situated learning, and the CA approach to foreign-language learning in classrooms are frameworks for understanding learning. We have looked first at children's participation in an adult community, then at learners' transition from peripheral participants to fuller participants in a community of practice, and finally at how CA can provide us with a methodology for understanding learner's changing identities as observed in their participation in discursive practices. In all examples of learning that we have included here, we have tried to show that while we naturally focus attention on the learner, in fact all participants – the adults, the old timers, and the teachers – change their participation to accommodate the learner's development. Without such accommodations, changes of participation are not possible.

SECTION B
Extension

Unit B1
The social nature of language and interaction

OVERVIEW OF UNIT

In Unit A1, we presented a number of different approaches to language and interaction considered as a social phenomenon, and we contrasted them with a view of language as an autonomous system independent of the context in which it is used. The approaches that we presented in Unit A1 addressed questions of who participates in the interaction, its spatial and temporal context, the means by which participants interact, and their purposes for interacting. Mikhail Bakhtin addressed these questions directly in his theory of the novel and his history of the novel's development in European literature. Ludwig Wittgenstein stressed that meanings of words are not isolated abstractions to be found in a dictionary, but must rather be interpreted according to their functions in the social activities of speakers – what he referred to as language games. Anthropologists studied the language games of exotic societies in order to understand how interactions between members of the societies created and reproduced the culture of the group. The methods anthropologists used were those of ethnography, and Dell Hymes, who pioneered work in this area, named the approach the ethnography of communication.

The reading in this unit is taken from Dell Hymes's introduction to the first collection of research papers by anthropologists inspired by the ethnography of communication. In this reading, Hymes presents his theory of the interconnection between the culture of a group and their ways of speaking, which he illustrates with copious examples from languages and cultures around the world.

From Hymes, D. (1972). 'Models of the interaction of language and social life.' In J. J. Gumperz and D. Hymes (eds), *Directions in sociolinguistics: The ethnography of communication* (pp. 35–71). New York: Holt, Rinehart and Winston.

Text B1.1
D. Hymes

Dell Hymes's influence on the study of language and interaction has been enormous, both through his own writing and through the research of his students, many of whom are cited in this book. Dell Hymes's research as a graduate student at Indiana University on the Kathlamet Chinook people grew into a lifelong interest in the relationship between ethnography and linguistics. Following academic appointments at Harvard University and the University of California, Berkeley,

D. Hymes

Hymes joined the Department of Anthropology at the University of Pennsylvania. During twenty-two years tenure at Penn he was a Professor of folklore, linguistics, sociology, and Dean of the Graduate School of Education.

★ Tasks B1.2.1–5: Before you read

➤ In this reading, Hymes never uses the names of the field with which he is most closely associated: 'ethnography of communication' or 'ethnography of speaking.' Instead, he refers to the field as 'sociolinguistics.' What do you understand by sociolinguistics?

➤ Can you think of a community in which most people use at least two different languages on a regular basis? Such communities (and the people who compose them) are called bi- or multilingual. Use the *who, where, when, how,* and *why* questions that we introduced in Unit A1 to discuss the use of the different languages in the community.

➤ Some communities and individuals claim to be monolingual, but even they can switch between different language varieties of the same language, for example between formal and informal talk, between essay writing and instant messaging. Who, where, when, how, and why do people use the different varieties?

➤ Hymes has been called a sociolinguist, an anthropologist, and a folklorist. What similarities or differences do you see among the field of sociolinguistics, anthropology, and folklore?

➤ In order to communicate, how important is it that people use the same language or the same dialect?

Diversity of speech has been singled out as the hallmark of sociolinguistics. Of this two things should be said. Underlying the diversity of speech within communities and in the conduct of individuals are systematic relations, relations that, just as social and grammatical structure, can be the object of qualitative inquiry. A long-standing failure to recognize and act on this fact puts many now in the position of wishing to apply a basic science that does not yet exist.

Diversity of speech presents itself as a problem in many sectors of life – education, national development, transcultural communication. When those concerned with such problems seek scientific cooperation, they must often be disappointed. There is as yet no body of systematic knowledge and theory. There is not even agreement on a mode of description of language in interaction with social life, one which, being explicit and of standard form, could facilitate development of knowledge and theory through studies that are full and comparable. There is not even agreement on the desirability or necessity of such a mode of description.

Bilingual or bidialectal phenomena have been the main focus of the interest that has been shown. Yet bilingualism is not in itself an adequate basis for a model or theory of the interaction of language and social life. From the standpoint of such a model or theory, bilingualism is neither a unitary phenomenon nor autonomous. The fact that two languages are present in a community or are part of a person's communicative competence is compatible with a variety of underlying functional (social) relationships. Conversely, distinct languages need not be present for the underlying relationships to find expression.

Bilingualism par excellence (e.g., French and English in Canada, Welsh and English in North Wales, Russian and French among prerevolutionary Russian nobility) is a salient, special case of the general phenomenon of linguistic repertoire. No normal person, and no normal community, is limited to a single way of speaking, to an unchanging monotony that would preclude indication of respect, insolence, mock seriousness, humor, role distance, and intimacy by switching from one mode of speech to another.

Given the universality of linguistic repertoires, and of switching among the ways of speaking they comprise, it is not necessary that the ways be distinct languages. Relationships of social intimacy or of social distance may be signaled by switching between distinct languages [Spanish: Guarani in Paraguay (Rubin 1962, 1968)]; between varieties of a single language (standard German: dialect), or between pronouns within a single variety (German Du:Sie). Segregation of religious activity may be marked linguistically by a variety whose general unintelligibility depends on being of foreign provenance (e.g., Latin, Arabic in many communities), on being a derived variety of the common language [Zuni (Newman 1964)], or on being a manifestation not identifiable at all (some glossolalia). Conversely, shift between varieties may mark a shift between distinct spheres of activity [e.g., standard Norwegian: Hemnes dialect (see Blom and Gumperz, Chapter 14)], or the formal status of talk within a single integral activity [e.g., Siane in New Guinea (Salisbury 1962)], Latin in a contemporary Cambridge University degree ceremony (e.g., *Cambridge University Reporter* 1969).

A general theory of the interaction of language and social life must encompass the multiple relations between linguistic means and social meaning. The relations within a particular community or personal repertoire are an empirical problem, calling for a mode of description that is jointly ethnographic and linguistic.

If the community's own theory of linguistic repertoire and speech is considered (as it must be in any serious ethnographic account), matters become all the more complex and interesting. Some peoples, such as the Wishram Chinook of the Columbia River in what is now the state of Washington, or the Ashanti of Nigeria, have considered infants' vocalizations to manifest a special language (on the Wishram, see Hymes 1966; on the Ashanti, Hogan 1967). For the Wishram, this language was interpretable only by men having certain guardian spirits. In such cases, the native language is in native theory a second language to everyone. Again, one community may strain to maintain mutual intelligibility with a second in the face of great differentiation of dialect, while another may declare intelligibility impossible, although the objective linguistic differences are minor. Cases indistinguishable by linguistic criteria may thus be now monolingual, now bilingual, depending on local social relationships and attitudes (discussed more fully in Hymes 1968).

Task B1.1.6: While you read

➤ These examples show how different communities categorize different forms of language. In your own community, how do you distinguish between one form

D. Hymes

of language and another? For example do you think that infants speak the same as adults? Do old people speak the same as young people? Do people from the north speak the same as people from the south? Where do you draw the line?

While it is common in a bilingual situation to look for specialization in the function, elaboration, and valuation of a language, such specialization is but an instance of a universal phenomenon, one that must be studied in situations dominantly monolingual as well. Language as such is not everywhere equivalent in role and value; speech may have different scope and functional load in the communicative economies of different societies. In our society sung and spoken communication intersect in song; pure speaking and instrumental music are separate kinds of communication. Among the Flathead Indians of Montana, speech and songs without text are separate, while songs with text, and instrumental music as an aspect of songs with text, form the intersection. Among the Maori of New Zealand instrumental music is a part of song, and both are ultimately conceived as speech. [It is interesting to note that among both the Flathead and Maori it is supernatural context that draws speech and music together, and makes of both (and of animal sounds as well among the Flathead) forms of linguistic communication.] With regard to speaking itself, while Malinowski has made us familiar with the importance of phatic communication, talk for the sake of something being said, the ethnographic record suggests that it is far from universally an important or even accepted motive (see Sapir 1949: 16, 11). The Paliyans of south India 'communicate very little at all times and become almost silent by the age of 40. Verbal, communicative persons are regarded as abnormal and often as offensive' (Gardner 1966: 398). The distribution of required and preferred silence, indeed, perhaps most immediately reveals in outline form a community's structure of speaking (see Samarin 1965; Basso 1970). Finally, the role of language in thought and culture (Whorf's query) obviously cannot be assessed for bilinguals until the role of each of their languages is assessed; but the same is true for monolinguals since in different societies language enters differentially into educational experience, transmission of beliefs, knowledge, values, practices, and conduct (see Hymes 1966). Such differences may obtain even between different groups within a single society with a single language.

★ Task B1.2.7: While you read

➤ If we are trying to understand how language functions in a particular society, why should we study silence? If we are interested in speaking, what's the point of asking under what conditions people don't speak?

What is needed, then, is a general theory and body of knowledge within which diversity of speech, repertoires, ways of speaking, and choosing among them find a natural place . . .

Its goal is to explain the meaning of language in human life, and not in the abstract, not in the superficial phrases one may encounter in essays and textbooks, but in the concrete, in actual human lives. To do that it must develop adequate modes of description and classification, to answer new questions and give familiar questions a novel focus.

Toward a Descriptive Theory

The primary concern now must be with descriptive analyses from a variety of communities. Only in relation to actual analysis will it be possible to conduct arguments analogous to those now possible in the study of grammar as to the adequacy, necessity, generality, etc., of concepts and terms. Yet some initial heuristic schema are needed if the descriptive task is to proceed. What is presented here is quite preliminary – if English and its grammarians permitted, one might call it 'toward toward a theory.' Some of it may survive the empirical and analytical work of the decade ahead.

Only a specific, explicit mode of description can guarantee the maintenance and success of the current interest in sociolinguistics. Such interest is prompted more by practical and theoretical needs, perhaps, than by accomplishment. It was the development of a specific mode of description that ensured the success of linguistics as an autonomous discipline in the United States in the twentieth century, and the lack of it (for motif and tale types are a form of indexing, distributional inference a procedure common to the human sciences) that led to the until recently peripheral status of folklore, although both had started from a similar base, the converging interest of anthropologists, and English scholars, in language and in verbal tradition.

The goal of sociolinguistic description can be put in terms of the disciplines whose interests converge in sociolinguistics. Whatever his questions about language, it is clear to a linguist that there is an enterprise, description of languages, which is central and known. Whatever his questions about society and culture, it is clear to a sociologist or an anthropologist that there is a form of inquiry (survey or ethnography) on which the answers depend. In both cases, one understands what it means to describe a language, the social relations, or culture of a community. We need to be able to say the same thing about the sociolinguistic system of a community.

Such a goal is of concern to practical work as well as to scientific theory. In a study of bilingual education, e.g., certain components of speaking will be taken into account, and the choice will presuppose a model, implicit if not explicit, of the interaction of language with social life. The significance attached to what is found will depend on understanding what is possible, what universal, what rare, what linked, in comparative perspective. What survey researchers need to know linguistically about a community, in selecting a language variety, and in conducting interviews, is in effect an application of the community's sociolinguistic description (see Hymes 1969). In turn, practical work, if undertaken with its relevance to theory in mind, can make a contribution, for it must deal directly with the interaction of language and social life, and so provides a testing ground and source of new insight.

Task B1.2.8: While you read

➤ Hymes claims that studying sociolinguistics is not just for academics but that it has a practical value, and he cites the example of bilingual education. How can the study of sociolinguistics improve bilingual education? Are there other practical uses of this kind of research?

Sociolinguistic systems may be treated at the level of national states, and indeed, of an emerging world society. My concern here is with the level of individual communities

D. Hymes

and groups. The interaction of language with social life is viewed as first of all a matter of human action, based on a knowledge, sometimes conscious, often unconscious, that enables persons to use language. Speech events and larger systems indeed have properties not reducible to those of the speaking competence of persons. Such competence, however, underlies communicative conduct, not only within communities but also in encounters between them. The speaking competence of persons may be seen as entering into a series of systems of encounter at levels of different scope.

An adequate descriptive theory would provide for the analysis of individual communities by specifying technical concepts required for such analysis, and by characterizing the forms that analysis should take. Those forms would, as much as possible, be formal, i.e., explicit, general (in the sense of observing general constraints and conventions as to content, order, interrelationship, etc.), economical, and congruent with linguistic modes of statement. Only a good deal of empirical work and experimentation will show what forms of description are required, and of those, which preferable. As with grammar, approximation to a theory for the explicit, standard analysis of individual systems will also be an approximation to part of a theory of explanation.

Among the notions with which such a theory must deal are those of speech community, speech situation, speech event, speech act, fluent speaker, components of speech events, functions of speech, etc.

★ Tasks B1.2.9–12: After you've read

➤ Hymes gives examples of language use in many different societies. Here are some of them: the Zuni, the Siane in New Guinea, the Wishram Chinook, the Ashanti of Nigeria, the Flathead Indians of Montana, and the Paliyans of south India. Find out what you can about these peoples.

➤ Hymes distinguishes between the 'macro' sociolinguistic study of national states and the 'micro' study of individual communities and groups, and he says that his concern is with the latter. What would a sociolinguistic study of national states consist of? And why does Hymes choose to focus on the micro?

➤ Hymes says that his theory must deal with 'speech community, speech situation, speech event, speech act, fluent speaker,' and so on. Define the five terms that the theory must deal with.

➤ Hymes mentions briefly the role of language in thought and culture, and refers to Benjamin Lee Whorf's theory that the language a person speaks influences the way that he or she thinks. Read Whorf's statement of his theory in his 1941 article 'The relation of habitual thought and behavior to language' at http://learn-gs.org/library/etc/1-4-whorf.pdf. What is your opinion?

UNIT SUMMARY

With this reading we have introduced a popular approach to the study of language and interaction. Hymes demonstrated the variety of codes, forms, and styles that language can take and described ways that the different varieties function in a community. The work of other scholars that we have reviewed in Unit A1 ranges from the theoretical insights of Bakhtin and Wittgenstein to the methods of microethnography and conversation analysis, in which language use is considered first and foremost as social action. Units A1 and B1 provide the groundwork for continuing study of the relationship between language and interaction in the remaining units. In the units that follow, we provide detailed analyses of language in use based on the concepts that we have introduced in this initial presentation.

Unit B2
Talk in context

OVERVIEW OF UNIT

In Unit A2, we presented several different interpretations of the word 'context.' We looked in dictionaries for the meaning of the word in ordinary language and then we considered the wider meanings that the word has accumulated in research on language and interaction. People who have studied language in interaction find it very important to understand the relationship between the two because, although we know that language forms have different meanings in different contexts, the relationship is quite complex, and an understanding of that relationship is at the basis of modern analysis by sociolinguists and linguistic anthropologists.

In fact, the quest to understand the effect of context on language in interaction leads us far beyond the normal sense of context. If we look at a slice of language in interaction, say one turn-at-talk in a conversation, the context of that slice is what happened in the interaction immediately before it: the sequential context. But Bourdieu has argued that we have to go far, far back, much further than the immediate sequential context in order to understand the values that people put on certain kinds of talk and certain ways of speaking that characterize a speaker. The context is also, most people would agree, where and when that slice of talk happened, but the where-and-when involves more than simply a physical descrip-tion of place and time; it is, rather, how the people involved in the interaction interpret that particular place at that particular time: what Hymes called the 'setting.' And also, of course, the context is the people who are speaking, but Goffman showed that if we limit our attention only to those people out of whose mouths words are articulated, then we ignore the influence on their language of other participants, some of whom may be present but not speaking and some of whom may not be physically present at all.

Although the examples that we have considered here seem to describe the influence of context (broadly understood) on language, we must also consider that we don't just talk *in* context, we also talk a context *into* existence by framing an interaction in order to provide a context for interpreting it. We sometimes do that with the collusion of other people; that is, we share a frame for interpreting an interaction with other people with whom we are interacting. But we also and often communi-cate at cross-purposes by constructing a frame for an interaction which differs from the frame that the other participants have constructed, and, although everybody understands the words that we use, they just don't get the meaning.

The richness and complexity of the interrelationship between language and context are explored further in the reading in this unit. It is a broad survey of the ways that 'context' has been interpreted in different traditions of social analysis.

From Goodwin, C., and Duranti, A. (1992). 'Rethinking context: An introduction.' In A. Duranti and C. Goodwin (eds), *Rethinking context: Language as an interactive phenomenon* (pp. 1–42). Cambridge and New York: Cambridge University Press.

Text B2.1
C. Goodwin and
A. Duranti

This reading is taken from the introductory chapter to a collection of essays by many of the leading figures in the social sciences. The authors of essays in the collection critically reexamine the concept of context from a variety of different angles and propose new ways of thinking about context in activities as diverse as face-to-face interaction, radio talk, medical diagnosis, political encounters, and the socialization of children. The collection is co-edited by Alessandro Duranti and Charles Goodwin. Alessandro Duranti is professor of anthropology at UCLA. His main areas of research are political discourse, agency and intentionality, orality and literacy, the history of linguistic anthropology, and jazz aesthetics. He has carried out fieldwork in Western Samoa and the United States. Charles Goodwin is professor of applied linguistics at UCLA. His research focuses on many aspects of language and interaction, including the co-construction of meaning, participation frameworks, the ethnography of science, aphasia as a social process, the social organization of perception through language use, as well as discourse in the professions. For many years he has videotaped daily life in the home of a man who, because of a stroke in the left hemisphere of his brain, could speak only three words: *Yes, No,* and *And.* Despite the severity of his language impairment this man was able to function as a powerful actor in conversation by getting others to produce the talk that he needed.

Tasks B2.1.1–3: Before you read

➤ Ask someone to tell you a story, and then write the story down. What is the difference between the live event of story telling and the transcription that you made of the story?

➤ Now tell the same story to someone else, and ask them to write it down. What is the difference between the way that you transcribed the story and the new transcription? Are the differences between the two transcriptions due to the two different story tellers?

➤ Study carefully the portrait of Elvis in Figure A2.1. Close the book and try to reproduce the picture as accurately as possible. When you have finished, compare your version with Figure A2.1. What are the differences between the figure you drew and the figure in A2.1? What are the differences between the background that you drew and the background in Figure A2.1?

In order to explore differences in approach to context it is useful to begin with a tentative description of the phenomenon, even if this will ultimately be found

C. Goodwin and
A. Duranti

Extension

inadequate. Consider first the behavior that context is being invoked to interpret. Typically this will consist of talk of some type. However, simply referring to an event being examined as talk is inadequate. Thus, talk can be seen as hierarchically organized, and different notions of context may be appropriate to different levels of organization . . . For example in the present volume Bauman analyzes both how prose-narration frames verse within a story, and how talk between teller and recipient frames the story as a whole as an event of a particular kind. Talk **within** the story (the prose frame) creates context for other talk (the verse), while yet other speech creates an appropriate context for the story itself. The **prose narration** in this story is thus at the same time, but from different analytical perspectives, **context** for something embedded within it, and talk that is itself **contextualized** by other talk. Use of the word 'talk' to identify one element in this process can thus lead to confusion. From a slightly different perspective behavior that is interpreted by reference to a context is by no means restricted to talk. Indeed just as nonvocal behavior can create context for talk . . . so talk can create context for the appropriate interpretation of nonverbal behavior . . . We will therefore use the term **focal event** to identify the phenomenon being contextualized. More generally an analyst can start with the observation, as Kendon does in this volume, that participants treat each other's stream of activity (talk, movement, etc.) in a selective way. The question then becomes **what** in each other's behavior do they treat as 'focal' and what as 'background'. The job of the analyst is to delineate this.

When the issue of **context** is raised it is typically argued that the focal event cannot be properly understood, interpreted appropriately, or described in a relevant fashion, unless one looks beyond the event itself to other phenomena (for example cultural setting, speech situation, shared background assumptions) within which the event is embedded, or alternatively that features of the talk itself invoke particular background assumptions relevant to the organization of subsequent interaction . . . The context is thus a frame (Goffman 1974) that surrounds the event being examined and provides resources for its appropriate interpretation:

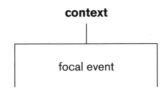

context

focal event

The notion of context thus involves a fundamental juxtaposition of two entities: (1) a focal event; and (2) a field of action within which that event is embedded . . .

Figure and ground

One key way in which context and focal event differ is in their perceptual salience. Generally the focal event is regarded as the official focus of the participants' attention, while features of the context are not highlighted in this way, but instead treated as background phenomena. The focal event is placed on center stage, while context constitutes the stage itself. In line with this, the boundaries, outlines, and structure of the focal event are characteristically delimited with far more explicitness and clarity than are contextual phenomena. Focal event and context thus seem to stand in a

C. Goodwin and
A. Duranti

fundamental **figure–ground** relationship to each other, a point developed in considerable detail by Hanks in this volume. These themes constitute the main focus for Kendon's chapter as well, in which he provides quite detailed analysis of how the *main attentional track* in an encounter is sustained, and indeed shaped, by ongoing interactive work in a *disattend track*, 'a stream of signs which is itself excluded from the content of the activity but which serves as a means of regulating it, bounding, articulating and qualifying its various components and phases.' Viewing the relationship between focal event and context in this fashion demonstrates its central relevance to one of the key issues that has emerged in contemporary studies of language and interaction: the use of **background information** to produce and understand action, and the question of how such background information is organized, recognized, invoked, and understood. We want to use the perspective advocated by Hanks as a point of departure for discussing some of the reasons why the analysis of context has proved so difficult and intransigent.

Focusing on the figure and ignoring the ground

In our view the fundamental asymmetry of the **figure–ground** relationship of focal event and its context has had enormous consequences on how these phenomena have been studied. First, differences in salience are accompanied by corresponding differences in structural clarity. The effect of this is that the focal event, with its far more clearly articulated structure, receives the lion's share of analytic attention while methods for analyzing, or even describing, the more amorphous background of context are not given anywhere near the same amount of emphasis. Thus linguists have taken the segmental structure of language as the key focal phenomenon that is relevant to the production and organization of talk. One result of this is a vast disparity between the incredible amount of work that has been done within formal linguistics on language structure, and the very small amount of research that has focused explicitly on the organization of context. With the exception of artificial intelligence researchers interested in simulation of discourse-based inferential processes . . ., formal linguists have been skeptical of psychologically oriented studies of mental units of behavior such as scripts, plans, and other such notions. . . . Indeed this disparity is found not only in formal analysis but also in the methodology available for simply describing the phenomena being examined. For thousands of years human beings have put great ingenuity and effort into the development of methods for accurately describing and writing down relevant distinctions within the stream of speech. Comparable attention to precise description of the context of a speech situation has been almost non-existent, and indeed a major task facing contemporary students of context is uncovering what are its constitutive features and how they are to be described, In our opinion this mixture of sharp, sustained focus on the details of language structure combined with a complementary neglect of its context is not accidental, but rather strong support for the arguments made by Hanks and Kendon about the intrinsic figure–ground relationship of focal event and context.

Extracting the focal event from its context for analysis

The structural articulation of the focal event is matched by an apparent clarity in its shape, outline, and boundaries. The effect of this is that it becomes easy for analysts

C. Goodwin and
A. Duranti

to view the focal event as a self-contained entity that can be cut out from its surrounding context and analyzed in isolation, a process that effectively treats the context as irrelevant to the organization of the focal event. Stories provide a classic example. In much research in anthropology, folklore, and sociolinguistics, stories have been analyzed as self-contained packages, entities that can be nicely 'collected' in an exotic setting and then safely transported back to the laboratory of the researcher. It is tacitly assumed that the process of removing the story from the setting in which it actually emerged and placing it in a new and often radically different context, the analytic collection of the investigator, does little if any damage to its intrinsic structure. Indeed a number of features of narrative readily lead to such a view. Thus a story told in one setting can be performed in another (as speakers demonstrate when they retell stories). Moreover, participants themselves often delimit the boundaries of a story . . . so that it stands out from other talk as a coherent entity. Many analysts have therefore found it both fruitful and unproblematic to devote their energies to description and analysis of the internal structure of stories while ignoring the interaction through which they were in fact told in the first place. The work of Lévi-Strauss (1963) on myth provides a classic example, although the chapters by Bauman and Basso in this volume suggest that much of what is important in a story or myth is not the 'content' but its inter-textuality . . . In brief it is very convenient to be able to extract speech forms from local contexts of production, a process that is facilitated by the clarity with which an event such as a story can be perceived as a discrete, self-contained unit.

There is however a range of work focusing on both the contributions made by the audience to a telling (see for example the special issue of *Text* on 'The Audience as Co-Author' [Volume 6.3, 1986] edited by Duranti and Brenneis, C. Goodwin 1984, Sacks 1974, and Schieffelin 1986) and on how the internal structure of stories reflects their embeddedness within larger interactive processes . . . that calls into question whether it is indeed appropriate to analyze stories in isolation from the local indigenous circumstances of their production. In the present volume Bauman demonstrates the major analytic gains that can be made by going beyond traditional assumptions about the ease with which stories can be extracted from their local context. By including within the scope of his analysis not only the story, but also the process of how it was told to the researcher, he is able to reexamine and reconceptualize a range of concepts that lie at the very heart of folklore, including **contextualization** (here approached as an active process), **tradition**, and **genre**, placing them within a dialogic, interactive framework.

 Tasks B2.1.4–8: After you've read

➤ Goodwin and Duranti distinguish between a focal event and a field of action within which that event is embedded. We have given examples of the distinction in representational painting such as the portrait of Elvis. Can you think of sports in which you can make the same distinction?

➤ Duranti and Goodwin (1992) argue that participants in interaction organize their attention along three tracks: '(1) a main-line, story-line track that is the official focus of attention; (2) a directional track that provides organization for the main-line track; and (3) a disattend track consisting of events that are officially treated as irrelevant to the activity in progress' (p. 324). Re-read the discussion of the different social roles that hearers and speakers can play in Section A2.1.2 and discuss participant roles in terms of these three attentional tracks.

➤ What are the advantages and disadvantages of extracting speech forms from the contexts in which they were produced?

➤ The development of recording technology has helped to expand the idea of context. At first, there was only writing; then came tape-recording of sounds and, later, pictures. How has recording technology helped to expand the notion of context? How could future development of technology represent contexts such as habitus and conversational frames?

➤ Write a new dictionary definition of 'context' that incorporates the dimensions of context that Goodwin and Duranti have described in this reading.

UNIT SUMMARY

This reading has laid out clearly some of the complexities of the relationship between language and context. Goodwin and Duranti used the visual trope that we developed in Unit A2 of the association between language and context as the relationship between figure and ground. They lamented the lack of attention that researchers have paid to the ground, i.e., the context. We hope in this unit and in Unit A2 to have restored some balance to the picture.

The importance of context in understanding language in interaction should now be clear, but we must develop a methodology for analyzing context that approaches in systematicity and rigor the methods that linguists have used in the analysis of language. In the next two units, we will present an ecological methodology for analyzing language in context. The figure in the figure–ground relation is considered as a set of linguistic and interactional resources and the context is defined as discursive practice. Participants employ linguistic and interactional resources to construct discursive practices, and the methodology is ecological in the sense that, just as the configuration of resources determines the discursive practice, so the practice entails the employment of those resources.

Unit B3
Interactional resources

OVERVIEW OF UNIT

In Unit A3, we described two methodologies for analyzing talk-in-interaction: systemic functional grammar and conversation analysis. The starting point of a systemic analysis is a text, examined by an analyst out of the context in which the text was created. In contrast, the context of interaction is at the heart of the fundamental question in conversation analysis: Why does this action happen in this conversation right now? Both approaches can provide insights into the relationship between language and interaction: The systemic approach makes tight connections between linguistic structure and the semantic functions which those structures serve, while in conversation analysis questions of social identity, preference, and stance are foregrounded.

The two readings in this unit develop these themes further. The first is an introduction to systemic functional grammar which focuses on the general principle of constituency in systemic analysis. The second is a discussion of the important difference between the generic linguistic resources that are available to participants and the actual language they use to create social identities and emotional stances in a particular interaction.

Text B3.1
M. A. K. Halliday
and
C. M. I. M.
Matthiessen

From Halliday, M. A. K., and Matthiessen, C. M. I. M. (2004). *An introduction to functional grammar* **(3rd ed.) (pp. 3–9). London: Arnold.**

Michael Halliday created a system of linguistic analysis that took as its starting point meaning rather than linguistic form. His radical approach, known as Systemic Functional Grammar (SFG) or Systemic Functional Linguistics (SFL), has become very influential especially in the field of education. It is an approach that is rooted in the general theories of language in context that were proposed by J. R. Firth and in the analysis of the communicative functions of language that were but forward by a group of linguists in Europe known as The Prague School. In SFG, the function of language is central (what language does, and how it does it), in preference to more structural approaches, which place the formal elements of language and their combinations as central. Halliday's approach is thus quite distinct from the formal theories of linguistics that are currently dominant in the United States and associated with Leonard Bloomfield and Noam Chomsky. Because of Halliday's appointments to chairs of linguistics in London and Sydney, there are large numbers of linguists who do research in systemic functional grammar in Britain and Australia, but relatively few in the United States.

Halliday has published widely, but since its first edition in 1985, *An introduction to functional grammar* has been the most extensive explanation of the theory and its methods. The reading below is taken from the third edition of *An introduction to functional grammar* published in 2004, which has been updated by Halliday in collaboration with Christian Matthiessen, professor of linguistics at Macquarie University in Sydney.[1]

Tasks B3.1.1–3: Before you read

➤ In Unit A2, we discussed Dr Martin Luther King's 'I have a dream' speech. Imagine that you heard Dr King speak on the National Mall in Washington, DC, in 1963. What is the difference between that experience and the experience of reading the speech or listening to a recording of it many years later?

➤ Many sacred texts are reports of a conversation that happened between a religious teacher and his disciples. For example, one of the texts in the Buddhist tradition is 'The Buddha Speaks of Amitabha Sutra,' in which the Buddha tells his disciple Shariputra about a world in the West called 'Utmost Happiness.' Find other examples of texts that are reports of dialogues from religious traditions that you know.

Figure B3.1 Little Miss Muffet. Source: http://www.landofmagic.co.uk/Picture%20Land.htm

➤ Review the definition of 'constituency' in Section A3.1.1. How could you apply the concept of constituency to a visual image such as Figure B3.1?

1.1 Text and grammar

When people speak or write, they produce text. The term 'text' refers to any instance of language, in any medium, that makes sense to someone who knows the language ... To a grammarian, text is a rich, many-faceted phenomenon that 'means' in many different ways. It can be explored from many different points of view. But we can distinguish two main angles of vision: one, focus on the text as an object in its own right; two, focus on the text as an instrument for finding out about something else. Focusing on text as an object, a grammarian will be asking questions such as: Why does the text mean what it does (to me, or to anyone else)? Why is it valued as it is? Focusing on text as instrument, the grammarian will be asking what the text reveals about the system of the language in which it is spoken or written. These two perspectives are clearly complementary: we cannot explain why a text means what it does, with all the various readings and values that may be given to it, except by relating it to the linguistic system as a whole; and equally, we cannot use it as a window on the system unless we understand what it means and why. But the text has a different status in each case: either viewed as **artefact**, or else viewed as **specimen**.

The text itself may be lasting or ephemeral, momentous or trivial, memorable or soon forgotten. Here are three examples of text in English.

Text 1–1

Today all of us do, by our presence here, and by our celebrations in other parts of our country and the world, confer glory and hope to newborn liberty.

Out of the experience of an extraordinary human disaster that lasted too long, must be born a society of which all humanity will be proud. Our daily deeds as ordinary South Africans must produce an actual South African reality that will reinforce humanity's belief in justice, strengthen its confidence in the nobility of the human soul and sustain all our hopes for a glorious life for all.

All this we owe both to ourselves and to the peoples of the world who are so well represented here today.

Text 1–2

Cold power is the **ideal brand for any family**.

We understand that there is more than one thing you want to achieve out of every wash load.

As such, we have developed a formula capable of achieving a wide range of benefits for all types of wash loads.

Text 1–3

'And we've been trying different places around the island that – em, a couple of years ago we got on to this place called the Surai in East Bali and we just go back there now every time. It is –'

'Oh I've heard about this.'
'Have you heard about it? Oh.'
'Friends have been there.'
'It is the most wonderful wonderful place. Fabulous.'

M. A. K.
Halliday and
C. M. I. M.
Matthiessen

Text 1–3 was a spontaneous spoken text, which we are able to transpose into writing because it was recorded on audio tape. Text 1–2 is a written text, which we could (if we wanted to) read aloud. Text 1–1 is more complex: it was probably composed in writing, perhaps with some spoken rehearsal; but it was written in order to be spoken, and to be spoken on an all-important public occasion (Nelson Mandela's inaugural speech as President, 10 May 1994).

When grammarians say that from their point of view all texts are equal, they are thinking of them as specimens. If we are interested in explaining the grammar of English, all these three texts illustrate numerous grammatical features of the language, in meaningful functional contexts, all equally needing to be taken into account. Seen as artefacts, on the other hand, these texts are far from equal. Text 1–1 constituted an important moment in modern human history, and may have left its imprint on the language in a way that only a very few highly-valued texts are destined to do. But here, too, there is a complementarity. Text 1–1 has value because we also understand texts like 1–2 and 1–3; not that we compare them, of course, but that each text gets its meaning by selecting from the same meaning-making resources. What distinguishes any one text is the way these resources are deployed.

Our aim in this book has been to describe and explain the meaning-making resources of modern English, going as far in detail as is possible within one medium-sized volume. When deciding what parts of the grammar to cover, and how far to go in discussion of theory, we have had in mind those who want to use their understanding of grammar in analysing and interpreting texts. This in turn means recognizing that the contexts for analysis of discourse are numerous and varied – educational, social, literary, political, legal, clinical and so on; and in all these the text may be being analysed as specimen or as artefact, or both (specimen here might mean specimen of a particular functional variety, or *register*, such as 'legal English'). What is common to all these pursuits is that they should be grounded in an account of the grammar that is coherent, comprehensive and richly dimensioned. To say this is no more than to suggest that the *grammatics* – the model of grammar – should be as rich as the grammar itself . . . If the account seems complex, this is because the grammar is complex – it has to be, to do all the things we make it do for us. It does no service to anyone in the long run if we pretend that *semiosis* – the making and understanding of meaning – is a simpler matter than it really is.

Task B3.1.4: While you read

➤   Halliday's distinction between text as artifact and text as specimen recalls the distinction that Bakhtin made between utterance and sentence. (See Unit A1.) What are the reasons why these scholars want to make this distinction? And can you think of examples that illustrate it.

M. A. K.
Halliday and
C. M. I. M.
Matthiessen

1.1.1 *Constituency*: (1) *phonological*

Perhaps the most noticeable dimension of language is its compositional structure, known as 'constituency'. If we listen to any of these texts – to any text, in fact – in its spoken form we will hear continuous melody with rising and falling pitch, and with certain moments of prominence marked by either relatively rapid pitch changes or extended pitch intervals. These moments of prominence define a snatch of melody – a melodic unit, or **line**; and within this melodic progression we will be able to pick up a more or less regular beat, defining some rhythmic unit, or **foot**. We can perhaps recognize that the 'line' and the 'foot' of our traditional verse metres are simply regularized versions of these properties of ordinary speech.

Each foot, in turn, is made up of a number of **syllables**; and each syllable is composed of two parts, one of which enables it to rhyme. We refer to this rhyming segment, simply, as the **rhyme**; the preceding segment to which it is attached is called the **onset**. Both onset and rhyme can be further analysed as sequences of consonants and vowels: consonant and vowel **phonemes**, in technical parlance.

The stretch of speech is continuous; we stop and pause for breath from time to time, or hesitate before an uncertain choice of word, but such pauses play no part in the overall construction. None of these units – melodic line (or 'tone group'), foot (or 'rhythm group'), syllable or phoneme – has clearly identifiable boundaries, some definite point in time where it begins and ends. Nevertheless, we can hear the patterns that are being created by the spoken voice. There is a form of order here that we can call **constituency**, whereby larger units are made up out of smaller ones: a line out of feet; a foot out of syllables; a syllable out of sequences of phonemes (perhaps with 'sub-syllable' intermediate between the two). We refer to such a hierarchy of units, related by constituency, as a **rank scale**, and to each step in the hierarchy as one **rank** . . .

What we have been setting up here is the rank scale for the sound system of English: the **phonological** rank scale. Every language has some rank scale of phonological constituents, but with considerable variation in how the constituency is organized (cf. Halliday, 1992, on Mandarin): in the construction of syllables, in the rhythmic and melodic patterns, and in the way the different variables are integrated into a functioning whole. We get a good sense of the way the sounds of English are organized when we analyse children's verses, or 'nursery rhymes'; these have evolved in such a way as to display the patterns in their most regularized form. Little Miss Muffet can serve as an example (Figure 1–1).

	foot			foot			foot			foot		
	syll.	syll.	syll.	syll.	syll.	syll.	syll.	syll.	syll.	syll.	syll.	syll.
line	Lit	tle	Miss	Muf	fet		sat	on	a	tuf	fet	
line	Eat	ing	her	curds	and		whey					There
line	come	a	big	spi	der	which	sat	down	be	side	her	And
line	frigh	tened	Miss	Muf	fet	a	way					

Figure 1–1 Example of phonological constituency

We will say more about phonology in Section 1.2 below. Meanwhile, we turn to the notion of constituency in writing.

Task B3.1.5: While you read

> Examine Halliday's presentation of phonological constituency in Figure 1–1. In the text, he mentions two phonological ranks below syllable: onset and rhyme. Add these two ranks to the phonological analysis in Figure 1–1.

1.1.2 *Constituency*: (2) *graphological*

As writing systems evolved, they gradually came to model the constituent hierarchy of spoken language, by developing a rank scale of their own. Thus, in modern English writing, we have the **sentence** (beginning with a capital letter and ending with a full stop), **subsentence** (bounded by some intermediate punctuation mark: colon, semicolon or comma), **word** (bounded by spaces) and **letter**. Figure 1–2 shows the same text written in orthographic conventional form.

The constituent structure is represented by a combination of **spelling** (combining letters to form words) and **punctuation** (using special signs, and also the case of the letter, to signal boundaries . . .). The system is more complex than we have illustrated here, in three respects: (1) word boundaries are somewhat fuzzy, and there is a special punctuation mark, the hyphen, brought in to allow for the uncertainty, for example, *frying pan*, *fryingpan*, *frying-pan*; (2) there is a further rank in the hierarchy of sub-sentences, with colon and semicolon representing a unit higher than that marked off by a comma; (3) there is at least one rank above the sentence, namely the paragraph. These do not affect the principle of graphological constituency; but they raise the question of why these further orders of complexity evolved.

The simple answer is: because writing is not the representation of speech sound. Although every writing system is related to the sound system of its language in systematic and non-random ways (exactly how the two are related varies from one language to another), the relationship is not a direct one. There is another level of organization in language to which both the sound system and the writing system are related, namely the level of **wording**, or 'lexicogrammar'. (We shall usually refer to this

		word	word	word	word	word	word	word
sent	subsent	Little	Miss	Muffet	sat	on	a	tuffet,
	subsent	eating	her	curds	and	whey.		
sent	subsent	There	came	a	big	spider,		
	subsent	which	sat	down	beside	her,		
	subsent	and	frightened	Miss	Muffet	away.		

Figure 1–2 Examples of graphological constituency

simply as 'grammar', as in the title of the book; but it is important to clarify from the start that grammar and vocabulary are not two separate components of a language – they are just the two ends of a single continuum.) The sound system and the writing system are the two modes of **expression** by which the lexicogrammar of a language is represented, or **realized** (to use the technical term).

Since language evolved as speech, in the life of the human species, all writing systems are in origin parasitic on spoken language; and since language develops as speech, in the life of every hearing individual, this dependency is constantly being re-enacted. Even with the deaf, whose first language uses the visual channel, this is not writing; Sign is more closely analogous to spoken than to written language. But as writing systems evolve, and as they are mastered and put into practice by the growing child, they take on a life of their own, reaching directly into the wording of the language rather than accessing the wording via the sound; and this effect is reinforced by the functional complementarity between speech and writing. Writing evolved in its own distinct functional contexts of book keeping and administration as 'civilizations' first evolved – it never was just 'speech written down'; and (at least until very recent advances in technology) the two have continued to occupy complementary domains.

So, still keeping for the moment to the notion of constituency, as a way in to exploring how language is organized, let us look at the phenomenon of constituency in lexicogrammar. This will help to explain the principles that lie behind this kind of hierarchic construction, and to understand what is common to different manifestations (such as melodic unit of speech, the line of metric verse and the sub-sentence of the written text).

 Task B3.1.6: While you read

> In Figure A3.2, the initial page of St Mark's Gospel in the Lindisfarne Gospels, boundaries between words are very fuzzy. Do a graphological analysis of the constituents of the text in order to identify the graphological constituents. They are probably different from the constituents of paragraph, sentence, and word into which we analyze constituency in modern texts.

1.1.3 *Constituency*: (3) *lexicogrammatical*

We will visit Little Miss Muffet just one more time. The punctuation of the text, in the previous section, clearly indicated its graphological composition, in terms of sentences, subsentences and words. When we now break down the same text into its grammatical constituents (Figure 1–3), we find a high degree of correspondence across the higher units: each written sentence is one **clause complex**, and each sub-sentence is one **clause**. This is obviously not a coincidence: the two sets of units are related.

But they are not identical; the correspondence will not always hold. Little Miss Muffet evolved as a spoken text, so when someone decided to write it down they chose to punctuate it according to the grammar. In Nelson Mandela's text, on the other hand, the first (written) sentence is grammatically a single clause – but it is written as five subsentences. Here, the punctuation is telling us more about the phonological structure (the division into tone groups) than about the grammar. There is nothing unusual about this: many writers punctuate phonologically rather than

		word group	word group	word group	word group
clause complex	clause	little miss muffet	sat	on	a tuffet
	clause	eating	her curds and whey		
clause complex	clause	there	came	a big spider	
	clause	which	sat down	beside	her
	clause	and	frightened	miss muffet	away

M. A. K.
Halliday and
C. M. I. M.
Matthiessen

Figure 1–3 Example of grammatical constituency

grammatically, or in some mixture of the two. And there are many kinds of written text that are carefully punctuated into sentences and sub-sentences (i.e. with full stops, colons and commas) but containing no clauses or clause complexes at all, like the following.

Text 1–4

CLASSIFIED RATES

£5.10 per line (average six words per line); display £12 per single column centimetre; box numbers £5.

Discounts: 20 per cent for four insertions, 30 per cent for eight insertions, 50 per cent for twelve insertions

Prices do not include VAT.

London Review of Books, 28 Little Russell Street, London WC1A 2HN.

It is often uncertain whether someone writing about grammar is talking about graphological units or grammatical units. To avoid this confusion we shall call them by different names (as has become the usual practice in systemic functional grammar). We will use **sentence** and **sub-sentence** to refer only to units of orthography. In referring to grammar we will use the term **clause**. When a number of clauses are linked together grammatically we talk of a **clause complex** (each single linkage within a clause complex can be referred to as one **clause nexus**).

Below the clause, the situation is rather different. Graphologically, sub-sentences consist of words – there is no written unit in between. The word is also a grammatical unit; and here we shall continue to use the same term for both, because the correspondence is close enough (both categories, orthographic word and grammatical word, are equally fuzzy!). Grammatically, however, the constituent of a clause is not, in fact, a word; it is either a phrase or a word group (which we shall call simply

M. A. K.
Halliday and
C. M. I. M.
Matthiessen

group from now on). (We have not shown phrases in Little Miss Muffet; there are two examples, *on a tuffet* and *beside her* . . . Grammatically, a word functions as a constituent of a group.

Words have constituents of their own, **morphemes**. These are not marked off in the writing system; sometimes they can be identified as the parts of a written word, for example *eat + ing, curd + s, frighten + ed*, or else recognized as traces of its history (*beside, away* were both originally dimorphemic). We shall not be dealing systematically with word morphology in this book . . . but it illustrates the limits of compositional structure in language (and hence the problems of trying to explain all of grammar in constituency terms). Grammarians used to worry a lot about whether to analyse *sat, came* as consisting of two morphemes (*sit/come* plus an abstract morpheme 'past' realized as a vowel change); but this is a problem created by the theory. Composition is an important semogenic (meaning-creating) resource; but it should not be allowed to dominate our thinking about grammar.

 Tasks B3.1.7–12: After you've read

> The rank scale of lexicogrammar can be represented as:
>   clause
>   phrase/group
>   word
>   morpheme

> Constituents at each rank can be linked together as complexes. In Figure 1–3, Halliday shows clause complexes. Can you think of examples of complexes of phrases, groups, words, or morphemes?

> Do an analysis of the lexicogrammatical constituents in Text 1–4.

> Do an analysis of the lexicogrammatical constituents of *Come!*

> Identify the morphemes in *Fashionably late.*

> All the examples in this unit so far have been of oral or written language, but the principle of constituency extends to other semiotic systems, including sign language. If you know a sign language, try to do a constituent analysis of how meaningless sign forms are organized into meaningful signs. This is similar to a phonological analysis of a spoken language.

> Compare the constituency structures of other languages that you know with English (say Chinese and German). Do some ranks in the lexicogrammatical scale of one language seem to do much more work than the same ranks in another language?

From Hall, J. K. (1995). '(Re)creating our worlds with words: A socio-historical perspective of face-to-face interaction.' *Applied Linguistics*, 16(2), 206–232.

Text B3.2
J. K. Hall

Joan Kelly Hall is professor of applied linguistics and education at Pennsylvania State University. She was one of the first applied linguists to recognize that it was important for language teachers and learners to understand the nature of social interaction. Like Halliday, Hall conceived of language as a set of resources, but she went further than Halliday's focus on linguistic function to consider the role that language-in-interaction plays in creating participants' identities and communities of learning. Like Halliday, Hall believed that the starting point for understanding interaction was not language; but where Halliday analyzed how language created meanings, Hall started her analysis with what she called interactive practices. Within this framework, she highlighted one very important feature of the discursive practice approach that we discuss in Unit A4: There is no fixed meaning in our utterances; rather, meaning is negotiated by participants online in each instance of a practice. Although most interactive practices are routine and therefore the configuration of linguistics and interactional resources that participants bring to a practice is well established as a genre, those same resources can be employed in ways by which participants create new meanings, individual identities, and personal stances that break the rules of the genre. This play between the pre-existing genre and the utterances of the moment, Hall called a sociohistorical perspective on face-to-face interaction.

Tasks B3.2.1–3: Before you read

➤ List some activities that you do very often. Which activities do you do with other people? Which activities involve language? Activities that you do regularly face-to-face with other people, Hall calls 'interactive practices.'

➤ In those interactive practices, are there language forms (words, sentences, pronunciations, modes of meaning) that you almost always use?

➤ Think again of the same interactive practices from the perspective of the interactional resources described in Unit A3. What are the interactional resources (the action sequences, the patterns of turn-taking and repair, and the participation frameworks) that participants employ in these practices?

A sociohistorical perspective of face-to-face interaction

Interactive practices

Much of our daily lives at home, at school, in the workplace, and in the community is taken up with talk. We must interact with others in order to accomplish whatever goals we have set, to become involved in those set by others, or to negotiate and work through a set of mutually defined goals. In our interactive participation we simultaneously develop two stances: we become affiliated to the social groups important to the accomplishment of our everyday lives at the same time that we

J. K. Hall

develop a unique stance towards ours and others' roles in these groups. And, contrary to some commonly held assumptions, our participation does not involve the individual creation of spontaneous, and freely chosen discourse, independent of any social (or other) constraints. Rather, our talk is comprised of interactive practices, structured moments of face-to-face interaction – differently enacted and differently valued – whereby individuals, come together to create, articulate, and manage their collective histories via the uses of sociohistorically defined and valued resources (Wertsch 1990, 1991; Hall 1993). Our participation in interactive practices involves the interplay of (at the minimum) three mutually-shaping spheres: a set of generic resources with the concomitant expectations of their uses (e.g. the practice(s) and goals they invoke), our social identities and those of the other participants, and the spatio-temporal conditions of the moment.

Interactive resources

One of the spheres influencing our participation in interactive practices is comprised of generic interactive resources. Specific aggregates of these resources are sets of prototypical uses, patterned regularities of use, or what Bakhtin eloquently terms 'crystallizations of events' (Morson and Emerson 1989, 1990), that correspond to typical interactive practices and typical themes, and include the accumulated, historical aspects of the practices to which they are connected. In their habits of use, constructed by their very uses in locally-situated moments of past time by particular groups of interactants, these sets of resources develop particular visions of the world, 'specific complexes of values, definitions of the situation, and meanings of possible actions' (Morson and Emerson 1989: 22), and come to any present interactive moment already imbued with these sedimented, historical meanings and attitudes. Elements particular to engagement in face-to-face interaction and which form in varying arrangements these aggregations, or genres, include such essential linguistically- and paralinguistically-instantiated resource as lexical and syntactic choices, participation structures act-sequences, and prosodic and other formulae to signal opening, transitional, and closing moves (e.g. Schegloff 1982; Jefferson 1990; Ford 1993).

★ Task B3.2.4: While you read

➤ In the preceding paragraphs, Hall introduces two important concepts that we develop throughout this book. The first is the idea of interactive practices, which we discuss in detail in Unit A4, under the heading of 'Defining Discursive Practice.' The second concept that Hall introduces here is the idea that participants use interactive resources in face-to-face interaction. In Unit A3, we discuss further linguistic and interactional resources that participants employ in order to construct practices.

Our uses of these resources at any particular moment of time are what Bakhtin (Morson and Emerson 1990) calls utterances, concrete responses to the conditions of the moment. In making these responses, we are ventriloquating (Wertsch 1991), i.e. using the conventional meanings of the resources available to us in the creation of our own voices. Our utterances have two simultaneously enacted functions: we (re)create the contexts of their uses by invoking the genres to which the utterances typically, i.e. sociohistorically, belong at the same time that we create our own voices in relation to the expectations of the uses of the resources and to the other participants with whom we are interacting. It is important to note that neither the generic resources nor our uses of them are reducible to the other. They exist as inseparable parts of a whole, of the dialogue, and are in a constant state of dialogic simultaneity (Bakhtin 1990; Morson and Emerson 1989). In other words, we can only come to understand the conventional meanings of the resources – genres – in terms of how they are used at particular moments of time – our utterances; and, conversely, our understanding of locally situated moves is developed only in terms of their positioning against their sociohistorical expectations. The following is an example of the dialogue that exists between the resources and our uses of them:

Husband: Take these shirts to the cleaners tomorrow, will you?
Wife: (stands and gives military salute by raising hand to forehead) Yes, sir.

The military salute and its accompanying response has a conventional meaning attached to it. Its use recognizes the saluted as a superior, and as such signifies, as well as creates an unequal status relationship between the person being saluted and whoever is doing the saluting. In this case, the wife uses its conventional meaning in such a way as to create a similar relation between her spouse and herself. Her move has two possible explanations: she is either (1) using the meaning of the resource *conventionally* to both indicate her understanding of and (re)create the unequal status relationship that exists between them; or (2) using the meaning of the resource *creatively* to indicate her stance, be it of humor or offense, towards the request, a response which can be either to the request itself or to its pragmatic realization – i.e. more versus less directly stated. Either way, there is a *dialogue* obtaining between the conventional meaning of and response to the salute, and its use by the woman at a particular moment, the investigation of which can tell us something about these participants, about their relationship, and about how each views her/his place within that situation. Viewed in this way, our moves take on a sociopolitical dimension in that by our every interactive move, consciously or not, we are sustaining or undermining our stance toward others, toward the world, and toward what we believe our social positioning is within that world. And, in this way, we make locally, i.e. interactively, visible the ideologies by which we live our lives (Thompson 1987).

According to Bakhtin (1990), then, consideration in the study of language use and meaning in interaction is neither the constructed system of elements removed from their practices and community of users nor, at the other extreme, the locally situated uses of language, whose meanings are assumed to be 'created on the spot', unbridled by any a priori factors, and thus equally shared among all participants. Instead, the concern is a dual one: it is the simultaneous investigation of the *dialogue* obtaining between the conventional, i.e. historical, meanings of the linguistic and paralinguistic resources and the constellation of practical strategies that interactants create with them in response to the conditions of any spatio-temporally bounded interactive moment. Bakhtin terms such study *translinguistics* (Gardiner 1992) and defines the dialogue as the negotiated relation between the two interdependent spheres which are in a continual state of 'intense and essential axiological interaction' (Bakhtin 1990: 10). Language study is, in other words, concerned with the concomitant focus on the conventionality of the resources being used and the specific ways in which the interactants use these resources to respond to and create specific locally-situated conditions. He argues specifically for giving particular attention to the study of

Extension

everyday, *ordinary* practices in which one engages, as he claims that it is in our everyday world where life's most fundamental meanings are created, and social change and individual innovation are born.

 ### Task B3.2.5: While you read

➤ Hall proposes a sociohistorical perspective on talk-in-interaction based on the theories of Mikhail Bakhtin. Hall borrows several terms from Bakhtin to describe this perspective. Refer to the discussions of Bakhtin's work in Unit A1.1 and Task C1.1 in order to determine what *utterance*, *dialogue*, and *genre* mean in the context of Hall's article.

It might be helpful to juxtapose the sociohistorical perspective of interaction with two common approaches to the study of language and meaning, the formal and the sociocultural, in order to develop a clearer understanding of its particular focus. In a formal perspective of language, which is arguably the view that has been more commonly attended to in SLL/A [second language learning and acquisition] circles, the various spheres are defined and handled as separate and unequal entities; genres are perceived as ideal models or fixed types of language use, while performances are treated as mere, and usually flawed, instantiations of these idealized models. The elements typically associated with various genres, for the most part defined as the syntactic and semantic pieces of the utterances, are abstracted from the practices with which they are associated, ranked in terms of what is thought to be some unambiguous and inherent order, and treated as such. The focus of one's attention (both analytic and pedagogic) becomes how the various parts of the larger, abstract syntactic, semantic, and discourse systems cohere: since it is assumed that there is an order that underlies all action, and meaning is thought to be determined by the relationships among these elements, *apart from their actual uses*. Bakhtin (Gardiner 1992) calls this a monologized perspective of language use in which privilege is given to those aspects of interaction that can be systematized and regulated, and thus disengaged from those whose resources they are. Ignored are the locally situated uses of these resources, since the individual moves are perceived to be too random, unimportant, and ordinary for focused attention.

 ### Task B3.2.6: While you read

➤ How would you analyze the dialogue between the husband and wife using the perspective of systemic functional grammar?

At the other extreme is the sociocultural approach to the study of language use and meaning. It is arguably this perspective that underlies many studies of practices undertaken within an 'ethnography of communication' framework. In these studies, the local configurations of language use are bracketed from broader sociohistorical and political concerns within which the interactive practices are embedded. From a sociocultural perspective, the meanings residing in the linguistic resources are thought to be historically unconstrained, i.e. locally created and negotiated among the group of interactants. Likewise, the individual's ability to use the resources, i.e. to create meaning, is thought to be unfettered by larger social, political, or historical constraints. Attention (again, both analytic and pedagogic) is given to the meanings constructed by a group of people at some spatio-temporally bounded moment with the intent of developing an understanding of the ways in which these individuals construct their realities and shared meanings *at that moment in time*. Meaning is thought not to reside in the resources, but in the locally situated uses of those resources. Their patterned uses are defined as that group's 'culture', and this cultural knowledge is assumed to be equally available to and shared among the participants (Cole and Engeström 1993). In its most extreme positioning, the sociocultural perspective claims that all knowledge about the meaning of the resources generated by such ethnographic investigation is context-dependent, unrecoverable at another time, and thus limited in its generalizability across moments.

Task B3.2.7: While you read

➤ How does a sociocultural perspective on the conversation between the husband and wife differ from a sociohistorical one?

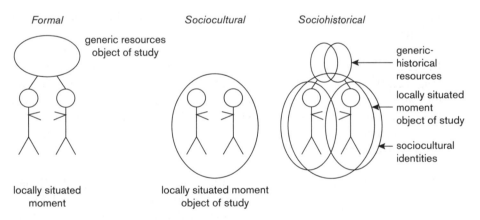

Figure 1 Approaches to the study of language use

Figure 1 is an illustration of the three perspectives. A primary difference among them is what counts as object of study. In the sociohistorical perspective of interaction, both the utterances and the sets of generic resources brought to the moment by a specific group of participants, as well as the identities of the participants themselves, are the focus of attention. What is of interest is the struggle between the historical meanings embedded in the resources and the locally situated moment, i.e. in discovering whose resources get used, which meanings are more or less malleable, how the individuals attempt to mold the resources for their own purposes, and the consequences of their doing so (or not). In contrast, the objects of study from a formal perspective are only the decontextualized generic resources themselves apart from their locally situated uses, and defined in formal (and ahistorical) terms. In the sociocultural position, it is the moment itself that is examined, with an eye toward the consensually determined meanings of the resources, which are thought to be socially constructed at that time and place with that group of people. Within these three perspectives, then, the linguistic and paralinguistic resources are defined and treated quite differently, and thus result in radically different research and pedagogic agendas: for the formalist, the agenda becomes the study of the systems of linguistic tools; for the socioculturalist, the stories and texts created by people at various moments in their lives; and for the sociohistorian, the locally situated contests between the conventional meanings of the resources brought to any particular moment and the ways in which people maintain or transform these meanings as they go about (re)creating their everyday worlds.

★ Tasks B3.2.8–12: After you've read

➤ In the title of Hall's article, she refers to '(re)creating our world with words.' What is the difference between 'creating' and 'recreating' our world? What is the function of the parentheses around the prefix 're-'?

➤ Where does 'history' figure in the sociohistorical perspective?

➤ What speech genres are invoked by the husband and wife in the dialogue that Hall reproduces?

➤ In the sociohistorical perspective on interactive practices, we take two views of language: We look at what people actually say in a specific interaction and we look at the genre of the practice; that is, the linguistic and interactional resources that are conventionally available to people in this practice and in others. Take a sociohistorical perspective on an interactive practice in which you have participated recently.

➤ Hall's sociohistorical perspective is influenced by the writings of Mikhail Bakhtin. Bakhtin was a Russian philosopher, literary critic and scholar who wrote influential works of literary and rhetorical theory and criticism. Find out as much as you can about Bakhtin's theories.

UNIT SUMMARY

The readings in this unit suggest ways in which we can analyze talk-in-interaction. We will find the methods of systemic functional grammar useful as we begin to analyze transcripts of complete real live interactions. The sociohistorical perspective will be useful in the latter part of the book when we come to discuss ways in which social identities and discourse communities are created through interaction. This perspective will also be important when we look at language development through social interaction. The article by Hall has also raised the important concept of interactive *practice*, an idea that we will explore in greater detail in Unit B4.

Unit B4
Discursive practices

OVERVIEW OF UNIT

How to characterize the relationship between language and context has been a problem of great interest to linguists, sociologists, and anthropologists for some time. In Unit A4, we have provided examples of one of the most recent approaches to the relationship put forward by linguistic anthropologists known as Practice Theory. Practice Theory does not take language as its basic unit, but instead focuses on practices, many of which involve language and those that we have called discursive practices. The discursive practice approach to language and context is grounded in four insights concerning interaction. One is the affirmation that participants create social realities through talk-in-interaction. The second is the appreciation that we stressed in Unit A2 of the context-bound nature of talk. The third is the idea that talk is social action. The fourth is the understanding that there is no fixed meaning in our utterances; rather, meaning is negotiated by participants in discursive practices.

Practice Theory originated in the writings of the French sociologist and anthropologist Pierre Bourdieu, and practices have been termed 'praxis,' 'actions,' 'interactions,' and 'activities' by other writers. Practice Theory seeks to explain the relationship between human action and social or cultural concepts such as power, identity, and beliefs. The theory focuses on specific instances of social interaction, many of which occur so regularly that they are the fabric of our daily lives, and some of which are of such value in a community that they have their own names. In Practice Theory the influence of cultural history is recognized explicitly for the influence that it has on the forms of practice and the social or cultural values that reproduce in practice.

From Hanks, W. F. (1996). *Language and communicative practices* (Chapter 1: 'Introduction: Meaning and Matters of Context'). Boulder, CO: Westview.

Text B4.1
W. F. Hanks

William Hanks is professor of linguistic anthropology at the University of California Berkeley. He has written extensively about routine language use in different cultures and has done fieldwork with the native Mayan peoples of the Yucatan peninsula in Mexico. Hanks is particularly interested in how people make reference to, describe, and orient themselves in space, and we have come across some of his work on indexicality in Unit A2. This reading is from the introductory chapter of his book on communicative practices (discursive practices as we call them), in which he contrasts two view of language: the view taken by formal linguists whose goal is to understand language as a phenomenon in its own right and the view taken by anthropologists and social theorists whose goal is to understand the use of language in context. Hanks believes that both views highlight different but interacting features of the same phenomenon.

★ Tasks B4.1.1–3: Before you read

➤ How important is language in comparison to communication by nonverbal means? Compare the lines (spoken language) and the stage directions (non-verbal information) in this short scene from Eugene Ionesco's play *Rhinoceros* (1960).

[Jean enters right, at the same time as Berenger enters left. Jean is very fastidiously dressed: brown suit, red tie, stiff collar, brown hat. He has a reddish face. His shoes are yellow and well-polished. Berenger is unshaven and hatless, with unkempt hair and creased clothes; everything about him indicates negligence. He seems weary, half-asleep; from time to time he yawns.]

Jean: [advancing from right] Oh, so you managed to get here at last, Berenger!
Berenger: [advancing from left] Morning, Jean!
Jean: Late as usual, of course. [He looks at his wrist watch.] Our appointment was for 11.30. And now it's practically midday.
Berenger: I'm sorry. Have you been waiting long?

➤ Do a grammatical analysis of a single line from the dialogue. Now, do a functional analysis; i.e., explain what social action the speaker is doing with his words. Does the functional analysis help you to explain the grammar? Does the grammatical analysis help to explain the action?

➤ Lift the four lines of spoken dialogue between Jean and Berenger and write a completely different scene between two different people. (Change the names if you want.)

START WITH A SIMPLE SCENARIO. It is 7:28 A.M. on September 19, 1993. Chicago. Jack has just walked into the kitchen. He is standing at the counter by the sink, pouring a cup of coffee. Natalia is wiping off the dining room table. Gazing vacantly at his coffee cup, still drowsy, Jack says,
    'D'the paper come today, sweetheart?'
She says,
    'It's right on the table.'
    Turning to the small table inside the kitchen, he picks up the paper and his cup of coffee. He joins her out in the dining room, where they sit in affectionate silence. She scribbles a list of the day's chores: 'Review headlines in Trib, Times, Globe, Post in re:

W. F. Hanks

UN role in peacekeeping efforts; prepare handout for PoliSci seminar; call AMH re: Friday; gym at 2:00; renew books at lib; dentist 4:15.' Unfocused, his eyes wander over the headlines: 'The Moment of Truth,' 'Duke Learns of Pitfalls in Promise of Hiring More Black Professors,' 'In a Less Arid Russia, Jewish Life Flowers Again (A Faith Reviving. Jews in Russia. A *Special Report*),' 'Perot, at Rally, Upsets Members of Both Parties.' They kiss. He lowers his face, rests it on the nape of her neck. After a moment, he turns back to the paper, still vague with sleep. She returns to her list. He sips his coffee, thinking of the day ahead.

In itself, language is neither the cause nor the measure of the world as we live it. Much of what makes the headlines would happen without talk, and we are instinctively wary of words for their ability to deceive. The dining room would still be there, and Jack and Natalia could still take their coffee, by habit, at the table. He would

Jack: D'the paper come today, sweetheart?
Natalia: It's right on the table.

Figure 1.1 Floorplan for a Routine Exchange

undoubtedly have found the paper on the table even if he never asked, and she could have just pointed. Virtually asleep, his words express little that we would call meaningful, and his eyes glaze over the paper, barely focusing on the information it announces. They embrace in the silence of intimacy. In other words, the consequential features of the scenario don't really depend upon the words spoken or even the speaking of words. The telegraphic exchanges between intimates can be virtually predictable or so idiosyncratic as to lack general interest. We need not even assume that they are wide awake. Next to disease, the environment, racism, and terror, speech seems oddly weightless. Talk is cheap.

True enough. But language permeates our daily lives, from the kitchen to the UN, and all the media in between. This sheer commonality should give us pause. The news might still happen without speech, but it would be difficult to call it news if it were never reported, and this happens only through language and other symbolic media. Jack and Natalia – or any other couple, for that matter – can do many things in silence, but this does not cut them loose from the horizon of words. There is always a history of conversation, intimate tellings. There are moments of withdrawal, when language is present by its painful absence. Common sense tells us that speech involves sound, but language inhabits silence, too (for the same reason that people are social beings even when they are alone). The truth has its moments because a pledge has been made. A university finds its present measured by a promise in the past. A third-party candidate breaks in with speech. And of course the newspaper is a printed form of language, whatever else it is. Sitting in the dining room in silence, Jack and Natalia are embedded in an unseen dialogue.

Task B4.1.4: While you read

➤ Together with a friend, act out the scene between Jack and Natalia.

The notion that talk is trivial compared to real action is often paired with the assumption that the meanings of words and utterances are transparent. We feel confident glossing Jack's utterance as a request for information about the paper or perhaps for the paper itself. Natalia's response appears equally simple and virtually literal. A closer look at their words, however, suffices to muddle this picture. Jack's question only asks whether the paper came that day, which should merit a simple yes or no response. Knowing that he reads the paper with breakfast and that he has no independent interest in newspaper delivery, Natalia hears his question as a request to locate the paper for him at that moment. It is this unspoken utterance that she answers. Her answer in turn introduces further tacit knowledge. Notice in Figure 1.1 that there are two tables on the scene, not one. The tables are in different rooms, as are the two people. Yet Jack hears her statement as making reference to the one nearest him, the one farthest from her. She cannot even see the table in the kitchen, and he knows this without having to think of it. How does he understand her? One might reason that he would expect her to say, 'It's in here,' or some such, if the paper were already on the dining room table. That she does not say this becomes meaningful. The assertive tone of her statement further reinforces the inference that she is giving him just the information he needs to find the paper. Maybe the words 'right on the table' convey that it is close to Jack, that he should be able to see it clearly.

But which inferences are actually made by such people, half asleep, in the familiar surround of their own home? Neither of them specifies that it was the newspaper of

W. F. Hanks

September 19 that Jack wants and not, say, the one from the day before. Yet this is implied, too. If the paper routinely came a day or a week late, then Natalia would understand him to be asking about that edition of the paper, and not the one of September 19. Papers can't move around by themselves anyway, so why does he ask if the paper 'came' instead of asking if it was delivered? Moreover, although he never says so, Jack is obviously referring to a certain newspaper and not the wax paper, the toilet paper, or the computer paper, and his use of the word 'today' suggests that there are some days on which it doesn't come (and therefore others on which it does). This gives the entire scenario an air of routine.

It should be clear that simple exchanges like this one can be tinkered with indefinitely and that much of the transparency that we sense on first hearing can be made opaque. The very telegraphic quality of the exchange, the presence of all that is unsaid, is part of what makes it appear routine. And we, as native actors, are curiously comfortable amidst an infinity of assumptions, beneath a horizon as familiar and unnoticed as the night sky. That is, provided we have the right kinds of background. Provided, for this example, that we come from a world in which people have dining rooms and read newspapers, in which men and women act as couples in certain common ways, in which English is spoken and coffee is drunk in cups in the morning. All of these things could be different, yet the coherence of words among silence would be similar – until something happens to break up the pieces, and the meanings shift about.

If the same exchange took place in a commercial kitchen in which large quantities of wax paper were needed, and Jack and Natalia were coworkers, he the short-order chef and she the manager, then it might be the wax paper that he was wondering about, taking for granted a history of problems with the supplier. Or Natalia might be the one who uses the paper because she works in the kitchen, and so Jack, the bartender, asks a real question, whether the paper was delivered, and not a request for information about its current whereabouts. What if Natalia, a native Spanish speaker, is actually practicing her English and the entire dialogue is a pedagogical exercise? Or if they are acting on the stage or running over an exchange they plan to perform at a later date in front of some third party, for reasons undisclosed? Back in the dining room, Natalia might know that Jack really wanted the newspaper, but she remembers that she happened to leave a new roll of toilet paper on the table when they returned from shopping the night before, and she playfully sends him to it, twisting his words mischievously. And so on. As we change the setting, making different assumptions, the meanings of the words shift around, become opaque, or change entirely.

The same applies to the boundary between language and gesture in much of everyday talk. Meanings understood without reflection turn out to depend in intricate ways on the cooperation of body posture and motion with speech. Jack's grasp of which table Natalia means is based on his body sense of her physical location outside the built space of the kitchen, relative to his own inside it. He is standing, about to walk to the dining room, and so can easily turn and pick up the paper as he comes to her. The two tables are in turn anchored to this relation and the habitual motion through the doorway between the two rooms. They sit close enough so that their embrace can happen as if by itself, without comment or preparation. Like the other tacit features of the scenario, most of this is so banal that a reader can digest the example easily. It takes a special effort and a certain perversity to make it strange. It takes a certain remove to unstick the words from their context, bringing their specific form into the foreground . . .

Task B4.1.5: While you read

➤ Hanks identifies two deictics in the conversation between Jack and Natalia: 'the paper' and 'the table.' How is it possible for Natalia to understand the referent of 'the paper'? And how is it possible for Jack to understand the referent of 'the table'?

W. F. Hanks

We will inevitably continue to trade on common sense throughout such an exercise. There is no other alternative. But the point is to make this part of the problem by examining the relation between what is actually said and what is understood. It is more a matter of bracketing, or temporarily suspending, contextual inferences rather than rejecting them outright. This first break, then, is what will allow us to separate the speech form from its own common-sense horizons, which in turn allows us to hear the words within the speech – which is in turn the first step toward language as a pure form with an inner logic of its own. 'D'the paper come today, sweetheart?' Yes-no question; past tense verb of motion with singular, inanimate subject; inverted word order of auxiliary verb and subject noun phrase; temporal adverb referring to the day of the utterance; utterance-final vocative, [+ familiar]; primary stress on first syllable of 'pépr'; intonation peak on primary stress and final syllable of 'tədéy.' This is the path of formalism, and that is why formalist understanding often runs counter to common sense.

To talk of an inner logic is to say that language is irreducible, that its structure and evolution cannot be explained by appeals to nonlinguistic behavior, to emotion, desire psychology, rationality, strategy, social structure, or indeed any other phenomenon outside the linguistic fact itself. We can pile on as many contingent facts of contexts as we wish, but language the code remains relatively autonomous. We associate this idea with such names as Ferdinand de Saussure, Leonard Bloomfield, Noam Chomsky, and Roman Jakobson, among the founders of modern linguistics, but its reach goes far beyond a single field. For ease of reference, we can call this the irreducibility thesis. It says simply that verbal systems have their own properties, and it fits well with a number of widely known facts: Languages are pervasively systematic in the sense of exhibiting patterned regularity across time and space. Sentences can be extracted from the ephemera of utterances, and languages are more than the accidents of speech. They have universal features such that regardless of the differences between any two anywhere in the world, one can predict that they share certain traits and exclude certain others. A verbal form, such as the sentence 'It's right on the table,' can be repeated a dozen times by speakers in as many different accents and for as many distinct purposes, and yet it is still recognizable and somehow the same. Jack could describe the table before him in great detail and you could photograph it without special effects; a comparison with the object itself would reveal that the verbal description employs things like nouns, definite articles, and verbs that have only tenuous analogues in the photo and none really in the physical thing.

Languages rest for their meaningfulness on a special sort of arbitrariness that is of a piece with irreducibility. In French one calls it *la table*, in German *der Tisch*, and in Spanish *la mesa*, yet these verbal differences appear to correlate with no differences in the thing itself, indeed no differences other than the ones we summarize in the names of the languages. Irreducibility is a grand way of saying what any working linguist or language learner already knows, namely, that languages have grammar and grammar has its own properties. The thresholds between grammar and utterance, expressions and things, may be difficult to draw, but this does not mean that they cannot be defined precisely. Moreover, the same common sense that obscures the line by making it invisible also affirms it. We know that words have relatively stable meanings fit for the dictionary, that they can be repeated, that a text can be separated from the situation in which it is read aloud, that a language can be written without being spoken, that it can be learned, to a degree, without being lived. The first break arises from the effort to make explicit this partial independence of language as a system.

Task B4.1.6: While you read

➤ One theory of language according to Hanks is that it is irreducible, and he writes that this theory is associated with Ferdinand de Saussure, Leonard Bloomfield, Noam Chomsky, and Roman Jakobson. What other theories of language can you contrast with irreducibility?

There is a second break that will concern us throughout this essay. If verbal forms are patterned, abstractable, universal, repeatable, and arbitrary, in brief sui generis, all the opposites also hold with equal force. They are variable, locally adapted, saturated by context, never quite the same, and constantly adjusting to the world beyond their own limits. And there is always an ideological dimension: people have ideas about their language, its value, meanings, history, and these ideas help shape the language itself. Here we come to the inverse thesis, which I call relationality. It is actually a family of approaches that have in common a focus on the cross-linkages between language and context and a commitment to encompass language within them. Irreducibility is of course built on a logic of relations, too, as we will see in Part 1 of this book. But the critical difference is that formalisms based on the irreducible system of language always posit a boundary between relations inside the system and relations between the system and the world outside of it. The former include things like the syntax or phonology of a language, and the latter things like the psychology or sociology of talk. Knowledge of a language, under this view, is inherently distinct from knowledge of the world. It is the idea of a boundary between language and non-language that makes all these other divisions possible. The system is at once more abstract, more general, and inherently longer lasting than any of the activities in which it is put to use. Proceeding from the break with particularity, formalist understanding leads to general laws of language and models of the combinatory potential of linguistic systems. This potential logically precedes any actual manifestation of speech. Relational understanding, on the contrary, proceeds from the break with formalist generality and leads back into particularity. It foregrounds the actual forms of talk under historically specific circumstances: not what could be said under all imaginable conditions but what is said under given ones. Here we come into contact with an endless array of particulars, with momentary circumstances and their contingencies. Language appears as a historical nexus of human relationships, a sudden patchwork that defies our ability to generalize. The line between knowing a language and knowing the world comes into question. It is unsurprising that social sciences in recent decades have seen a return to historical specificity, partly in reaction to the universalizing sweep of structuralist thought. Formalism loses in verisimilitude what it gains in internal rigor. Yet the really hard part is to achieve this second break without merely replicating the pathways of common sense, since this would mistake the problem for the solution.

Relationality has been argued for by Franz Boas, Edward Sapir, and their students in anthropology, for whom the interaction among language, culture, and individual lived worlds was, and still is, of basic import. It fits the later Ludwig Wittgenstein, for whom actions in the world were formative of and not dependent upon the regularities that we summarize as a grammar. It fits Nelson Goodman's irrealism, according to which language provides the means of formulating versions of the world that are comparable to musical scores, pictures, and other nonverbal representations. It applies to phenomenologists such as Roman Ingarden. Maurice Merleau-Ponty, and Alfred Schutz, for whom one of the primordial facts of language is its interpenetration with experience. It applies to the work of the Marxist V. N. Voloshinov, the psycho-linguist Ragnar Rommetveit, and the political philosopher Charles Taylor, who have attempted to synthesize inner logics with relational dependencies in interestingly different ways.

Task B4.1.7: While you read

➤ The second theory of language that Hanks discusses is that language is relational. How do relationality and irreducibility compare with the dichotomy that Bakhtin proposed between utterance and sentence?

Relationality can combine with irreducibility in various ways. One could say simply that the irreducible uniqueness of language lies precisely in how it relates to the world around itself. This yields a view in which what is essential is not inside the linguistic system as such but in its potential for entering into further relations in the world. Alternatively, one could maintain that language is capable of entering into coherent relations because in fact it remains stable, repeatable, and sui generis. It is precisely because an expression like 'the table' has the meaning it does that it can be used in reference to both a kitchen table and a dining room table. This yields an expanded version of irreducibility, for it amounts to the claim that the sui generis system is a precondition and relationality is a contingent factor. First we define form, and then we add an overlay of context. Only by combining the two do we arrive at meanings as full as the ones in our opening exchange between Natalia and Jack. We need not try to decide among such alternatives in the abstract, as though we could legislate an answer. Rather, we ought to take the general point that the two theses are just that: propositions about the foundation of language, not exhaustive descriptions or categories of things that one could sort out like so many marbles. Indeed, irreducibility and relationality are best seen as foregrounding different but interacting aspects of a single phenomenon, for it is in attempts to unify and transcend them that we arrive at the starting point for our analysis.

Tasks B4.1.8–12: After you've read

➤ Hanks writes that the irreducibility thesis and the relationality thesis are different ways of interpreting the same phenomenon. Which way best agrees with the way that you prefer to analyze language?

➤ Consider the ten words listed in Task A4.2.1. How would you analyze these words assuming the irreducibility thesis? Could these ten words be analyzed from a relational point of view?

➤ Using the model of Natalia and Hank's morning, write a scenario of an ordinary encounter that you participated in recently. In addition to the words, be sure to describe the setting and the actions of participants.

➤ In the scenario that Hanks describes, do you perceive either participant exerting power over the other?

➤ Hanks writes that the irreducibility thesis is associated with Ferdinand de Saussure, Leonard Bloomfield, Noam Chomsky, and Roman Jakobson; and the relationality thesis is associated with Franz Boas, Edward Sapir, Ludwig Wittgenstein, Nelson Goodman, and others. Who are these people and what did they write?

UNIT SUMMARY

Hanks draws our attention to two contrasting ways of looking at the same practice of talk-in-interaction and has challenged our common-sense ways of looking at talk, but he has not proposed a methodology by which we can relate systematically human action and social or cultural concepts such as power, identity, and beliefs, which is the goal of Practice Theory. In the next unit, two other linguistic anthropologists, Dell Hymes and Elinor Ochs, will describe means by which that relationship can be described and ways in which practices are acquired by children.

Unit B5
A framework for describing discursive practices

OVERVIEW OF UNIT

In this unit, we will read contributions to our understanding of the relationship between talk-in-interaction and social context by two distinguished anthropologists: Dell Hymes and Elinor Ochs. Hymes developed *the ethnography of speaking*, a theory and method of analyzing language and culture that became extremely influential and on which the discursive practice approach is based. Ochs extended Hymes's approach to the role of language use in children's acquisition of the values and cultural beliefs of the society into which they are born. Ochs's theory of *language socialization* helps us to understand how people learn discursive practices and the role of practices in learning culture.

Anthropologists have always been interested in how different cultures use language and applied linguists worked on the assumption that language use was a social activity but, before the pioneering work of Dell Hymes, the connections between language and context of use were never systematically described. Although earlier work on the relationship of language to context had been carried out at the University of London by Bronislaw Malinowski and J. R. Firth, Hymes's innovative proposal was that just as anthropologists studied people and cultures with the tools of ethnography, so understanding of language use and social context could be achieved by an ethnography of speaking. Ethnography involves fieldwork with people often in exotic societies that results in qualitative descriptions of human social phenomena, and ethnographers stress that social phenomena cannot be understood independently of one another. Hymes had done fieldwork with Native American peoples and, like the distinguished American ethnographers and linguists Franz Boas, Edward Sapir, and Leonard Bloomfield, Hymes observed that Native American ways of speaking are very different from the ways of speaking in the Anglo-American mainstream. The grammar of Native American languages differs from European languages, and ways of using their languages are also very different. In Native American communities, who can say what to whom and under what circumstances and how people value different kinds of talk and silence are very different from the ways of speaking outside those communities.

The focus of Unit A5 is a specific methodology for analyzing the relationship between talk and context, and the discursive practice framework exemplified there started with Hymes's pioneering work. The terms and methods of discursive practice and ethnography of speaking are very different but their approach to language and interaction is the same. Both start with a unit of interaction, which Hymes called a speech event and which we have called a discursive practice, and then proceed by an analysis of a small number of what Hymes called factors in speech events and what we have called interactional and linguistic resources available to speakers. A close reading of the following article by Hymes will show the similarities and differences between the ethnography of speaking and discursive practice approaches.

From Hymes, D. (1962). 'The ethnography of speaking.' In T. Gladwin and W. Sturtevant (eds), *Anthropology and human behavior* (pp. 15–53). Washington, DC: Anthropological Society of Washington.

Text B5.1
D. Hymes

This reading is an extract from a much longer article in which Hymes proposes the theory and methods of an ethnography of speaking.

Tasks B5.1.1–3: Before you read

➤ Think of societies where people speak languages different from your own. Ignore for a moment the linguistic differences between their language and yours and try to focus of how the way they speak differs from your ways of speaking. Here are a few things to consider: When do they talk a lot? When do they prefer to remain silent? Do they alternate between different languages or do they use primarily one language? Are there things that they say in their culture that sound very funny to you? Do they find some things very funny in your language?

➤ What do you understand by the word 'event'? How is an event different from a practice?

➤ What do you understand by the word 'function'? What is the function of 'uhuh' in a conversation between two people?

There seem to be three aspects of speech economy which it is useful to consider separately: *speech events*, as such; the *constituent factors* of speech events; and the *functions of speech*. With each aspect, it is a question of focus, and a full description of one is partly in terms of the rest.

Speech Events

For each aspect, three kinds of questions are useful. Taking first the speech events within a group, what are instances of speech events? What classes of speech events are recognized or can be inferred? What are the dimensions of contrast, the distinctive features, which differentiate them? (This will include reference to how factors are represented and functions served.) What is their pattern of occurrence, their distribution vis-à-vis each other, and externally (in terms of total behavior or some selected aspect)?

Extension

One good ethnographic technique for getting at speech events, as at other categories, is through words which name them. Some classes of speech events in our culture are well known: Sunday morning sermon, inaugural address, pledge of allegiance. Other classes are suggested by colloquial expressions such as: heart-to-heart-talk, sales-talk, talk man-to-man, woman's talk, bull session, chat, polite conversation, chatter (of a team), chew him out, give him the lowdown, get it off his chest, griping, etc. I know no structural analysis. Clearly the material cannot be culled from a dictionary alone: instances and classes of speech events may be labelled by quite diverse means, not only by nouns, but also by verbs, phrases, and sentences. In response to the question, 'Nice talk?', a situation may be titled by the response 'Couldn't get a word in edgewise.'

Insofar as participants in a society conceive their verbal interaction in terms of such categories, the critical attributes and the distribution of these are worth discovering . . .

An interesting question about speech events concerns what can serve to close them, or to close a sequence within one.

 Task B5.1.4: While you read

➤ Hymes describes speech events and provides a number of examples. Consider the clarinet lesson that we analyzed in Unit A5. What are the features of clarinet lesson that would make it a speech event? What kinds of spoken interactions would Hymes not consider speech events?

Factors in Speech Events

Any speech event can be seen as comprising several components, and the analysis of these is a major aspect of an ethnography of speaking. Seven types of component or factor can be discerned. Every speech event involves 1. a Sender (Addresser); 2. a Receiver (Addressee); 3. a Message Form; 4. a Channel; 5. a Code; 6. a Topic; and 7. Setting (Scene, Situation).

The set of seven types of factor is an initial ('etic') framework. For any group, the indigenous categories will vary in number and kind, and their instances and classes must be empirically identified. For example, Sender and Addresser, or Receiver and Addressee, need not be the same . . .

The form of a Message, or the typical form of a class of Messages, is a descriptive fact that becomes significant especially as an aesthetic and stylistic matter, whether in relation to the resources of a code (Newman [1940] has shown that Yokuts and English stand in sharp contrast), to a particular context (Riffaterre [1959] takes this relation as fundamental to analysis of style), or to a particular referential content (as when some linguists find that the modifier 'Trager-Smith' fits their sentence rhythms better as 'Smith-Trager').

Cross-cultural differences in Channels are well known, not only the presence of writing, but also the elaboration of instrumental channels among West African peoples such as the Jabo, the whistling of tones among some of the Mazatecs of Mexico, etc.

It has already been noted that the Code factor is a variable, given a focus on the speech habits of a population. The range is from communities with different levels of a single dialect to communities in which many individuals command several different languages. The presence of argots, jargons, forms of speech disguise, and the like enters here. Terms such as 'dialect,' 'variety,' 'vernacular,' 'level,' are much in discussion now (see Ferguson and Gumperz 1960, Hill 1958, Kenyon 1948). It is clear the status of a form of speech as a dialect, or language, or level, cannot be determined from linguistic features alone, nor can the categories be so defined. There is a sociocultural dimension (see Wolff 1959, on the non-coincidence of objective linguistic difference and communicative boundary), and the indigenous categories must be discovered, together with their defining attributes and the import of using one or another in a situation. Depending on attitude, the presence of a very few features can stamp a form of speech as a different style or dialect.

The Topic factor points to study of the lexical hierarchy of the languages spoken by a group, including idioms and the content of any conventionalized utterances, for evidence and knowledge of what can be said. To a large extent this means simply that semantic study is necessary to any study of speaking. An ethnography of speaking does also call special attention to indigenous categories for topics. One needs to know the categories in terms of which people will answer the question, 'What are they talking about?', and the attributes and patterns of occurrence for these categories. The old rhetorical category of topoi might go here as well.

The Setting factor is fundamental and difficult. It underlies much of the rest and yet its constituency is not easily determined. We accept as meaningful such terms as 'context of situation' and 'definition of the situation' but seldom ask ethnographically what the criteria for being a 'situation' might be, what kinds of situations there are, how many, and the like. Native terms are one guide, as is the work of Barker and Wright (1955) to determine behavior settings and to segment the continuum of behavior.

Some of the import of these types of factors will be brought out with regard to the functions of speech. With regard to the factors themselves, let us note again that native lexical categories are an important lead, and that contrast within a frame is a basic technique for identifying both instances and classes, and for discovering their dimensions of contrast.

Given the relevant instances and classes for a group, the patterning of their distribution can be studied. One way is to focus on a single instance or class, hold it constant, and vary the other components. As a sort of concordance technique, this results in an inventory, a description of an element in terms of the combinability of other elements with it. As a general distributional technique, this can discover the relations which obtain among various elements: whether co-occurrence is obligatory, or optional, or structurally excluded. Sometimes the relation will hold for only two elements (as when a certain category of Receiver may be addressed only by a certain category of Sender), sometimes for several. The relation may characterize a class of speech events . . .

Task B5.1.5: While you read

➤ Consider again the Clarinet Lesson that we analyzed in Unit A5. Identify in the lesson the seven factors that Hymes describes: sender, receiver, message form, channel, code, topic, and setting.

Functions in Speech Events

The third aspect of speech events is that of function. Within anthropology the functions of speech (or language) have usually been discussed in terms of universal functions. While it is important to know the ways in which the functions of speaking are the same in every group and for every personality, our concern here is with the ways in which they differ. One way to approach this is to reverse the usual question, 'what does a language contribute to the maintenance of personality, society, and culture?' and to ask instead, 'what does a personality, society, or culture contribute to the maintenance of a language?' Especially if we ask the question in situations of culture change, we can see the various functional involvements of speech and of given languages.

Some students of standard languages have defined for them functions and correlative attitudes. These in fact apply to all languages, and serve to contrast their roles. To illustrate: among the Hopi-Tewa the language serves prestige, unifying, and separatist functions, and there is great language pride as well as language loyalty. Among the Eastern Cherokee the hierarchy of functions seems just the reverse; the retention of the language serves mainly a separatist function, and there is an attitude of loyalty, but hardly of pride. Perhaps we think too much in terms of nineteenth-century European linguistic nationalism to notice that some languages do not enjoy the status of a symbol crucial to group identity. The Fulnío of Brazil have preserved group identity over three centuries by giving up their territory to maintain their language and major ceremony, but the Guayqueries of Venezuela have preserved group identity by maintaining a set of property relations. Of indigenous language and religion there has been no trace for generations. One suspects that the Guayqueries' involvement with their language differed from that of the Fulnío.

When only a few speakers of a language are left in a community, the survival of the language becomes almost entirely dependent on its manifest and latent functions for the personalities concerned. Thus Swanton rescued an important and independent Siouan language, Ofo, partly by luck; he happened to be in the unsuspected presence of the last speaker, and followed up a chance remark. But it was partly due to the personality of the woman, who could be an informant because she had practiced the language frequently to herself in the years since all other speakers had died.

These examples of the broad functional involvements of speech, and of languages, raise questions that can be answered only within general ethnography or social anthropology. While the same holds for an ethnography of speaking at other points, insofar as it is a special focus and not a separate subject-matter, it looms large here because the necessary conceptual framework exists almost entirely outside linguistics. There are still points and progress to be made, however, by concentrating on the linguistic discussions of the function of speech in terms of the constructive factors of the speech event.

 ## Tasks B5.1.6–7: While you read

> In the preceding paragraphs, Hymes discusses the broad functions of a language for its speakers. A language may function as a source of prestige for its speakers (or not), as a unifying force for a community (or not). Does your language function in these ways?

> ➤ In the next paragraph, Hymes uses the word 'function' in a different sense. How do the two senses of 'function' differ?

Within the tradition of linguistics, functions of speech have commonly been an interpretation of factors of the speech event in terms of motive or purpose, obtaining a set of functions one for each factor discriminated. Sometimes a particular feature, a linguistic category, or literary genre is associated with a function. For example, the 1st person pronoun, interjections, and the lyric poem have been associated with expressive function (focus on the Sender within the speech event); the 2nd person pronoun, imperatives, and rhetoric or dramatic poetry with the directive function; and the 3rd person pronoun, and epic poetry, with the referential function.

Some conception of speech functions must figure in any theory of behavior, if it is to give any account of speaking. The same holds for an account of language in a theory of culture. Indeed, rival views on many issues involving speech can best be interpreted as involving differing assumptions about the importance or existence of various functions. For an ethnography of speaking, then, the question is not, should it have a conception of speech functions, but, what should that conception be?

There can be only a preliminary outline at present, and, as a guide for field work, its concern should be for scope and flexibility. It should not conceive the functions of speech too narrowly, as to number or domain, and it should not impose a fixed set of functions. While some general classes of function are undoubtedly universal, one should seek to establish the particulars of the given case, and should be prepared to discover that a function identifiable in one group is absent in another.

One can point to seven broad types of function, corresponding to the seven types of factor already enumerated. (Each type can be variously named, and the most appropriate name may vary with circumstances; alternatives are given in parentheses.) The seven are: 1. Expressive (Emotive); 2. Directive (Conative, Pragmatic, Rhetorical, Persuasive); 3. Poetic; 4. Contact; 5. Metalinguistic; 6. Referential; 7. Contextual (Situational).

In the simplest case, each of the types of function can be taken as focusing upon a corresponding type of factor, and one can single out questions and comments, and units as well, that primarily are associated with each.

'You say it with such feeling' points to expressive function, and a language may have units which are conventionally expressive, such as French [h] ('Je te H'aime') and English vowel length ('What a fiiiiiiine boy'), used to convey strong feeling. (A feature can be conventionally an expressive device only where it is not referential, i.e., for phonic features, not functioning phonemically to differentiate lexical items.) 'Do as I say, not do as I do' points to directive function, and imperatives have been cited as primarily directive units. 'What oft was thought, but ne'er so well expressed' points to poetic function, focused on message form, as does 'The sound must seem an echo to the sense.' Feet, lines, and metrical units generally are primarily poetic in function. 'If only I could talk it instead of having to write it' and 'Can you hear me?' point to contact function; breath groups may be channel units, in the case of speaking, as are pages in the case of print. 'Go look it up in the dictionary' points to meta-linguistic function, to concern with the code underlying communication; words such as 'word,' and technical linguistic terms, which make talk about the code possible, serve primarily metalinguistic function. Quotation marks have metalinguistic function when they signal that a form is being cited or glossed, but channel function when enclosing quoted or imagined speech. 'What are you going to talk about?', 'What did he have to say?' focus on topic and point to referential function. Most lexical and grammatical units are primarily referential, and are analyzed by descriptive linguistics in terms of that function. 'When will you tell him?', 'As mentioned above,' 'You can't talk like that here!!', 'If you're going to use that scene at all, you'll have to put it later in the play,' are primarily contextual in function as are a sign flashing 'On the Air' and the statement of scene at the beginning of an act of a play '(Elsinore. A platform before the castle)'.

Tasks B5.1.8–12: After you've read

➤ In 1974, Hymes published a revision of his seven components of speech events. He called these Setting and Scene, Participants, Ends (purposes or outcomes), Act Sequence, Key (the tone or manner of the event), Instrumentalities (channel and form), Norms (social rules governing the event), and Genre (the kind of event). The seven components formed the acronym SPEAKING, and, thanks to its useful mnemonic, Hymes's 'SPEAKING model' became well known. How does the SPEAKING model differ from the list of factors involved in speech events that he described in 1962?

➤ Compare Hymes's discussion of sender and receiver with Goffman's differentiation of the roles of speaker and hearer that we presented in Unit A2.1.2.

➤ The terms 'emic' and 'etic' were coined by Kenneth Pike (1967) to distinguish two ways of interpreting social behavior. An *emic* approach to the analysis of social interaction is a description treated by insiders (the people being studied) as relevant to their system of behavior, while an *etic* approach analyzes interaction in terms of theories or categories that the outside analyst uses, which are not necessarily accepted or understood as relevant by insiders. Is Hymes's analysis of speech events emic or etic?

➤ Roman Jakobson's model of the functions of language had a decisive influence on Hymes. Jakobson (1960) writes that all acts of communication, be they written or oral, are contingent on these six constituent elements.

CONTEXT

MESSAGE

ADDRESSER . . . . ADDRESSEE

CONTACT

CODE

A message is sent by an addresser to an addressee. For this to occur, the addresser and addressee must use a common code, a physical channel, or contact, and the same frame of reference, or context. (Though Jakobson stipulates that by 'context' he means 'referent,' the term is confusing, since it could be mistakenly construed as pointing to the circumstances of utterance rather than to what the message is about.) Each of the constituent elements of the communicative act has a corresponding function; thus:

REFERENTIAL

POETIC

EMOTIVE . . . . CONATIVE

PHATIC

METALINGUAL

How are the functions that Hymes describes in speech events different from Jakobson's?

➤ Compare the factors that Hymes describes in speech events with the seven resources employed by participants in creating discursive practices described in Unit A5.1.

From Ochs, E. (1996). 'Linguistic resources for socializing humanity.' In J. J. Gumperz and S. C. Levinson (eds), *Rethinking linguistic relativity* (pp. 407–437). Cambridge and New York: Cambridge University Press.

Text B5.2
E. Ochs

Hymes laid out a framework for understanding talk as part of human culture, and the research of Elinor Ochs has shown how the culture of a community is reproduced in the next generation through talk-in-interaction with children. For Ochs, the acquisition of a language by children and their learning to be a member of society are both integrated in a process she called *language socialization*. In the article that is extracted below, Ochs uses the principle of indexicality to explain how social concepts and values such as identity, social acts and activities, and feelings are associated with language. Indexicality is a meaning-making process that we discussed in Unit A5.3.3, where we showed how the teacher's and student's use of indexicals such as 'here' and 'there' invoked a third participant in their interaction. The indexicality principle, however, is much broader than spatio-temporal relationships. In Unit A2.2.3, we gave examples of regional accent indexing the speaker's provenance and verbal politeness indexing social relationship among speakers; Ochs goes even further to show how language indexes emotion, social rank, and in fact a complete range of cultural phenomena. She argues that it is through experiencing the indexicality principle in discursive practices that children are socialized to a culture.

Tasks B5.2.1–3: Before you read

➤ In many cultures, information about the gender, age, and social status of speakers is indexed by language. How does language index this information in the cultures that you know?

➤ When a person is speaking, how do you know if they are excited, happy, or afraid? Are there different ways of indexing these affective stances in other cultures and languages that you know?

➤ Is sociocultural information and affective stance important in *all* cultures that you know?

E. Ochs

1 Language socialization

A basic challenge of language socialization research has been to articulate the role of language praxis in the process of becoming a member of society. This challenge has been addressed largely by detailed studies of language socialization in particular communities and settings . . . The present chapter draws upon these studies to address two critical dilemmas.

The first dilemma concerns how language practices encode and socialize information about society and culture. Since, typically, information about social identities, actions, stances, and the like is not made explicit (e.g. 'This woman is an honoured guest,' 'We are telling a story,' 'This is a scientific fact'), how is such information otherwise conveyed? To say simply that the meaning of utterances is indeterminate is not itself illuminating vis-à-vis understanding the relation of linguistic form to the socialization of culture. We need to delve into the notion of indeterminacy to see if there is an architecture therein, much like other researchers seek order within chaos (Prigogine & Stengers 1984, Briggs & Peat 1989). In the discussion to follow, the process of language socialization will be related to the capacity of language practices to index socio-cultural information.

A second dilemma is the relation of language socialization not just to local culture but to human culture as a species phenomenon. We have for so long pigeon-holed culture as antithetical to universals of human nature that we have scarcely attended to culture as a singularly human enterprise. 'Cultural universal' is not an oxymoron. A universal of human behavior is not necessarily an outcome of innate mechanisms; it may be an outcome of pan-species commonalities in the human accommodation to, and structuring of, social life. Without diminishing the importance of differences, it is important to recognize these commonalities as facilitating social co-ordination across social groups. What does this imply about language socialization? One implication is that human beings across societies may be using language in similar ways to both structure their environment and socialize novices. One challenge of language socialization research is to present candidate universals in the relation of language to socialization and the structuring of culture.

To this end, in this chapter I draw on diverse studies in pragmatics, sociolinguistics, conversation analysis, and linguistic anthropology to formulate three principles (the principles of indexicality, universal culture, and local culture) concerning the indexing and socializing of culturally relevant information through language practices and the scope of these processes across human societies. For purposes of this discussion, culture is here conceptualized as a set of socially recognized and organized practices and theories for acting, feeling, and knowing, along with their material and institutional products, associated with membership in a social group.

2 The Indexicality Principle

The fields of pragmatics, linguistic anthropology, sociolinguistics, conversation analysis, and ethnomethodology all articulate ways in which the meaning of cultural forms, including language, is a function of how members engage these forms in the course of their social conduct. By now it is generally appreciated that members use cultural forms, including linguistic forms within their code repertoires, variably according to their conceptualization of the social situation at hand. In the social sciences 'situation' is usually broadly conceived and includes socio-cultural dimensions a member activates to be part of the situation at hand such as the *temporal and spatial locus* of the communicative situation, the *social identities* of participants, the *social acts* and *activities* taking place, and participants' *affective and epistemic stance*. For purposes of this discussion, situational dimensions other than space and time are preliminarily defined as follows:

social identity encompasses all dimensions of social personae, including roles (e.g. speaker, overhearer, master of ceremonies, doctor, teacher, coach), relationships (e.g. kinship, occupational, friendship, recreational relations), group identity (e.g. gender, generation, class, ethnic, religious, educational group membership), and rank (e.g. titled and untitled persons, employer and employee), among other properties;

social act refers to a socially recognized goal-directed behavior, e.g. a request, an offer, a compliment;

activity refers to a sequence of at least two social acts, e.g. disputing, storytelling, interviewing, giving advice;

affective stance refers to a mood, attitude, feeling, and disposition, as well as degrees of emotional intensity vis-à-vis some focus of concern (Ochs & Schieffelin 1984, Labov 1984, Levy 1984);

epistemic stance refers to knowledge or belief vis-à-vis some focus of concern, including degrees of certainty of knowledge, degrees of commitment to truth of propositions, and sources of knowledge, among other epistemic qualities (Chafe & Nichols 1986).

Every novice enters a fluid, sometimes volatile, social world that varies in certain conventional, non-random ways. Membership is accrued as novices begin to move easily in and out of linguistically configured situations. As they do so, novices build up associations between particular forms and particular identities, relationships, actions, stances, and the like. A basic tenet of language socialization research is that *socialization is in part a process of assigning situational, i.e., indexical, meanings* (e.g. temporal, spatial, social identity, social act, social activity, affective or epistemic meanings) to particular forms (e.g. interrogative forms, diminutive affixes, raised pitch and the like). I will refer to this tenet as the Indexicality Principle. To index is to point to the presence of some entity in the immediate situation-at-hand. In language, an index is considered to be a linguistic form that performs this function (Lyons 1977, Peirce 1955). Peirce, for example, defines index as follows:

> [An index is] a sign, or representation, which refers to its object not so much because of any similarity or analogy with it, nor because it is associated with general

characters which that object happens to possess, as because it is in dynamical (including spatial) connection both with the individual object, on the one hand, and with sense or memory of the person for whom it serves as a sign, on the other hand.

(Peirce 1955: 107)

A linguistic index is usually a structure (e.g. sentential voice, emphatic stress, diminutive affix) that is used variably from one situation to another and becomes conventionally associated with particular situational dimensions such that when that structure is used, the form invokes those situational dimensions.

An example of linguistic indexing of *affective stance* is provided in (1) below. Affect is richly indexed in all languages of the world (see Ochs & Schieffelin 1984). In addition to indexing particular kinds of affect (e.g. positive affect, negative affect), languages also index degrees of affective intensity. 'Intensity operates on a scale centered about the zero, or unmarked expression, with both positive (aggravated or intensified) and negative (mitigated or minimized) poles' (Labov 1984: 44). In (I), a stance of heightened affect is indexed in the immediate situation through the use of the following structures in English: quantifiers ('all over,' 'a lot') as well as emphatic stress (e.g. 'a lot,' 'that long'), phonological lengthening (e.g. 's::-so,' 'jus::t'), interjections ('Go:d'), laughter, and repetition (e.g. 'I didn't eat one bit I didn't take one bite').

★ Task B5.2.4: While you read

Text B5.2 continues with a transcription of an interaction between a mother and her two children. Read the transcript of the interaction below, then take the roles of the mother and her two children and act out the interaction. Make sure that you give emphatic stress to words that are underlined and stre-e-e-etch the sounds that are indicated by a colon (:). Square brackets denote the beginning of overlapping talk, and equals signs indicate contiguous utterances where the second is latched on to the first. Focus on the lines of the dialogue that are highlighted by arrows. How are the affective stances of the mother and the children indexed by their language?

(1) Mother approaches her two children (Jimmy and Janet), who are eating dinner. Jimmy has just commented that Janet has drowned her meat in A1 sauce and compares this with how he used to drown his pancakes in syrup:

→ Jimmy: when I had pancakes one – pancakes (that) one time?
→   I like syrup? I put syrup? – <u>all over</u> my pancakes
→   and a <u>lot</u> – an – I didn't eat one bit I didn't take one
→   bite – I took some bites but =
    Mother: = when was that?
    Jimmy: a long time ago? – bout ((tosses head)) ten? – ten years old?
               – a:nd – the: [(Ja)
→ Mother: [(that wasn't <u>that</u> long
→ Jimmy: (well who knows) – but um th- the <u>pan</u>cake – it was
→   s::-so soft (you) could – like (break) it with your –

→   – ju::st (pull it off) – <u>Go:d</u> hh
                  ((pause))
Jimmy: (I) tried to scrape some of it <u>off</u> but hchehe
           ((pause)) ((TV going))
Mother: just sinks in

A second example of indexicality focuses on the indexing of social identity. This example is taken from interaction between two siblings in a Western Samoan household. Western Samoan society is elaborately hierarchical, with ranking on the basis of title, generation, and age among the variables. Traditional expectations assume that higher-ranking parties to an interaction will be less physically active than lower-ranking parties. Hence directives using the deictic verbs sau, 'come,' and alu, 'go,' are appropriately addressed to those of lower rank (Platt 1986). Within the analytic framework of the present chapter, we consider these verbs to index not only spatial dimensions but social relational dimensions of the social situation as well. In particular, the verbs sau and alu index that the speaker is of a higher rank than the addressee. In example (2), Mauga addresses her younger sibling Matu'u (2 years 2 months), with each instance of the deictic verbs indicating the asymmetrical nature of their relationship:

(2) Matu'u's older sister, Mauga, is sitting at the front edge of the house. Matu'u is at the back of the house:

→ Mauga: *Matu'u sau*
            'Matu'u, come here.'
→   *Matu'u sau*
            'Matu'u, come here.'
            ((Matu'u goes to Mauga))
→   *alu mai sau 'ie*
            'Go get a piece of clothes (for you).'
→   *Alu amai le mea solo ai lou isu*
            'Go get it to wipe your nose.'
→   *kamo' e, alu e amai le solosolo 'ua e loa 'ua e loa*
            'Hurry, go get the handkerchief, you know, you know.'

3 The Universal Culture Principle

Section 2 of this chapter addressed 'The display dilemma' (i.e., how does language display and socialize cultural knowledge?) by articulating ways in which linguistic practices index, constitute, and entail socio-cultural dimensions of situations. But what about 'The scope dilemma' (i.e., what are the cultural boundaries of language socialization?)? Do these principles preclude the possibility of non-absolute universals in the linguistic structuring of human culture? I think not. Culture is not only tied to the local and unique, it is also a property of our humanity and as such expected to assume some culturally universal characteristics across communities, codes, and users. Principle 2, the Universal Culture Principle, proposes that there are certain commonalities across the world's language communities and communities of practice in the linguistic means used to constitute certain situational meanings. This principle suggests that human interlocutors use certain similar linguistic means to achieve certain similar social ends. In this sense, the Universal Culture Principle is a limited (linguistic) means-ends principle. The principle is limited in the sense that it applies to some but not all indexical practices, in the sense that the common indexical practices may characterize many but not all communities, and in the sense that the indexical practices may give rise to unpredictable consequences; that is, linguistic means/social ends relations are inherently non-linear. Given these limitations, what is the basis for the Universal Culture Principle?

First, in all societies, linguistic forms are exploited to constitutively index the *general situational dimensions* of time and space, epistemic and affective stance, acts, activities, and identities (e.g. roles, relationships).

Second, within the dimensions of stance and social act, there are certain comparable categories of *stance and act meaning* across communities of speakers. For example, within the dimension of stance, epistemic categories such as relative certainty/uncertainty and experiential vs. reported knowledge are distinguished in many communities. Similarly, affective categories such as intensity/mitigation, surprise, positive and negative affect are indexed universally. Within the dimension of social act meanings, acts such as greeting, asserting, prompting, thanking, agreeing, disagreeing, accepting, rejecting, refusing, approving, disapproving, reporting, announcing, prompting, asking questions, and requesting goods and services appear across the world's communities. Furthermore, there are common valences linking stance and act meanings across communities. Certain stance meanings are common critical meaning components of social acts that characterize culture universally; for example, uncertainty is an epistemic stance component of questioning, negative affect is an affective stance component of rejecting; positive affect is an affective stance component of thanking. . . .

These commonalities characterize our humanity, our human culture. They afford, i.e. allow for the possibility of (Gibson 1979), a singularly human conversation in which some ways of displaying stances, some ways of acting, and some ways of meaning are recognizable as we traverse local borders. As each of us treads on 'foreign' territory, we discern some common indexical threads that link us to one another as members of one human cultural fabric. The challenge to all cultural travellers is to go beyond these commonalities to recognize distinctly local ways of indexing and constituting social situations and cultural meanings.

 Task B5.2.5: While you read

➤ Ochs claims that the following cultural concepts are indexed by language across the world's communities. Can you think of any exceptions?
   – Relative certainty/uncertainty
   – Experiential vs. reported knowledge
   – Intensity/mitigation, surprise
   – Positive and negative affect
   – Acts such as greeting, asserting, prompting, thanking, agreeing, etc.

4 The Local Culture Principle

The Local Culture Principle proposes that local culture is constituted in part by the myriad of situationally specific valences that link time, space, stances, acts, activities, and identities. (I am not trying to reduce the texture of local culture to these variables.) Culturally distinct patterns in stance-act-activity-identity relations lie in cultural expectations regarding (a) the *scope* of stances and acts associated with particular activities and identities, (b) the *preferences* for particular stances and acts within particular activities and for particular social identities, and (c) the *extent* of particular stance and act displays within particular activities and for particular identities.

4.1 *Local scope*

Local cultures may differ in expectations concerning the kinds of stances and social acts to be displayed in a particular activity or by a person of a particular status and/or in a particular social relationship among interlocutors. Thus while certain stances and acts associated with relatively low and high rank may be universal (i.e. accommodating stances and acts), others may be quite particular to a local group. For example, while the social identity of high chief in traditional communities in Western Samoa entails certain of the same stances and social acts of high-ranking persons across societies (e.g. receiving deference, rights to direct certain other parties to gain access to desired goods and services), other stances and acts are particular to Samoan chiefs. For example, in decision-making activities, chiefs have the right, and are expected, to express opinions to lower-ranking persons (in this case, orators), whereas lower-ranking persons are expected to make suggestions when invited to do so (Duranti 1981). For members of the Samoan community, the social identity of chief (and orator) has distinctly local act entailments. Another way of looking at this relation is to say that in this community, the act of giving an opinion in decision-making councils constitutively indexes the social identity of high chief. The act of giving an opinion in decision-making councils in other communities does not necessarily index and constitute such an identity or even high rank more generally. This particular constellation of act-identity valences/entailments is constitutive of local cultural knowledge that Samoan children eventually come to grasp and some may even come to challenge in light of their experiences in New-Zealand- and Australian-style school classrooms.

Task B5.2.6: While you read

➢ Think of the ways that the high status of teachers is indexed in Western societies. What differences in how high status is indexed would Samoan children find when they attend school in New Zealand or Australia? What effect might this have on their education?

4.2 *Local preference*

In addition to differences in which stances and acts are linked to particular identities and activities, there are local differences in the stances and acts preferred by particular identities and for certain activities. For example, in the sequence of acts comprising the activity of clarification, language communities and communities of practice will differ in their preferences for one or another act strategy for achieving clarification of an unintelligible or partially intelligible message. These preferences may be across the board for all speakers and settings or may be tuned to specific situational conditions. In traditional communities of Western Samoa, speakers have available in their pragmatic repertoire all the clarification strategies . . . as possible universals. Certain of these strategies, however, are highly preferred and others highly dis-preferred. In particular, in most circumstances, Samoan interlocutors overwhelmingly prefer either the act strategy of directing the party producing the unintelligible utterance to repeat or simply asserting non-comprehension and overwhelmingly disprefer the act strategy of verbally guessing the nature of the message (Ochs 1988). The dispreference for making an explicit guess is strongest in the condition where the party producing the unintelligible utterance is a young child. Of all the possible clarification strategies, explicit guessing requires the most cognitive accommodation in that the guesser presumably tries to assume the perspective of what the other may be thinking/intending, whereas simply stating that one does not understand or directing the other to repeat does not demand the same degree of accommodation. As noted earlier, accommodation is a stance/act that constitutively indexes actors of lower rank. In the case where the child produces the troublesome utterance, others co-present are higher rank than the child, rendering inappropriate acts of explicit guessing.

4.3 Local extent

Communities are particular not only in their preferences for one act or stance strategy over another vis-à-vis particular identities and particular activities but also in the extensiveness of those stance and act displays by those identities and in those activities. For example, members of communities the world over engage in prompting activities constituted by discrete acts of prompting. These same communities, however, may differ quite dramatically in the extensiveness of the prompting activities, i.e., how long and complex the prompting is in general and in particular situational conditions (Ochs 1990, Schieffelin & Ochs 1988). It is certainly one of the more frustrating experiences for language socialization researchers to report on the cultural import of prompting activities among the Kaluli or Kwara'ae or White working-class Baltimore families only to hear from a member of the audience that prompting goes on among mainstream American families as well. Yes it does. Indeed it goes on in all communities as far as we can see. What gives prompting a cultural importance among Kaluli (Schieffelin 1990) or Kwara'ae (Watson-Gegeo & Gegeo 1986) or White working-class Baltimore (Miller 1982) families, among other things, is its complexity and duration. In these communities, prompting talk covers pages of transcript and is used in triadic (A prompts B to tell C) as well as dyadic (A prompts B to tell A) interactions across a wide range of interlocutory relationships to elicit a vast range of stance, act, and activity displays. The use of prompts in mainstream American families pales in comparison: prompting activities tend to boil down to a two-turn prompt sequence between an adult and a child to display politeness ('Say "thank you"') or in routines such as labeling objects ('say "bird"'), or occasional prompts in dyadic or triadic interactions to facilitate a child's storytelling . . .

5 Socializing humanity

The three principles of indexicality, universal culture, and local culture together suggest that indexicality is at the heart of language socialization. Even more strongly, the principles suggest that a theory of indexicality is a theory of socialization and that a theory of socialization is only as strong as the theory of indexicality that underlies it.

Tasks B5.2.7–12: After you've read

➤ Summarize what you understand by Ochs's three principles: the Indexicality Principle, the Universal Culture Principle, and the Local Culture Principle.

➤ Do you see any contradictions between the Local Culture Principle and the Universal Culture Principle?

➤ In the conversation illustrated by the cartoon of the three people and the monkey in Unit A5, how do the participants index gender in their talk?

➤ In the clarinet lesson analyzed in Unit A5, how do the teacher and student index their relative social statuses?

➤ In the clarinet lesson analyzed in Unit A5, how does the student index her negative feelings?

➤ Have you had the experience of living in a different country where people speak a different language? If so, does your experience confirm or contradict Ochs's principles of universal culture and local culture?

UNIT SUMMARY

In this unit, we have read and discussed two classic articles by linguistic anthropologists. In the first, Hymes presented a method for understanding the relationship between language and culture by first identifying units of interaction which he called speech events (which later we have called discursive practices), and then by describing in detail the components of speech events. The methodology that we have used in Section A to describe the resources employed by participants to co-construct discursive practices is based on Hymes's ethnography of speaking. In the second article by Elinor Ochs, describing language in use ('praxis' in Ochs's term) and understanding human cultures and the organization of social groups are two aspects of the same question, just as understanding how children learn language and understanding how they come to participate as members of an adult society are for Ochs the same process. It is simply a question of a scholar's disciplinary focus whether they choose to focus on one or the other: Developmental psychologists study child cognitive and social development while linguists study the processes of language acquisition. Even as adults, we acquire new languages and new cultures, and Ochs's theory of how the two are integrated is a topic that will be discussed in the readings in Unit B6.

Unit B6
Interactional competence

OVERVIEW OF UNIT

In Unit A6, we discussed several theories of how people use language in social interaction. We discussed how the term 'competence' is used in ordinary language and contrasted the ordinary meaning of the term with its use by linguists, socio-linguists, and anthropologists. At the conclusion of the review of theories of competence we defined 'interactional competence' as a relationship specific to a single discursive practice between linguistic and interactional resources and the social context in which the resources are employed. The resources employed by all participants to co-construct a participation framework are: register and modes of meaning, speech acts, turn-taking, repair, and interactional boundaries. We recognized that co-construction of a discursive practice assumes that participants are able to share the mental states of others, which we called intersubjectivity. Finally, we recognized the difference between competence and expertise, and we discussed how interactional resources are used to create the identities of expert and novice in a discursive practice.

The two fundamental concepts of interactional competence and expertise are developed further in this unit in the writings of Aaron V. Cicourel, emeritus professor of cognitive science at the University of California, San Diego.

Text B6.1
A. V. Cicourel

From Cicourel, A. V. (1995). 'Medical speech events as resources for inferring differences in expert-novice diagnostic reasoning.' In U. M. Quasthoff (ed.), *Aspects of oral communication* (pp. 364–387). Berlin and New York: W. de Gruyter.

Aaron Cicourel was interested in how, through interaction, people construct knowledge and status. Cicourel worked with doctors and medical students in a training hospital in California and in this article he discusses differences in the ways that medical students interact with patients, and how they display their knowledge to a senior doctor. His work on language in interaction has shown how medical personnel construct status and expertise through interaction. Although Cicourel's argument is grounded very firmly in an analysis of talk-in-interaction, he argues against the methodology of conversation analysis which rejects the application of social or cultural context to conversation unless social or cultural facts are invoked by participants in their talk. Cicourel believes that it is not possible for an analyst to understand the construction of expertise in medical interactions without considerable ethnographic and personal knowledge of medical settings. For this reason, before we read Cicourel's analysis, it's a good idea to become familiar with some the medical settings in which the interactions occurred.

In the United States, medical care is provided primarily in institutions such as hospitals and clinics. Access to medical care by people who need non-urgent care is controlled by an institutional process of making an appointment through a receptionist. When a person enters a medical institution to seek care, the person takes on the role of 'patient' and the roles of care providers are similarly clear and labeled as 'nurses,' 'doctors,' and at a teaching hospital 'medical students.' In the interaction that Cicourel describes, the patient is first met by a nurse who takes the patient's temperature, weight, and blood pressure, and asks about the purpose of the patient's visit. The patient then is taken to a small examination room where, after a short while, the patient is examined. In the teaching hospital where Cicourel observed, the first person to examine the patient in the examination room was a 'training fellow.' The training fellow was an advanced medical student who had already completed a residency in physical medicine and was pursuing specialist training in rheumatology (the study of people with arthritis and rheumatic and musculo-skeletal diseases). After the initial examination, the training fellow left the examination room and met with the attending physician. The 'attending' was a physician who had completed residency and practiced medicine in the hospital focusing on rheumatology. The attending also supervised residents and medical students. In his exchange with the attending, the training fellow described his examination of the patient and answered to the best of his knowledge any questions that the attending posed. Cicourel analyzed the two conversations between the teaching fellow and the patient and between the teaching fellow and the attending. In this article, Cicourel did not describe any further interactions but, after their private discussion, the attending and training fellow would normally return together to the examination room, where the attending would examine the patient again and discuss a treatment plan.

The participants that Cicourel studied were the patient, the training fellow, and the attending, and he was interested to discover how in the initial interview the patient and the training fellow constructed the training fellow's expertise and how in the discussion of the case with the attending, the statuses of novice and expert were constructed. He described expertise 'by reference to the differential way sources of potential information are perceived and understood by novices and experts, particularly in the way they use language to authenticate their status vis-à-vis one another' (Cicourel, 2000, p. 67).

Tasks B6.1.1–3: Before you read

➤ Consider conversations in which one participant is considered an expert and another participant a novice (for example, teacher and student, football coach and player, research scientist and post-doc, chef and cookery student, etc.).

A. V. Cicourel

What linguistic and interactional resources do participants employ in order to construct expertise?

➤ How do questions asked by experts differ from questions asked by novices?

➤ Besides how they talk, can you tell who's the expert and who's the novice in a practice just by how they dress, how they stand, and how they gesture?

Introduction

The relationship between novices and experts is at once an issue of knowledge representation and language use in a specifiable task (that is, institutional) environment. For example, I examine the role of oral communication as part of the institutional implementation of a health care delivery system. Several levels of explanation are presupposed. Each level (oral versus, say, written communication) interacts with and creates constraints for related levels. The paper builds on the collaborative oral discourse routinely produced in a medical setting between house staff (interns, residents, training fellows), patients and attendings (the expert in charge of the patient or service) that leads to a differential diagnosis. Socially distributed knowledge and cognition (Cicourel, 1964; 1974; 1990; Hutchins, 1989; Polanyi, 1958; Schutz, 1945; 1953) drive the oral exchanges at several levels of analysis. For example, there are socially distributed authority and power relations between novices, patients and attendings. The participants presume of and display to each other differences in knowledge attributions, communicative competence and reasoning strategies that contribute to the socially distributed cognition needed in everyday problem solving (Hutchins, 1989).

Medical diagnostic reasoning requires the physician to elicit symptoms and signs, assess the patient's complaints or problems, create an appropriate treatment plan and, in teaching hospitals, is an occasion for the expert to evaluate the novice's performance and progress. These exchanges and their assessment help to legitimate the novice's status with the patient. The exchanges also perform an institutionalized bureaucratic function. They indirectly confer credentials and status symbols as part of the novice's gradual achievement of expertise. . . .

★ Task B6.1.4: While you read

➤ In Cicourel's article, he compares the interactions of the teaching fellow with those of a more advanced medical student, the resident. That's why he refers to 'two novices.' For reasons of space, we have included here only the interactions involving the teaching fellow.

In the Western world, a micro environment consisting of four 'walls', a 'ceiling', something often called an 'examining table', ready access to water and a place to store supplies are often found in structures called the equivalent of 'hospitals', 'clinics', 'medical offices', 'infirmaries', and 'surgeries'. Men and women, often dressed in white garments, routinely visit individuals placed in an 'examining room' because of alleged ailments or complaints. A number of rituals are necessary in order to gain access to those rooms. Persons with alleged ailments require some kind of advance proof that economic resources are available when notifying someone in advance about when it might be possible to visit the 'clinic' or particular cultural setting.

In the proceding [sic] paragraph, I have sought a vocabulary that would appear more 'neutral'. A quick glance at my efforts, however, will reveal how difficult it is for an observer to escape the cultural and linguistic framing all descriptions impose. Every description inevitably presumes tacit expectations about what is activated in the reader's mind as a consequence of the opening lines presented.

An American hospital provides the ethnographic context for my tale of two novices and an expert in a rheumatology clinic. A fairly clear set of normative status and power relationships can be identified in the clinic that mirrors all teaching hospitals in the United States. For example, authority and power are instantiated when someone designated as an object, the 'patient,' calls to set up an appointment with a 'doctor'. The person becomes an object within a bureaucratic structure unless known personally to the receptionist. The available times are seldom under the control of the patient. Some amount of negotiation is necessary. When the patient arrives at the clinic, it is the physician's time that again controls the order in which assessment and treatment will be dispensed. The bureaucratic processing of the patient as object occurs. There may be several gatekeepers; a receptionist who attends to information about one's background and financial matters, a nurse who may weigh the patient, take her temperature, blood pressure and perhaps inquire as to the purpose of the visit. Patients are distributed into examining rooms that facilitate routine ways for processing them with dispatch. The opening line of a physician's medical history (e.g., 'What seems to be the problem? [or] Please tell me what seems to be the matter?') shifts the patient back to subject status. In a teaching hospital, shifting the patient to object status enables medical novices and experts to employ a metalevel of discussion that links the patient to the medical literature and prior clinical experiences.

Medical decision making begins when the physician learns about the patient's reason for the visit. For example, a referral slip or the nurse's notes or perhaps a remark from a member of the house staff (intern, resident or training fellow). If the clinic is devoted to patients who are part of teaching activities, an advanced medical student, resident or training fellow is likely to introduce themselves as the physician . . .

Task B6.1.5: While you read

➤ The following transcript is from the initial interview between the teaching fellow (TF) and the patient (P). With a partner, take on the two roles and play the interview.

1	TF:	Ummm, who sent you to Arthritis?
2	P:	Uh, uh, Oncology
3	TF:	Oncology, (unclear) that's okay. (other voice)
4		Now let me just get a piece of paper (7 seconds)
5		(Closing drawers).
6		How old are you?
7	P:	44.
8	TF:	Okay (9 seconds) and (do you?) have any problems?
9	P:	Oooooh, the whole body.

10	TF:	Whole body.
11	P:	Joints, really bad.
12	TF:	Uhuh, yeah, okay.
13	P:	And ummm, breakout in these big red spots, (mumbling)
14		tops and toes.
15	TF:	Uhummm.
16	P:	But only when I sit in the hot water, they come out
17		quite a bit, my hands get, like this, they stiffen up.
18	TF:	Uhummm.
19	P:	They stiffen all the way up.
20	TF:	Ummkay, so now how long as this been happening?
21	P:	Oh, quite a while.
22	TF:	Couple months? Er,
23	P:	Longer than that, cuz I was taking Dr. Blumberg
24		(Door/drawer slamming closed) up in San Miguel.
25	TF:	But is he an arthritis doctor?
26	P:	Mmhuh (?)
27	TF:	Okay, what did doc, now, so, it's maybe uh 9 months? Or
28	P:	No, it's been about a year'n a half.
29	TF:	'Bout a year a'half.
30	P:	Uhummm, seems to get worse though . . .

★ Task B6.1.6: While you read

The next transcript is from the exchange between the teaching fellow (TF) and the attending (A). With a partner, take on the two roles and play the interview.

1	TF:	Ok, next is Elena Louis, (background voices) anway
2		She's 44 years of age and sent here from (the?)
3		Oncology group.
4		So the past two years she has had episodes initially
5		of Erythema followed by swelling involving the second
6		and third metacarpal and pip joint of both hands,
7		alternating, one time this hand, one time this hand.
8		She's also had arthritis of her ankles, which includes
9		redness on a lateral border of the lateral malleolus
10		followed by swelling.
11		Comes on, first the redness, and she has pain and
12		swelling within 24 hours,
13		lasts for several days, and then it goes away.
14		But when she has it, the pain is quite severe.
15		It greatly limits her hand function, and her walking
16		function.
17		Ummm, she really has minimal joint complaints other
18		than back stiffness and her other joints.
19		She has had no difficulty with her elbows really, or
20		her shoulders.

21		Uhh, she's not had any nodules.
22		She has no Raynaud's (disease).
23		She has no Sjogrens.
24		She is tired all the time.
25		She is now getting a lot of leg cramping.
26		Ummm, she has no family history of arthritis
27		She has no occasional morning sickness, but it's
28		not real (?) . . .
29	A:	How long, has this been a problem?
30	TF:	Two years. She has seen by a Doctor Blumberg,
31		San Miguel, and told she had BJD (degenerative joint
32		disease).
33		She previously had seen another physician and was
34		told she had Rheumatoid Arthritis.
35		She has tried at one point in time on Tolectin and
36		she didn't feel it helped her, and at this point in
37		time she's on no medication . . . uh.

Tasks B6.1.7–12: After you've read

➤ Analyze the vocabulary and grammatical structures used by the teaching fellow in the two transcripts. Does the register that the teaching fellow uses with the patient differ from the register that he uses with the attending? If so, why?

➤ What mode of meaning does the patient use to describe her symptoms? Does the teaching fellow use the same mode of meaning to describe the patient's symptoms to the attending?

➤ Analyze the turn-taking system in both transcripts. Who selects the next speaker?

➤ Analyze the sequence of acts in both transcripts. Are they the same or different?

➤ On the basis of your analysis of register, modes of meaning, turn-taking, and act sequences, how is expertise constructed between the patient and the teaching fellow? Between the teaching fellow and the attending?

➤ In co-constructing unequal expertise in a conversation, participants must create reciprocal statuses; that is, one participant must be authenticated as an expert and the other as a novice or non-expert. How do the participants in these two transcripts co-construct their roles?

UNIT SUMMARY

In this unit, we have looked at ways in which interactional competence differs from communicative competence and ways in which participants use interactional competence to co-construct identities in talk-in-interaction. The context that we have examined is institutional discourse in a hospital. We have said that interactional competence is a relationship between linguistic and interactional resources and the social context in which the resources are employed, and that the relationship is specific to a single discursive practice, but we have considered very few practices. In the next few units we will consider whether interactional competence can be transported from one practice to another and whether participants learn something which is specific to a single practice.

Unit B7
Co-constructing identity

OVERVIEW OF UNIT

Identity, we argued in Unit A7, is a complex and shifting attribute of a person. Identity is projected by the self and altercast by others and, ultimately, co-constructed in interaction between the self and others. The role of talk-in-interaction in co-constructing identity is discussed and exemplified in the article that we present in this unit. Dennis Day analyzes workplace conversations between Swedish workers and their immigrant colleagues at two factories in Sweden and shows how ethnic identities are constructed for the immigrants and how those colleagues resist the ethnic identities that are available to them. The kinds of identities that are being negotiated are gender and ethnicity – which in Unit A7 we have called master identities and claimed that they are aspects of personhood that are relatively stable and unchanging. What Day's research shows, however, is that even these aspects of master identity are relational; that is, they are negotiated from moment to moment and are highly variable.

From Day, D. (1998). 'Being ascribed, and resisting, membership in an ethnic group.' In C. Antaki and S. Widdicombe (eds), _Identities in talk_ (pp. 151–170). London: SAGE Publications.

Text B7.1
D. Day

Ethnicity is a social construction that indicates identification with a particular group which is often descended from common ancestors. Members of the group share common cultural traits (such as language, religion, and dress) and are an identifiable minority within the larger nation-state. The concepts of race and ethnicity are closely related, but, because of the pejorative implications in contemporary society of the word 'race' ethnicity is the preferred term. In its etymology, however, the word 'ethnic' has a sense of otherness. The first definition of 'ethnic' given in _Webster's third new international dictionary_ is 'of or relating to the Gentiles or to nations not converted to Christianity,' and 'heathen,' and 'pagan' are given as synonyms.

In contemporary industrial societies, transnational migration is common, and individuals who migrate to find work in another country are often perceived as ethnic by citizens who can trace their ancestry back many generations in the host country: The immigrants speak different languages, they eat different foods, and they have different religious views and social values. These differences are sometimes felt to enrich the economy and culture of the host society, but oftentimes immigration by ethnically diverse people is perceived to be a threat. Businesses employ immigrant workers and it is rational for them to be concerned that immigrant workers are received well by their work mates. The business community has therefore sponsored much research and training regarding intercultural communication with immigrants. In England in the 1970s, for example, the National Centre for Industrial Language Training was set up in order to facilitate interethnic communication in the workplace, and one of the most enduring outcomes of this initiative is the film *Crosstalk* (Gumperz, Jupp, and Roberts, 1979).

The work that Dennis Day describes in his article continues in this tradition of research into interethnic communication in the workplace. Day describes interactions between Swedish workers and their Chinese immigrant colleagues at two factories in Sweden and he focuses on the ways in which ethnic identity is constructed (or ascribed) by the Swedish workers and how that ethnic identity is resisted by the Chinese workers. Dennis Day knows the situation that he describes very well. He lives in Sweden and teaches intercultural communication and anthropological linguistics at the University of Southern Denmark in Odense.

⭐ **Tasks B7.1.1–4: Before you read**

➤ Would you call yourself ethnic? Why? Or why not?

➤ If you or someone you know identifies as ethnic, what are the characteristics that go to make up ethnic identity? How does ethnic identity relate to the language that people speak?

➤ Describe a workplace that you know in which some workers are recent immigrants and others consider themselves 'mainstream.' Describe some interactions that you have noticed among individuals from these two groups.

➤ In 2006, there was a great debate in the United States about immigration. The US Senate proposed a plan that would allow illegal immigrants to earn citizenship, while also tightening border security and enforcing existing bans on the hiring of undocumented workers. A very different proposal was made in the House of Representatives that would, among other things, make it a felony to be an illegal immigrant in the United States. What is your position on legal and illegal immigration in your country?

D. Day

It has often been suggested that much of what it means to be social resides both in our language and in our linguistic communicative practices. Likewise, it has also often been suggested that those studying language need to bear in mind that the language people use in interaction can join them together – or, indeed, keep them apart – in particular social ways. Group categorizations, I will suggest, are both orientations to our sociality and social actions themselves. The identity categories you use in talking to the people around you are tools by which you organize your activities with them, and, at the same time, they are ways in which you constitute them as members of the same, or a different, social group.

The specific sort of group I want to focus on in this chapter is the *ethnic* group. Sometimes people around you can pick out your membership in an ethnic group in contrast to theirs and that may, so to speak, be used against you, casting doubt on your capacities to be a member of the social group pursuing the activity at hand. In my study of linguistic ethnic group categorization at two workplaces in Sweden, I have found that people react against their membership in minority ethnic groups being made relevant for the task at hand. One understanding of this reaction is that they do so in order to alleviate doubt as to their capacities as members of the social group jointly doing what the others are doing. My purpose with this chapter is to describe briefly how I have arrived at this understanding . . .

Two Workplace Studies

During 1988 and 1989, and 1992 and 1993, I conducted field studies at two factories in Sweden, Mat AB and Komponenter AB, whose workforces were composed to a large extent of immigrants (the names of the companies, as well as of all informants, are pseudonyms). Field work covered a range of activities, although the data in this chapter will come from recordings of interviews with employees, a video-recording of an arranged 'party-planning' discussion, and recordings of coffee breaks. The data are in Swedish and I will provide glosses, with a rough approximation of some speech features like overlap, in English. I have not attempted to render the Swedish into 'transcription-like' English translations, however, as that would give, I believe, a false impression of authenticity to the translations as examples of spoken language . . .

The first study was initiated through contacts at the factory who were disconcerted by problems they had implementing a job-rotation scheme. Top management personnel at the factory felt their problems were a result of workers having built ethnic 'cliques'. Initially my ambition was to show how their problems were communicative in nature, that communication between different ethnic groups had led to misunderstandings which, in their turn, had led to a breakdown in group relations. After some time at the factory, however, I found that such a description of the workplace was only one of many and that 'ethnic group' categorizations – such as a Chinese group, a Polish group, etc. – were often inappropriate and even contested categorizations.

The second workplace I studied was organized quite differently from the first one. Whereas the first workplace reminded one of a typical assembly line, the second was designed along more innovative 'team-work' lines. I found there that ethnicity was rarely a resource in interactions among members of the work team I studied. This was obviously, however, a 'multiethnic' workplace. In fact, the very first thing the foreman of the work team I studied told me, quite spontaneously, was something like the following which I recall from memory:

> One thing I don't understand is how outsiders, [workers not involved in the work teams organization] say we're 'all white'. Look at us, I'm Finnish but a Swedish citizen, Kaarlo was born in Sweden but is a Finnish citizen, Ahmad is from Ethiopia, Aina's family is Finnish, and Johan and Björn are Swedish.

These observations led me to reconsider the notion of interethnic communication taking the following question as a point of departure: how does one go about identifying communication as interethnic from an interlocutor's perspective? In other words, how can one show that interlocutors are orienting to their communication as something we can gloss as 'interethnic communication'? My attempt to answer this question led to what I have termed ethnification processes (Day, 1994), by which I mean processes through which people distinguish an individual or collection of individuals as a member or members respectively of an ethnic group. A communicative variant of ethnification processes, linguistic ethnic group categorization, will be discussed here. One way of seeing interethnic communication from an interlocutor's perspective, then, is to view it as communication where at least one interlocutor orients to at least one other interlocutor or oneself through direct or indirect linguistic categorization as a member of a differing ethnic group. Interethnic communication in this view is the result of a particular type of social identity work in the course of intentional communicative interaction.

Linguistic Ethnic Group Categorizations

Linguistic ethnic group categorizations, I suggest, ascribe people to a particular sort of social group, namely an ethnic group. I take it that to categorize a person as a member of an ethnic group is to say he or she is ready to share in some action or attribute with other members and there is some particular institutionalized collection of 'owned' characteristics, such as a shared history, common language, etc., which follow from this . . .

A speaker can categorize a person directly, by referring to him or her with a lexically obvious ethnic group label such as 'Swede'. Alternatively, a speaker may succeed in categorizing someone into a certain linguistic ethnic group not by direct naming, but, more subtly, by some oblique work in his or her description of some other person or thing. That description may serve to set up what I will term a case of special relevance. The description is now as it were 'in the air' and will be taken to be relevant to the participants in the group. That is to say, rather formally: if among a group of interlocutors where at least one interlocutor A is describable as a member of X ethnic group and someone ethnically categorizes something or someone other than A as of an X ethnic group type, then X ethnicity can be taken to be of special relevance for A given that neither A nor any other interlocutor has any other special attachment to the thing or person ethnically categorized. I exemplify such a categorization from the 'party planning' activity below.

Task B7.1.5: While you read

➤ In the present article, Day claims that ethnic identity is procedurally relevant to the conversations that he reports, and he shows the interactional work that participants do to make ethnicity relevant. What are the advantages and disadvantages of using procedural relevance to limit the aspects of identity that are considered in analyzing a conversation?

(1) Party planning

| 58 | → | M: | eh entertainment one could have chin chon |
| 59 | → | | huang ((laughter)) but it's a little |

60		hard
61	MA:	mm
62	T:	yeah it is
63	M:	entertainment first and then we can take
64		which food and drink and then entertainment,
65		we'll take it last
66	MA:	⌐yeah
67	T:	∟mm

M: eh: (0.5) underhållning (.) man skulle kunna ha med chin chon huang (skratt) men det är lite svårt.

MA: mm:,

T: ah! >det år det<

M: underhållning (0.2) å först å sen ska vi ta vilken mat (.) å drick o sen underhållning. det tar vi sist.

MA: ⌐ja!

T: ∟mm

At lines 58–9, Malia (M) suggests that at the party they have 'chin chon huang' for entertainment. I take this to be Malia's guess at what a Chinese expression might be like. In this way, Malia has initiated an 'identity-rich puzzle' (Schenkein, 1978[. . .]). By using a stereotypically 'Chinese-like', but still rather ambiguous, expression, she implicitly nominates anyone with appropriate expertise to clarify, or comment on the proposal – and, among these participants, that person is potentially MA or T. MA passes the turn with a minimal 'mm' while T (Tang) takes it up only slightly less minimally; it is surely hearable that were she to pass further comment on 'chin chon huang', Tang would identify herself as a member of the linguistic category group Malia has thrown into the air. I take Malia's expression 'chin chon huang', then, to be an example of linguistic ethnic group categorization by special relevance. There is a suggestion of what I assume is Chinese entertainment among a group where there is one interlocutor, Tang, who, for others there, can be described as Chinese. Thus, the suggestion is made to be of special relevance for Tang . . .

Task B7.1.6: While you read

➤ What is it about the expression 'chin chon huang' that makes it sound like a stereotypically Chinese-like expression? Can you think of any other expressions that sound stereotypical of particular ethnic groups?

Ascription of Membership as a Prerequisite for Group Activity

Linguistic ethnic group categorizations, being descriptions of people as members of a social group, may also be seen as relevant to the prerequisite constitution of the social group jointly pursuing the social activity at hand. From this perspective it is possible to talk of the prerequisites for being a member of a social group in conjunction with the pursuance of a social activity.

A first concern for presumptive members/interactants would be whether a candidate member/interactant can be taken to have committed him- or herself to taking part in

Extension

the interaction. A second concern would be if he or she can be trusted to pursue the joint purpose of the interaction. A final concern would be the availability to him or her of resources for achieving the joint purpose. I will term these three concerns 'prerequisite conditions' with the understanding that they are prerequisite for participation in a social activity.

The first prerequisite noted above can be seen as dealing with establishing oneself as ready for membership in a social group; the second with having that membership ratified, that is that one will cooperate as a group member; and the third with the availability of resources to use the social activities of that group. In brief, then, we can talk of readiness, trust and resources as explorable dimensions of social groups in relation to social activities. These are, of course, matters which have to be done interactionally – in visible signs and in talk. And, equally, they can all be *resisted*, and in the same way. This is what I shall be showing in the workplace talk below.

Resistance to Ethnic Group Categorizations

On almost every occasion where a speaker offered or asserted an ethnic categorization of an interlocutor, that interlocutor resisted it in some way. I noted five different ways in which resistance was done.

1 One can Dismiss the Relevance of the Category

Consider, for example, Xi's comment (at line 54 in extract (4) below), which might be glossed as her saying that they need not have Chinese food on her account.

(4) Party planning

```
51  L:   don't we have something that, one can eat
52       that, China or
53  R:   Chinese food is really pretty good
54  X:   haha ( ) it doesn't matter, I'll eat anything
55  R:   ah (that's [what I that)
56  L:              [yeah, but this concerns everyone
57       doesn't it?
```

```
    L:   har vi inte nånting som man kan äta som' (.) kina eller
    R:   kinamat är i och för sig bra
    X:   haha ( ) spelar ingen roll jag äter allt
    R:   ah: (det jag som)
    L:              ja men det gäller alla dom andra också va?
```

Lars (L) suggests that they have Chinese food (lines 51–2) at the party, a suggestion which Rita (R) upgrades but neither directly refuses nor accepts. It would appear that it is left for Xi (X) to decide whether what Lars has said is a suggestion which projects an acceptance or refusal. The suggestion may be taken to be of special relevance for Xi by how she responds to it – 'haha, it doesn't matter, I'll eat anything' (line 54). For Lars to suggest 'Chinese food' among this group of interlocutors, where Xi may be taken as 'Chinese', is to make the suggestion specially relevant for her. Her response at line 54 indicates that this was indeed the way it was heard. If this were not the case, then her response that she will eat anything could be heard as a literal, if obtuse, acceptance of the suggestion of Chinese food. Lars, however, does not appear to hear Xi's utterance this way; rather, he hears her response as not wanting Chinese food (line 57). The fact that she says it does not matter can be heard as a denial of the relevance of the ethnic category to which she is being ascribed.

Tasks B7.1.7–11: After you've read

➤ Day mentions five different ways in which a participant can resist being ethnified (i.e., altercast as a member of an ethnic group different from that of other participants), but we have included only one here. The other ways that Day mentions are: (1) Minimize the supposed 'difference' between ethnic categories, (2) Reconstitute the category so that one is excluded, (3) Ethnify the ethnifier, and (4) Resist ethnification by actively avoiding it. Provide examples of these four ways of resisting ethnification.

➤ An ethnic identity has different meanings according to who claims or who altercasts that identity. In the examples that Day provides, it is the immigrant from a minority background who is being altercast as ethnic by people from the majority. But claiming ethnicity for oneself can be act of solidarity with others and it can be or an act of resistance against the majority (non-ethnic) society. How can participants construct a solidary ethnicity in interaction with others? How can a claim of ethnicity be an act of resistance?

➤ Ethnic identity is not only constructed through language but also through other nonverbal semiotic systems. Take a particular ethnic identity and describe the nonverbal means by which it is created.

➤ In Section A7.6, we introduced the notion of 'crossing': adopting the language, dress, and lifestyle of conspicuously different groups in society. Some white middle class youth like to cross into a hip hop African-American identity, and some middle-class women in Baltimore like to cross nostalgically into a working-class identity. Yet, there are some ethnic identities into which people don't often cross. What are these identities? And why are they not popular identities to cross into?

➤ Here is the first verse of Bob Dylan's song 'I Pity the Poor Immigrant.' You can easily find the complete lyrics on the web. Discuss Dylan's song in the context of ethnicity and ethnification as Day interprets them in his article.

I pity the poor immigrant
Who wishes he would've stayed home,
Who uses all his power to do evil
But in the end is always left so alone.
That man whom with his fingers cheats
And who lies with ev'ry breath,

Who passionately hates his life
And likewise, fears his death.

UNIT SUMMARY

The text in this unit has focused exclusively on how ethnic identities are constructed through talk-in-interaction. Day closely examined the moment-by-moment development of specific instances of talk-in-interaction, and he has not gone beyond the aspects of identity that are procedurally relevant to talk in those interactions. For this reason he has not exemplified how accent constructs identity nor how identity is constructed nonverbally; he has not focused on the aspects of identity that we have called 'personal identities' that are created on the basis of how others evaluate a person's attitudes and behavior; and he has not discussed the role of political institutions in imposing and coercively applying identities. Nonetheless, Day's data show the quicksilver-like way in which relational identities appear, become relevant, and disappear as they become no longer relevant to subsequent talk. Finally, the data confirm the co-constructed nature of identity through negotiation between the self and others as we work to establish the identity that is relevant to a particular moment in interaction.

Unit B8
Discourse communities

OVERVIEW OF UNIT

Community and identity are inextricably linked because groups are composed of individuals and individuals are members of groups. To understand individual identity we must understand an individual's membership in a community and, to understand community, we need to investigate how members of the community perceive the world, think, and act in concert with others. The text that we present here gives one perspective on the relationship between community and identity. Shirley Brice Heath provides a vivid description of how one particular practice helps to construct a community and how language use within that practice both reflects community-wide usage and helps to define it.

From Heath, S. B. (1983). *Ways with words: Language, life, and work in communities and classrooms.* **Cambridge and New York: Cambridge University Press. (Excerpts from pp. 201–211.)**

Text B8.1
S. B. Heath

Shirley Brice Heath's prize-winning book *Ways with words* is a classic study of children learning to use language at home and at school in two communities only a few miles apart in the south-eastern United States. 'Roadville' is a White working-class community of families steeped for generations in the life of textile mills; 'Trackton' is a Black working-class community whose older generations grew up farming the land but whose current members work in the mills. In tracing the children's language development, Heath shows the deep cultural differences between the two communities, whose ways with words differ as strikingly from each other as either does from the pattern of the townspeople, the 'mainstream' Blacks and Whites who hold power in the schools and workplaces of the region.

Shirley Brice Heath is professor of English and dramatic literature at Stanford. She is a linguistic anthropologist whose primary interests are oral and written language, youth development, race relations, and organizational learning. She is widely known for her work with young people as co-researchers in the townships of Johannesburg, South Africa, as well as economically disadvantaged communities in the United States.

Tasks B8.1.1–4: Before you read

➤ The following extract from *Ways with words* describes part of a practice which is central to the community of 'Trackton' – the Sunday church service. Ways of speaking in the Trackton community are often similar to the ways that language is used in the Sunday church service, and the organization of the service is a natural reflection of ways of speaking in the community. The Sunday church service is also a time when members of the Trackton community come together face to face. Are you a member of a group which has regular meetings in which the organization of talk affects the language of everyday life?

➤ Refer to Erickson's description of the dinner-table conversation of the Italian-American family that we presented in Unit A8. How did that family's 'ways with words' help to construct a community?

➤ In some communities, the written word is considered to have a special value greater than the spoken word, and it is believed to be important not to change what is written. In other communities, the written word may simply be the starting point for spoken discourse, and it is spoken eloquence that is most valued. What is the relative importance of speech and writing for you?

➤ In Unit A2, we studied the 'I have a dream' speech by Dr Martin Luther King, Jr. In his early career, Dr King was pastor of a Baptist Church, in Montgomery, Alabama. Read the 'I have a dream' speech again and consider ways in which it demonstrates Dr King's skill with the spoken word.

In attempting to understand the unconscious rules members of a group follow in their lives, we often look for patterns and themes of behavior which are carried from the home life into other institutions community members themselves control. The churches attended by Trackton families and their friends were such institutions. Most went to country churches for Sunday services, usually held twice a month. In these churches, the pastor serves not one, but several churches, and he often also holds one or two other jobs during the week. The pastor, often called 'reverend,' is always a male. Few have had formal training at a theological seminary. Many are known to have lived 'sinful' lives in their younger days and to have 'come to the Lord' after recognizing the evil of their ways. Their training has usually been in one of the black colleges of the South, where they have majored or taken courses in religion, and they have supplemented this training with additional work at summer programs, through correspondence courses, or in graduate programs at nearby integrated state schools. . . .

The Sunday service as a whole is a harmonious blend of uses of highly formal written materials, lists of items and informally written announcements, oral performances which draw from the written words, and spontaneous oral performances which take the formulae of either written or oral expressions and expand these. Hymns, prayers, and sermon are intertwined in patterns which defy analytic description by their complication in overlapping and simultaneous pieces. Outsiders, unfamiliar with the routines of the service and the norms of participation by members of the congregation, cannot understand the service in many parts, and often report their feeling that 'too much is going on at the same time.' A personal testimony provokes a spontaneous response in song, which ends abruptly as a prayer begins; throughout the prayer, as many as three different songs may be hummed or sung; as the prayer ends, the sermon may begin, the preacher speaking slowly and deliberately at first, and only gradually moving into a series of chants, each with its own crescendo, punctuated by spontaneous bursts of song, prayers, or verbal expressions of agreement from the congregation.

Task B8.1.5: While you read

➤ To understand an unfamiliar practice like this Sunday service in Trackton, use the framework for describing discursive practices introduced in Unit A5. Use Heath's description of the community's ways with words to sketch members' linguistic, interactional, and identity resources employed in the Sunday service.

Almost all parts of the service – hymns, prayers, and sermon – have in their background written sources. There are hymn books, and the hymn board at the front of the church gives the hymn numbers, as does the bulletin. Those who are called on by the minister to pray have always been asked to prepare in advance, and most bring a card or small piece of paper with their prayer written out on it. The sermon is based on a Biblical text, and the pastor always writes out portions of the sermons in preparation for Sunday services and revival meetings. Yet in each of these parts of the service, there is a pattern of movement away from the form and formality of the written sources. For example, most of the country churches still 'raise' their hymns, though they have hymn books with prepared words. In raising a hymn, the choir leader may begin the hymn by announcing the hymn number from the book, then reading the first verse of the hymn, slowly and dramatically, pausing often to look at the congregation. The congregation then begins singing and may continue through the entire first verse before a member of the choir or congregation breaks in with new words which may be a phrase or set of phrases from an earlier prayer, the hymn, or one of several formulaic phrases that may raise a hymn. The congregation is quiet while the new self-appointed leader raises a set of phrases, and they then join in repeating it, then pause for another leader to offer another set. This pattern of alternation continues until the hymn ends. . . .

The following illustration of a raised hymn occurred at a point in the church service when a member of the congregation – a hospital orderly – recounted an experience he had faced in his work the past week. He told of his own sense of emptiness as he tried to help a dying patient. The choir leader continued after the story by saying 'After all, I'm gonna tell ya, there are some times . . .'

S. B. Heath

Task B8.1.6: While you read

➤ The transcript below is Heath's attempt to represent in writing the oral event of 'raising' a hymn. When you read it, try to recreate the oral version by treating the transcript as film script and assigning parts to different people to read aloud. Don't omit the slaps and foot stomping.

Trackton text XI

A single voice on the other side of the church repeated in a chant, slowly rising in
pitch –
> *There are some times*

The choir leader picked up as his chant died, and chanted –
> *When things be rough.*

The congregation then began humming the tune to Kumbaya, a familiar song often
heard in popular recordings of Afro-American music. A portion of the congregation
then repeated with the new melody –
> *There are some times*

The choir leader introduced in chant –
> *When there is no other help.*

The congregation had by this point joined together to sing –
> *There are sometimes, yea Lord*
> *There are sometimes, yea Lord*

Another leader added in chant –
> *Yea, oh Lord, yea sometimes*

The choir leader then chanted while the congregation hummed –
> *When we be back at twelve o'clock [a metaphorical expression for birth and death, the beginning
> and the end].*

While the congregation returned to humming, another single male voice raised from
the congregation –
> *We need yay Lord*

The choir leader added in chant –
> *Sometimes, yea*

The single male voice which had emerged as the lead voice in the congregation then
chanted –
> *So, come by here, Lord*

and the congregation immediately sang the phrases –
> *Come by here*
> *Come by here*
> *Yea Lord.*

The congregational leader then chanted –
> *Somebody needs ya, Lord.*

The congregation sang –
> *Somebody need ya, Lord*
> *Somebody yea*
> *Somebody need ya Lord*
> *Come by here.*

Another congregational member chanted –
> *Aye, aye, come by here*
> *Come by here*
> *Yea, somebody need ya, Lord*
> *Come by here.*

Two sharp claps came from the congregation, there was a momentary pause, and the
choir leader chanted softly –
> *Somebody's waitin', Lord.*

The congregation sang –
> *Come by here*

Somebody's waitin', Lord
Come by here.
A congregational leader shouted shrilly –
Somebody's waitin', Lord.
The congregation sang quietly –
Come by here.
The choir leader chanted slowly and with crescendo –
My Jesus, come by here, Lord
Yea, come by here
Yea, Lord, come by here
Come by here.
Yea, Lord, come by: here.
The congregation sang softly –
Oh, Lord, come by here
Yea, Lord, come by here
Come by here, Lord
Come by here.
As the congregation finished, the leader chanted with a falling cadence –
Yea, Lord, come by here.
Following this hymn, simpler by far than most performed in the church because the melody and word patterns were somewhat predictable, there was quiet for slightly over one minute before a female voice in the back of the church raised a shrill crying chant –
Oh my Lord, which way to go?
Only the women in the congregation picked up this phrase and sang to a melody different from that of the last hymn –
Which way, Oh Lord?
Another female added in a chant –
I feel so alone, Lord.
These and subsequent words of this hymn were all contributed by women, though near its end, men joined in the humming, and at one point, the choir leader shouted 'Sing it, sing it,' and added 'I'll be somewhere with Him.'

It is important to remember that this singing, punctuated by claps and foot stomping on the second and fourth beats, and shouts of praise are participated in by educated and uneducated, literate and illiterate alike in the church. When I asked those in the church who had had formal training in music or graduate-level training in education how they had learned to raise hymns, they answered my questions as follows:
Well, you just begin singing and the others join in.
I asked: 'But how do they know when and what to sing?'
Well, they sing the words.
I persisted: 'Which words?'
The ones they hear and the ones that belong.
I tried a different avenue of questioning: 'But when?'
When they feel it's right.
This type of questioning about a practice apparently so unsuitable for analyzing step-by-step in terms of the respective bits and pieces and the particular cues for different roles was fruitless. I asked the same questions of members of the congregation who had no education, and the answers were similar. Neither formal music training nor a college education in which one learns to analyze some parts of the world about one seems to carry over to hymns on Sunday morning. As one leader chanted to the congregation –

S. B. Heath

Yea, yea, now Christian friends
Now, I'm gonna say it
I know dat I feel good
I know dat I know de Lord
'n I'm gonna tell sump'n
If ya'll don't feel good
It's sump'n wrong.

The congregation responded:

Yea, yea sump'n.

It is a 'sump'n' which allows the raising of hymns that leaders and congregation compose during, in, and for the performance. It is a 'sump'n,' which cannot be articulated by the members that accounts for the process and force by which they sing, tell a tale, compose a story, or pray a prayer. . . .

Throughout the sermons, prayers, and raised hymns of the church, there appears a familiar pattern which marks many other features of Trackton life: the learning of language, telling of stories, and composing of hand-clap and jump-rope songs. Throughout these habits and the shifts from oral to written language, there is an oral performance pattern of building a text which uses themes and repetitions with variations on these themes. The young children follow this pattern in practicing and playing in their language learning; older siblings use it when they entertain the community with their songs and games; it permeates greetings, and leavings, and parts of stories. Often a formulaic phrase expresses an essential idea, but this phrase is for building from, and as such is continually subject to change as individuals perform and create simultaneously.

 Tasks B8.1.7–12: After you've read

➤ An interactional resource that participants in the Sunday service use regularly is call-and-response. This is defined as 'spontaneous verbal and non-verbal interaction between speaker and listener in which all of the statements ('calls') are punctuated by expressions ('responses') from the listener' (Smitherman, 1977, p. 104). How is call-and-response used in the church service?

➤ Do you think that call-and-response can be used to help African-American students learn in classrooms?

➤ Recall Philips's description of participation structures in the Warm Springs Indian community and participation structures in school. Compare Heath's 'ways with words' with Philips's 'participation structures.'

➤ Recall Erickson's use of musical notation to represent the speech rhythms and nonverbal activity of the Pastore family's conversation over dinner. Try to use musical notation to represent the Sunday service.

➤ How are written texts used in the Trackton Sunday church service? Compare the function of written texts in Trackton with their use in other religious or civic ceremonies that you know.

➤ Heath asked members of the Trackton congregation how they learned to raise a hymn but, despite her persistent questioning, they were unable to explain to her; they said that they just did what they felt was right. Why couldn't they explain?

UNIT SUMMARY

The text in this unit has shown how communities are constructed by what people do, and in particular the ways that people use language. As a linguistic anthropologist, Heath's approach is to look first at the ways that members of a community use language, which she does so insightfully in her description of members' participation in the Trackton Sunday church service. She analyzes the ways in which Trackton folks' ways with words differ from the mainstream, focusing on their creative 'raising' of the written word into a spoken form and their use of call-and-response. Similar close analyses were carried out by Erickson with his description of the Pastore's dinner table conversation and by Philips when she contrasted participation structures on the Warm Springs Indian reservation and in the public schools. Such close description of oral practices as these authors perform inevitably limits the amount of data that they can analyze, and so the question then arises of how much we can generalize from a single instance of a practice to ways of speaking in the community at large. Heath's book, *Ways with words: Language, life, and work in communities and classrooms,* shows how by long-term participant observation of a community and a variety of its practices, an ethnographer can paint a much fuller picture of a discourse community.

Unit B9
Learning in cultural communities

OVERVIEW OF UNIT

In Unit A9 we presented three theories of learning as social interaction: language socialization, situated learning (also known as legitimate peripheral participation), and the analysis of classroom discourse. Here we include an excerpt from an article that exemplifies research within the theory of language socialization. The article is written by the leading researcher in the field of language socialization, and we have chosen this article because the author uses a cultural context that may be familiar to many of us: American children playing a game of softball and how one child is socialized to the rules of the game and the identities that participants construct.

Text B9.1 E.
Ochs

From Ochs, E. (2002). 'Becoming a speaker of culture.' In C. J. Kramsch (ed.), *Language acquisition and language socialization: Ecological perspectives*. London: Continuum. (Excerpts from pp. 99–120.)

Young children acquire the activities, language, and beliefs of the society into which they are born almost effortlessly, and the way that young children's socialization is mediated by language has become the focus of concern of linguistic anthropologists such as Elinor Ochs. Ochs is professor of anthropology at the University of California, Los Angeles, where she directs the UCLA Center on Everyday Lives of Families. Researchers in the Center examine how members of middle-class working families create a home life through culturally and situationally organized social interactions.

In this article, Ochs starts by examining children engaged in a common social activity – playing softball at school – and focuses on how the children interact with Erin, a young girl with autism. She uses this example to show how Erin is being socialized to social and cultural rules and beliefs of her community. After grounding language socialization in this concrete example, Ochs goes on to develop a more general theory of how language indexes participants' actions, stances, identities, and activities. She concludes by discussing how actions and stances are indexed in different cultural communities, and she finds that, although there are many similarities across different cultures, there are significant differences 'in the *frequency, elaboration, and sequential positioning* of actions and stances expected in carrying out a particular activity or assuming a particular identity' (p. 114). These differences often lead to cross-cultural miscommunication.

Figure B9.1 A girl at bat in a game of softball. Source: Downloaded from iStockphoto, File Number 575574

To help situate us in the cultural context of Ochs's example, there are a few things that we need to know about softball. Figure B9.1 shows a girl at bat in a softball game. The ball has just been pitched and the batter is about to bat the ball. In the interaction transcribed by Ochs, there is disagreement between the two teams about a ball that was pitched at Erin and where the ball hit. This is an important issue in the game of softball because if the ball hit Erin's bat, it is considered a strike and, after three strikes, the batter is out. On the other hand, if the ball hit Erin's body and she made no attempt to avoid being hit, then it is not considered a strike.

Tasks B9.1.1–3: Before you read

➤ Language socialization research aims to explain how language practices encode and socialize information about society and culture. The methods that most researchers use involve ethnographic descriptions of child rearing practices in different contexts. In researching these practices, what are the advantages of studying interactions of adults with children compared with studying child–child interactions?

➤ In this article, Ochs describes how language indexes the speaker's stance – her attitude to what she is saying. Consider ways in which a speaker's stance can be indexed in your language and other languages you know.

➤ What do you know of child rearing practices in different cultures? How are they similar to or different from the way in which you were reared?

Premises of language socialization

Language socialization is rooted in the notion that the process of acquiring a language is part of a much larger process of becoming a person in society. As originally formulated, the discipline articulates ways in which novices across the life span are socialized into using language and socialized through language into local theories and preferences for acting, feeling, and knowing, in socially recognized and organized practices associated with membership in a social group (Schieffelin and Ochs 1986). Language socialization research analyzes how and why young children are apprenticed through language into particular childhood identities and activities and how older children and adults learn the communicative skills necessary for occupational and other community identities. Language socialization studies also examine how members of multilingual communities are socialized into using different codes, and how language socialization practices impact language maintenance and language change (Baquedano-Lopez, 2001; Kulick 1992; Schieffelin 1994). . . .

In language socialization research, social interactions are mined for culturally rooted ways in which veteran and novice participants co-ordinate modes of communication, actions, bodies, objects, and the built environment to enhance their knowledge and skills. Drawing on the cultural psychological notion that human development is facilitated by participation in socially and culturally organized social interactions, an important unit of analysis in language socialization research is the social activity in which more or less experienced persons participate (Leont'ev 1979). Activities such as playing a game, sharing a meal, or planning an event are analyzed for the psychological stances and actions that experts and novices routinely provide or elicit. Such moves shape the direction of activities and apprentice less knowledgeable and less skilled persons into activity competence. In the softball game involving Erin, for example, members of each team and the referee use the following linguistic structures to both configure Erin's actions and mentor her into the rudiments of the game.

Novices become acquainted with activities not only from their own and others' attempts to define what transpires in an activity, but also from how those participating in the activity respond to them. Are the expressed stances, actions, and ideas acknowledged or ignored? Do others display alignment, as when the referee initially supports the judgment that the pitcher's ball hit Erin?

```
Teacher:    Did it hit her?
Teammates:  Yes!
Teacher:    [That's what I thought.
```

Or do others display nonalignment, as when members of the opposing team disagree with Erin's team mates?

```
Opposing team:  No! ( ?)
Catcher:        [n–
Gary:           ((touches his own wrist, indicating where the
                ball hit Erin))
Catcher:        [No it hit the [bat Miss Ruby
```

And is the uptake minimal, as when Erin displays attention to Gary's explanation but otherwise offers no facial or vocal feedback? Or do others provide elaborate responses, including not only tokens of attention but also elaborate assessments, descriptions, justifications, explanations, analogies, anecdotes, and the like? For example, the catcher of the opposing team successfully convinces the teacher-referee that the ball hit the bat, not Erin's hand, through an eyewitness demonstration of what transpired:

```
Catcher:        [Miss Ruby, (.) Miss Ruby
                [((standing opposite teacher))
                I saw it hit [her on the bat right here.
                            [((looks down and taps bottom of
                her face guard))
Teacher:        ((looks down to where catcher is indicating))
Opposing team:  It hit her on the ba:t.
Team mates:     ( ?    )
Teacher:        OKA:Y. IT'S COUNTED AS A:: (.8) stri::ke.
```

From this perspective, socialization is an interactional achievement, and language socialization researchers are in the business of articulating the architecture of such interactions . . .

Task B9.1.4: While you read

➤ Ochs writes that language socialization research analyzes how and why young children are apprenticed through language into particular childhood identities. What evidence is there in the transcripts that the participants (the girls and the teacher) are constructing particular identities?

Understanding social context

Vital to competent participation in social groups is the ability to understand how people use language and other symbolic tools to construct social situations. In every community, members draw upon communicative forms to signal social information; indeed, one of the important functions of grammar and lexicon is to key interlocutors into what kind of social situation is taking place (Gumperz 1982; Hanks 1989; Silverstein 1993). Four dimensions of the social context are particularly relevant to the socialization of cultural competence: the ability to signal the *actions* one is performing, the psychological *stances* one is displaying, the social *identities* one puts forward, and the *activities* in which one is engaged. A social *action* is here defined as a socially recognized goal-directed behavior, e.g. responding to a question, asking for clarification, hitting a softball with a bat, catching a softball, running the bases (Leont'ev 1979). Psychological *stances* include both affective and epistemic orientation toward some focus of concern. *Affective stance* includes a person's mood, attitude, feeling, or disposition as well as degrees of emotional intensity (Biber and Finegan 1989; Besnier 1990; Ochs and Schieffelin 1989; Labov 1984; Levy 1984). In the softball game, for example, participants use a variety of lexical and grammatical affect markers to assess Erin's actions:

'It **did** hit the **ba::t**.
↑O::::H↓!
'**YA::Y! ALRI:::GHT!**'
'**Good** hit Erin!'

E*pistemic stance* refers to a person's knowledge or belief, including sources of knowledge and degrees of commitment to truth and certainty of propositions (Chafe and Nichols 1986). The softball players and referee used epistemic stance markers, for example, to establish the truth of the claim that the pitcher's ball hit Erin's bat:

'Miss Ruby, Miss Ruby I **saw** it hit her on the bat **right here**.'
'OKA:Y, IT'S COUNTED AS A:: (.8) stri::ke . . . (Claudia) said it hit the ba:t.'
'**See**! She even **said** it (.) **almo::st**.'
'I'm **tellin**' the ↑**tru:th**.'

The contextual dimension of social identity comprises a range of social personae, including, for example, social roles, statuses, and relationships, as well as community, institutional, ethnic, socioeconomic, gender, and other group identities. In the softball game, Erin is apprenticed into the identities of softball player and team member. At the same time, the way her peers mentor Erin and speak on her behalf construct her as a classmate with certain impairments and special needs.

Finally, *social activity* refers to at least two co-ordinated, situated actions and/or stance displays by one or multiple persons. Typically, these actions and stance displays relate to common or similar topics and goals. As noted earlier, activity is a vital unit of analysis in cultural psychology and language socialization research, because it establishes a social milieu or medium for less and more competent persons to perceive, collaborate with, and potentially be transformed by one another in culturally meaningful ways. A game of softball, in this sense, offers Erin repeated opportunities to watch, listen, have contact with artifacts (e.g. bat, ball, bases), and enact the game.

As this discussion implies, children and other novices are exposed to dimensions of social context not in isolation but in concert, as they are drawn into the life of the community. The four contextual dimensions of action, stance, identity, and activity are interdependent in that social groups associate particular stances with particular actions, associate these linked stances and acts with particular social identities and activities, and associate particular activities with particular identities (Ochs 1996):

Actions ∪ Stances

Actions ∪ Stances ∪ Identities

Actions ∪ Stances ∪ Activities

Activities ∪ Identities

Moreover, identities and activities are more complex than actions and stances, in the sense that particular social identities and activities culturally entail particular actions and stances. That is, actions and stances are the cultural building blocks of social identities and activities.

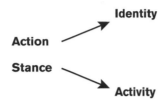

The building of activities and identities is generative, in the sense that activities and identities themselves build more complex activities and identities. Thus, for example, the activity of one player being up at bat is part of the larger activity of one team being up at bat, which in turn is part of an activity unit called an inning, which is part of the larger activity of playing softball. Activity theorist Yrjo Engeström (1990, 1993) conceptualizes social structures such as medical clinics, courts, professions, workplaces, and schools as activity systems, i.e. a set of interconnected, situated activities. Thus, we might think of the activity of playing softball as one of many activities that structure the public school as a community institution. In this vein, Erin's competence and participation in the institutional life of the school depends on her understanding and participation in recreational activities such as softball. Similarly, social identities can help build other identities. Erin's identity as a more or less successful softball player helps to instantiate her as a more or less successful student and classmate in this school community.

Language and social context

Where does language fit into this perspective on the construction of and socialization into culturally and situationally organized actions, stances, activities, and identities? Every social group has available to its members a repertoire of linguistic forms. Like a communicative palette, members draw upon this repertoire to portray particular stances, acts, activities, and identities. I have argued, however, that few linguistic forms explicitly and exclusively encode activities or identities. Rather, linguistic forms generally encode psychological stances and actions that are linked to activities and identities:

$$\text{Linguistic Form} \longrightarrow \begin{bmatrix} \text{Stance} \\ \text{Action} \end{bmatrix} \longrightarrow \begin{bmatrix} \text{Activity} \\ \text{Identity} \end{bmatrix}$$

For example, linguistic forms that express negative psychological stances are linked to the activity of disagreement, yet these forms index this activity only indirectly because they encode a stance that is culturally associated with disagreements. This does not mean that everyone who engages in disagreements always uses certain negative forms, but rather that if one wants to engage in disagreement, one can do so by using linguistic forms such as 'No!' and 'not' in English.

E. Ochs

The relation between language and the construction of social context can be useful in understanding the emergence of language and cultural competence across the life span. Most children and other novices learn to use and recognize linguistic markers of stance and actions, and learn how to use these stance and action markers to instantiate certain social activities and identities. We can use this framework to discern levels of sociolinguistic competence (Ochs 1993).

First, we can determine whether or not and how a child or other novice *linguistically indexes an action or stance*. Did he use action or stance markers that are part of the group's sociolinguistic repertoire? . . . In other cases, sociolinguistic incompetence may be due to a lack of knowledge concerning local conventions for act or stance production. Second, we can examine whether or not and how novices linguistically encode actions and stances that are appropriate to particular activities and identities . . .

The research framework presented here is useful in understanding cross-cultural similarities and differences in the relation of language to action, stance, activity, and social identity and their implications for second-language socialization. In this perspective, there is considerable overlap across speech communities in how language users signal actions and psychological stances but considerable differences in how communities use actions and stances to realize particular activities and identities (Ochs 1993). For example, actions such as requests, contradictions, affirmations, and summons are marked similarly across languages (Gordon and Ervin-Tripp 1984; Gordon and Lakoff 1971; Grimshaw 1990). Similarly, psychological stances of certainty and uncertainty, emotional intensity, and politeness have corresponding forms cross-linguistically (Brown and Levinson 1987; Labov 1984; Ochs and Schieffelin 1989; Besnier 1990). These commonalities assist novice second-language acquirers who venture across geographical and social borders. Alternatively, those who enter new speech communities face cultural differences in the kinds of actions and stances considered appropriate in carrying out a particular activity or assuming a particular identity, and in the *frequency, elaboration, and sequential positioning* of actions and stances expected in carrying out a particular activity or assuming a particular identity. These cross-cultural differences often thwart the language socialization of novices trying to access second cultures. Communication breaks down because the action or stance is not expected by one or another interlocutor, or went on too long or too briefly or at the wrong time and place in the particular activity underway, or for the particular social role, status, or relationship attempted. Because *some* but not all relations between language and social context are familiar and expected, novice and veteran language users may be disturbed at how the other is communicating.

★ Tasks B9.1.5–8: After you've read

➤ The four dimensions of social context that Ochs mentions are (1) the *actions* one is performing, (2) the psychological *stances* one is displaying, (3) the social *identities* one puts forward, and (4) the *activities* in which one is engaged. How does she define these four dimensions?

➤ Ochs indicates the interdependence of the four contextual dimensions by the symbol for the union of sets. For example, she represents the association in some social groups of particular stances with particular actions by 'Actions [∪]

Stances.' Consider carefully the four associations that Ochs proposes. Can you find examples of those associations in cultural groups with which you are familiar? (For example, consider the association in your culture between an action of arguing and the epistemic stance of doubting the truth of a proposition.)

➤ Ochs claims that the sociolinguistic competence of an individual can be assessed by how she uses linguistic stance and action markers to instantiate certain social activities and identities. Discuss how you would use this idea as the basis of a formal test of sociolinguistic competence. How does sociolinguistic competence differ from communicative and interactional competence? (We introduced these last two ideas in Unit A6.)

➤ Ochs writes that breakdowns in communication across cultures occur when the action or stance is not expected by one or another interlocutor, or went on too long or too briefly or at the wrong time and place in the particular activity under way, or for the particular social role, status, or relationship attempted. Reflect on breakdowns in cross-cultural communication that you have experienced or witnessed. Can they be explained in the ways that Ochs proposes?

UNIT SUMMARY

In the interaction that we have studied in this unit, we observed people who are developing interactional skill. We considered what is learned: Is it language, interactional skill, actions, stances, identities, or some combination? Learning is presented as participation in a discursive practice: a softball game. In the Ochs article, she examines a short segment of one interaction in which the language, stances, and identities of participants are made clear by the children and by the teacher. The focal learner is Erin, and we do not know what Erin had learned from the interaction because Erin's contributions to the interaction (if there were any) were not transcribed and because we have no further information about Erin's development as a child at school or as a softball player.

SECTION C
Exploration

Unit C1
Exploring the nature of
language and interaction

INTRODUCTION

This introductory unit contains four activities that will help you become more familiar with tasks associated with conducting research on language and interaction. Because the writings of Bakhtin, Wittgenstein, Hymes, and other scholars that have been mentioned in Units A1 and B1 may not be familiar to you, this unit provides opportunities for you to read some of their work in the original. In addition to this library work, several of the activities in this unit are action-oriented and encourage you to look at language in interaction from the perspective of the theories that we have introduced in Units A1 and B1.

C1.1   READING BAKHTIN

In his writings over a period of about fifty years, Bakhtin introduced several concepts that are the foundations of the study of language and interaction. Bakhtin's presentation of his ideas is often obscure and in some cases his thinking developed over the years so that some of his later writings may present ideas that are developments from what he wrote at an earlier time. Here are some of the concepts that Bakhtin introduced that are of importance in the study of language and interaction. Read the English translations of his own writing and the relevant parts of the comprehensive study of Bakhtin's thought in Morson and Emerson (1990), and write a short evaluation of each of the following ideas.

- Utterance: Bakhtin, 'The problem of speech genres': Morson and Emerson, pp. 125–127
- Addressivity: Bakhtin, 'The problem of speech genres': Morson and Emerson, pp. 131–133
- Dialogue: Bakhtin, 'Problems of Dostoevsky's poetics': Morson and Emerson, pp. 131–133
- Heteroglossia: Bakhtin, 'The problem of speech genres': Morson and Emerson, pp. 139–145
- Genre: Bakhtin, 'Problems of Dostoevsky's poetics': Morson and Emerson, pp. 271–305

C1.2 LANGUAGE GAMES

Wittgenstein invented the theory of language games to explain certain aspects of the way that people use language in interaction. He also said that our normal theory of language as simply a way of representing reality blinded us to the way that language is related to action. He united the two when he wrote: 'I shall also call the whole [of language], consisting of language and the actions into which it is woven, the "language-game"' (Wittgenstein, 2001, I, 7). Wittgenstein's ideas were later developed into the theory of speech acts by J. L. Austin (1962) and John Searle (1969).

Read Searle's essay 'What is a Speech Act?' in which Searle describes a set of 'rules' for the act of promising and write a critique of Searle's description of the language game of promising. 'What is a Speech Act?' was originally published in 1965 as a chapter in *Philosophy in America*, edited by Max Black, published in the US by Cornell University Press and in the UK by Allen and Unwin. The essay has been reprinted eleven times and translated into seven languages.

C1.3 THE ETHNOGRAPHY OF SPEAKING

Hymes's initial list of the contextual features included:

- a sender (addresser)
- a receiver (addressee)
- a message form
- a channel
- a code
- a topic
- a setting (scene, situation).

Read Hymes's article (1962/1974) in order to discover exactly what he meant by these seven terms. Then take a notebook and an audio- or video-recorder and record a short spoken interaction between people that you know. Transcribe the interaction and describe its contextual features under the seven headings that Hymes provided. Is your description complete?

C1.4 CONVERSATION ANALYSIS

Read one of the short introductions to CA listed below. Make a list of the questions and points for debate which the reading raises for you. Discuss these issues with friends and colleagues who have read a different reading from you.

- Hutchby, I., and Wooffitt, R. (1998). 'What is conversation analysis?' in their *Conversation analysis: Principles, practices and applications*. Cambridge and Malden, MA: Polity.

- Heritage J. (1984). 'Conversation analysis' in his *Garfinkel and ethnomethodology*. Cambridge: Polity.
- Zimmerman, D. H. (1988). 'On conversation: The conversation analytic perspective' in J. A. Anderson (ed.), *Communication yearbook* (Vol. 11, pp. 406–432). Beverly Hills, CA: Sage.

QUESTIONS AND ACTIVITIES FOR FUTURE EXPLORATION

In this unit we have considered several different approaches to the analysis of language and interaction: the dialogic perspective of Bakhtin, the action-oriented perspective of Wittgenstein and Searle, the ethnographic perspective of Hymes, the microethnographic approach of Erickson, and the strictly empirical approach of Conversation Analysis. What do you consider to be the strengths and weaknesses of these five approaches?

Unit C2
Exploring the nature of context

INTRODUCTION

In Unit A2, we presented the many different ways in which language and context affect one another. We saw examples of how a certain moment of interaction is influenced by what went before, of how participants' cultural understanding of where they are and when the interaction is happening affect what happens in the interaction. We expanded the notions of participation to include not only those participants who produce the words and those to whom the words are addressed but also other participants who influence what goes on in interaction by being there or by being invoked. We showed that the contributions of all participants are an image of the historical cultural conditions in which they grew up. And we recognized that individuals do not create interaction or any other meaningful social reality alone, but these conditions are co-constructed.

These features of context influence language, but they must not obscure the influence of language on context. By creating frames by which all participants can interpret their words and actions, human agents construct contexts through language as much as context influences language. The two data examples that you will meet in this unit are transcripts of stories told by two very different people and, although the voices of both speakers are recorded without interaction from anybody else, each of the stories cannot be fully understood without careful analysis of their contexts and the contexts which the speakers create.

C2.1 PRESENTATION OF DATA 1

The data transcript below is a story told by Jerome Smith to StoryCorps.[1] StoryCorps is an oral history project in the United States intended to instruct and inspire people to record one another's stories in sound. The recordings are housed at the American Folklife Center at the Library of Congress in Washington, DC, and they are available on air through National Public Radio.

Mr Smith grew up in New Orleans and still lived there when his story was recorded in 2006. He recalled riding a streetcar (a tram) when he was ten years old in New Orleans in 1950.

My father was on a streetcar here, and he took the screen down that separated the blacks from the whites, put it in the middle of the floor. Some months later, I did the same thing. And I put the screen down, took a seat, and the streetcar became very hostile. An old black woman came from the back and slapped me aside my head. It felt like there was a bell ringing in my head, and she said, I'm going to fix him for disrespecting these white folks. You should never do that – disrespect white people. You have no business trying to sit with them. And she told I'm a take him home and she pushed me down as I was trying to get off the streetcar.

And she came behind me, and she took me behind a auto store on St. Bernard and St. Claude. And this was the moment. This was the moment that make me stand like I stand today. She told me never, ever stop, she started crying. She hugged me and said I'm proud of you, don't you ever quit. And even though I didn't know the words that were right then, that opened up the door.

In Unit A2, we presented several dimensions of context. In the following activities, we will take each dimension in turn and investigate how it relates to the story.

C2.1.1 Activity 1: sequential context

Here again are the sentences from the first paragraph of the story, but they are arranged here in alphabetical order by the first word of the sentence. When you place them back in the sequence in which they appear in the transcript, what clues do you use to sequence the sentences?

A. *An old black woman came from the back and slapped me aside my head.*
B. *And I put the screen down, took a seat, and the streetcar became very hostile.*
C. *And she told I'm a take him home and she pushed me down as I was trying to get off the streetcar.*
D. *It felt like there was a bell ringing in my head, and she said, I'm going to fix him for disrespecting these white folks.*
E. *My father was on a streetcar here, and he took the screen down that separated the blacks from the whites, put it in the middle of the floor.*
F. *Some months later, I did the same thing.*
G. *You have no business trying to sit with them.*
H. *You should never do that – disrespect white people.*

C2.1.2 Activity 2: setting

Mr Smith's story was recorded in a traveling recording studio, called a MobileBooth that visited New Orleans in 2006. The MobileBooth is a trailer that travels around the country to provide people with a welcoming space where they can record an interview with someone important to them. StoryCorps facilitators provide

Figure C2.1 A StoryCorps MobileBooth. Source: `http://www.hhcc.com/?m=200605`

professional audio and photographic equipment and one copy of each interview for the participants, with an additional copy to be archived at a local repository. Figure C2.1 shows the outside of a MobileBooth. Recall that 'setting' refers to the spatial and temporal context of an event, as they are interpreted by the participants. How do you think the setting influenced Mr Smith's story?

C2.1.3 Activity 3: participants

Recall that Goffman included among the participants in a speech event the production roles of *animator, author*, and *principal*; and the reception roles of *official, unofficial* and *ratified, unratified* hearers. Given what we know of the context of StoryCorps, who were the participants when Mr Smith told his story in 2006?

In his story, Mr Smith tells about his two interactions in 1950 with an old black woman, the first on the streetcar and the second behind the auto store. Who were the participants in the two interactions?

C2.1.4 Activity 4: habitus

You can listen to Mr Smith's story and see a picture of him at `http://www.npr.org/templates/story/story.php?storyId=6562915`. Recall that *habitus* refers to people's socially acquired predispositions, tendencies, propensities, or inclinations, which are shown in mental phenomena such as opinions and outlooks, linguistic phenomena such as ways of talking, and physical phenomena such as deportment, posture, as well as ways of walking, sitting, and dressing. From looking at Mr Smith's picture and from hearing his voice, what can you tell about the habitus that was laid down in his formative years by the cultural environment of Mr Smith's home?

Consider the other people on the streetcar. Some were white and some were black. Given what you know about racial identities in the United States in the 1950s, what can you guess about the habitus of the other riders?

Commentary on data 1

The sociopolitical context of Mr Smith's story is racial segregation in postwar America. For Black Americans the act of refusing to sit in the place on a streetcar that had been allocated to them was an important act of resistance to the apartheid that existed in America at the time. In fact, one act of resistance very similar to Mr Smith's has gained epic status in the history of civil rights. The heroine was Rosa Parks, a black seamstress who refused to relinquish her seat to a white man on a city bus in Montgomery, Alabama, in 1955. Here is the story of the consequences of Mrs Parks's action as told in her obituary in *The New York Times* (October 25, 2005).

> For her act of defiance, Mrs. Parks was arrested, convicted of violating the segregation laws and fined $10, plus $4 in court fees. In response, blacks in Montgomery boycotted the buses for nearly 13 months while mounting a successful Supreme Court challenge to the Jim Crow law that enforced their second-class status on the public bus system.

> The events that began on that bus in the winter of 1955 captivated the nation and transformed a 26-year-old preacher named Martin Luther King Jr. into a major civil rights leader. It was Dr. King, the new pastor of the Dexter Avenue Baptist Church in Montgomery, who was drafted to head the Montgomery Improvement Association, the organization formed to direct the nascent civil rights struggle.

> 'Mrs. Parks's arrest was the precipitating factor rather than the cause of the protest,' Dr. King wrote in his 1958 book, *Stride Toward Freedom*. 'The cause lay deep in the record of similar injustices.'

> Her act of civil disobedience, what seems a simple gesture of defiance so many years later, was in fact a dangerous, even reckless move in 1950s' Alabama. In refusing to move, she risked legal sanction and perhaps even physical harm, but she also set into motion something far beyond the control of the city authorities. Mrs. Parks clarified for people far beyond Montgomery the cruelty and humiliation inherent in the laws and customs of segregation.

> That moment on the Cleveland Avenue bus also turned a very private woman into a reluctant symbol and torchbearer in the quest for racial equality and of a movement that became increasingly organized and sophisticated in making demands and getting results.

> 'She sat down in order that we might stand up,' the Rev. Jesse Jackson said yesterday in an interview from South Africa. 'Paradoxically, her imprisonment opened the doors for our long journey to freedom.'

Perhaps you knew about Rosa Parks before you read Mr Smith's story, but if you did not, does this knowledge change your view of the context of Mr Smith's story?

C2.2 PRESENTATION OF DATA 2

The second data transcript is from the video *American Tongues* (Kolker and Alvarez, 1987). The speaker is Philip, a young man from the North End of Boston. Sitting on a stoop in his neighborhood surrounded by his friends he talks to the camera about the advantages that he sees about growing up in the city. We have tried to reproduce Philip's way of speaking as accurately as possible in this transcript, but if you want to hear and see the original, you should watch the video.

```
I would never change growin up in da city. (.5) da best t'ing
dat ever happened to me. (.) really was. it s- it's such an
advantage over people. c's you go to a club, you start talkin
to a babe, and she says you ita:yan? (.) and sh- what makes you
t'ink dat. and she s's you talk like an itayan. (.5) and den
you start givin her de accent ((speaks with an Italian accent))
yeah youse guy:s. and uh where youse fro:m. and (.8) I'm wid
t'ree o my frie:ns, I t'rew da football all day:, and uh (1.0)
dis dat and de od-. mudda. ((resumes normal accent)) an stuff
like dat an- (.) an da women dey eat it up. dey love dat. dey
really do dey t'rive on dat. and den you get a guy right? and
you tell im (.4) don fuck wid me I break ya mudderfuckin head.
and den right away da guy he says wow dis kid's from the city,
he's gonna pull a shank on me, an capi:, you can intimidate
people (.5) wid ya (1.0) verbal actions.
```

C2.2.1 Activity 1: habitus

A person's accent is part of their habitus because most people acquired their accents in their early years from their family and the neighborhood where they grew up. Some people try to change their accent when they become adults, but such a change is hard to effect. Everybody has an accent, but we normally pay more attention to the accents of people who *didn't* grow up in our neighborhood and whose accent is different from ours. In what ways is Philip's accent different from yours?

Certain accents are prestigious because they are associated with people who have wealth and power in our society. Other accents are undervalued because the people with those accents do not. How would you evaluate Philip's accent?

C2.2.2 Activity 2: frames and conversational inference

Participants in social interaction do not simply respond to the context of an interaction by modifying what they say and how they say it; people are creative. Goffman and Gumperz showed that speakers are human agents and we can create contexts for our talk. Speakers use contextualization cues in order to provide a frame for other parties to interpret what is happening in an interaction. What conversational cues does Philip use when he meets a woman at a club?

Philip says that he can intimidate people with his verbal actions. How does he do that?

Philip paints himself as being successful with women: 'They love that. They really do. They thrive on that.' He says that he is just as successful in intimidating men, who fear him: 'Wow, this kid's from the city, he's going to pull a knife on me.' When a speaker tells a story about himself, he is presenting a picture of himself to the listeners, who go away from the interaction with some opinion about his character. What impression do you have of Philip?

Commentary on data 2

The North End of Boston has always been the place where new immigrants settled, first Irish, then Eastern European Jews, and by 1900 the Italian population in the North End was 14,000. Over the next twenty years it would more than double to 37,000 and at its peak, in 1930, 44,000 Italians were packed into an area less than one square mile in size. It was a tough radical neighborhood where the two anarchists Nicola Sacco and Bartolomeo Vanzetti grew up. Today, Italian-Americans still comprise more than 41 percent of the resident population of the North End. The neighborhood is packed with restaurants, virtually all of them Italian, and the neighborhood is still deeply rooted in Italian culture. Residents hold annual festivals to honor patron saints of Italian villages. Italian remains the lingua franca throughout the district and it is one of the most vibrant and thriving neighborhoods of its kind.

QUESTIONS AND ACTIVITIES FOR FUTURE EXPLORATION

Although Mr Smith makes no mention of Rosa Parks, he tells his story in the context of that historic event in the civil rights movement in the United States. Can you find another storyteller whose personal story evokes either implicitly or explicitly a famous historical event?

Philip's roots in the North End of Boston are an important part of the context of his story. Research a neighborhood that you know that has strong traditions. How do these traditions influence the way that people speak?

We have presented these two stories as transcriptions of oral data in a textbook on language interaction. In other words, we have entextualized the stories of Mr Smith and Philip. What effect does the process of entextualization have on our understanding of the stories? Record a story from someone you know and then transcribe it. How has the story changed in the transcription?

Unit C3
Exploring ways of making meaning

INTRODUCTION

We began Unit A3 with a consideration of Dr Martin Luther King Jr's 'I have a dream speech' as a communicative event and we argued that it can be seen from two complementary perspectives. We can use the tools of systemic functional grammar (SFG) to analyze the ways in which meaning is constructed in a communicative event considered as a text. And we can understand the way in which a communicative event works in real time by analyzing the interactional resources that participants use. In the activities that we present here, we will practice how to analyze the meaning making resources of language in a text and we will explore the very different procedures that are needed to understand the interactional resources that speakers use in the moment-to-moment organization of conversation.

C3.1 PRESENTATION OF DATA 1

The text below is taken from the first few minutes of Dr Martin Luther King Jr's 'I have a dream speech.' You can watch and listen to a 17-minute video of the whole speech online at the Google video website. King gave the speech on the steps of the Memorial to President Abraham Lincoln at one end of the National Mall in Washington, DC. He begins by recognizing Lincoln's role in emancipating the slaves.

1 *Five score years ago, a great American in whose symbolic shadow we stand*
2 *today, signed the Emancipation Proclamation. This momentous decree came*
3 *as a great beacon light of hope to millions of Negro slaves who had been seared*
4 *in the flames of withering injustice. It came as a joyous daybreak to end the*
5 *long night of their captivity.*

6 *But one hundred years later, the Negro still is not free. One hundred years*
7 *later, the life of the Negro is still sadly crippled by the manacles of segregation*
8 *and the chains of discrimination. One hundred years later, the Negro lives on*
9 *a lonely island of poverty in the midst of a vast ocean of material prosperity.*
10 *One hundred years later, the Negro is still languishing in the corners of*
11 *American society and finds himself an exile in his own land. And so we have*
12 *come here today to dramatize a shameful condition.*

13 *In a sense we have come to our nation's capital to cash a check. When the*
14 *architects of our republic wrote the magnificent words of the Constitution and*
15 *the Declaration of Independence, they were signing a promissory note to which*
16 *every American was to fall heir. This note was a promise that all men, yes,*
17 *black men as well as white men, would be guaranteed the inalienable rights*
18 *of life, liberty, and the pursuit of happiness.*

19 *It is obvious today that America has defaulted on this promissory note insofar*
20 *as her citizens of color are concerned. Instead of honoring this sacred*
21 *obligation, America has given the Negro people a bad check, a check which*
22 *has come back marked 'insufficient funds.' But we refuse to believe that the*
23 *bank of justice is bankrupt. We refuse to believe that there are insufficient funds*
24 *in the great vaults of opportunity of this nation. So we have come to cash this*
25 *check – a check that will give us upon demand the riches of freedom and the*
26 *security of justice. We have also come to this hallowed spot to remind America*
27 *of the fierce urgency of now. This is no time to engage in the luxury of cooling*
28 *off or to take the tranquilizing drug of gradualism. Now is the time to make*
29 *real the promises of democracy. Now is the time to rise from the dark and*
30 *desolate valley of segregation to the sunlit path of racial justice. Now is the time*
31 *to lift our nation from the quick sands of racial injustice to the solid rock of*
32 *brotherhood. Now is the time to make justice a reality for all of God's children.*

C3.1.1 Activity 1: phonological constituency

The fundamental process in SFG is to analyze a text into a hierarchy of levels, each of which is both a constituent of a higher level and the composition of one or more constituents of a lower level. The dimensions of language that Halliday and Matthiessen discuss are phonology, graphology, and lexicogrammar. Since the original of Dr Martin Luther King Jr's speech is an oral text, we will not do an analysis of graphological constituents (although if you wish, you can do a graphological analysis of the transcription given above).

Listen to a recording of the speech online from the Google video website, and analyze the phonological constituents of part of the speech (for example lines 6–12). The phonological ranks are line, foot, syllable, onset, and rhyme. A *syllable* is composed of a rhyming part, known as the *rhyme*; if a syllabic segment precedes the rhyme, it is called the *onset*. A *foot* is a grouping of two or more syllables into a rhythmic unit, and a *line* is a grouping of two or more feet into a melodic unit or tone group. You can use these symbols to indicate the boundaries between phonological constituents: Double slash // for a line boundary and single slash / for a foot boundary.

C3.1.2 Activity 2: lexicogrammatical constituency

The ranks of the lexicogrammar are morpheme, word, word group (or phrase), clause, and clause complex. Morphemes are the lowest rank and are the smallest unit of meaning, and a word may be constituted by one or more morphemes. A word group or phrase (often simply called a group in SFG) is the next rank and groups are the constituents of clauses. A clause functions as a message and has two elements of information structure: the Theme and the Rheme: Theme is the point of departure of the message which locates and orients the clause within its sequential context and Rheme is the remainder of the message in which Theme is developed. A clause complex is the highest rank and is constituted by two or more clauses linked together. Very often a clause complex in lexicogrammar corresponds to a sentence in the graphological system. Take, for example the clause complex in lines 28–29: *Now is the time to make real the promises of democracy*. This complex is constituted by the two clauses

> now is the time
> to make real the promises of democracy

The Theme of the first clause is *now* and the Rheme is *is the time*. *Now, is,* and *the time* are words or groups, and each is composed of a single morpheme. The second clause has three constituent groups: *to make* + *real* + *the promises of democracy*. All the words that constitute the groups are single morphemes except *promise+s* (though you could argue about the morphemic constituents of *democracy*).

Take another part of the text and show its lexicogrammatical constituency.

C3.1.3 Activity 3: metafunction

Systemic functional grammar recognizes three broad purposes to which texts are put. Texts may serve to influence others people's thoughts, beliefs, or actions; texts are also ways in which we describe, represent, analyze and explain internal experiences such as our thoughts and feelings and external experiences that happen in the world outside our bodies; and finally, language enables us to make connections between different parts of a text – in other words to create textuality. These three broad purposes are labeled metafunctions in SFG and they correspond to the interpersonal, ideational, and textual metafunctions. Metafunctions operate at the clausal level, which is to say that, in a multi-clausal text like the 'I have a dream' speech, many different metafunctions may operate within the same long text.

Examine each of the clauses in the extract from the 'I have a dream' speech, paying particular attention to the verbal elements, and identify the metafunction of each clause.

C3.1.4 Activity 4: textuality

Textuality is what enables texts to hang together instead of being a random jumble of clauses, and understanding textuality involves identifying the Theme and Rheme of each clause. Theme is the starting point of the message – what the clause is going to be about, and the Rheme is that part of the clause in which the Theme is developed. One characteristic of all texts is the way in which Theme develops and SFG recognized three patterns of thematic development: Thematic iteration, the zigzag pattern, and the multiple Rheme pattern. Thematic iteration involves making the same lexicogrammatical participant Theme on a regular basis. The zigzag pattern we diagrammed in Section A3.1.3 and it involves introducing a lexico-grammatical element as Rheme in one clause and then promoting the same element to Theme in the next clause. The multiple-Rheme pattern involves introducing several elements within a complex Rheme and then promoting each of those elements in turn to thematic status in the following clauses.

One characteristic of a great orator is the thematic development of his speeches. Identify the Themes and Rhemes in the clauses in the extract from Dr Martin Luther King Jr's speech and describe the patterns of thematic development. Why does he use this pattern?

C3.2 PRESENTATION OF DATA 2

Understanding the interactional resources of talk-in-interaction is a very different task from the analysis of how meaning is created in text. When a text is analyzed using the methods of systemic functional grammar, it is extracted from the sequential, cultural, and historical context in which the text was originally produced. Talk in interaction is very different because we want to preserve the online nature of the talk; and this means that what we say and what we do at a particular moment of interaction with other speakers is crucially dependent on how we interpret what has gone before in the interaction. The basic analytical question that we must ask is 'Why did this speaker do this action at this particular point in the interaction?'

The methodology of conversation analysis has brought many insights into that basic question and in this book we cannot provide any more than a superficial treatment of the methods of conversation analysis. Doing conversation analysis is a skill that requires many, many hours of practice with actual data. There are several books that introduce the methods of CA, but one of the most useful is Paul ten Have's *Doing conversation analysis: A practical guide*. There are also a number of websites that provide an introduction together with some online data. The introductory tutorial on CA at `http://www-staff.lboro.ac.uk/~sscai/sitemenu.htm` is designed by Charles Antaki at Loughborough University in the United Kingdom, and this site allows practice with British English data. For those who prefer to work with data from speakers of American English, the best introduction is the transcription module on Emanuel Schegloff's home page at `http://www.sscnet.ucla.edu/soc/faculty/schegloff/TranscriptionProject/index.html`.

C3.2.1 Activity 1: transcribing sequences and silence

In order to study talk-in-interaction in a book such as this, it is necessary to first record the talk with a high quality audio- or video-recorder, and then to convert the talk to text on the printed page so that it can be analyzed. We commented in Unit C2 that the process of entextualization of talk removes the talk from its original context and locates it in a new context, and we should be aware that the new context influences the talk in a different way from the original context. This difference is recognized by conversation analysts, who make every effort to try to interpret the talk from the perspective of the participants in the interaction rather than from their own perspective as analysts. This approach, which focuses on the ways in which participants make sense of their world, display their understanding to others, and produce the mutually shared social order in which they live, is known as ethnomethodology. An ethnomethodological approach also implies that the information from talk in interaction that was available to the original participants must also be available to the conversation analyst.

Unfortunately, in the process of transcribing a spoken interaction as text a tremendous amount of information is lost. When we transcribe dialogue, we often use a play script or screenplay format in which each participant's turn at talk is written on separate lines, but in so doing we have lost information about how much time elapses between one speaker's turn and the next and whether speakers overlap and where the overlap begins and ends. Even within a single speaker's turn, does the speaker pause in the middle of the turn? And how much time elapses during that pause? The transcription system that is used in CA is an attempt to overcome these problems of transcription by using the following symbols to indicate overlap, latching, and elapsed silent time.

[ ]	Square brackets indicate the beginning and end of over-lapping talk.
=	Equals signs, one at the end of one line and one at the beginning of the next indicate that there is no hearable silence between adjacent turns.
(0.5) and (.)	Numbers in parentheses indicate elapsed silent time in units of one-tenth of a second. Shorter silences are indicated by a dot.

Here is a transcript of part of a telephone conversation between two American women. The conversation is transcribed here as a play script. Go to the transcription module on Emanuel Schegloff's home page and compare his transcription with the one provided here. What differences do you find?

Bee: Because they are going to do the operation on the tear duct first.
Ava: Mhm.
Bee: Before they can do the cataracts.
Ava: Right. Yeah.

C3.2.2 Activity 2: transcribing speech delivery

Another big difference between speech and writing is that graphological ranks do not correspond to phonological ranks and the symbols such as period (or full stop), comma, colon, semicolon, and so on that we use in writing to indicate boundaries between constituents do not mark boundaries between constituents in talk. Unless we use the phonetic punctuation system of the legendary pianist and humorist Victor Borge, we don't speak with punctuation and, equally, when we transcribe speech we need to find a different way of indicating phonological information. The system that has been devised for CA *does* in fact use punctuation symbols, although their meaning in a CA transcript is very different from how they function in writing. Here are the symbols used in CA transcription and an explanation of each.

be<u>ware</u>	Underscoring indicates some form of stress on a syllable.
oh::	Colons indicate a lengthening (or stretching) of the preceding sound, and more colons indicate a longer stretch.
don't be stup–	A dash indicates a cut-off.

Punctuation marks are used to indicate intonation of the preceding utterance.

.	A period indicates a falling tone.
,	A comma indicates a low-rising intonation, like when you are reading items from a list
?	A question mark indicates rising intonation, not necessarily a question.

Other aspects of speech delivery are indicated by the following symbols.

°	An utterance bracketed by degree signs is relatively quieter than the surrounding talk, and more degree signs signal even quieter talk.
	An arrow pointing up or down marks a shift in the following syllable to a relatively higher or lower pitch.
< >	Less/greater than signs bracket talk that is noticeably faster than the surrounding talk.
> <	Greater/less than signs bracket talk that is noticeably slower than the surrounding talk.
hhh, (hh), ·hh	Hearable aspiration (breathing) is shown where it occurs in the talk by the letter *h*. More *h*'s indicate more aspiration.
() (guess) ((smiles))	Empty parentheses indicate that the transcriber could not hear what was said; parenthesized words indicate the transcriber's best guess at that what was said; double parentheses indicate descriptions of nonverbal action.

Here is a transcript of the beginning of the telephone conversation between Ava and Bee. The conversation is transcribed here as a play script. Go to the transcription module on Emanuel Schegloff's home page and compare his transcription with the one provided here. Listen carefully to the audio and discuss how effectively the CA transcription captures the speech of the two women.

1	*Ava:*	Hello
2	*Bee:*	Hi.
3	*Ava:*	Hi.
4	*Bee:*	How are you?
5	*Ava:*	Okay.
6	*Bee:*	Good. You sound . . .
7	*Ava:*	I wanted to know did you get a what-you-may-call-it, a parking
8		place this morning?
9	*Bee:*	A parking place.
10	*Ava:*	Mhm.
11	*Bee:*	Where?
12	*Ava:*	Oh just anyplace. I was just kidding you.
13	*Bee:*	No?
14	*Ava:*	No.
15	*Bee:*	Why? What's the matter with you? You sound happy.
16	*Ava:*	Nothing. I sound happy?
17	*Bee:*	Yeah.
18	*Ava:*	No.
19	*Bee:*	No?
20	*Ava:*	No.
21	*Bee:*	You sound sort of cheerful.
22	*Ava:*	Anyway, how have you been?
23	*Bee:*	Oh surviving, I guess.
24	*Ava:*	That's good. How's Bob?
25	*Bee:*	He's fine.
26	*Ava:*	That's good.

C3.2.3 Activity 3: transcribing non-standard English

Another difference that you have probably noticed between Schegloff's CA transcriptions and the play scripts presented here is in the way that the words are transcribed. Compare Schegloff's transcription of these three lines with a transcription in standard written English.

```
Ava:  I 'ave    [a lotta t]ough courses.
Bee:            [Uh really?]
Bee:  On I c'n ima:gine.=<wh'tche tol' me whatchu ta:kin(.)/(,)
```

> *Ava:* I have a lot of tough courses.
> *Bee:* Oh really?
> *Bee:* I can imagine with you told me what you're taking.

Some differences to note between the words in the CA transcription and their Standard English equivalents are *'ave* for *have, lotta* for *lot of, c'n* for *can,* and *whatchu takin* for *what you're taking.* The CA transcription attempts to render features of a nonstandard English accent, and it does so in a way that speakers of Standard English can understand. Some linguists object to this convention of transcribing nonstandard English, saying that the convention devalues the speech of people who do not speak Standard English, and the only equitable solution is to use a broad phonetic transcription for both standard and nonstandard accents.

You can decide for yourself how best to transcribe nonstandard accents. Record someone you know who speaks English with a nonstandard accent and transcribe their speech in the way that you feel is most appropriate. Then show your transcription to the speaker and ask for their reactions to your transcription.

C3.2.4 Activity 4: collecting data

Make an original audio or video recording of a naturally occurring verbal interaction between at least two people. The recording should take no longer than ten minutes. Write a detailed account of the process by which you obtained the recording, including the equipment that you used, the set-up, the reactions of the participants, and the sound (and video) quality of the recording.

QUESTIONS AND ACTIVITIES FOR FUTURE EXPLORATION

Share the recording that you made in Activity C3.2.4 with a friend or colleague. Both you and your colleague should work independently to write a transcription of the recording. When you both have finished, compare your transcriptions.

In Section A3.2.1, we discussed action sequences in conversation. Locate and identify any adjacency pairs in the transcript that you have made.

In Section A3.2.2, we introduced two features of turn-taking: transition-relevance place and selection of next speaker. Analyze each transition between speakers in the transcript that you have made and explain *when* the transition was accomplished and *how* the next speaker was selected.

Recall that repair in conversation can be classified according to who initiated the repair and who completed it. Identify repairs in the transcript that you have made and discuss whether they are *self-initiated self-repair, self-initiated other repair, other-initiated self-repair,* or *other-initiated other repair.*

Unit C4
Different communities,
different practices

INTRODUCTION

We presented Practice Theory in Unit A4 and defined practice as human activities that have their own rules, their own constraints, and their own structures. We limited our attention to those practices involving language and quoted Karen Tracy's definition of a discursive practice as 'talk activities that people do.' We study discursive practice because it is through participation in discursive practices that people co-construct personal identities, values, and other socially and culturally meaningful realities. This is a very different way of arriving at an understanding of these concepts from saying that realities such as identity, belief systems, and values are pre-existing in advance of interaction, that somehow people schlep these things around with them in some sort of psychological back pack. Another important idea that a practice approach can illuminate is that the notion of community can be understood by investigating what kinds of practices community members do and the extent to which they share knowledge about the rules, constraints, and structures of the practices. We will discuss the important issues of identity construction in discourse communities in Units C7 and C8, but for the time being we will look closely at two discursive practices to develop our analytical skills.

The two discursive practices that we will examine here are practices which occur regularly and, for that reason, it is easier to relate the features of the particular instances that we present here to discussions of other practices that share some of the same features. That does not mean that all practices are iterations or routines because, as Tracy defined them, discursive practices are *any* talk activities that people do. It is, however, easier to look at those practices that occur regularly because it is perhaps easier to recognize their structure. The analytical procedures that we will use to identify the linguistic and interactional resources are those that we presented in Unit A4. Linguistic resources we mentioned include register and modes of meaning. Identifying the linguistic register of a practice means the features of pronunciation, vocabulary, and grammar that typify it; identifying the modes of meaning means using systemic functional grammar to understand how participants construct interpersonal, experiential, and textual meanings in the practice. Understanding how participants in a practice employ interactional resources means describing the selection of speech acts and their sequencing, the organization of turn-taking and repair, and how the practice is bounded by opening and closing acts. Taken together, the analysis of linguistic and interactional resources employed will provide a basis for understanding the participation framework of the practice.

C4.1 PRESENTATION OF DATA 1

The first practice is a story told to a group of friends. The setting is the thirty-first birthday party for Corey at his house. He and his wife are joined at their apartment in a town in the American Midwest by a group of three friends. The group of five has known each other for six to eight years since the time when they were all students at the same private liberal arts and science college and, although they now live in different places, they have kept in touch since graduating. The five friends are hanging out, drinking beer, listening to a Bob Marley CD, and telling each other stories. The story below is told by Greg and the rest are listening as they prepare food, Corey is the only one who speaks during Greg's narrative. The transcript is an entextualization of the recording made by Wortman (2000) and it is transcribed here according to the conventions of conversation analysis.

```
 1   Greg:   coupla weekends ago we went to uh, (1.0) Bill:
 2           an´ Christie an´ (.8) bunch o´ people from the
 3           program, (.5) went to >Indian Summer<?
 4   Corey:  hehe Gre(h)g´s the o(h)nly dru(h)nk in the
 5           programs.
 6   Greg:   yeah I ended up staying there but, (1.0) we we
 7           went to the Indian Summer which is down in
 8           Summerfest grounds. it´s like, (1.8) a weekend
 9           celebration f´ the Native American culture. (1.0)
10           an:d Freddy Fender and the: Texas Tornados were
11           playing.
12   Corey:  woo:h.
13   Greg:   yeah was good, (.2) but they all left before-,
14           (.5) it was like nine o´clock an´ they´d just
15           gotten started, an´ they go we´re gonna go, so I
16           stayed and walked home. ( ) but: (.5) u:m,
17           (.5) we saw, (0.5) I saw two guys dancing (.5)
18           the real Fat Man (1.0) up in front there=
19   Corey:  [=yeah    ]
20   Greg:   [and they] were weren´t even fakin´ it like we
21           were but they were doin´ (.2) all the moves an´
22           Bill saw it too, an´ (.5) these two guys were
23           just totally drunk, an´ they had- they even had
24           the arm thing goin´, and=
25   Corey:  =yeah.
26   Greg:   they weren´t fat though but they were, (.2) they
27           still had goin´ in the one leg and
```

```
28  Corey:  I wish I could show people that some time. show
29          'em like oh yeah ( ) but it's a rip-off of The
30          Fat Man.
31   Greg:  [oh yeah. ]
32  Corey:  [that particu]lar:, Midwestern: [(    )]
33   Greg:  but when we walked          [up, we] came
34          around this corner and saw these two guys
35          dancing, Bill and I both looked at each other
36          (1.5) ye::ahhhh. ((Greg pumps his arm in
37          imitation of a move from The Fat Man dance.))
38  Corey:  haha
```

C4.1.1 Activity 1: the structure of narrative

In his research on Black English vernacular, William Labov (1972a) suggested that a fully formed narrative may show the following acts in this sequence.

1. abstract: one or two clauses summarizing the main story
2. orientation: identification of the time, place, persons, and their activity or situation
3. complicating action
4. evaluation: the means used by the narrator to indicate the point of the narrative
5. result or resolution
6. coda: a signal that the narrative is finished

How far does Greg's narrative conform to the sequence of acts proposed by Labov? Make audio recordings of two spontaneous narratives told by speakers with different ethnic backgrounds. To what extent is the structure of their narratives similar to or different from Greg's? Does Labov's framework fit all three narratives or does it have to be modified? If Labov's framework doesn't fit, develop your own framework that fits all three.

C4.1.2 Activity 2: register

Consider Greg's pronunciation and grammar. How is it different from standard written English? Unless you live in the Midwest, there are probably some words or phrases that Greg uses that you are unfamiliar with. What are they? What does the register of Greg's narrative imply about his relationship with Corey and the others?

C4.1.3 Activity 3: modes of meaning

Recall the metafunctions of a text that we listed in Unit A3. The interpersonal metafunction is to influence others people's thoughts, beliefs, or actions; the ideational metafunction is to describe experience, represent it, analyze it, and explain it; and the textual metafunction allows us to connect utterances to their linguistic context. Analyze each clause of Greg's story separately and identify its metafunction. Do the metafunctions change as the story progresses?

C4.1.4 Activity 4: turn-taking

Focus on Corey's contribution to the narrative. How does Corey know when to take a turn-at-talk? During Greg's turns, who selects Corey as next speaker? Narratives in some Pacific cultures take the form of 'talk story.' In Hawai'i, for example, people do 'talk story' in which collaboration and cooperation are highly regarded. Karen Watson described these conversations as 'rambling personal experience narratives mixed with folk materials' (1975, p. 54). In talk story, a person shares a story while others corroborate or add to it as it is being told. In what ways is The Fat Man story similar to or different from talk story?

C4.1.5 Activity 5: community and participation framework

Greg indexes a lot of information that he believes that Corey and the other people listening to him know. He mentions Bill and Christie, who are known to everybody; Summerfest is a big music festival held in Milwaukee; Freddy Fender is vocalist/guitarist in the Tex-Mex supergroup, the Texas Tornados; and 'The Fat Man' is a dance that is popular in the American Midwest. You can see a video clip of someone doing The Fat Man at the BuzzHumor website at `http://www.buzz humor.com/videos/1882/Fat_Man_Dance`. How does Greg's indexical work in his narrative create community among the people at Corey's birthday party?

C4.2 PRESENTATION OF DATA 2

The second practice that we will examine in this unit is from a radio call-in show. This is an interactive public forum, where listeners can call a radio station and talk on air with the host of the program. The program presented here is *The Mark Belling late afternoon show*, broadcast on Radio WISN in Milwaukee, Wisconsin. Discussions on the program, hosted by Mark Belling, range widely and include topics from sports to politics. The show is regularly rated the most popular afternoon show in Milwaukee and is among the highest-rated afternoon political talk shows in the country.

The particular segment presented here was broadcast on November 7, 2000, the day of the general election in the United States. Democratic president Bill Clinton had served for two terms and, although the country was prosperous and at peace, President Clinton's last years in office had been marred by a number of scandals. The presidential election of 2000 was hotly contested between the Republican and

Democratic Parties and there was also a popular Green Party candidate: Ralph Nader. The Democratic candidate was Al Gore, who had served as Vice President under President Clinton, and the Republican candidate was George W. Bush, the son of the president who had preceded Clinton in office. The election was very close and the national campaigns of all parties had been followed with intense interest by many Americans. Radio programs hosted by politically conservative personalities such as Rush Limbaugh and Mark Belling were considered to have had a significant influence in bringing many conservatives voters to the polls. The popular election of the president did not result in a clear victory for either candidate, and the final decision to award the presidency to George W. Bush was made by the United States Supreme Court.

It was broadcast shortly after 3 o'clock in the afternoon of November 7, 2000, when polling places across the country were still open. The show begins with a monologue by the host, who then opens the telephone line to the first caller. The segment ends when the host closes the conversation with the first caller and moves on to another caller.

```
 1 Mark:  bigger government a:nd no cut in taxes, (1.0) leave
 2         social security run down the drain, (1.0) expand
 3         Medicare without trying to save it, (1.5) and lie to
 4         the people whenever it serves your purpose, (1.0) or
 5         the direction that Governor Bush would like to take
 6         the country in. (1.0) that's in front of us. (2.0)
 7         safe to say that no-one knows (1.0) six hours before
 8         the last votes are cast on the West Coast, (0.5) two
 9         hours before the last votes are cast in the state
10         that may decide it all, Florida, (1.0) who's going
11         to win the election. (1.5) those wh're predicting ay
12         Bush blowout look idi otic, (2.0) to those that said
13         that this thing would be close (.5) look prescient,
14         (1.0) the pollsters who had this race within a
15         couple of points either way (1.0) have been
16         vindicated, those who (.5) had a wider margin (.8)
17         appear to be silly. who will win, (.5) no one knows,
18         (.5) television networks and the candidates
19         themselves do exit polls of voters leaving the
20         polls, (2.0) the networks have not released those
21         polls, (1.0) nobody's talking openly. (1.5) Matt
22         Drudge who runs an internet web site (1.2) quotes
23         campaign sources  whatever that means I fear it's
24         just Bush spin (.2) meaning this is the best look
25         they could put on it >but I don't know that< (1.0)
26         indicates apparently a very very close race, (.8)
27         Bush winning a number of the smaller battleground
28         states (1.0) Gore seemingly ahead in Michigan, (1.0)
```

```
29        dead heat in Pennsylvania and Florida. (1.0)
30        California goin´ big for Gore. (2.0) if you take a
31        look at the electoral map, it´s seems impossible for
32        Gore to win without sweeping Michigan Pennsylvania
33        and Florida, (2.0) but it also looks possible that
34        he may do that. (.8) Bush wins either Florida or
35        Pennsylvania and hold most of the rest of the
36        battleground I  think he wins. (2.0) some of these
37        states may turn out to be extre:::mely close. (3.0)
38        I am extremely  worried. (3.0) I also think that if
39        Bush loses, (.5) the Bush supporters will be a lot
40        more upset than the Gore supporters will be happy,
41        (3.0) >somebody said to me today< you know, (.2) if
42        Gore wins I´m not going to be able to stand to watch
43        it, (1.0) when he gives his victory speech. (1.0)
44        well I I gonna  have to watch it so I can comment on
45        it, (.5) imagine how  nauseating that would be? (.8)
46        you don´t want that to occur, you BETTER GET TO THE
47        POLLS BETWEEN NOW AN´ EIGHT O´CLOCK, (2.0) (      )
48        worse than Clinton´s? ye ah. because (1.5) even
49        with Clinton won the second term we didn´t know how
50        bad it was gonna get. (1.0) ´member if Clinton´s
51        second term Monika and none o´ that stuff had
52        occurred, the Chinese secrets, (2.0) lying under
53        oath? twice? (.5) waggin´ his finger at us and sayin´
54        now you ((lowered voice)) listen up I never: messed
55        around with that little bimbo, ((normal voice)) (.2)
56        y´know al- none o´ that ´d occurred. (2.0) not to
57        mention four years now of Gore´s serial lying (.8)
58        this whole campaign? (.2) oh this ´d be far worse.
59        (.8) plus. (.5) you did have the feeling that with
60        Clinton at least that some point this gonna end,
61        eight years is the most he can serve, (1.0) Gore
62        wins it looks like it´s eternal, (2.0) oh this´d be
63        way worse. (2.0) s´d be way worse. (1.0) makes you
64        feel as though there´s no hope. (1.5) way worse.
65        (6.0) West Side. Dave y´re on >radio eleven thirty
66        double you eye ess enn.<=
67 Dave:  =hey Mark thanks for takin´ my call, (.5) uhm, (.2)
68        I have had such a stressful day, because, (.) as an
69        educator: that´s like the one issue that I:
70        completely agree with Gore on an´ (.5) >I guess I
71        can´t say completely agree but I disagree with Bush
72        on< an:d I gotta admit right [(              )]
73 Mark:                               [you don´t believe] in
74        better schools?
```

75 Dave: par´n me?
76 Mark: you don´t believe in better schools?
77 Dave: I believe in better schools, I just believe in a
78   different road to get there. (.5) uhm, (.) but
79   that´s that´s for another show that I´d love to call
80   back on,
81 Mark: >well I don´ know< uh ye- I decide what´s on this
82   show.
83 Dave: oh that´s true.
84 Mark: what has what has Al Gore done to improve our
85   schools.
86 Dave: well that´s why I took back that I bel- I agree with
87   Gore.=
88 Mark: =>he´s not done anything< to improve our [schools.]
89 Dave: [I agree.]
90   I [(   )]
91 Mark: [you know George doubleyou] Bush, under George
92   doubleyou Bush, in Texas schools improved.
93   (2.0)
94 Dave: okay.
95 Mark: it´s a matter of <u>fact</u>. ºthat´s all. º
96 Dave: okay. but I I guess,
97 Mark: have you already voted?
98 Dave: yes I have.
99 Mark: who did you vote for.
100 Dave: I voted for Bush.=
101 Mark: =then I´ll leave ya alone.
102 Dave: ok- I appreci(h)ate it tha(h)nks for the,
103 Mark: I mean if you were gonna say you´re still undecided,
104 Dave: [no actually (   )]
105 Mark: [a::nd this   ] issue had you- totally in
106   conflict, I would have <u>pum</u>meled you. but,
107 Dave: [(   )]
108 Mark: [well   ] that you voted for Bush, uh what do I
109   care if you´ve got this hang-up on schools.
110 Dave: I wore my uh (.5) Clinton with the nose growing
111   watch all day to remind myself how sick I am of the
112   (.5) way he´s: (.5) uhm (.8) completely destroyed
113   morality in this country, him and his (.2) his
114   administration (.5) .hh and uhm (.4) I gotta tell ya
115   when I walked outta that uh (.5) voting booth, which
116   by the way I had no wait for either, sorry to
117   disappoint ya, but uh (1.0) it was uh (.2) I I felt
118   incredibly relieved. I hope I feel [(   )]
119 Mark: [oh <u>I</u>´m sure.]
120   (.5) I can tell you this, (.5) the people who walked

121   away from today´s vote voting for Bush, (.8) feel
122   better about themselves than those who voted for
123   Gore. (.4) >first thing< you got all these Nader
124   supporters (.2) who r- in their <u>heart</u> wished they
125   would´ve voted for Nader, (.5) but (.) in the end
126   din´t want to waste their vote, (.5) so their vote
127   for Gore is half-hearted at best,
128 Dave: [right.]
129 Mark: [>secondly] you can jus´ <u>see</u>< by their re<u>action</u> (.2)
130   <u>most</u> of them won´t be that disappointed if Gore
131   loses, (.5) most Bush supporters are going to
132   <u>de</u>vastated.
133 Dave: yeah I [ah ( )]
134 Mark: [you know if] if if if Bush loses. the people
135   who voted for Bush, an <u>I</u> y´know as bad the lat- last
136   eight years have been, (.2) I at least have had the
137   moral superiority of being able to say (.2) that <u>I</u>
138   was not part of empowering that slug. (.5) and the
139   next four years, as miserable as they´ll be, (.4)
140   and the horrible things that are gonna occur in the
141   courts (.5) and th´ awful- awful direction that the
142   country is gonna continue to take, (.2) and the
143   inability to fix social security or any of these
144   other things, (.5) I will at least be able to say,
145   (.2) that I wasn´t part of this, I was one of those,
146   (1.0) who dis sented.
147   (1.0)
148 Dave: true. (.) and I I´m [gonna feel the same way.]
149 Mark: [I think the people who voted]
150   for Bush feel <u>much</u> better about themselves, (.5)
151   <u>even</u> if Bush goes on to lose.
152 Dave: well it was- it was actually the first time of the
153   day that I actually felt like the stress was lifted
154   off my shoulders. (.) I y´know [I mean ( )]
155 Mark: [well I it´s]
156   because by you´re, because you´re conflicted, you
157   don´t really care who wins?
158 Dave: oh no that´s not true at all. (1.0) uhm, if I really
159   didn´t care who won I don´t know if I would´ve gone
160   and voted. (1.0) uhm. (1.5) instead I I (1.0) I made
161   a d- I guess I guess it´s more that I made a
162   decision that, (.8) <u>one</u> issue was not worth uh (1.0)
163   the morality and the: the bigger: the bigger picture
164   to me, (.) and that´s just an issue I have to fight
165   on a different front if I can.
166 Mark: okay. thanks for the call. ´preciate it.

C4.2.1 Activity 1: power in discursive practice

Politics is about power, a nation's president has the power to make laws, the power to redistribute wealth among the people, and the power to go to war. But power is also exerted in discursive practices by controlling and constraining the contributions of non-powerful participants. In this segment from the Mark Belling late afternoon show, do you perceive a difference in discursive power between the host and the caller? If you do perceive a power differential, does the non-powerful participant resist the power that the other exercises over him?

C4.2.2 Activity 2: interactional resources for constructing discursive power

Consider carefully the sequence of topics in the conversation. Which participant gets to introduce a topic? Does the same topic continue in the next turn of the other participant? Consider also the turn-taking in the data segment: When does one speaker perceive a transition-relevance place in the other speaker's turn? How is the next speaker selected? Now consider the trajectories of repair. Identify instances of repair in the data. Which participant initiates the repair and which participant completes it?

C4.2.3 Activity 3: discursive practice and the creation of a community

According to The Pew Research Center (June 8, 2004), news audiences in America are increasingly politicized, with more conservatives than liberals listening to and participating in radio talk shows.

> Fully 24% of Republicans regularly listen to radio shows that invite listeners to call in to discuss current events, public issues and politics. Only about half as many Democrats (13%) regularly listen to these types of shows. Similarly, 21% of conservatives listen to talk radio compared with 16% of liberals. The partisan gap in the talk radio audience has grown in recent years. In 2002, more Republicans than Democrats listened to talk radio programs regularly (21% vs. 16%, respectively). Today Republican attention has increased to 24%, while Democratic interest has dropped to 13%. (p. 14)

Why should talk radio appeal more to conservatives than to liberals?

QUESTIONS AND ACTIVITIES FOR FUTURE EXPLORATION

The two data segments that we have presented in this unit have demonstrated ways in which practices create solidarity among participant and ways in which power is exercised over non-powerful participants. Collect and analyze a narrative told to a group of friends and a segment from a radio call-in show. Do the practices that you have researched show similar patterns of power and solidarity that we have found in the data examined in this unit?

Unit C5
Patterns of classroom discourse

INTRODUCTION

The framework for describing discursive practices that we introduced in Unit A5 can be applied to talk-in-interaction in all the practices that we have introduced so far: to the conversation between Donnie and his mother on the bus, to the patient consultation with the pharmacist, to Dr Martin Luther King's 'I have a dream' speech, to the conversation between Natalia and Jack that Hanks reported, and to the classroom discussion of the word 'habitat' that Markee recounted. In Unit A5, we used the framework to analyze the conversation between teacher and student in a clarinet lesson, and in this unit we will continue to practice applying the discursive framework to other conversations in classrooms. The first set of activities is based on a recording of a classroom interaction in an American elementary school and data for the second set of activities are conversations in classrooms where the focus is on learning a new language, in this case English as a second language.

C5.1 PRESENTATION OF DATA 1

The first data segment is from a lesson taught by an elementary-school teacher to a class of about a dozen young students.[1] The teacher had spent previous lessons with this class introducing them to geometrical concepts with the help of quilts and now, just before this segment, she has just read to the class from 'The bedspread' by Sylvia Fair, in which two elderly sisters embroider the house of their childhood at either end of a white bedspread. The segment is transcribed below.

```
1   Teacher:   there´s two places in the book that I want to
2              re-read to you quickly, ·h and  the: n, (2.0)
3              um >an´ then I want us to talk about the question
4              that Amanda asked during the story,< you probably
5              didn´t hear her if you were sitting in the back,
6              because she said it pretty quietly, ·h but it was
7              a good question, and you might have been thinking
8              this question while I was reading too, ·h back
9              when: Amelia and Maude were <first beginning,> ·h
```

10		u:m, the- they were still in the planning stages,
11		they hadn´t sewed anything yet, ·h this is what
12		Maude said, ·h u:m, <we´ll each make a house,
13		(.5) one at each end of the bedspread, <then it
14		will be symmetrical.>> (.5) ·h and Ama(h)nda
15		while she was listening to the story said, (.2)
16		<what´s symmetrical.> let´s talk about that word,
17		symmetrical, who can share um (.5) share with the
18		group. what do you think, what- what´s your
19		guess. what do you think it might have to do
20		with. ·h Paul, what´s your guess.
21	Paul:	a house?
22	Teacher:	·h k(h)ay symmetrical might be a word that only
23		has to do with houses. ·h okay, what would it
24		mean. (.8) what about houses would: <symmetrical
25		have to do with.>
26		((jump cut in recording))
27	Teacher:	what else could be symmetrical.
28	S1:	the carpet.
29	Teacher:	the carpet could be symmetrical? what would—
30		what would a carpet be like that was symmetrical.
31		(2.0)
32	S2:	like— if it was all like: grey?
33	Teacher:	if it was all grey it would be symmetrical? (.5)
34		and what are you thinking about the word
35		symmetrical.
36	S3:	I think symmekrical means u:m (.5) things that
37		are um like the- sa:me?
38	Teacher:	(1.0) tell me more about that. cuz I don´t know
39		exactly what you mean when it says they´re ·h the
40		same. you— you mean you agree with Nicole that
41		symmetrical means identical? (.2) exactly the
42		same, can´t tell them apart.
43	S3:	(1.0) well you can sort of tell them apart.
44	Teacher:	how could you tell ´em apart if they were
45		exactly the same.

C5.1.1 Activity 1: linguistic resources

Listen carefully to the teacher's talk in this data segment. What features of her
pronunciation, grammar, and choice of vocabulary do you notice? Take each clause
of the teacher's talk at a time, and identify the mode of meaning that she is using in
each clause: Is it interpersonal, experiential, or textual?

C5.1.2   Activity 2: interactional resources

Now consider the interactional resources that the teacher and her students employ. First, consider which actions are done by the teacher and which actions are done by the students. What do you notice about the sequential organization of actions in this data segment? When it comes to selecting the next speaker, recall that there are several ways in which this may be done: current speaker selects next, next speaker self-selects, or current speaker continues. Which techniques of turn-allocation are used in this lesson?

C5.1.3   Activity 3: spatial configuration

Watch the video of this data segment and draw a diagram of the seating arrangement of the teacher and the students. How does this seating arrangement influence participants' employment of interactional resources?

C5.1.4   Activity 4: language socialization

If you can, get hold of a copy of 'The bedspread' by Sylvia Fair. One of the teacher's aims in this data segment and the series of lessons on quilting of which it forms a part is to teach geometrical concepts like symmetry. Another way of teaching these concepts is by drawing abstract geometrical figures such as triangles and rectangles to illustrate the concepts. Recall in Ochs's article on language socialization in Unit B5 that one of the aims of language socialization is to understand how language practices encode and socialize information about society and culture. What does the language socialization approach imply about the two methods of teaching geometry?

C5.1.5   Activity 5: community and practice

Most people in the Midwestern community where the segment was recorded would recognize it as part of an elementary school math lesson. Because the practice has social and cultural value to the community and because similar instances of this practice happen regularly, the practice has a name. How does this practice correspond to your own knowledge and expectations of a math lesson in an elementary school?

C5.2   PRESENTATION OF DATA 2

In Unit A3, we introduced the notion of repair, which has been studied extensively by conversation analysts. Repair is the treatment of any sort of trouble in interaction, and one of the contexts in which you find a lot of trouble is the discourse of classroom interaction. You can probably identify some sources of trouble in the students' talk in the first data segment in this unit, and it is fairly easy to see how the teacher repairs that trouble. Repairing trouble in classroom interaction is, however, not the same as correction, which McHoul (1990) understands as indicating unacceptable student answers and providing correct information. Correction is thus an identifying task and an achievement of classroom teaching (Macbeth, 2004, p. 705), while repair is a much more general procedure that is found in all kinds of talk-in-interaction.

The different kinds of repair that can be found in second- and foreign-language classrooms were studied by Paul Seedhouse (2004) in his wide-ranging discussion of the application of conversation analysis to talk in language classrooms. Seedhouse discovered that repair functioned very differently in four kinds of language classrooms, which are differentiated by the teacher's instructional goals in the lesson. The goals that Seedhouse identified, he termed the pedagogical contexts of (1) form and accuracy, (2) meaning and fluency, (3) task orientation, and (4) a procedural context. In a form-and-accuracy context, 'the teacher expects that learners will produce precise strings of linguistic forms and precise patterns of interaction which will correspond to the pedagogical focus which he/she introduces' (Seedhouse, 2004, p. 102). In a meaning-and-fluency context,

> the aim is on maximizing the opportunities for interaction presented by the classroom pedagogical environment and the classroom speech community itself. Participants talk about their immediate environment, personal relationships, feelings, and meanings, or the activities they are engaging in. The focus is on the expression of personal meaning rather than on linguistic forms, on promoting fluency rather than accuracy.
>
> (ibid., p. 111)

The task-oriented context develops from the philosophy of task-based learning, in which instead of an explicit focus on language, learners do activities where the target language is used by the learner for a communicative purpose in order to achieve an outcome (Willis, 1996). In a task-oriented lesson, the teacher introduces a pedagogical focus by allocating tasks to learners and often leaves learners alone to manage the interaction themselves.

Finally, a procedural context is a part of almost every lesson and the teacher's aim is to give information to the students concerning the classroom activities which are to be accomplished in the lesson. Procedural information is usually delivered by the teacher with little spoken interaction with the students.

Troubles may, of course, occur in all of these four contexts but it is interesting that the trajectory of repair is different in each context. The three data segments below are taken from classrooms with three of these four language learning pedagogical contexts, as reported in Seedhouse (2004, pp. 146–155).

Data segment 2.1

```
 1 L1:  they are watch televi— television
 2  T:  okay now. yesterday at eight o´clock (.) they (.)
 3 L1:  they ar[e they watche [s       watched [ they were=
 4  T:         [they-         [they:::        [they ( )
 5 L1:  = (.) watching
```
                                        (van Lier, 1988, p. 197)

Data segment 2.2

```
 1  T:  could you tell me something about marriage in Algeria?
 2      who is married here?
 3 L1:  Azo, only Azo.
 4  T:  alright, your opinion about that.
 5 L2:  he will marry.
 6  T:  oh, he is engaged, engaged. tell me something about the
 7      institution of marriage in Algeria. tell me something
 8      about it.
 9 L3:  there are several institutions.
10  T:  you don´t have marriage in Algeria. what do you have
11      then?
12 L4:  only women and men.
13  T:  yes, that´s what marriage is.
14 L1:  the marriage in Algeria isn´t like the marriage in
15      England.
16  T:  what do you mean?
17 L2:  for get marriage you must pay two thousand.
18 L5:  yes more expensive than here.
19  T:  why do you have to pay money?
20 L6:  no. It´s our religion.
21 L7:  not religion but our tradition.
22 L8:  no, religion, religion. in religion we must pay women,
23      but not high price, but tradition.
24 L5:  between women, women does not like to married to a low
25      money because it is not, it is (.)
26  T:  oh, dowry, oh dear.
```
                                        (Hasan, 1988, pp. 258–259)

Data segment 2.3

```
 1 LL:  Paul what´s this?
 2  T:  it´s a flood you had a flood
 3 L1:  what´s a flood?
```

```
 4   T:  inundation ((tr: flood))
 5  L1:  uh uh
 6   T:  OK?
 7  L2:  and why?
 8   T:  ah well (.) how many people did you have?
 9  L1:  in the field?
10  L2:  in the dyke?
11   T:  in the dyke
12  LL:  100
13   T:  100 not enough
14  LL:  ah ha
```

(Seedhouse, 1994, p. 309)

C5.2.1   Activity 1: trajectory of repair

Schegloff, Jefferson, and Sacks (1977) identified three distinct moments in the trajectory of repair: the source of the trouble, the initiation of the repair, and the resolution of the repair; and in each moment we can identify the participant in whose turn the action occurs and we can count the number of turns that elapse from the trouble source to the conclusion of the repair. Instead of naming them, the participants are referred to as 'self' and 'other.' In each of the three data segments above, identify one or more sources of trouble, the initiation of repair, and the repair conclusion.

C5.2.2   Activity 2: turn-taking and repair

How many turns does it take from trouble source to repair in each of the data segments? Why is repair concluded immediately in the same turn in some cases, and why does it take several turns to conclude in others?

C5.2.3   Activity 3: repair and 'correction'

What do you understand by 'correction'? In which of these data segments would you call the repair a correction? On the basis of your analysis of repair, what would you say is the pedagogical focus of each of these data segments?

QUESTIONS AND ACTIVITIES FOR FUTURE EXPLORATION

Now you have had some practice applying the discursive practice framework to analyzing talk-in-interaction in several educational contexts, try to collect some data of your own by video and/or audio recording a classroom, teacher, and students that you have access to. Although you may find it easy to get access to classroom data, it is very important to realize your responsibilities as a researcher to the people who you record. Many universities have instituted procedures for reviewing requests to collect data from human subjects and it is important to find out what procedures are in place at your institution. Protection of human subjects in research in the United States is guided by three basic ethical principles determined in the Belmont report of The National Commission for the Protection of Human Subjects of Biomedical and Behavioral Research (1979). These principles are:

- *Respect for persons*: Most people should be treated as autonomous individuals and some people such as children and medical patients should be protected because of reduced autonomy.

- *Beneficence*: Researchers should maximize the benefits of research and minimize any potential harm.

- *Justice*: The risks of participating in research and the beneficial results of research should be distributed fairly across both the groups to which research subjects belong and the larger society.

Unit C6
Assessing interactional competence

INTRODUCTION

We present in this unit a series of data segments taken from conversations between learners of English and native speakers, we examine reports of a child with autism, and we compare autistic behavior with interaction between a mother and her normal 12-week-old son. The aim of the activities that we present here is for you to consider the importance of some fundamental features of inter-actional competence: it is practice-specific, it is co-constructed, and it requires intersubjectivity.

C6.1 PRESENTATION OF DATA 1

In Unit A6, we defined interactional competence as a relationship between the participants' employment of linguistic and interactional resources and the contexts in which they are employed. The resources that interactional competence highlights are those of language (register and modes of meaning) and interaction (sequential organization, turn-taking, and repair), which together create identities for participants in the participation framework of a specific discursive practice. A discursive practice is anything that participants do through language that is bounded by opening and closing acts. Unlike communicative competence, interactional competence is not the ability of an individual to employ those resources in any and every discursive practice; interactional competence is how those resources are employed mutually and reciprocally by all participants in a specific practice.

Some researchers (Young and He, 1998) have criticized a particular kind of assessment of oral foreign language proficiency that takes the form of an interview because, although the interview is designed to be a general assessment of global speaking ability, the nature of the discursive practice in which the assessment is made limits the role identity of the candidate. In order to investigate the extent to which a candidate's interactional competence is constrained by the practice in which they are participating and by the role of the other participant, we present here two data segments, one from a formal oral proficiency assessment and the other from a dorm room conversation. Both are dyadic conversations (involving only two speaking participants) and both interactions involve one learner of English and one native speaker. The learner of English is identified in the transcripts as NNS (nonnative speaker) and the native speaker by NS. Data segment 1 is from Johnson (2001, p. 94) and data segment 2 is from Riggenbach (1998, pp. 59–60).

Data segment 1

```
 1   NS: How long does it take you to to get from Salt Lake City
 2       to Provo?
 3  NNS: I took a bus this morning so it took me about an hour
 4       and twenty minutes to get here.
 5   NS: Oh you rode the bus?
 6  NNS: Yeah I did.
 7   NS: Did they have a good bus service from between the two
 8       cities?
 9  NNS: Yeah they have UTA Utah Transit Service and it´s real
10       good.
11   NS: (clears throat) What kind of buses are they uh do they
12       have? Are they big ones?
13  NNS: It´s really big one.
14   NS: Oh I see I see. Interesting! Now, is there any kind of
15       train connection between the two cities?
16  NNS: Uh usually I I think they do but I never take a train.
17       They have Amtrak from Provo to Salt Lake and I don´t
18       know how much it costs but they have it a Amtrak from
19       Provo to Salt Lake.
20   NS: Now, (clears throat) you say that you have lived in
21       Provo for four years now?
22  NNS: Yeah.
23   NS: Is that the only place in Utah that you´ve lived?
24  NNS: Yeah, I came I came here in nineteen . . . ninety.
25   NS: Oh nineteen ninety. And from where did you come?
```

Data segment 2

```
 1   NS: Well what do you think about um mothers who um have
 2       their baby [and they leave them in garbage
 3  NNS:            [Uh-huh
 4   NS: cans
 5       (1.5)
 6  NNS: Huh? What do you (s [
 7   NS:                    [They have— they have their baby?
 8  NNS: My mom?
 9   NS: No no (hh) Not your(hh hh) — Mothers.
10  NNS: Uh huh. Mothers uh huh
```

```
11   NS: They have their baby?
12  NNS: Uh huh
13   NS: And then— they leave it in garbage cans.
14       (.8)
15  NNS: Garbage?
16   NS: Garbage cans. Like big garbage c(hh)ans. Outside of
17       businesses.
18  NNS: Uh h[uh
19   NS:      [and apartments
20  NNS: Ahh:: [
21   NS:        [You know what I mean?
22  NNS: No I don't know. I d— I understand Garbage.
23   NS: Ye[ah. You know dumpsters? where— You know
24  NNS: [Garbage.
25   NS: our garbage?
26  NNS: Garbage?
27   NS: Uh huh
28  NNS: Ah yeah
29   NS: Yeah. And they'll have a baby and they'll leave it in
30       there
31       (2.0)
32  NNS: Uh yu:h? ((tone displays shock))
33   NS: Yeah. For someone to- to take it or for it to die.
34  NNS: Die? Ahh:: Like a (just lea[ve it)
35   NS:                            [Mm-hm
36  NNS: I know. ((clears throat)) What do yo [u
37   NS:                                      [It's mean.
38  NNS: What's mean?
39   NS: No— It's mean. It's mean.
40  NNS: Mean.
41   NS: Yeah(hh hh) It's bad.
42  NNS: It's bad. Uh— I know (( unintelligible [x xx))
43   NS:                                        [Mm-hm
44  NNS: Because baby is not thing is y' [know
45   NS:                                 [Baby's what?
46  NNS: Not thing. Baby is a animal— (hh) I(hh)don't know.
47       Humor.
48   NS: Human ye [ah
49  NNS:          [So I can't do that. I ca:n't do that. I can't
50       sell, I can't— I can't throw garba [ge
51   NS:                                    [Throw it awa[y.
52  NNS:                                                 [Throw
53       away.
54   NS: Yeah.
55  NNS: But— I can't kill because it's human.
```

C6.1.1   Activity 1: practice-specific interactional resources

Consider the interactional resources that participants employ in these two practices: that is, describe the organization of turn-taking, the sequential organization of speech acts, and the processes of repair that you find in these two practices. Put your descriptions of the interactional resources in the practices side by side and compare and contrast their interactional structure.

C6.1.2   Activity 2: practice-specific linguistic resources

Consider now the linguistic resources that participants employ in these two practices: that is, describe the registers and the modes of meaning that participants employ in the two practices. What differences and similarities and differences do you find? Are the interactional differences greater or less than the linguistic differences?

C6.1.3   Activity 3: interview or conversation?

One of these practices was recorded in a dormitory room where the learner had lived for six months with her native-speaking interlocutor. This data segment is ten minutes into the recording, following a discussion on similar topics that the learner had been discussing that week in her ESL conversation class. The other data segment was taken from a regularly scheduled oral proficiency interview conducted by telephone by a trained assessor working for an agency of the US federal government. Which data segment is taken from which practice? Use interactional and linguistic evidence to support your answer.

C6.1.4   Activity 4: transfer of interactional competence

What are the differences between an interview and an informal conversation? What can you infer about a participant's interactional competence from those two practices? If someone is a good conversationalist, would you expect them to interview well?

C6.2   PRESENTATION OF DATA 2

One way to understand interactional competence is to define it and to contrast interactional competence with communicative competence and linguistic competence, but another way is to consider conditions where interactional competence does not exist. To do so, we can consider interaction in which the basis for interactional competence is absent, and we can do that by examining the case of people who find it very difficult to perceive the intentions and desires of others, who exhibit very little intersubjectivity.

Autism is the name for a broad spectrum of mental diseases that affect thought, perception, and attention. An aspect of interactional competence that tends to be disturbed in people with autism has to do with knowing how to use language appropriately and in context. That includes knowing how to hold a conversation, thinking about what the other person in a conversation understands and believes, and tuning in to the metalinguistic signals of the other person, such as facial expression, tone of voice, and body language. It is important to remember that communication is as much nonverbal as it is verbal, and people with autism have great difficulty understanding nonverbal language. One way of interpreting this reaction is to say that people with autism have difficulty with intersubjectivity, and often this is observable because people with autism have great difficulty making eye contact with others.

People with autism may have other symptoms besides lack of intersubjectivity, and the range of autistic symptoms is quite wide. Some people with autism like to live very organized lives, to make lists, and dislike too much novelty or new information. Mark Haddon wrote *The curious incident of the dog in the night-time*, a novel in which the narrator is Christopher, a 15-year-old boy who suffers from autism, whom Haddon portrays with sympathy and understanding. The following passage from Mark Haddon's novel is Christopher's description of some of his own feelings about communication and about other people.

> *I find people confusing. This is for two main reasons. The first main reason is that people do a lot of talking without using any words. Siobhan says that if you raise one eyebrow it can mean lots of different things. It can mean 'I want to do sex with you' and it can also mean 'I think what you just said was very stupid.'... The second main reason is that people often talk using metaphors. These are examples of metaphors*
>
> **I laughed my socks off.**
> **He was the apple of her eye.**
> **They had a skeleton in the cupboard.**
>
> *... When I try and make a picture of the phrase in my head it just confuses me because imagining an apple in someone's eye doesn't have anything to do with liking someone a lot and it makes you forget what the person was talking about.*

C6.2.1   Activity 1: autism and intersubjectivity

What evidence is there in the passage that Christopher has difficulty with intersubjectivity? If you have read the book, you might want to find other examples of the problems that Christopher has taking the perspective of other people.

C6.2.2 Activity 2: autism and lying

Christopher is unable to lie about the events he recounts in the book, and many individuals with autism are known to 'tell it as it is' or to never tell a lie. In fact, the advent of lying behavior in people who are being treated with autism is viewed as a cognitive milestone in their treatment and can be seen as a reason to celebrate. Why is the inability to lie associated with autism? Why would lying require intersubjectivity?

C6.3 PRESENTATION OF DATA 3: MOTHER–INFANT INTERACTION

In this activity we look at the normal development of very young infants in order to identify the onset of intersubjectivity. Figure C6.1 shows a communicative exchange between a mother and her normal child. The exchange is analyzed frame by frame from a film recording. The levels of general animation displayed by the body movements of the infant and mother are indicated by Levels I–IV. The horizontal scale is frames of the film and there are 16 frames per second. The pictures below the chart show the disposition of mother and infant at 29 frames (1.8 seconds), 53 frames (3.3 seconds), and 109 frames (6.8 seconds). The mother talks and moves her head; the infant babbles, smiles, waves his arm, and opens his hand.

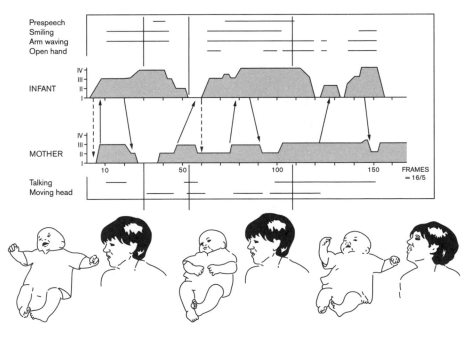

Figure C6.1 Conversation-like exchange between a mother and her 12-week-old boy.
Source: Trevarthen (1977, Figure 2, p. 240)

Look at the chart in Figure C6.1, which shows the degree of interaction between the mother and her child. Do you see any evidence that the actions of the mother and child are related? As we discussed in Units A4–6, turn-taking is one of the interactional activities in which the onset of a new turn is very finely tuned to the turn-in-progress. Do you see any evidence of that fine attunement in the activities of mother and child in Figure C6.1?

QUESTIONS AND ACTIVITIES FOR FUTURE EXPLORATION

How is oral proficiency in foreign languages assessed at your institution? Ask permission to record an oral proficiency assessment. How valid do you think the procedure is as a measurement of interactional competence?

Read as much as you can about autism and other disorders of social communication. Do you think that Mark Haddon's portrayal of Christopher in *The curious incident of the dog in the night-time* is a valid depiction of a child with autism?

Unit C7
Constructing identities

INTRODUCTION

We present in this unit several opportunities for you to explore further how identities are created through language. Most of the tasks that we present here do not involve talk-in-interaction but are, instead, ways in which you can investigate how individuals present their identities to an audience and how others describe an individual's identity. We first ask you to consider stories in which a person changes physical shape. The questions to think about are: Does the person's identity change when they are in a different body? What remains the same? How do other people know that this is the 'same' person? You can then go on to listen to voices of ordinary people telling stories about their lives, and you may like to reflect on the impression that their voices make on you. On the printed page, our impressions of fictional characters in literature are based on a skillful author's description but also on our own experiences with real people who we see as similar in some way to the fictional character. In the third activity, you get to read a short story and reflect on the identity of one of the characters. After that, we move into a different medium – computer-mediated communication – and reflect on the great and growing popularity of social networking websites. How do members of these sites use the computer to create images of themselves? What do they include? What do they exclude? And we conclude the unit with a final summation of a person's life in obituaries. Obituaries make fascinating reading because they show what aspects of a person's life make the news, and they often show that tiny details of a person's life are more memorable aspects of their identity than their official accomplishments.

Identities are fascinating because we all have them, and we are often dissatisfied with the way that we project our own identities and with the ways that some people altercast us. Maybe these activities will make you more skillful in creating the identity that you desire.

C7.1 SHAPESHIFTING

Stories of shapeshifting involve a change of the physical form or the shape of a person or animal. One example is the Orcadian story of the selkie-man that we told in Unit A7; shapeshifting is a common theme in folklore and science fiction, and stories of shapeshifters are found in most world literatures. Shapeshifting is not a natural process such as aging or metamorphosis, but it does involve a change of identity as well as a change of physical form. Read some of the following stories of shapeshifting and discuss how the identities of the shapeshifter change from shape to shape and how those identities are altercast by the other characters in the story.

- *The picture of Dorian Gray* by Oscar Wilde. This novel was first published in 1890 and tells of a young man named Dorian Gray, the subject of a painting by artist Basil Hallward. After Hallward paints a beautiful, young man's portrait, his subject's frivolous wish that the picture change and he remain the same comes true. Dorian Gray's picture grows aged and corrupt while he continues to appear fresh and innocent. Several film adaptations of the novel have been made including an excellent 1945 MGM version.

- In Book Ten of *The Odyssey*, Homer tells the story of Circe, the goddess and enchantress on the Island of Aeaea, who changes Odysseus's men into swine.

- The collection of Chinese folktales 聊斋志异 (Liaozhai Zhiyi) by 蒲松龄 (Pu Songling) was translated into English by Herbert Giles as *Strange stories from a Chinese studio*. The collection contains several tales about fox spirits, who usually appear as beautiful young women. These shapeshifters are also common in Japanese and Korean folklore.

You can read more about shapeshifting in *The encyclopedia of fantasy* by John Clute and John Grant. An updated edition of the encyclopedia was published in 1999 by Orbit in the UK and by St Martin's Press in the US.

C7.2 VOCAL IMPRESSIONS

An individual's voice and the language variety that they use are often more important in helping them create an identity than the words that they say. Because this is so important, many people (not just actors) pay money to enroll in 'accent reduction' classes or to attend 'voice training.' Their motivation is to project an identity that they believe is more desirable to them and pleasing to others.

In order to understand the emotional values that hearers attach to voices, here are some links to voices on the Web. First, complete an evaluation of the speaker's voice. Does the speaker sound hesitant or confident? friendly or unfriendly? credible or untrustworthy? old or young? serious or humorous? shy or confident? talkative or taciturn? Try to express how the voice sounds to you. For example, listeners to the National Public Radio show *All things considered* said that the American actor Morgan Freeman's voice brought to mind front porches, rocking chairs, brandy, sandpaper, the fireside, walnuts, grandfathers, and the voice of their conscience.

Now transcribe all or part of the audio in the way that you think best represents the speaker's voice. (You can use a conventional phonetic transcription or invent your own way of transcribing; just don't use Standard English.) Then, try to do an imitation of the speaker and ask someone to compare your imitation with the original. Finally, consider what it is about a voice that indexes these aspects of master identity: age, gender, social class, ethnicity, national or regional origin; and these aspects of personal identity: courageous, tough, honest, sexy, smooth talker, and big shot.

You can hear some audio samples of American voices on the web site of DARE (The Dictionary of American Regional English) at `http://polyglot.lss.wisc.edu/dare/dare.html`. Many of the clips are of speakers telling the same story, 'Arthur the Rat,' which is a short tale devised to obtain phonetic representation from speakers throughout the country of all phonemes in American English. Recordings were made all over the United States of speakers reading this passage in 1965–70. Some other more personal stories are told by these informants:

- A 23-year-old black woman with a college education from Memphis, Tennessee, described when she first heard Stokely Carmichael talk about 'black power.'

- A 77-year-old white man with a grade-school education from Beals, Maine, describes to an interviewer how to make a small rowboat.

- A 76-year-old white man with a grade-school education from Roswell, New Mexico, describes the rules that cowboys have to follow at mealtimes on a cattle drive.

- A 70-year-old white woman with a college education from Brooklyn, New York, talks about sailing back to New York during the prohibition era from a vacation in Cuba.

- A 79-year-old white woman with a grade-school education from Picayune, Mississippi, talks about men from the government moving her out of her home.

You can listen to audio recordings of voices from various parts of England online at The British Library's collection of 650 English accents and dialects at `http://www.collectbritain.co.uk/collections/dialects/`. Here are five voices chosen by the curator of the collection, Jonathan Robinson.

- Retired bus conductress Mary Jane Anderson was 77 when she was recorded in Backworth, North Tyneside. She describes the old colliery houses at Backworth and the pride people took in keeping their yards and doorsteps presentable.

- Farmer Les Oakes was 60 when he was recorded in Cheadle, Staffordshire. He talks passionately about his collection of old artifacts and architectural items.

- Garage clerk Bryan Tungate was 59 when he was recorded in Mulbarton, Norfolk. He describes the changes he has witnessed in the last sixty years in Mulbarton and talks about people's over-dependence on the car as a means of transport.

- Retired farm labourer Dick Gilbert was 79 when he was recorded in Weare Giffard, Devon. He recalls the treatment he received from three different farmers as a young farm hand.

- Housekeeper Miss Dibnah was 65 when she was recorded in Welwick, Yorkshire. She explains how to make white bread, brown bread and spice bread.

Do the same thing with the voices of nonnative speakers of English on *The speech accent archive at* `http://accent.gmu.edu/index.php`.

C7.3 IDENTITIES IN LITERATURE

Find a short story with a major character and a few minor ones. Here are some stories you might try, but feel free to choose your own: *The duel* by Anton Chekhov, *The green suit* by Dwight Allen, *The ambitious guest* by Nathaniel Hawthorne, *A very old man with enormous wings* by Gabriel Garcia Marquez, *The hitch-hikers* by Eudora Welty, *The best girlfriend you never had* by Pam Houston.

- Focus on one of the main characters in the story.

- Describe how master, interactional, personal, and relational identities are created for that character.

- How does the 'direct speech' of your character and others help to create their identities?

C7.4 IDENTITIES ON LINE

MySpace and *FaceBook* are two very popular social networking websites offering an interactive, user-submitted network of friends, personal profiles, blogs, groups, photos, music, and videos. Most users of these websites are teenagers or young people in their 20s and 30s. Both sites allow users to create Personal Profiles which can be viewed by any other member. Users of these networks spend some time to create an identity that they promote by an attractive personal page with personal details including their marital status, sexual orientation, body type, ethnicity, religion, zodiac sign, whether they smoke or drink, any children they have, their education, and occupation. Most personal pages are attractively designed and include pictures, videos, music, lists of things they have read, movies they have seen, and a blog.

■ Do you have a personal page on a social networking site? Share your site with friends and tell them why you have included certain information about yourself and why you have excluded other information.

■ Research other people's personal pages on *MySpace* and *FaceBook*. Which aspects of identity are most commonly included? Which aspects are rarely mentioned?

■ *FaceBook* was founded in February 2004 by Harvard University sophomore Mark Zuckerberg and, as of February 2007, the website had over 25 million members worldwide. *MySpace* is believed to have been founded in July 2003 by students from the University of California and a small team of programmers. It is currently controlled by Rupert Murdoch's News Corporation (the parent company of Fox Broadcasting and other media enterprises). Research the history of these two social networking websites. What is the reason for their immense popularity?

C7.6 OBITUARIES

As we mentioned in Unit A7, obituaries published in local or national newspapers are an attempt to finally altercast an individual's identity, and no matter what is written in the obituary, the individual cannot contest it. Research obituaries published in these national newspapers, three published in the United States and three in the United Kingdom.

■ *The Dallas Morning News* www.dallasnews.com

■ *The New York Times* www.nytimes.com

■ *The Washington Post* www.washingtonpost.com

■ *The Daily Telegraph* www.telegraph.co.uk

■ *The Independent* www.independent.co.uk

■ *The Times* www.timesonline.co.uk

Find the obituaries from these newspapers for a single individual – the person will obviously be quite famous if you are to find obituaries in American and British newspapers. Compare how the identity of the individual is created in different obituaries. Use as a basis for your comparison the four aspects of personhood that Tracy specified. According to Marilyn Johnson (2006), obituaries published in Britain tend to be written in a different style from those published in the United States. To Johnson (p. 148), an American writer, a great British obit:

doesn't read like a prosaic résumé. It's an opinionated gem of a biography, informed by all kinds of history, high and low, including gossip. It has the clear-eyed view of an op-ed piece and the drama of the news. It doesn't pull its punches in consideration of the dead; it aims not just for factual truth . . . but for some sort of 'higher truth' – and it takes pleasure in its aiming. Most of all, it is, in its individual state, a highly particular and layered creation, and something of an acquired taste.

Do you agree with Johnson's take on British obits? How would you characterize the American variety? And how about obituaries written in your local newspaper?

QUESTIONS AND ACTIVITIES FOR FUTURE EXPLORATION

The activities listed in this unit have focused on identities created in writing or by a person's vocal monolog. In other words, in these activities we have considered only identities as projected or interpreted. The readings in Unit B7 and some of the excerpts in Unit A7, however, showed how identities are *negotiated* in talk-in-interaction. If you wish to explore how identities are co-constructed, you may wish to videotape interactions between people who don't know each other very well (academic counseling encounters, first dates, and dinner parties are some examples). Watch your recordings many times and then carefully transcribe the interaction using the methods of conversation analysis and analyze how the participants in these encounters negotiate identities. Here are two references that may help with your analysis.

Bucholtz, M., and Hall, K. (2004). Language and identity. In A. Duranti (ed.), *A companion to linguistic anthropology* (pp. 369–394). Malden, MA and Oxford: Blackwell.

Gumperz, J. J. (ed.). (1982). *Language and social identity.* Cambridge and New York: Cambridge University Press.

Unit C8
Discovering communities

INTRODUCTION

The concept of community is important in understanding how individuals construct their identities, but the notion of 'community' itself has been defined in different ways by different scholars. Traditionally, linguists have interpreted communities as groups of people who share knowledge of a language and attitudes toward that language. In studies of groups of people who remain in the same place over generations, for example, dialectologists have distinguished different communities according to their members' pronunciation and their use of particular vocabulary. In the modern world, with much greater movement of people across national boundaries, the concept of community has become much less bound to physical location. Members of a virtual community, for example, may have very little face-to-face contact and still create a community by shared uses of language as well as a common medium for communication: over the internet. Use of language is just one way in which individuals create a community. As Erickson pointed out in his study of the dinner-table conversation among members of an Italian-American family, coordination of talk with gesture, posture, and gaze is a crucial part of creating and maintaining a community.

Cultural communities are created in two ways: by a shared sense of heritage and by shared participation in daily activities. The distinction between cultural insiders and outsiders is particularly noticeable in the ways that insiders and outsiders name members of a cultural group. And as outsiders, we have to do a lot of work in order to understand how insiders participate and what the meanings of participation are.

In this unit, you have the opportunity to investigate some or all of these questions about community. The activities that follow encourage you to study speech communities, virtual communities, discourse communities, communities of practice, and cultural communities.

C8.1 SPEECH COMMUNITIES

Speech community (sometimes called a linguistic community) is a core concept in linguistic theory, particularly for sociolinguists and other linguists working with language data. Peter Patrick (2002) has provided a historical survey of how the term has been used by linguists, in which he reviews, among others, these writings by major figures in the field.

- Bloomfield, Leonard. (1926). A set of postulates for the science of language. *Language*, 2, 153–154.

- Bucholtz, Mary. (1999). 'Why be normal?' Language and identity practices in a community of nerd girls. *Language in Society*, 28(2), 203–223.

- Duranti, Alessandro. (1988). Ethnography of speaking: Towards a linguistics of the praxis. In F. J. Newmeyer (ed.), *Linguistics: The Cambridge survey, vol. IV. Language: The socio-cultural context.* Cambridge: Cambridge University Press.

- Gumperz, John. (1962). Types of linguistic communities. *Anthropological Linguistics*, 4(1), 28–40. Reprinted in J. Fishman (ed.) (1965), *Readings in the sociology of language* (pp. 460–472). The Hague: Monton.

- Gumperz, John. (1968). The speech community. In D. L. Sills and R. K. Merton (eds), *International encyclopedia of the social sciences* (pp. 381–386). New York: Macmillan. Reprinted in P. Giglioli (ed.), *Language and social context* (pp. 219–231). Harmondsworth: Penguin.

- Hymes, Dell. (1972). Models of the interaction of language and social life. In J. J. Gumperz and D. Hymes (eds), *Directions in sociolinguistics: The ethnography of communication* (pp 35–71). New York: Holt, Rinehart and Winston.

- Labov, William. (1972). *Sociolinguistic patterns.* Philadelphia: University of Pennsylvania Press.

- Romaine, Suzanne. (1994). *Language in society: An introduction to socio-linguistics.* Oxford and New York: Oxford University Press.

- Silverstein, Michael (1996). Monoglot 'standard' in America: Standardization and metaphors of linguistic hegemony. In D. Brenneis and R. Macaulay (eds), *The matrix of language: Contemporary linguistic anthropology* (pp. 284–306). Boulder, CO: Westview.

Read Patrick's article and a selection from the original writings in this list. Prepare an essay in which you critique the use of the term 'speech community' and develop your own definition of the term. Be sure to provide examples of speech communities in your essay.

C8.2 VIRTUAL COMMUNITIES

Unlike members of a speech community, members of a virtual community maintain their contacts with each other by computer-mediated communication. There are many virtual communities but perhaps some of the most interesting are blogs co-constructed by current and former members of the military services and their spouses at home. Called 'milblogs,' these provide very different views on current wars and military life from the perspectives provided by the print and television media. By reading milblogs like `www.blackfive.net`, compiled by Mathew Burden, a former paratrooper, you get a strong sense of the comradeship and common interests of people serving in the United States military. A collection of posts from the BlackFive blog has been published by Burden (2006) as *The blog of war: Front-line dispatches from soldiers in Iraq and Afghanistan.*

Take one month's worth of postings on a site like BlackFive and investigate how the bloggers' language creates a community. Here are some ways of approaching the question.

1   How busy is the site: how many postings and how long is the average post?
2   Consider whether a handful of posting can be considered as instances of a discursive practice. Analyze the postings using the framework for describing discursive practices that we presented in Unit A5. Here are some ways to do that.
  ■   What are the boundaries of one posting? Can you identify the opening and closing acts?
  ■   What is the register of the posting? Are there vocabulary, spelling, or grammatical structures that seem to be common to postings on this site?
  ■   What are the modes of meaning that bloggers use? Do they use a pre-dominantly interpersonal, experiential, or textual mode?
  ■   Do postings reference other postings on the site? How do they do so?
  ■   Are there instances of repair? How do bloggers repair the postings of others? Are there any instances of self-repair?
3   Is computer-mediated communication the only way that members of this virtual community communicate? Is there evidence from the site that some members communicate face to face?

C8.3   DISCOURSE COMMUNITIES

Make a video recording of an ordinary dinner at the home of a family. (The family could be your own, but make sure that you have informed consent from all people concerned.) Carefully transcribe the verbal and nonverbal activities that occur, paying particular attention to how participants coordinate their talk with their bodily movements and with the built environment of the space in which the dinner happens. You may find it particularly interesting to look at how participants coordinate the following three elements of nonverbal behavior with talk.

  ■   *Gaze*: When does a participant gaze at another participant? When does the participant gaze at an object? When do they avert their gaze? When does a participant's gaze transfer from one object or participant to another?

- *Posture*: Are all participants seated? Do participants stand up or move around the table? In what direction does a participant orient the upper part of their body? When does a participant's posture change?

- *Gesture*: This refers primarily to the movement of the hands and arms, but you should consider also facial gestures such as yawns, smiles, and grimaces. If participants are eating, how do they coordinate movement of food, between plate and mouth with talk?

In doing this project, you will probably want to focus on a short section of the conversation because the amount of detail that you include will be an obstacle to a clear presentation of a longer slice of data; and also the more information that you include in a transcript, the more time it will take to transcribe. In addition to Erickson (1992), which we reviewed in Unit A9, here are some resources that you may find useful.

- Blum-Kulka, S. (1997). *Dinner talk: Cultural patterns of sociability and socialization in family discourse.* Mahwah, NJ: Lawrence Erlbaum Associates.

- Goodwin, C., and Goodwin, M. H. (1992). Context, activity and participation. In P. Auer and A. Di Luzio (eds), *The contextualization of language* (pp. 77–99). Amsterdam and Philadelphia: John Benjamins.

- Schegloff, E. A. (1984). On some gestures' relation to talk. In J. M. Atkinson and J. Heritage (eds), *Structures of social action: Studies in conversation analysis* (pp. 266–296). New York: Cambridge University Press.

When you have completed your transcript, analyze to what extent your data support the claim that we made in Unit A8:

> Timing of nonverbal activity in relation to the timing of talk is a general phenomenon found in all human interaction, but it is an index of a discourse community when participants treat timing as a shared resource. That means that when we observe focused face-to-face interactions in which participants' movements are out of sync with each other, we may begin to doubt the existence of a community.

C8.4 COMMUNITIES OF PRACTICE

Read Vignette I from Etienne Wenger's book (1998) *Communities of practice.* The vignette is a description of a working day in the life of a young woman, Ariel, who works as a medical insurance claims processor at the fictitious ALINSU Insurance Company. You can read the vignette on line at: `http://www.analytictech.com/mb119/excerpted_from_wenger.htm`. Review Wenger's description of the three dimensions of practice in a community of practice that we presented in Unit A8 (mutual engagement in a joint enterprise in which participants employ a shared repertoire), and discuss how the vignette illustrates those dimensions.

Research an organization in your community (a company, a school, a seminar group, a social club, or some other organization) by shadowing a member of that organization through one day. Prepare a description of their day using Wenger's vignette as a model and discuss how your data illustrates Wenger's dimensions of community of practice. Use these guidelines in your research.

- Make sure that you have informed consent to record and write about the day's activities from the person that you are shadowing and from the people in the organization with whom she interacts.

- Interview the person you are shadowing before the day, and ask her to describe to you a normal working day. Her description should include time at work as well as time traveling to and from work. Take written notes of the interview.

- On the day that you will shadow, meet the person at her home and travel to work with her. Accompany her throughout her working day but try not to interact with her. Simply observe, take notes, and if possible take copies of any written documents that she uses. Travel home with her at the end of her working day.

- Afterwards, write as detailed an account as you can of the day. Show a draft of your account to the person and ask her to comment on it. Focus particularly on the person's mutual engagement with others in a joint enterprise, in which members employ a shared repertoire.

Use your written record as a basis of an essay in which you discuss Wenger's theory of community of practice.

C8.5 CULTURAL COMMUNITIES

Communities are defined to some extent by the names that members of the community use to describe themselves, the names used by outsiders, and the emotional associations that those names bear. Naming is an important issue, especially for ethnic minority communities, because of people's belief that words influence the way that people think about the world.

Investigate the importance of naming cultural communities by first reading 'Finding a name that fits: Significance of ethnic labels Hispanic, Latino' by Kendra Hamilton (2001) and answer the five questions below. The article describes how members of cultural communities contest naming practices. It is available online at: `http://find articles.com/p/articles/mi_m0DXK/is_16_18/ai_79743148`. It is also reproduced in Walters and Brody (2005), from which these questions are taken:

1   What do the terms *Hispanic* and *Latino* denote and connote for those interviewed in this article? What are the sources of those meanings? Why is the distinction important?

2   What is the history of the term *Hispanic*? Why is Latin America called *Latin America*? (Remember that Portuguese, not Spanish, is the main language of Brazil.) In what ways do the labels *Hispanic* and *Latino* reflect and create a linguistic division from a colonial past?

3   Consider two other minority groups in the U.S. – African Americans and Asian Americans. What are some terms of self-reference that have been used by members of these groups? What might account for variations in these naming practices?

4   An Asian American students' association posted a sign entitled 'The Ten Things Asian Americans Hate Most.' Number 1 on the list was 'The hyphen.' Why all the fuss about a hyphen?

5   Outsiders who do not wish to offend ethic groups (and even more so those who wish to demonstrate support or solidarity) often find it difficult to choose terms to describe the group and its members. Why? How might outsiders decide which term or terms to use or not to use?

QUESTIONS AND ACTIVITIES FOR FUTURE EXPLORATION

In this unit, we have treated speech communities, virtual communities, discourse communities, communities of practice, and cultural communities separately. Each of the five sections has focused on one interpretation of the word 'community' and we have used as examples different groups of people that we have called communities. What are the similarities and differences among the five treatments of community that we have presented here?

Unit C9
Developing interactional skills

INTRODUCTION

In this unit we present two different kinds of learning activities. The close analysis of interaction will provide insights into the participation metaphor for learning and also the ways that classroom discourse reflects the pedagogical aims of the teacher. Further reading and reflection on classic studies in the fields of language socialization and situated learning show how those approaches have been used to construct understandings of learning.

C9.1 PARTICIPATION FRAMEWORKS FOR LEARNING

David Shea (1994) analyzed four conversations in English between Japanese studying in the US and Americans. The Japanese students had acquired approximately the same level of proficiency in English, although their knowledge of the language was not paralleled by their knowledge of ways of thinking, acting, and participating in conversations in English. Shea's analysis shows that, in different conversations with different interlocutors, learners of English with the same level of proficiency appear to have very different knowledge of English. He explains this difference by invoking two dimensions of the participation framework of conversation: participation and perspective. On the participation dimension, a native speaker of English may allow learners to cooperatively share the floor, recognize the learner's right to speak, and value their ideas. Alternatively, the native speaker may interrupt or exclude the learner and usurp the rights to shape the direction of talk. On the dimension of perspective, the native speaker may acknowledge the learner's orientation and commitment to the topic of discussion; alternatively, the native speaker may index a distinct orientation and a different commitment.

The four conversations from Shea (1994) are reproduced below.

■ Do a close comparative analysis of the discourse of each of the four, basing your analysis on Shea's two dimensions of participation and perspective.

■ Now read Shea's article to see if you agree with his analysis.

■ Work with a learner of English and record the learner's conversations with four different interlocutors. Does the learner's proficiency in English vary in the four conversations?

■ If you find differences in the learner's English, discuss the implications of those differences (1) for the acquisition and participation metaphors for learning and (2) for the assessment of proficiency in a second language.

■ Shea uses a few transcription conventions in addition to those presented in Unit C3. These are his additional conventions:

,,	Pause of approximately one-half second per comma
{ }	Overlapping speech inserted as backchannels: e.g. "unhun" and "right"
`	Distinctly falling intonation
/	Distinctly rising intonation
hhh	Laughter
<...>	Ellipsis: conversation not included, either within or across turns
' '	Verbal quotation: speaker adopts a distinctly different voice
???	Speech not understood in transcription
!	Distinctly excited emotion

(1) Jiro is an undergraduate junior majoring in International Business with two semesters remaining before graduation. His advisor is attempting to judge whether Jiro has met university requirements for graduation.

```
 1 Advisor: Okay I need to get that and your phone number.
             Have you changed your phone number also?
 2    Jiro: Yes, er, [uh
 3 Advisor:         [I have that you are Town Apartment # 891
 4    Jiro: Yes that´s right [uh but uh
 5 Advisor:                  [That´s correct
             <. . .>
 6 Advisor: What else did you take?
 7    Jiro: 1 took Chemistry 2—, er, Chemistry/
 8 Advisor: 215?
 9    Jiro: [215
10 Advisor: [okay that showed up. What else´ Anything else/
11    Jiro:       [a::nd uh-
12 Advisor:       [at your other College?
13    Jiro: I took the tennis/
14 Advisor: Okay, the PE, that´s fine. Okay! good, we´re okay,
             , o:kay, let´s se::e, , , , Okay, I have that you
             ha:ve, two major required courses left, to take, ,
             {unhun/} And your choices for those are PS 571 and
             Business 663.
             You must [get==
```

```
15   Jiro:              [yes
16   Advisor:  ==these classes because see PS 571's only offered,
                  once a year,
17   Jiro:     Oh really?
18   Advisor:  So if you don't get it, you will have to wait till
                  next Spring. And if you don't get it when you
                  register, you need to go to the PS department and
                  tell them that you must have this class because
                  you' won't' be' here' next Spring, and you have to
                  get it to graduate
19   Jiro:     [I see
20   Advisor:  [Because see, <. . .> that, department must, grant
                  you permission to take that class, so if you don't
                  get it during registration, , you need to go to
                  the department directly and tell them, that you
                  have to have it to graduate, u::m,
21   Jiro:     You mean [Political Studies?
22   Advisor:           [In fact I'll write it on your sheet,
                  'Must, have, to, graduate'
                  <. . .>
23   Advisor:  Do you still have your check-sheet? This thing
                  that I gave you?
24   Jiro:     Yes, I [have
25   Advisor:         [Okay let me go and update it, and make
                  sure everything's—, see! you keep all these old
                  ones and I want you to throw, them, aw::ay!
26   Jiro:     Yeah hhh I er, [I uh-
27   Advisor:                 [This is the one I want you to
                  keep, this in the only one I want you to have
                  {yeah} I want you
```

(2) Fumiko is a new first-year graduate student. Dr Hughes is a professor in her department. Fumiko has made an appointment with Dr Hughes in the hope of getting ideas for her upcoming thesis. Fumiko has just expressed surprise that a telephone interview of local businesses would be more costly than a written interview. She then suggests a telephone survey, to which Dr Hughes responds.

```
1   Dr Hughes:  Yeah I don't think we could use the same survey,
                  over the phone because, {hhh} people won't be
                  able to, it would be harder to, you know,
                  {unhun} elicit responses
2   Fumiko:     You have to keep them for an hour hhh, you just
                  say, 'yes yes yes'
3   Dr Hughes:  So, (7 sec pause)
4   Dr Hughes:  Uh, wh-, what's your, objective?
```

```
   5     Fumiko:   Um, I´m, , I´m interested in any movement
                   that´s, like against for, against the, the
                   regular flow of, of maybe capitalist system of
                   this society movement, {um} so like—,
   6  Dr Hughes:   I would say this um, , , , this is really, the
                   intent of this study is to influence the attitude
                   of the consumer, {unhun} but it´s not to impose,
                   , uh, rules, in other words, it allows free
                   markets to work, but try to influence the
                   attitude of the consumer so that he realizes,
                   the benefits and costs, associated with his
                   purchases and purchase decisions
```

(3) Two of Kazuko's academic colleagues, Sandy and Valerie, are in town for a
professional conference and are having dinner at Kazuko's house. The three women
are all post-doctoral researchers in chemistry, approximately the same age. In this
excerpt, Sandy and Valerie are asking Kazuko about her present position and her
impressions of the United States.

```
   1  Valerie:  Do you feel accustomed to it yet?
   2  Kazuko:   Yeah, , after, we—, you know we spent a three
                nights, four nights at the conference, we feel
                this our home hhh {hhh}
   3   Sandy:   Oh so it´s good to go away
   4  Kazuko:   [Yeah, right
   5   Sandy:   [So you can do that
   6  Valerie:  And this is your first time to be, in the United
                States? [or have been—
   7  Kazuko:           [For her but,
   8  Valerie:  not for you
   9  Kazuko:   not for me, yeah
  10  Valerie:  Where were you before?
  11  Kazuko:   In the North/[University of—
  12  Valerie:               [And were you working there?
  13  Kazuko:   Yeah with Dr Mary Brown/ um,
  14  Valerie:  Was that the same woman you´re working with here?
  15  Kazuko:   Yeah
  16   Sandy:   Valerie asked, how did you get this post doc,
                I couldn´t remember, Now, {K: oh) did she write
                you?
  17  Kazuko:   Yeah, when, she decided to come here, from the
                North to here, she-, I think she sent letters to
                many people to announce about it and <. . .> so I
                was, I was unhappy with my position hhh, I was,
                sort of looking for, {S: unhun} looking for a
                chance [to
```

```
18   Sandy:        [Which boss was this?
                [hhh
19   Kazuko:   [Well, well hhh {S: hhh} You know that hhh,
               so I wonder, if I could be uh, her post doc
               then, ,
20   Sandy:   This is delicious. Prize winning food
21   Kazuko:   Okay hhh yeah
22   Valerie: And this is a, a one year/ or a two year post doc?
23   Kazuko:   Uh, Mary says two years, and,
24   Sandy:   Kikuchi-san/ Japan said one year [hhh
25   Kazuko:                                    [Yeah
26   Sandy:   So who knows,
```

(4) This is a lunch conversation between Kazuko and Lilly, the technician in the lab where Kazuko conducts her research. Kazuko has just turned on the tape recorder and commented about being the subject of Shea's research.

```
1   Kazuko:   But it's, rather strange to see my conversation on
              a neat typed written, {hhh} he even, he even, he
              pointed out what does this mean and, {unhun}
              that's rather embarrassing hhh {hhh} , , , ,
2   Lilly:    Yeah, I can't imagine what, , what it would be
              like to record your, everyday/ {unhun/} for the
              whole day what it would be like, (right) you know
              after you recorded it, {unhun/} and run it out,
              it's like, 'I said that? Boy, I sound stupid!'
              [hhh
3   Kazuko:   [hhh right yeah, , I hate to hear my speaking in—,
              from a you know a tape recorder or a videotape,
              it's always very—, sounds stupid hhh {hhh} 'Am I
              that stupid?' [hhh
4   Lilly:              [hhh well, I don't know if you
              noticed this or not but, when you hear yourself
              talking inside your head, {right} you sound like
              one tone, {right} and then when you hear it on a
              recording {unhun} it's like you're in a different
              {right} tone and it's like, {unhun} 'I don't sound
              like that do I!?' {unhun} you know, {right} cause
              there's,
5   Kazuko:   Yeah maybe we, hear from, inside of you know
              {unhun} head or something,
6   Lilly:    unhun, cause—, cause—, you know to me, I think I
              have somewhat of a low voice/ {oh} and in reality,
              I have a quite high voice, {hhh} and it's like,
              hhh {hhh} well how come it sounds low here {ah}
              and it, sounds high there
```

```
 7  Kazuko    Unhun, yeah, , but it´s not only a matter of, you
                know, sound difference, {unhun/} but also a sound
                stupid hhh
 8   Lilly:   Yeah cause you actually end up completing what
                you´re trying to say in your head {unhun} and you
                don´t actually say it {unhun} completely, {unhun}
                I do that all the time,
 9  Kazuko:   So maybe everybody must think themselves {unhun}
                little bit clever than every other people think
                [hhh
10   Lilly:   [hhh ´What do you mean you don´t understand?
                {unhun/} I understood myself completely!´ {unhun/}
                hhh
11  Kazuko:   ´You should know what I mean´ {hhh} hhh
```

C9.2 LANGUAGE SOCIALIZATION

Language socialization means both socialization through language and socialization to use language. Children acquire tacit knowledge of principles of social order and systems of belief through exposure to and participation in language-mediated interaction. The approach used by language socialization researchers is to examine closely the verbal interactions of infants and small children with older children and adults. These interactions are socially organized and carry information concerning social order and express local conceptions and theories about the world. Language use is then a major if not the major tool for conveying sociocultural knowledge and a powerful medium of socialization. As Ochs has written, 'children acquire a world view as they acquire a language' (Ochs, 1986, p. 3). The following are three classic studies of language socialization.

■ Clancy, P. M. (1986). The acquisition of communicative style in Japanese. In B. B. Schieffelin and E. Ochs (eds), *Language socialization across cultures* (pp. 213–250). New York: Cambridge University Press.

■ Miller, P. J. (1982). *Amy, Wendy, and Beth: Learning language in South Baltimore.* Austin, TX: University of Texas Press.

■ Heath, S. B. (1982). What no bedtime story means: Narrative skills at home and school. *Language in Society,* 11(1), 49–76.

Read these three studies and write an essay in which you reflect in the same light as these studies on your own childhood and the means through which you acquired the values, culture, and world view that you have as an adult.

C9.3 SITUATED LEARNING

In Lave and Wenger's (1991) book *Situated learning: Legitimate peripheral participation*, the authors argue for an approach to learning that mostly involves personal and physical involvement of both newcomers and old timers in a formal or informal apprenticeship. Some of the examples they cite of situated learning are described in detail in these four articles:

■ Cain, C. (1991). Personal stories: Identity acquisition and self-understanding in Alcoholics Anonymous. *Ethos*, 19(2), 210–253.

■ Hutchins, E. (1993). Learning to navigate. In S. Chaiklin and J. Lave (eds), *Understanding practice: Perspectives on activity and context* (pp. 35–63). New York: Cambridge University Press.

■ Jordan, B. (1989). Cosmopolitan obstetrics: Some insights from the training of traditional midwives. *Social Science and Medicine*, 28(9), 925–944.

■ Marshall, H. M. (1972). Structural constraints on learning: Butchers' apprentices. *The American Behavioral Scientist*, 16(1), 35–44.

Read these reports of situated learning by nondrinking alcoholics, quartermasters in the U.S. Navy, Yucatec midwives, and meat cutters in American supermarkets. How do they show the following features of situated learning: the characteristics of the community of practice, the transition from newcomer to old timer, the help that both newcomers and old timers provide each other, the repertoire of skills that the learner develops, and the acquisition of a new identity? How does the process of situated learning differ from teaching and learning in traditional courses of instruction?

C9.4 CLASSROOM DISCOURSE

Seedhouse (2004) claimed that interaction in classrooms where students are learning a foreign or second language differs according to the pedagogical focus of the lesson. He showed that interactional patterns of turn-taking, sequential organization, and repair are inextricably intertwined with the pedagogical context created by the teacher. Focus on the patterns of repair in the following three excerpts from classroom interaction in ESL classes. Where is the trouble source? Which speaker initiates the repair? Which speaker completes the repair? On the basis of your analysis of repair, decide if the pedagogical context of the excerpt is (1) form and accuracy, (2) meaning and fluency, (3) task-based, or (4) procedural. Can you say what is being learned in these excerpts?

(5) From Nunan, 1989, p. 142

```
Teacher:   what about in China? well, Hong Kong. China. do you
           have a milk van?
Learners:  er, China (.) no, no milk.
Teacher:   no milk?
Learners:  yeah, shop, er, city, city.
Teacher:   ah, at the shop, the shop.
Learners:  er, yes, yes.
Learner:   Hong Kong. Hong Kong.
Teacher:   yeah, in Hong Kong, yes.
Learners:  in China, yes er ( ) city.
Teacher:   in the big cities.
Learners:  big city (.) city, yeah.
Teacher:   ah huh!
Learners:  Guangdong. Peking. Shanghai, Shanghai.
Learner:   yes, er city, very big, big milk car.
Teacher:   big milk van. ah! and city, country. in the country,
           no?
Learners:  no.
Teacher:   no. shh, shh, shh (gestures)
Learner:   that's right.
Teacher:   yes (laughs)
Learner:   I'm, er, I'm (.) no, is China, er city.
Teacher:   uh huh!
Learner:   er, I'm house, near, near city er, I'm go to city
           shopping, er, how many?
Teacher:   buy milk.
Learner:   buy milk, yeah. buy milk.
Teacher:   buy milk.
Learner:   buy milk, go to home, yes.
```

(6) From Lightbown and Spada, 1993, p. 76

```
Learner:   it bug me to have=
Teacher:   =it bugs me. it bugzzz me
Learner:   It bugs me when my brother takes my bicycle
```

(7) From Seedhouse, 1994, p. 309

```
Learners:  Paul what's this?
Teacher:   it's a flood you had a flood
Learner 1: what's a flood?
Teacher:   inundation ((tr: flood))
Learner 1: uh uh
Teacher:   OK?
```

```
Learner 2:  and why?
  Teacher:  ah well (.) how many people did you have?
Learner 1:  in the field?
Learner 2:  in the dyke?
  Teacher:  in the dyke
 Learners:  100
  Teacher:  100 not enough
 Learners:  ah ha
```

QUESTIONS AND ACTIVITIES FOR FUTURE EXPLORATION

What is meant by *learning*? In this unit we have considered four different approaches to learning: participation frameworks for learning, language socialization, situated learning, and classroom discourse. How do those theories relate to our normal use of the word? Consider these two dictionary definitions of the transitive verb 'learn.' How do the theories of learning that we have explored in this unit help us to understand what we normally mean by learning? Explore other theories of learning in the fields of psychology and education. How do these theories explain the development of interactional skills?

The first definition of 'learn' in the *Oxford English dictionary* is:

> To acquire knowledge of (a subject) or skill in (an art, etc.) as a result of study, experience, or teaching. Also, to commit to memory (passages of prose or verse), *esp.* in phrases *to learn by heart, by rote*

In *Webster's third new international dictionary, unabridged*, the first definition is:

> to gain knowledge or understanding of or skill in by study, instruction, or experience : receive instruction in <*learn* a language> <*learn* arithmetic> <*learn* a trade> <*learn* dancing> <a law which must . . . be *learnt*, but can never be taught – Havelock Ellis> <only just *learnt* how to enjoy life – Joyce Cary>

Notes

UNIT A1

1 Bakhtin's term for the time-space context of utterance is *the chronotope.*
2 Wittgenstein's thinking about language games was first sketched in English in *The Blue and Brown Books* (1969) and then summarized and expanded in German in his *Philosophical investigations* (2001). This approach is markedly different from the views of meaning that he expounded earlier in the *Tractatus* (1933).
3 The book that Gumperz and Hymes edited in 1972 titled *Directions in sociolinguistics: The ethnography of communication* contains many of the earliest contributions to our understanding of language and interaction.

UNIT A2

1 'context.' Webster's third new international dictionary, unabridged. Merriam-Webster, 2002. http://unabridged.merriam-webster.com (18 Sep. 2005).
2 Kiss me, kiss me my darling / As if tonight was the last INS raid. / Kiss me, kiss me my honey / Cos I'm afraid of losing you somewhere in LA. // Who knows maybe tomorrow I'll be in jail / Longing for your ass (I mean eyes) / And maybe they'll deport me back to Tijuana / Cos I'm an illegal alien.

UNIT A3

1 See Tannen (1989) for a discussion of the relation between Dr King's written speech and its performance.
2 'language.' *Webster's third new international dictionary, unabridged. Merriam-Webster, 2002. http://unabridged.merriam-webster.com (25 May 2006).*
3 *You can watch and listen to a streaming video of Dr Martin Luther King's 'I have a dream' speech at* http://video.google.com/videoplay?docid=1732754907698549493&q=i+have+a+dream.
4 British Library, Cotton MS Nero D. iv, f. 27. Lindisfarne Gospels: initial page to St Matthew's Gospel (England, Lindisfarne, c. 698).
5 The ideational metafunction is also referred to as experiential (Halliday and Matthiessen, 2004).
6 Michelob or 'Mich' is a popular beer in the United States.
7 The conversation is taken from Antaki's 'An introductory tutorial in Conversation Analysis.' Video, audio, and transcripts of the conversation are available on the web at http://www-staff.lboro.ac.uk/~ssca1/intro1.htm.

8 Sacks, Schegloff, and Jefferson (1974, p. 709)
9 Participation framework is discussed in greater detail in Section A5.3.3.

UNIT A4

1 You can view the picture online at iStockphoto `http://www.istockphoto.com/index.php`, `File Number: 1725834`.
2 'Yalie' – A person who attends or attended Yale University.
3 'Sparta' – A town in Georgia.
4 Although the term 'register' is used in slightly different senses by different linguists (some use 'style,' others prefer 'register'), it invariably relates linguistic form to social practice. So while some linguists talk about a formal or an informal register others prefer to use the term to refer to the language of a professional or disciplinary group as in 'legal register' or 'medical register' (Armstrong, 1997).

UNIT A5

1 See Section A4.2 for an explanation of how participants use register as a resource to construct discursive practices.
2 See the explanation of these three modes of meaning in Section A3.1.3.
3 Interactional resources including action sequences, turn-taking, repair, and participation framework were discussed in Section A3.2.
4 See Richards (2006) for a discussion of the relationship between classroom discourse features such as the IRE sequence and aspects of personal and institutional identity.

UNIT A6

1 Quotes taken from `http://www.brainyquote.com/` on January 29, 2007.
2 My interpretation of this conversation builds on Schegloff (1992) but goes further in locating the conversation in a discursive practice.

UNIT A7

1 The character descriptions are of Falstaff, Hamlet, Kitty, and Hester. Sir John Falstaff appears in the plays *Henry IV Parts I and II* and *The merry wives of Windsor* by William Shakespeare. Hamlet, Prince of Denmark, is the title character and protagonist of Shakespeare's play. Ekaterina Alexandrovna Shcherbatskaya (better known as Kitty) is a character in Leo Tolstoy's novel *Anna Karenina*. Hester Prynne is the protagonist of Nathaniel Hawthorne's novel *The scarlet letter*. SparkNotes Online Study Guides are available at `http://www.sparknotes.com/`.
2 *The I.M.s of Romeo and Juliet*, 2006 Wall Calendar by Roz Chast, published by Cartoon Bank.com.
3 *Argot* is defined in *Webster's third new international dictionary* as 'a special vocabulary and idiom used by a particular underworld group especially as a means of private communication.'

4   Translation: As young men . . . we would style our hair, powder our faces, climb into our fabulous new clothes, put on our shoes, and wander off to some fabulous little bar. In the bar we would stand around with our gay companions, look at the fabulous genitals on the butch man nearby who, if we fluttered our eyelashes at him sweetly, might just wander over to offer a light for the unlit cigarette clenched between our teeth.

5   This scene is from an episode of *Seinfeld* titled 'The Wizard,' originally aired on February, 26, 1998 (Season 9, Episode 15). *Seinfeld* is produced by Sony Pictures Television.

UNIT A8

1   Both Dell Hymes (1972, p. 55) and Suzanne Romaine (1994, p. 23) attribute the term 'Sprechbund' to the Czech linguist Jiří V. Neustupný.

2   A video record of the family's conversation at the dinner table is available on Erickson's website at `http://www.gseis.ucla.edu/faculty/ferickson/resources/talk.html`.

3   In the United States, children enter the first grade of elementary school at age 5 or 6. Children in the third grade are usually between 7 and 8 years old. Most eighth graders are between 13 and 14.

UNIT B3

1   A less demanding introduction to systemic functional grammar is available in Butt *et al.* (2000).

UNIT C2

1   Copyright ©1990–2005 National Public Radio®. All rights reserved. No quotes from the materials contained herein may be used in any media without attribution to National Public Radio. This transcript may not be reproduced in whole or in part without prior written permission. For further information, please contact NPR's Rights and Reuse Associate at (202) 513–2030.

UNIT C5

1   The video of this classroom interaction is part of the demonstration video for *Transana*, a computer program that allows researchers to transcribe and analyze large collections of video and audio data. You can download the video from the Transana website, http://www.transana.org/download/index.html. The data segment begins about three minutes into the demonstration video.

References

Alim, H. S. (2004). Hip Hop Nation Language. In E. Finegan and J. Rickford (eds), *Language in the USA: Themes for the twenty-first century* (pp. 387–409). Cambridge and New York: Cambridge University Press.

Alvarez, L., Kolker, A., Center for New American Media, WETA-TV (Television station: Washington, DC), Independent Television Service, CNAM Film Library, *et al.* (2001). *People like us: Social class in America* [Videocassette]. Hohokus, NJ: Center for New American Media.

American Council on the Teaching of Foreign Languages. (1986). *ACTFL provisional proficiency guidelines.* Hastings-on-Hudson, NY: Author.

Antaki, C. (n. d.). *An introductory tutorial in conversation analysis.* Retrieved March 2 2007 from http://www-staff.lboro.ac.uk/~ssca1/sitemenu.htm.

Armstrong, N. (1997). *Review of the book 'Dimensions of register variation. A cross-linguistic comparison.'* Retrieved August 29, 2006, from http://wjmll.ncl.ac.uk/issue02/armstrong2.htm.

Austin, J. L. (1962). *How to do things with words.* Cambridge, MA: Harvard University Press.

Bachman, L. F. (1990). *Fundamental considerations in language testing.* Oxford and New York: Oxford University Press.

Bachman, L. F., and Palmer, A. S. (1996). *Language testing in practice: Designing and developing useful language tests.* Oxford and New York: Oxford University Press.

Bakhtin, M. M. (1981). *The dialogic imagination: Four essays.* Edited by M. Holmquist, translated by C. Emerson and M. Holmquist. Austin, TX, and London: University of Texas Press.

Bakhtin, M. M. (1984). *Problems of Dostoevsky's poetics* (C. Emerson, trans.). Minneapolis: University of Minnesota Press.

Bakhtin, M. M. (1986). The problem of speech genres (V. W. McGee, trans.). In M. M. Bakhtin and C. Emerson (eds), *Speech genres and other late essays* (pp. 60–102). Austin, TX, and London: University of Texas Press.

Bakhtin, M. M. (1990). *Art and answerability: Early philosophical essays* (V. Liapunov, trans.). Austin: University of Texas Press.

Bales, Robert F. (1970). *Personality and interpersonal behavior.* New York: Holt, Rhinehart and Winston.

Baquedano-López, P. (2001). Creating social identities through *doctrina* narratives. In A. Duranti (ed.), *Linguistic anthropology: A reader* (pp. 343–358). Oxford: Blackwell.

Barker, R. G., and Wright, H. F. (1955). *Midwest and its children: The psychological ecology of an American town.* Evanston, IL: Row, Peterson.

Barnes, D. (1976). *From communication to curriculum.* Harmondsworth: Penguin.

Barnes, D., and Shemilt, D. (1974). Transmission and interpretation. *Educational Review*, 26(3), 213–228.

Basso, E. B. (1992). Contextualization in Kalapalo narratives. In A. Duranti and C. Goodwin (eds), *Rethinking context: Language as an interactive phenomenon* (pp. 253–269). Cambridge: Cambridge University Press.

Basso, K. H. (1970). 'To give up on words': Silence in Western Apache culture. *Southwestern Journal of Anthropology*, 26(3), 213–230.

Bauman, R. (1992). Contextualization, tradition, and the dialogue of genres: Icelandic legends of the *kraftaskáld*. In A. Duranti and C. Goodwin (eds), *Rethinking context: Language as an interactive phenomenon* (pp. 125–145). Cambridge: Cambridge University Press.

Bell, A. (1984). Language style as audience design. *Language in Society*, 13(2), 145–204.

Besnier, N. (1990). Language and affect. *Annual Review of Anthropology*, 19, 419–451.

Biber, D., and Finegan, E. (1989). Styles of stance in English: Lexical and grammatical marking of evidentiality and affect. *Text*, 9(1), 93–124.

Birdwhistell, R. L. (1960). Kinesics and communication. In E. S. Carpenter and M. McLuhan (eds), *Explorations in communication: An anthology* (pp. 54–64). Beacon Hill, NC: Beacon Press.

Birdwhistell, R. L. (1970). *Kinesics and context: Essays on body motion communication.* Philadelphia, PA: University of Pennsylvania Press.

Blom, J.-P., and Gumperz, J. J. (1972). Social meaning in linguistic structure: Code switching in Norway. In J. J. Gumperz and D. Hymes (eds), *Directions in sociolinguistics: The ethnography of communication* (pp. 407–434). New York: Holt, Rinehart and Winston.

Bloomfield, L. (1927). Literate and illiterate speech. *American Speech*, 2(10), 432–439.

Bloomfield, L. (1933). *Language.* New York: H. Holt and Company.

Bourdieu, P. (1977). *Outline of a theory of practice* (R. Nice, trans.). Cambridge and New York: Cambridge University Press.

Bourdieu, P. (1984). *Distinction: A social critique of the judgment of taste* (R. Nice, trans.). Cambridge, MA: Harvard University Press.

Bourdieu, P. (1990). *In other words: Essays toward a reflexive sociology* (M. Adamson, trans.). Oxford: Polity.

Briggs, J., and Peat, F. D. (1989). *Turbulent mirror: An illustrated guide to chaos theory and the science of wholeness.* New York: Harper and Row.

Britton, J. (1971). Talking to learn. In D. Barnes, J. Britton, and H. Rosen (eds), *Language, the learner and the school* (revised ed., pp. 81–115). Harmondsworth: Penguin.

Brouwer, C. E., and Wagner, J. (2004). Developmental issues in second language conversation. *Journal of Applied Linguistics*, 1(1), 29–47.

Brown, P., and Levinson, S. C. (1987). *Politeness: Some universals in language usage.* Cambridge and New York: Cambridge University Press.

Bryant, S., Forte, A., and Bruckman, A. (2005, November 6–9). *Becoming Wikipedian: Transformation of participation in a collaborative online encyclopedia.* Paper presented at the GROUP International Conference on Supporting Group Work, Sanibel Island, FL.

Burden, M. C. (2006). *The blog of war: Front-line dispatches from soldiers in Iraq and Afghanistan.* New York: Simon and Schuster.

Burton, P. G. (1985). *Parallel lives.* London: GMP.

Butt, D., Fahey, R., Feez, S., Spinks, S., and Yallop, C. (2000). *Using functional grammar: An explorer's guide* (2nd ed.). Sydney: National Centre for English Language Teaching and Research.

Cain, C. (1991). Personal stories: Identity acquisition and self-understanding in Alcoholics Anonymous. *Ethos*, 19(2), 210–253.

Cambridge University Reporter, January 15, 1969, p. 890.

Canale, M., and Swain, M. (1980). Theoretical bases of communicative approaches to second language teaching and testing. *Applied Linguistics*, 1(1), 1–47.

Chafe, W. L., and Nichols, J. (eds). (1986). *Evidentiality: The linguistic coding of epistemology*. Norwood, NJ: Ablex.

Chomsky, N. (1965). *Aspects of the theory of syntax*. Cambridge, MA: MIT Press.

Chomsky, N. (1976). *Reflections on language*. Glasgow, Scotland: Fontana/Collins.

Cicourel, A. V. (1964). *Method and measurement in sociology*. New York: Free Press.

Cicourel, A. V. (1974). *Cognitive sociology: Language and meaning in social interaction*. New York: Free Press.

Cicourel, A. V. (1990). The integration of distributed knowledge in collaborative medical diagnosis. In J. R. Galegher, R. E. Kraut, and C. Egido (eds), *Intellectual teamwork: Social and technological foundations of cooperative work* (pp. 221–242). Hillsdale, NJ: Erlbaum.

Cicourel, A. V. (1995). Medical speech events as resources for inferring differences in expert-novice diagnostic reasoning. In U. M. Quasthoff (ed.), *Aspects of oral communication* (pp. 364–387). Berlin and New York: W. de Gruyter.

Cicourel, A. V. (2000). Expert. *Journal of Linguistic Anthropology*, 9(1–2), 72–75.

Clancy, P. M. (1986). The acquisition of communicative style in Japanese. In B. B. Schieffelin and E. Ochs (eds), *Language socialization across cultures* (pp. 213–250). New York: Cambridge University Press.

Cole, M., and Engeström, Y. (1993). A cultural-historical approach to distributed cognition. In G. Salomon (ed.), *Distributed cognitions: Psychological and educational considerations* (pp. 1–46). Cambridge and New York: Cambridge University Press.

Comrie, B. (1987). *The world's major languages*. New York: Oxford University Press.

Cran, W., and McNeill, R. (2005). *Do you speak American?* Retrieved August 21, 2007 from http://www.pbs.org/speak/words/sezwho/hiphop/.

Cutler, C. A. (1999). Yorkville crossing: White teens, hip hop, and African American English. *Journal of Sociolinguistics*, 3(4), 428–442.

Day, D. (1994). Tang's dilemma and other problems: Ethnification processes at some multicultural workplaces. *Pragmatics*, 4, 315–336.

Day, D. (1998). Being ascribed, and resisting, membership in an ethnic group. In C. Antaki and S. Widdicombe (eds), *Identities in talk* (pp. 151–170). London: SAGE Publications.

DiNozzi, R., Tannen, D., Georgetown University. Dept of Linguistics, George Washington University. Columbian School of Arts and Sciences, George Washington University. Committee on Linguistics, Pulse Media, *et al.* (2001). *He said, she said: Gender, language, communication* [Videocassette]. Los Angeles: Into the Classroom Media.

Duranti, A. (1981). *The Samoan fono: A sociolinguistic study*. Canberra: Dept of Linguistics, Research School of Pacific Studies, Australian National University.

Duranti, A., and Brenneis, D. (eds). (1986). *The audience as co-author*. Special issue of Text vol. 6, no. 3. New York: Mouton de Gruyter.

Duranti, A., and Goodwin, C. (eds). (1992). *Rethinking context: Language as an interactive phenomenon*. New York: Cambridge University Press.

Durkheim, É. (1969). *L'évolution pédagogique en France* (2nd ed.). Paris: Presses universitaires de France.

Egbert, M. M. (2004). Other-initiated repair and membership categorization: Some conversational events that trigger linguistic and regional membership categorization. *Journal of Pragmatics*, 36(8), 1467–1498.

Engeström, Y. (1990). *Learning, working and imagining*. Helsinki: Orienta-Konsultit Oy.

Engeström, Y. (1993). Developmental studies of work as a testbench of activity theory: The case of primary care medical practice. In S. Chaiklin and J. Lave (eds), *Understanding practice: Perspectives on activity and context* (pp. 64–103). New York: Cambridge University Press.

Erickson, F. (1992). They know all the lines: Rhythmic organization and contextualization in a conversational listing routine. In P. Auer and A. Di Luzio (eds), *The contextualization of language* (pp. 365–397). Amsterdam and Philadelphia: John Benjamins.

Erickson, F. (2004). *Talk and social theory: Ecologies of speaking and listening in everyday life.* Cambridge and Malden, MA: Polity.

Fair, S. 1982. *The bedspread.* New York: William Morrow.

Fairclough, N. (2001). *Language and power* (2nd ed.). London: Pearson Education.

Falvey, M. (1983). *Teacher attitude and learner behaviour.* Unpublished MA thesis, University of Birmingham, Birmingham.

Ferguson, C. A. (1977). Baby talk as a simplified register. In C. Snow and C. A. Ferguson (eds), *Talking to children: Language input and acquisition* (pp. 209–235). Cambridge: Cambridge University Press.

Ferguson, C. A., and Gumperz, J. J. (1960). *Linguistic diversity in South Asia: Studies in regional, social, and functional variation.* Bloomington, IN: Indiana Research Center in Anthropology, Folklore, and Linguistics.

Figlio, D. N. (2005). Boys named Sue: Disruptive children and their peers. *NBER Working Paper,* 11277.

Ford, C. E. (1993). *Grammar in interaction: Adverbial clauses in American English conversations.* Cambridge and New York: Cambridge University Press.

Ford, C. E., and Thompson, S. A. (1996). Interactional units in conversation: Syntactic, intonational, and pragmatic resources for the management of turns. In E. Ochs, E. A. Schegloff, and S. A. Thompson (eds), *Interaction and Grammar* (pp. 134–184). Cambridge: Cambridge University Press.

Gardiner, M. (1992). *The dialogics of critique: M. M. Bakhtin and the theory of ideology.* London and New York: Routledge.

Gardner, P. M. (1966). Symmetric respect and memorate knowledge: The structure and ecology of the individualistic culture. *Southwestern Journal of Anthropology,* 22, 389–415.

Gibson, J. J. (1979). *The ecological approach to visual perception.* Boston, MA: Houghton Mifflin.

Goffman, E. (1974). *Frame analysis.* New York: Harper and Row.

Goffman, E. (1979). Footing. *Semiotica,* 25(1), 1–29. Reprinted in Goffman (1981).

Goffman, E. (1981). *Forms of talk.* Philadelphia: University of Pennsylvania Press.

Gómez-Peña, G. (1996). *The new world border: Prophecies, poems and loqueras for the end of the century.* San Francisco: City Lights.

Goodwin, C. (1984). Notes on story structure and the organization of participation. In J. M. Atkinson and J. C. Heritage (eds), *Structures of social action* (pp. 225–246). Cambridge and New York: Cambridge University Press.

Goodwin, C., and Duranti, A. (1992). Rethinking context: An introduction. In A. Duranti and C. Goodwin (eds.), *Rethinking context: Language as an interactive phenomenon* (pp. 1–42). Cambridge and New York: Cambridge University Press.

Gordon, D., and Ervin-Tripp, S. M. (1984). The structure of children's requests. In R. L. Schiefelbusch and J. Pickar (eds), *The acquisition of communicative competence* (pp. 298–321). Baltimore: University Park Press.

Gordon, D., and Lakoff, G. (1971). Conversational postulates. *Papers from the seventh regional meeting of the Chicago Linguistic Society,* 63–84.

Grice, H. P. (1989). Logic and conversation. In H. P. Grice (ed.), *Studies in the way of words* (pp. 3–143). Cambridge, MA: Harvard University Press.

Grimshaw, A. D. (ed.). (1990). *Conflict talk: Sociolinguistic investigations of arguments in conversations.* Cambridge and New York: Cambridge University Press.

Gumperz, J. J. (1982). *Discourse strategies.* Cambridge and New York: Cambridge University Press.

Gumperz, J. J. (2000). Inference. *Journal of Linguistic Anthropology*, 9(1–2), 131–133.

Gumperz, J. J., and Hymes, D. (eds). (1972). *Directions in sociolinguistics: The ethnography of communication*. New York: Holt, Rinehart and Winston.

Gumperz, J. J., Jupp, T. C., and Roberts, C. (1979). *Crosstalk: A study of cross-cultural communication* [Film]. London: BBC Enterprises.

Haddon, M. (2003). *The curious incident of the dog in the night-time*. London: Jonathan Cape.

Hall, J. K. (1993). The role of oral practices in the accomplishment of our everyday lives: The sociocultural dimension of interaction with implications for the learning of another language. *Applied Linguistics*, 14(2), 145–166.

Hall, J. K. (1995). (Re)creating our worlds with words: A sociohistorical perspective of face-to-face interaction. *Applied Linguistics*, 16(2), 206–232.

Halliday, M. A. K. (1992). A systemic interpretation of Peking syllable finals. In P. Tench (ed.), *Studies in systemic phonology* (pp. 98–121). London: Pinter.

Halliday, M. A. K., and Matthiessen, C. M. I. M. (2004). *An introduction to functional grammar* (3rd ed.). London: Arnold.

Hamilton, K. (2001). Finding a name that fits: Significance of ethnic labels Hispanic, Latino. *Black Issues in Higher Education*, September 27.

Hanks, W. F. (1989). Text and textuality. *Annual Review of Anthropology*, 18, 95–127.

Hanks, W. F. (1991). Foreword. In J. Lave and E. Wenger, *Situated learning: Legitimate peripheral participation* (pp. 13–24). Cambridge and New York: Cambridge University Press.

Hanks, W. F. (1992). The indexical ground of deictic reference. In A. Duranti and C. Goodwin (eds), *Rethinking context: Language as an interactive phenomenon* (pp. 43–76). Cambridge: Cambridge University Press.

Hanks, W. F. (1996). *Language and communicative practices*. Boulder, CO: Westview.

Hasan, A. S. (1988). *Variation in spoken discourse in and beyond the English foreign language classroom: A comparative study*. Unpublished doctoral thesis, University of Aston, Birmingham.

Have, P. ten (1999). *Doing conversation analysis: A practical guide*. Thousand Oaks, CA: Sage.

Heath, S. B. (1983). *Ways with words: Language, life, and work in communities and classrooms*. Cambridge and New York: Cambridge University Press.

Henderson, T. (2004). *The physics classroom*. Retrieved August 30, 2006, from `http://www.glenbrook.k12.il.us/gbssci/phys/Class/refln/u13l1c.html`.

Hill, T. (1958). Institutional linguistics. *Orbis*, 7, 441–455.

Hogan, H. M. (1967). *An ethnography of communication among the Ashanti*. Unpublished M.A. thesis, University of Pennsylvania, Philadelphia.

Hutchby, I., and Wooffitt, R. (1998). *Conversation analysis: Principles, practices and applications*. Cambridge and Malden, MA: Polity.

Hutchins, E. (1989). *Organizing work by adaptation*. Paper presented at the conference on Organizational Learning at Carnegie Mellon University, May 18–20.

Hymes, D. (1962/1974). The ethnography of speaking. In T. Gladwin and W. Sturtevant (eds), *Anthropology and human behavior* (pp. 15–53). Washington, DC: Anthropological Society of Washington. Reprinted in B. G. Blount (ed.) (1974) *Language, culture, and society: A book of readings* (pp. 189–223). Cambridge, MA: Winthrop.

Hymes, D. (1966). Two types of linguistic relativity. In W. Bright (ed.), *Sociolinguistics* (pp. 114–165). The Hague: Mouton.

Hymes, D. (1968). Linguistics – the field. *International encyclopedia of the social sciences*, 9, 351–371.

Hymes, D. (1969). Linguistic aspects of comparative political research. In R. T. Holt and J. E. Turner (eds), *The methodology of comparative research: A symposium from the Center* for Comparative Studies in Technological Development and Social Change and the Department of Political Science, University of Minnesota. New York: Free Press.

Hymes, D. (1971). *On communicative competence*. Philadelphia: University of Pennsylvania Press. Reprinted in J. B. Pride and J. Holmes (eds) (1972), *Sociolinguistics: Selected readings* (pp. 269–293). Harmondsworth: Penguin.

Hymes, D. (1972). Models of the interaction of language and social life. In J. J. Gumperz and D. Hymes (eds.), *Directions in sociolinguistics: The ethnography of communication* (pp. 35–71). New York: Holt, Rinehart and Winston.

Hymes, D. (1974). *Foundations in sociolinguistics: An ethnographic approach*. Philadelphia: University of Pennsylvania Press.

Ionesco, E. (1960). *Rhinoceros, and other plays*. New York: Grove Press.

Jacoby, S., and Ochs, E. (1995). Co-construction: An introduction. *Research on Language and Social Interaction*, 28(3), 171–183.

Jakobson, R. (1960). Closing statement: Linguistics and poetics. In T. A. Sebeok (ed.), *Style in language* (pp. 350–377). Cambridge, MA: MIT Press.

Jefferson, G. (1990). List construction as a task and interactional resource. In G. Psathas (ed.), *Interaction competence* (pp. 63–92). London and Washington, DC: University Press of America.

Johnson, Marilyn. (2006). *The dead beat: Lost souls, lucky stiffs, and the perverse pleasures of obituaries*. New York: HarperCollins.

Johnson, Marisia. (2001). *The art of non-conversation: A re-examination of the validity of the oral proficiency interview*. New Haven, CT: Yale University Press.

Jordan, B. (1989). Cosmopolitan obstetrics: Some insights from the training of traditional midwives. *Social Science and Medicine*, 28(9), 925–944.

Kelley, W. (2000). Instrumental music lessons [VHS video]. Madison, WI: University of Wisconsin-Madison.

Kendon, A. (1992). The negotiation of context in face-to-face interaction. In A. Duranti and C. Goodwin (eds.), *Rethinking context: Language as an interactive phenomenon* (pp. 323–334). Cambridge: Cambridge University Press.

Kenyon, J. S. (1948). Cultural levels and functional varieties of English. *College English*, 10, 31–36.

Kolker, A., and Alvarez, L. (1987). *American tongues* [Video recording]. New York: The Center for New American Media.

Kramsch, C. (1986). From language proficiency to interactional competence. *The Modern Language Journal*, 70(4), 366–372.

Kroskrity, P. V. (2000). Identity. *Journal of Linguistic Anthropology*, 9(1–2), 111–114.

Kulick, D. (1992). *Language shift and cultural reproduction: Socialization, self, and syncretism in a Papua New Guinean village*. Cambridge and New York: Cambridge University Press.

Labov, W. (1966). *The social stratification of English in New York City*. Washington, DC: Center for Applied Linguistics.

Labov, W. (1972a). *Language in the inner city: Studies in the Black English Vernacular*. Philadelphia: University of Pennsylvania Press.

Labov, W. (1972b). *Sociolinguistic patterns*. Philadelphia: University of Pennsylvania Press.

Labov, W. (1984). Intensity. In D. Schiffrin (ed.), *Meaning, form, and use in context: GURT '84* (pp. 43–70). Washington, DC: Georgetown University Press.

Lave, J., and Wenger, E. (1991). *Situated learning: Legitimate peripheral participation*. Cambridge and New York: Cambridge University Press.

Lee, J. (2006). *Talking to the self: A study of the private speech of adult bilinguals*. Unpublished Ph.D. dissertation, Program in Second Language Acquisition, University of Wisconsin-Madison.

Leont'ev, A. N. (1979). The problem of activity in psychology (J. V. Wertsch, trans.). In J. V. Wertsch (ed.), *The concept of activity in Soviet psychology* (pp. 37–71). Armonk, NY: M. E. Sharpe.

Levinson, S. (1983). *Pragmatics.* Cambridge and New York: Cambridge University Press.

Lévi-Strauss, C. (1963). *Structural anthropology* (C. Jacobson and B. G. Schoepf, trans.). New York: Basic Books.

Levy, R. (1984). Emotion, knowing and culture. In R. A. Shweder and R. A. LeVine (eds), *Culture theory: Essays on mind, self, and emotion* (pp. 214–237). Cambridge and New York: Cambridge University Press.

Lightbown, P. M., and Spada, N. (1993). *How languages are learned.* Oxford and New York: Oxford University Press.

Linell, P. (1998). *Approaching dialogue: Talk, interaction and contexts in dialogical perspectives.* Amsterdam and Philadelphia: Benjamins.

Linell, P. (2005). *The written language bias in linguistics: Its nature, origins and transformations.* London and New York: Routledge.

Lyons, J. (1977). *Semantics* (2 volumes). New York and Cambridge: Cambridge University Press.

Macbeth, D. (2004). The relevance of repair for classroom correction. *Language in Society,* 33(5), 703–736.

McCall, G. J., and Simmons, J. L. (1978). *Identities and interactions: An examination of human associations in everyday life* (rev. ed.). New York: Free Press.

McHoul, A. (1990). The organization of repair in classrooms. *Language in Society,* 19, 349–377.

Markee, N. (2000). *Conversation analysis.* Mahwah, NJ: Lawrence Erlbaum Associates.

Mifflin, M. (2000). Who are you calling "Ms."? Why have women suddenly rejected the politically charged courtesy title? *Salon.com.* Retrieved April 25, 2007, from http://archive.salon.com/mwt/feature/2000/07/27/ms/index.html.

Miller, G. A. (1974). Psychology, language, and levels of communication. In A. Silverstein (ed.), *Human communication: Theoretical explorations* (pp. 1–17). Hillsdale, NJ: Erlbaum.

Miller, P. J. (1982). *Amy, Wendy, and Beth: Learning language in South Baltimore.* Austin, TX: University of Texas Press.

Morgan, M. (2004). Speech community. In A. Duranti (ed.), *A companion to linguistic anthropology* (pp. 3–22). Malden, MA, and Oxford: Blackwell.

Morson, G. S., and Emerson, C. (1989). *Rethinking Bakhtin: Extensions and challenges.* Evanston, IL: Northwestern University Press.

Morson, G. S., and Emerson, C. (1990). *Mikhail Bakhtin: Creation of a prosaics.* Stanford, CA: Stanford University Press.

Nation, I. S. P. (2001). *Learning vocabulary in another language.* Cambridge and New York: Cambridge University Press.

National Commission for the Protection of Human Subjects of Biomedical and Behavioral Research, The. (1979). *The Belmont report: Ethical principles and guidelines for the protection of human subjects of research* Retrieved March 6, 2007, from http://www.hhs.gov/ohrp/humansubjects/guidance/belmont.htm.

Newman, S. S. (1940). Linguistic aspects of Yokuts style. In A. H. Gayton and S. S. Newman (eds), *Yokuts and Western mono myths* (pp. 4–8). Berkeley: University of California Press.

Newman, S. S. (1964). Vocabulary levels: Zuni sacred and slang usage. In D. Hymes (ed.), *Language in culture and society: A reader in linguistics and anthropology.* New York: Harper and Row.

Nguyen, H. T. (2003). *The development of communication skills in the practice of patient consultation among pharmacy students.* Unpublished Ph.D. dissertation, University of Wisconsin-Madison.

Nunan, D. (1989). *Understanding language classrooms.* Hemel Hempstead: Prentice Hall.

Ochs, E. (1986). Introduction. In B. B. Schieffelin and E. Ochs (eds), *Language socialization across cultures* (pp. 1–13). Cambridge and New York: Cambridge University Press.

Ochs, E. (1988). *Culture and language development: Language acquisition and language socialization in a Samoan village.* New York and Cambridge: Cambridge University Press.

Ochs, E. (1990). Indexicality and socialization. In J. W. Stigler, R. A. Shweder, and G. H. Herdt (eds), *Cultural psychology: Essays on comparative human development* (pp. 287–308). Cambridge and New York: Cambridge University Press.

Ochs, E. (1993). Constructing social identity: A language socialization perspective. *Research on Language and Social Interaction,* 26(3), 287–306.

Ochs, E. (1996). Linguistic resources for socializing humanity. In J. J. Gumperz and S. C. Levinson (eds), *Rethinking linguistic relativity* (pp. 407–437). Cambridge and New York: Cambridge University Press.

Ochs, E. (2002). Becoming a speaker of culture. In C. J. Kramsch (ed.), *Language acquisition and language socialization: Ecological perspectives* (pp. 99–120). London: Continuum.

Ochs, E., and Schieffelin, B. B. (1984). Language acquisition and socialization: Three developmental stories and their implications. In R. A. Shweder and R. A. LeVine (eds), *Culture theory: Essays on mind, self, and emotion* (pp. 276–320). New York: Cambridge University Press.

Ochs, E., and Schieffelin, B. B. (1989). Language has a heart. *Text,* 9(1), 7–25.

Ortner, S. B. (1984). Theory in anthropology since the sixties. *Comparative Studies in Society and History,* 126(1), 126–166.

Patrick, P. J. (2002). The speech community. In J. K. Chambers, P. Trudgill, and N. Schilling-Estes (eds), *Handbook of language variation and change* (pp. 573–597). Oxford, UK and Malden, MA: Blackwell.

Peirce, C. S. (1955). *Philosophical writings of Peirce.* New York: Dover Publications.

Peirce, C. S., Hartshorne, C., and Weiss, P. (1933). *Collected papers of Charles Sanders Peirce.* Cambridge, MA: Harvard University Press.

Pew Research Center for the People and the Press, The. (June 8, 2004). *Media consumption and believability study.* Retrieved March 4, 2007, from http://people-press.org/reports/pdf/215.pdf.

Philips, S. U. (1970). Acquisition of rules for appropriate speech usage. In J. Alatis (ed.), *Report of the twenty-first annual round table meeting on linguistics and language studies* (pp. 77–96). Washington, DC: Georgetown University Press.

Philips, S. U. (1972). Participant structures and communicative competence: Warm Springs children in community and classroom. In C. B. Cazden, V. P. John, and D. Hymes (eds), *Functions of language in the classroom* (pp. 370–394). New York: Teachers College Press.

Philips, S. U. (1976). Some sources of cultural variability in the regulation of talk. *Language in Society,* 5, 81–95.

Philips, S. U. (1982). *The invisible culture: Communication in classroom and community on the Warm Springs Indian Reservation.* New York: Longman.

Philips, S. U. (1985). Indian children in Anglo classrooms. In N. Wolfson and J. Manes (eds), *Language of inequality* (pp. 311–323). Berlin: Mouton.

Pike, K. L. (1967). *Language in relation to a unified theory of the structure of human behavior* (2nd, rev. ed.). The Hague: Mouton.

Platt, M. (1986). Social norms and lexical acquisition: A study of deictic verbs in Samoan child language. In B. B. Schieffelin and E. Ochs (eds), *Language socialization across cultures* (pp. 127–152). Cambridge and New York: Cambridge University Press.

Polanyi, M. (1958). *Personal knowledge: Towards a post-critical philosophy.* Chicago: University of Chicago Press.

Prigogine, I., and Stengers, I. (1984). *Order out of chaos: Man's new dialogue with nature.* Toronto and New York: Bantam Books.

Rampton, B. (1998). Language crossing and the redefinition of reality. In P. Auer (ed.), *Code-switching in conversation: Language, interaction and identity* (pp. 290–320). London: Routledge.

Rampton, B. (ed.). (1999). *Styling the other.* Special issue of the *Journal of Sociolinguistics,* 3(4).

Rampton, B. (2005). *Crossing: Language and ethnicity among adolescents* (2nd ed.). Manchester: St Jerome Press.

Ranney, S. (1992). Learning a new script: An exploration of sociolinguistic competence. *Applied Linguistics,* 13(1), 25–50.

Rheingold, H. (2000). *The virtual community: Homesteading on the electronic frontier* (rev. ed.). Cambridge, MA: MIT Press.

Richards, K. (2006). 'Being the teacher': Identity and classroom conversation. *Applied Linguistics,* 27(1), 51–77.

Riffaterre, M. (1959). Criteria for style analysis. *Word,* 15, 154–174.

Riggenbach, H. (1998). Evaluating learner interactional skills: Conversation at the micro level. In R. Young and A. W. He (eds), *Talking and testing: Discourse approaches to the assessment of oral proficiency* (pp. 53–67). Amsterdam and Philadelphia: John Benjamins.

Rogoff, B. (2003). *The cultural nature of human development.* Oxford and New York: Oxford University Press.

Romaine, S. (1994). *Language in society: An introduction to sociolinguistics.* Oxford and New York: Oxford University Press.

Rubin, J. (1962). Bilingualism in Paraguay. *Anthropological Linguistics,* 4(1), 52–58.

Rubin, J. (1968). *National bilingualism in Paraguay.* The Hague: Mouton.

Sacks, H. (1974). An analysis of the course of a joke's telling in conversation. In R. Bauman and J. Sherzer (eds), *Explorations in the ethnography of speaking* (1st ed., pp. 337–353). New York: Cambridge University Press.

Sacks, H., Schegloff, E. A., and Jefferson, G. (1974). A simplest systematics for the organization of turn-taking for conversation. *Language,* 50, 696–735.

Salisbury, R. F. (1962). Notes on bilingualism and linguistic change in New Guinea. *Anthropological Linguistics,* 4(7), 1–13.

Salomon, G. (1993). Editor's introduction. In G. Salomon (ed.), *Distributed cognitions: Psychological and educational considerations* (pp. xi–xxi). Cambridge and New York: Cambridge University Press.

Samarin, W. (1965). The language of silence. *Practical Anthropology,* 12, 115–119.

Sapir, E. (1949). *Selected writings in language, culture and personality,* edited by D. G. Mandelbaum. Berkeley: University of California Press.

Saussure, F. de, Bally, C., Sechehaye, A., and Riedlinger, A. (1966). *Course in general linguistics* (W. Baskin, trans.). New York: McGraw-Hill Book Co.

Shea, D. P. (1994). Perspective and production: Structuring conversational participation across cultural borders. *Pragmatics,* 4(3), 357–389.

Schegloff, E. A. (n. d.). *Emanuel A. Schegloff's home page.* Retrieved March 2, 2007, from `http://www.sscnet.ucla.edu/soc/faculty/schegloff/`.

Schegloff, E. A. (1982). Discourse as an interactional achievement: Some uses of 'uh huh' and other things that come between sentences. In D. Tannen (ed.), *Analyzing discourse: Text and talk* (pp. 71–93). Washington, DC: Georgetown University Press.

Schegloff, E. A. (1992). Repair after next turn: The last structurally provided defense of intersubjectivity in conversation. *American Journal of Sociology,* 97(5), 1295–1345.

Schegloff, E. A., Jefferson, G., and Sacks, H. (1977). The preference for self-correction in the organization of repair in conversation. *Language*, 53(2), 361–382.

Schenkein, J. N. (1978). Identity negotiation in conversation. In J. N. Schenkein (ed.), *Studies in the organization of conversational interaction* (pp. 57–78). New York: Academic Press.

Schieffelin, B. B. (1979). *How Kaluli children learn what to say, what to do, and how to feel: An ethnographic study of the development of communicative competence.* Unpublished Ph.D. dissertation, Columbia University, New York.

Schieffelin, B. B. (1986). *Context and interpretation in Kaluli story telling.* Paper presented at the annual meeting of the American Anthropological Association.

Schieffelin, B. B. (1990). *The give and take of everyday life: Language socialization of Kaluli children.* Cambridge and New York: Cambridge University Press.

Schieffelin, B. B. (1994). Code-switching and language socialization: Some probable relationships. In J. F. Duchan, L. E. Hewitt, and R. M. Sonnenmeier (eds), *Pragmatics: From theory to practice* (pp. 20–42). Englewood Cliffs, NJ: Prentice Hall.

Schieffelin, B. B., and Ochs, E. (1988). *Micro-macro interfaces: Methodology in language socialization research.* Paper presented at the annual meeting of the American Anthropological Association.

Schieffelin, B. B., and Ochs, E. (eds). (1986). *Language socialization across cultures.* Cambridge and New York: Cambridge University Press.

Schiffrin, D. (1987). *Discourse markers.* Cambridge and New York: Cambridge University Press.

Schutz, A. (1945). On multiple realities. *Philosophy and Phenomenological Research*, 5, 533–575.

Schutz, A. (1953). Common-sense and scientific interpretations of human action. *Economica*, 14.

Searle, J. R. (1969). *Speech acts: An essay in the philosophy of language.* London: Cambridge University Press.

Seedhouse, P. (1994). Linking pedagogical purposes to linguistic patterns of interaction: The analysis of communication in the language classroom. *International Review of Applied Linguistics*, 32(4), 303–320.

Seedhouse, P. (2004). *The interactional architecture of the language classroom: A conversation analysis perspective.* Malden, MA, and Oxford: Blackwell.

Sfard, A. (1998). On two metaphors for learning and on the dangers of choosing just one. *Educational Researcher*, 27(2), 4–13.

Shameem, N. (2007). Social interaction in multilingual classrooms. In Z. Hua, P. Seedhouse, L. Wei and V. Cook (eds), *Language learning and teaching as social inter-action* (pp. 199–217). Basingstoke: Palgrave Macmillan.

Shea, D. P. (1994). Perspective and production: Structuring conversational participation across cultural borders. *Pragmatics*, 4(3), 357–389.

Silverstein, M. (1993). Metapragmatic discourse and metapragmatic function. In J. A. Lucy (ed.), *Reflexive language: Reported speech and metapragmatics* (pp. 33–58). Cambridge and New York: Cambridge University Press.

Sinclair, J. M., and Coulthard, M. (1975). *Towards an analysis of discourse: The English used by teachers and pupils.* Oxford and New York: Oxford University Press.

Smitherman, G. (1977). *Talkin and testifyin: The language of Black America.* Boston: Houghton Mifflin.

Sorabji, S. J. (2001, March 4). Racism, name-changing and toilets. *Times of India.*

Tannen, D. (1989). *Talking voices: Repetition, dialogue, and imagery in conversational discourse.* Cambridge and New York: Cambridge University Press.

Tannen, D. (2004). Talking the dog: Framing pets as interactional resources in family discourse. *Research on Language and Social Interaction*, 37(4), 399–420.

Thomas, C. (1994). Lecture games (real): Games to play, on paper, during a lecture. Retrieved February 8, 2007, from `http://www.galactic-guide.com/articles/2R60.html`.

Thompson, J. B. (1987). Language and ideology: A framework for analysis. *Sociological Review*, 35, 516–536.

Tracy, K. (2002). *Everyday talk: Building and reflecting identities*. New York: Guilford.

Trappes-Lomax, H. (2004). Discourse analysis. In A. Davies and C. Elder (eds), *The handbook of applied linguistics* (pp. 133–164). Malden, MA: Blackwell.

Trevarthen, C. (1977). Descriptive analyses of infant communicative behaviour. In H. R. Schaffer (ed.), *Studies in mother-infant interaction: Proceedings of the Loch Lomond symposium, Ross Priory, University of Strathclyde, September, 1975* (pp. 227–270). London and New York: Academic Press.

Trudgill, P. (1974). *The social differentiation of English in Norwich*. Cambridge and New York: Cambridge University Press.

Tsui, A. B. M. (1995). *Introducing classroom interaction*. London: Penguin.

Twitchin, J. (Producer), and Gumperz, J. J., Jupp, T. C., and Roberts, C. (Director). (1979). *Crosstalk: A study of cross-cultural communication*. London: BBC Enterprises.

Urban, G. (1996). Entextualization, replication, and power. In M. Silverstein and G. Urban (eds), *Natural histories of discourse* (pp. 21–44). Chicago: University of Chicago Press.

van Lier, L. (1988). *The classroom and the language learner*. New York: Longman.

Vocate, D. R. (1994). Self-talk and inner speech: Understanding the uniquely human aspects of intrapersonal communication. In D. R. Vocate (ed.), *Intrapersonal communication: Different voices, different minds* (pp. 3–31). Hillsdale, NJ: Erlbaum.

Voloshinov, V. N. (1973). *Marxism and the philosophy of language* (L. Matejka and I. R. Titunik, trans.). New York: Seminar Press.

Vygotsky, L. S. (1978). *Mind in society: The development of higher psychological processes*. Cambridge, MA: Harvard University Press.

Walters, K., and Brody, M. (eds). (2005). *What's language got to do with it?* New York: Norton.

Watson, K. A. (1975). Transferable communicative routines: Strategies and group identity in two speech events. *Language in Society*, 4, 53–72.

Watson-Gegeo, K. A., and Gegeo, D. W. (1986). Calling-out and repeating routines in Kwara'ae children's language socialization. In B. B. Schieffelin and E. Ochs (eds), *Language socialization across cultures* (pp. 17–50). New York: Cambridge University Press.

Watson-Gegeo, K. A., and Nielsen, S. (2003). Language socialization in SLA. In C. J. Doughty and M. H. Long (eds), *The handbook of second language acquisition* (pp. 155–177). Malden, MA, and Oxford, UK: Blackwell.

Wells, B., and Macfarlane, S. (1998). Prosody as an interactional resource: Turn-projection and overlap. *Language and Speech*, 41(3–4), 265–294.

Wenger, E. (1998). *Communities of practice: Learning, meaning, and identity*. Cambridge and New York: Cambridge University Press.

Wertsch, J. V. (1990). The voice of rationality in a sociocultural approach to mind. In L. C. Moll (ed.), *Vygotsky and education: Instructional implications and applications of sociohistorical psychology* (pp. 111–126). Cambridge and New York: Cambridge University Press.

Wertsch, J. V. (1991). *Voices of the mind: A sociocultural approach to mediated action*. Cambridge, MA: Harvard University Press.

Whorf, B. L. (1941). The relation of habitual thought and behavior to language. In L. Spier, A. I. Hallowell, and S. S. Newman (eds), *Language, culture, and personality: Essays in memory of Edward Sapir* (pp. 75–93). Menasha, WI: Sapir Memorial Publication Fund.

Willis, J. (1996). *A framework for task-based learning*. London: Addison Wesley Longman.

Wittgenstein, L. (1933). *Tractatus logico-philosophicus*. New York: Harcourt, Brace.

Wittgenstein, L. (1969). *Preliminary studies for the 'Philosophical investigations', generally known as the Blue and Brown books* (2nd ed.). Oxford: Blackwell.

Wittgenstein, L. (2001). *Philosophical investigations: The German text, with a revised English translation* (G. E. M. Anscombe, trans. 3rd ed.). Oxford and Malden, MA: Blackwell.

Wolff, H. (1959). Intelligibility and inter-ethnic attitudes. *Anthropological Linguistics*, 1(3), 34–41.

Wortman, B. (2000). *Effective storytelling in a social setting*. Unpublished paper for English 905 seminar on 'Interactional Competence.' University of Wisconsin-Madison.

Young, R., and He, A. W. (eds). (1998). *Talking and testing: Discourse approaches to the assessment of oral proficiency*. Amsterdam and Philadelphia: John Benjamins.

Young, R. F., and Miller, E. R. (2004). Learning as changing participation: Negotiating discourse roles in the ESL writing conference. *The Modern Language Journal*, 88(4), 519–535.

Index